A WORD FROM THE CREATORS

IT DIDN'T BECOME A RISING STAR...OR A BESTSELLER. IT PAINS ME THAT *CROQUIS POP* DIDN'T TURN OUT AS WELL AS I'D HOPED. I APOLOGIZE FOR THIS AND THANK YOU FOR TRUSTING US SO FAR.

— KwangHyun Seo

IT FEELS LIKE I'M GOING THROUGH PUBERTY AGAIN! YEAH, I KNOW IT SOUNDS FUNNY AT MY AGE, BUT EVER SINCE I FIRST DREW DA-IL, MY HEART STARTED BEATING A MILE A MINUTE. ^^ I'M NOT SURE IF I'LL SEE DA-IL AGAIN AFTER THIS VOLUME, BUT I REALLY WANT TO MAKE HIS DREAMS COME TRUE. I'D LIKE TO SAY THANKS TO THOSE OF YOU WHO'VE READ *CROQUIS POP* SO FAR. AND I'LL BE BACK. YOU GO, DA-IL!!

— JinHo Ko

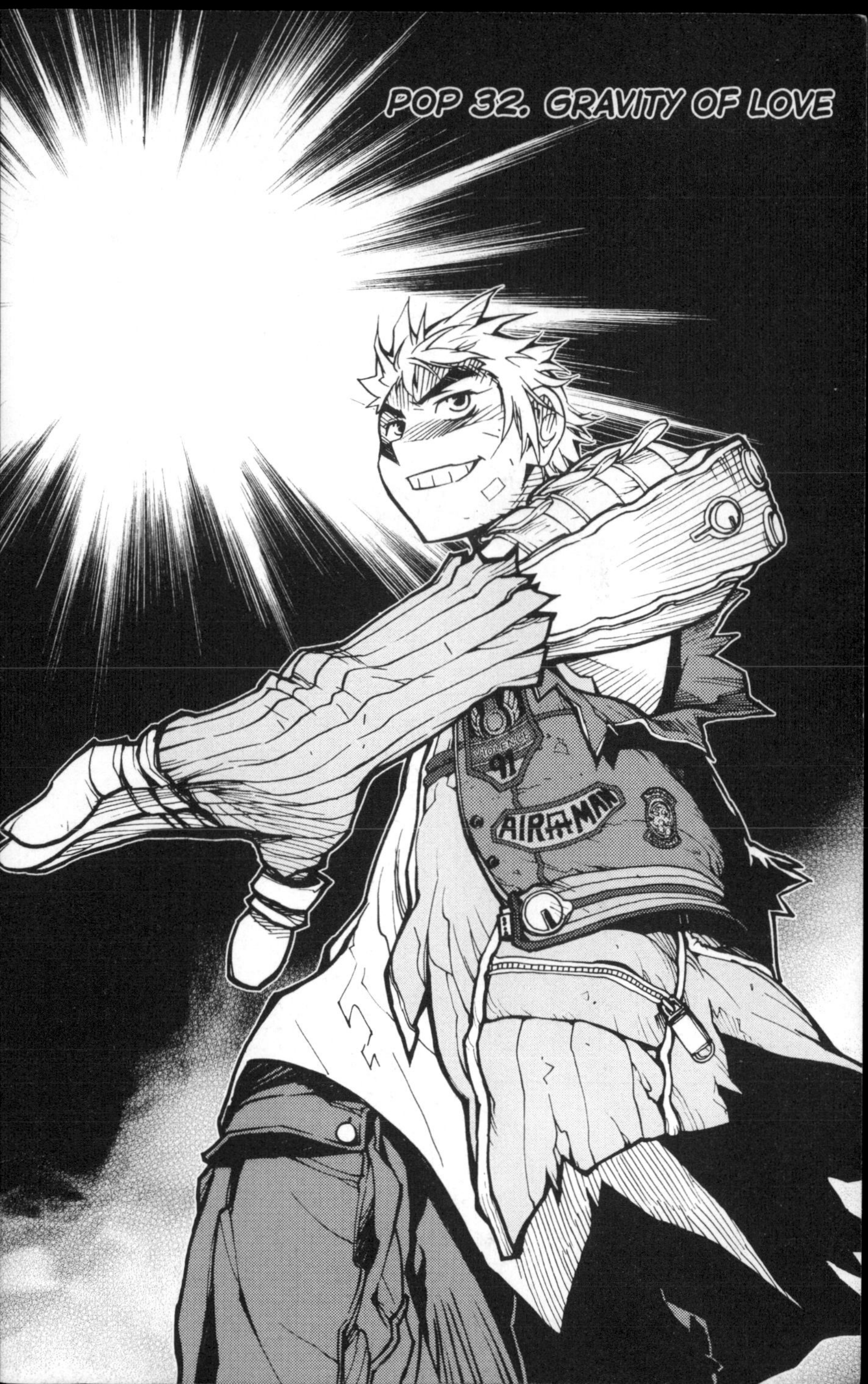
POP 32. GRAVITY OF LOVE

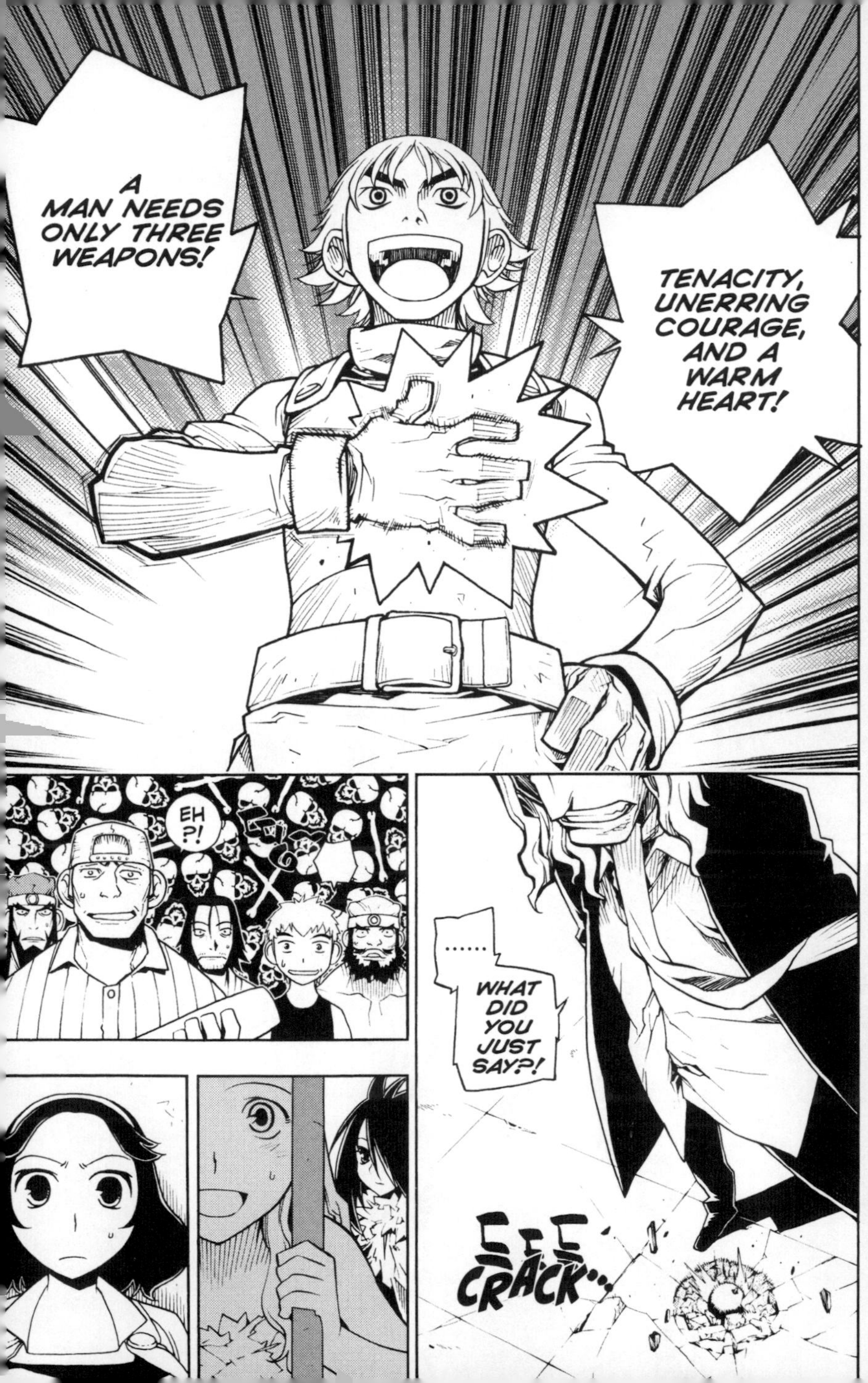
A MAN NEEDS ONLY THREE WEAPONS!
TENACITY, UNERRING COURAGE, AND A WARM HEART!
EH ?!
......
WHAT DID YOU JUST SAY?!
CRACK...

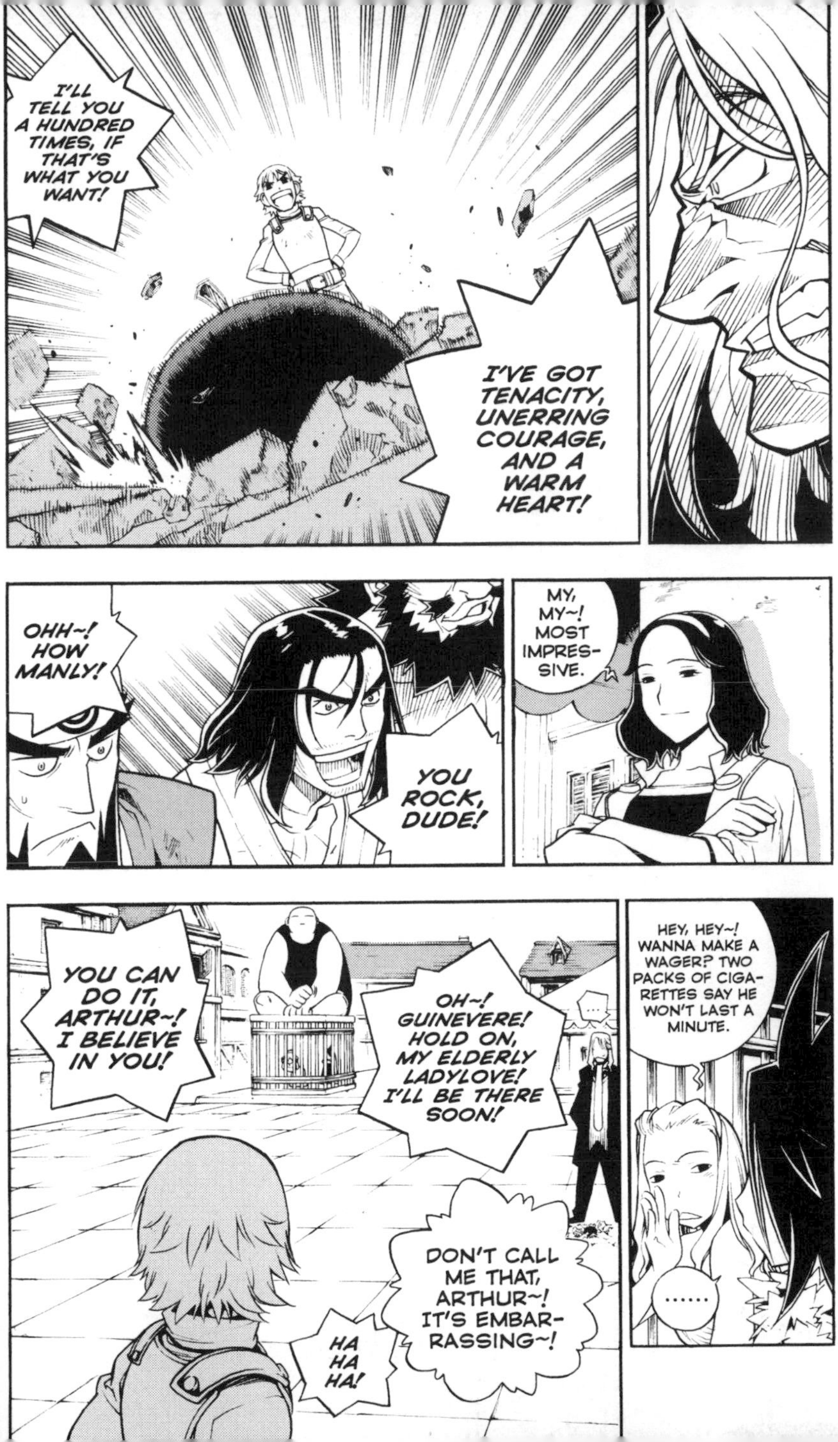
I'LL TELL YOU A HUNDRED TIMES, IF THAT'S WHAT YOU WANT!
I'VE GOT TENACITY, UNERRING COURAGE, AND A WARM HEART!
OHH~! HOW MANLY!
YOU ROCK, DUDE!
MY, MY~! MOST IMPRES-SIVE.
YOU CAN DO IT, ARTHUR~! I BELIEVE IN YOU!
OH~! GUINEVERE! HOLD ON, MY ELDERLY LADYLOVE! I'LL BE THERE SOON!
...
DON'T CALL ME THAT, ARTHUR~! IT'S EMBAR-RASSING~!
HA HA HA!
HEY, HEY~! WANNA MAKE A WAGER? TWO PACKS OF CIGA-RETTES SAY HE WON'T LAST A MINUTE.
......

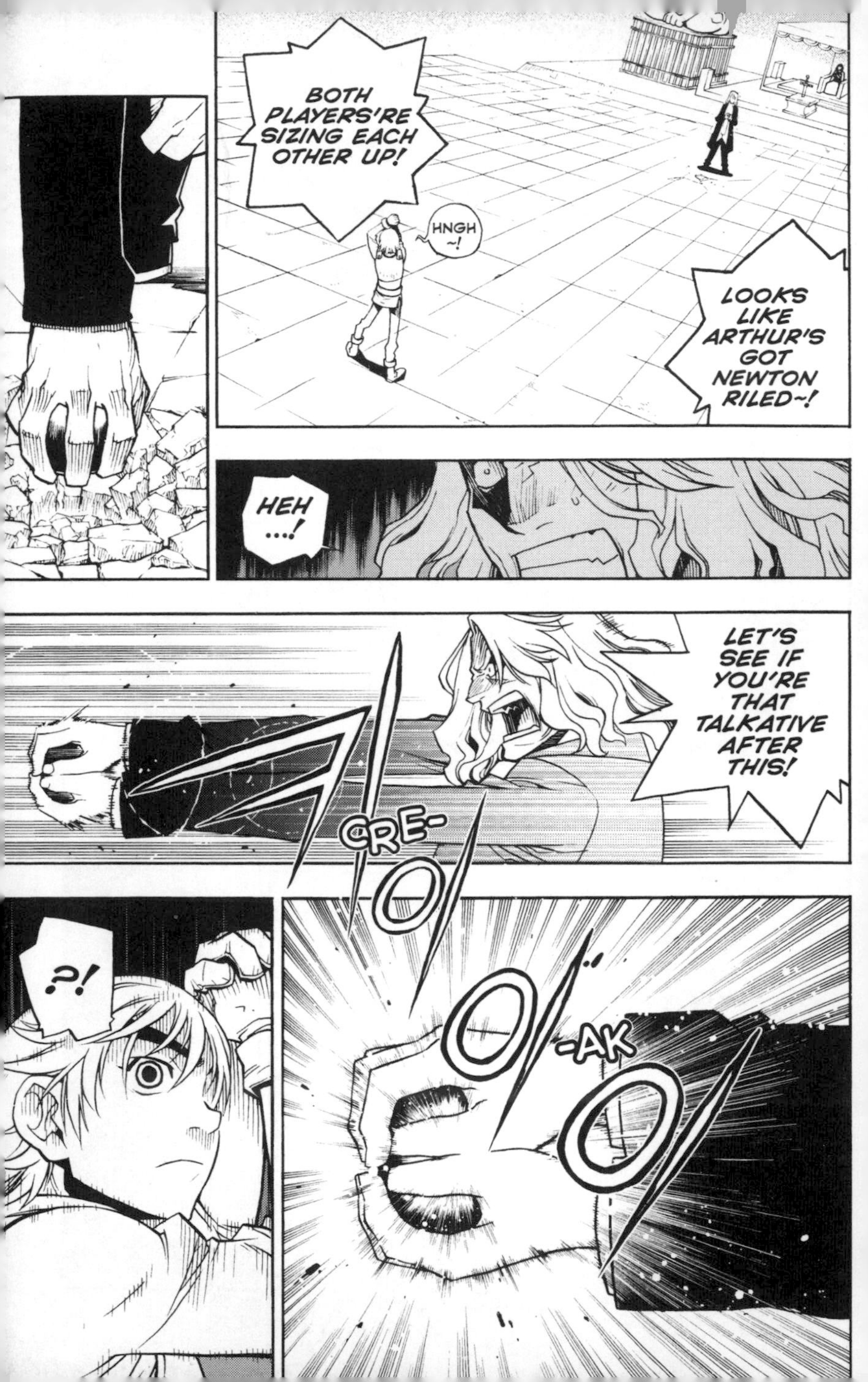
BOTH PLAYERS'RE SIZING EACH OTHER UP!
HNGH ~!
LOOKS LIKE ARTHUR'S GOT NEWTON RILED~!
HEH ...!
LET'S SEE IF YOU'RE THAT TALKATIVE AFTER THIS!
CRE-
?!
-AK

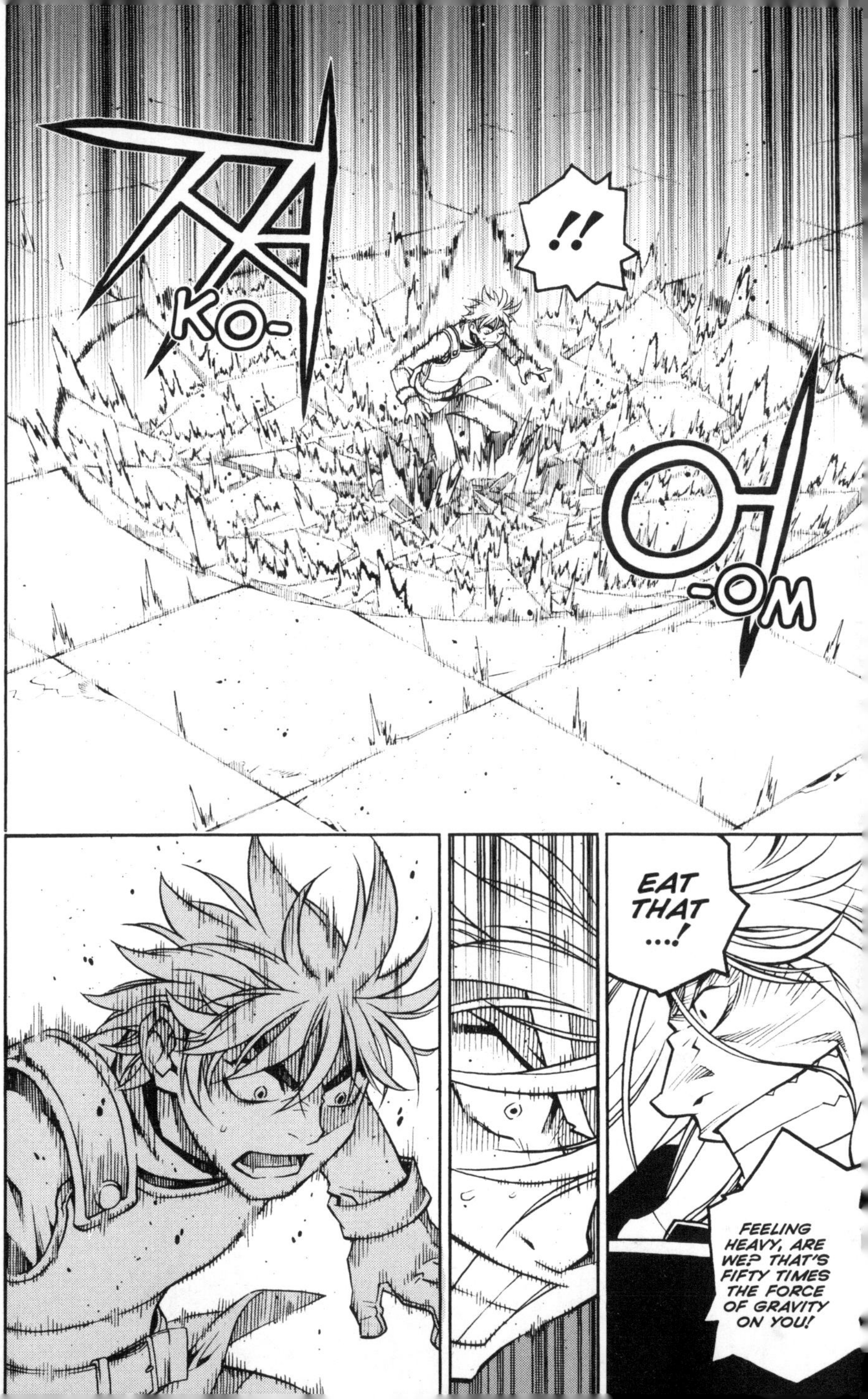
KO-
!!
-OM
EAT THAT ....!
FEELING HEAVY, ARE WE? THAT'S FIFTY TIMES THE FORCE OF GRAVITY ON YOU!

THAT'S WHAT YOU GET FOR UNDERESTIMATING ME!

KOO-

-NG

ENJOY THE PAIN, YOU SPOILED BRAT!!

T-THE FLOOR COLLAPSED?!

YOU...

...YOU WHELP! I WANT TO HEAR YOU SCREAM!

AND ADMIT YOUR PRIDE WAS YOUR DOWNFALL!

HNG...

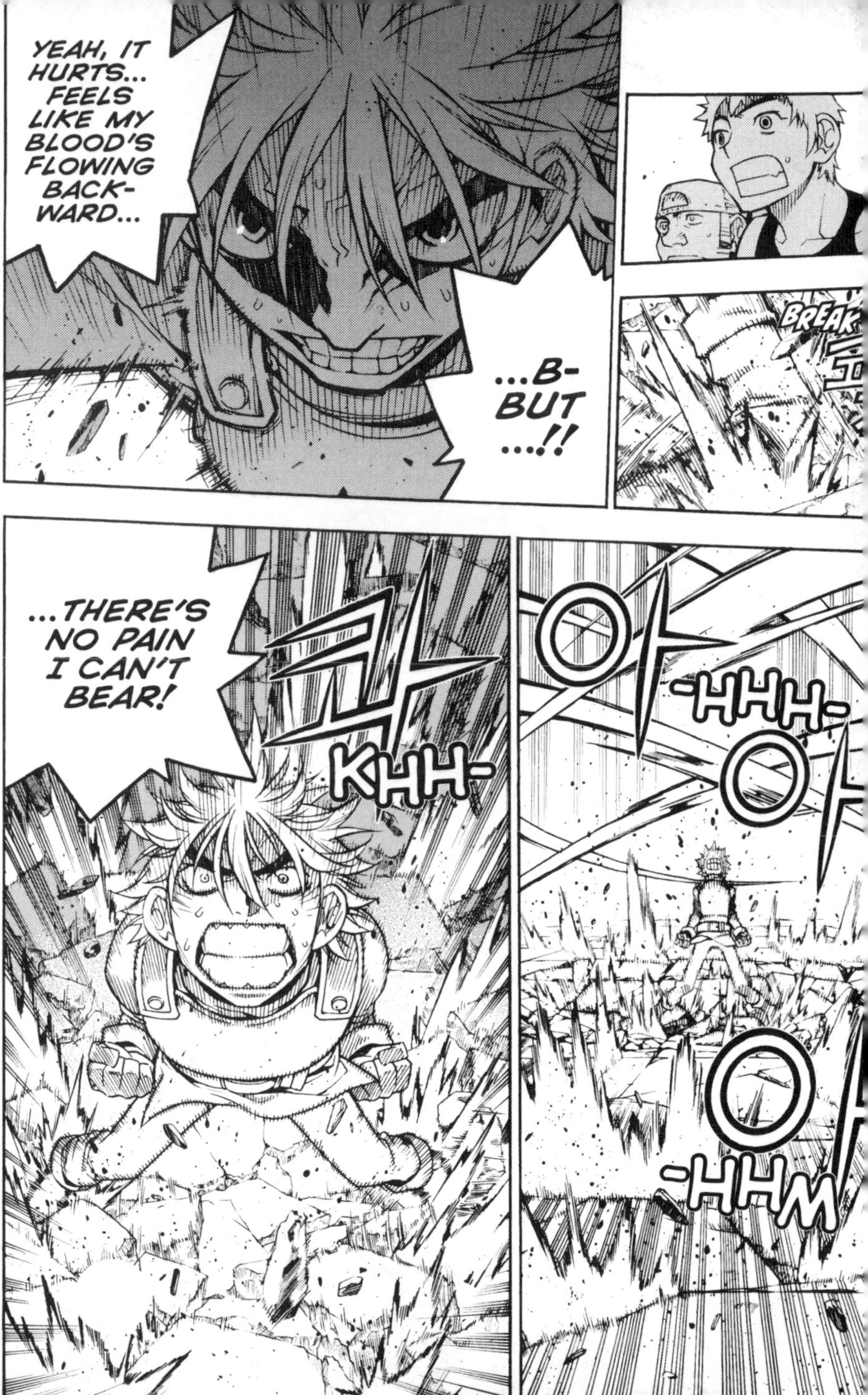
YEAH, IT HURTS... FEELS LIKE MY BLOOD'S FLOWING BACK-WARD...
...B-BUT ...!!
BREAK
...THERE'S NO PAIN I CAN'T BEAR!
KHH-
-HHH-
-HHM

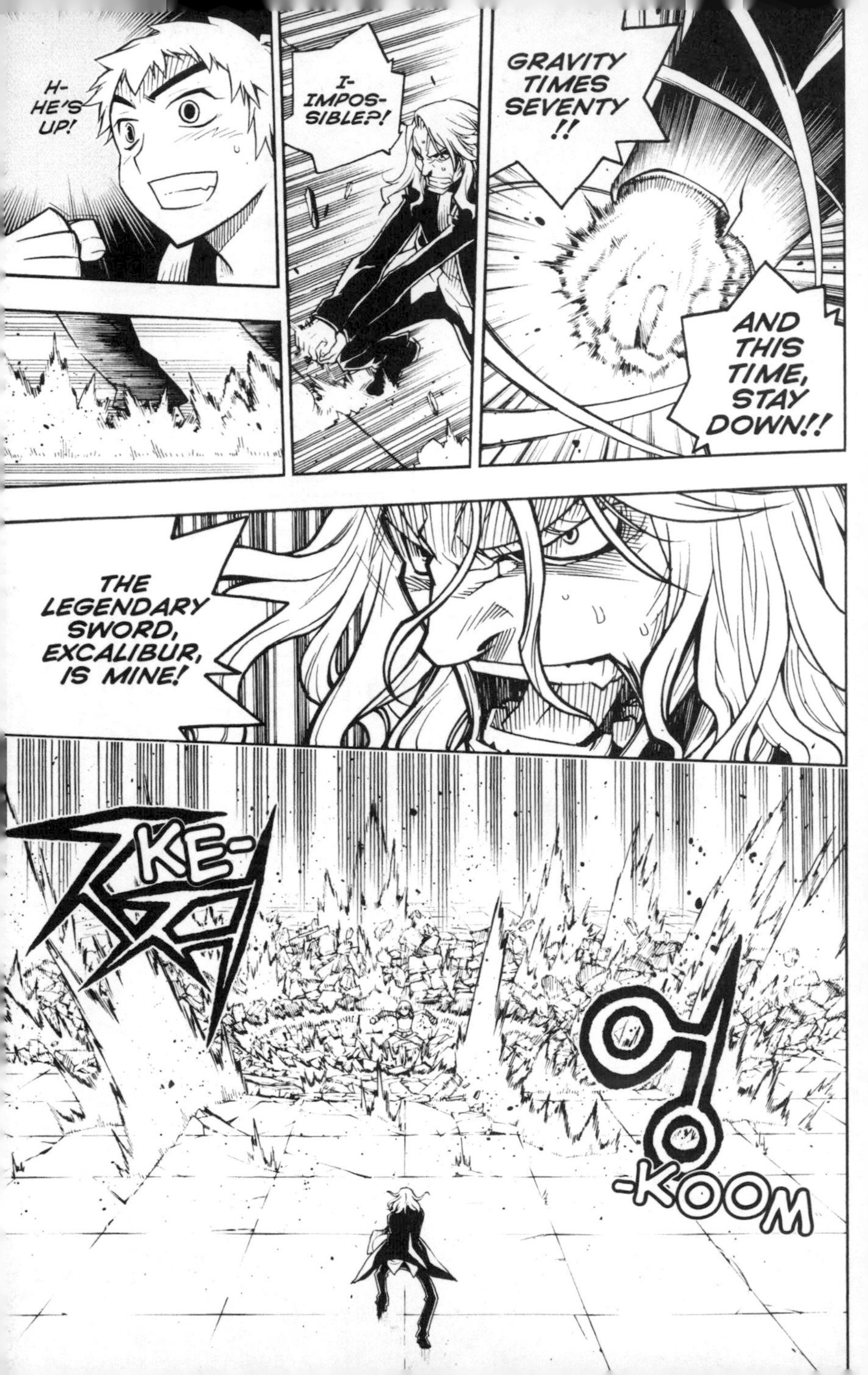
H-HE'S UP!
I-IMPOSSIBLE?!
GRAVITY TIMES SEVENTY!!
AND THIS TIME, STAY DOWN!!
THE LEGENDARY SWORD, EXCALIBUR, IS MINE!
KE-
-KOOM

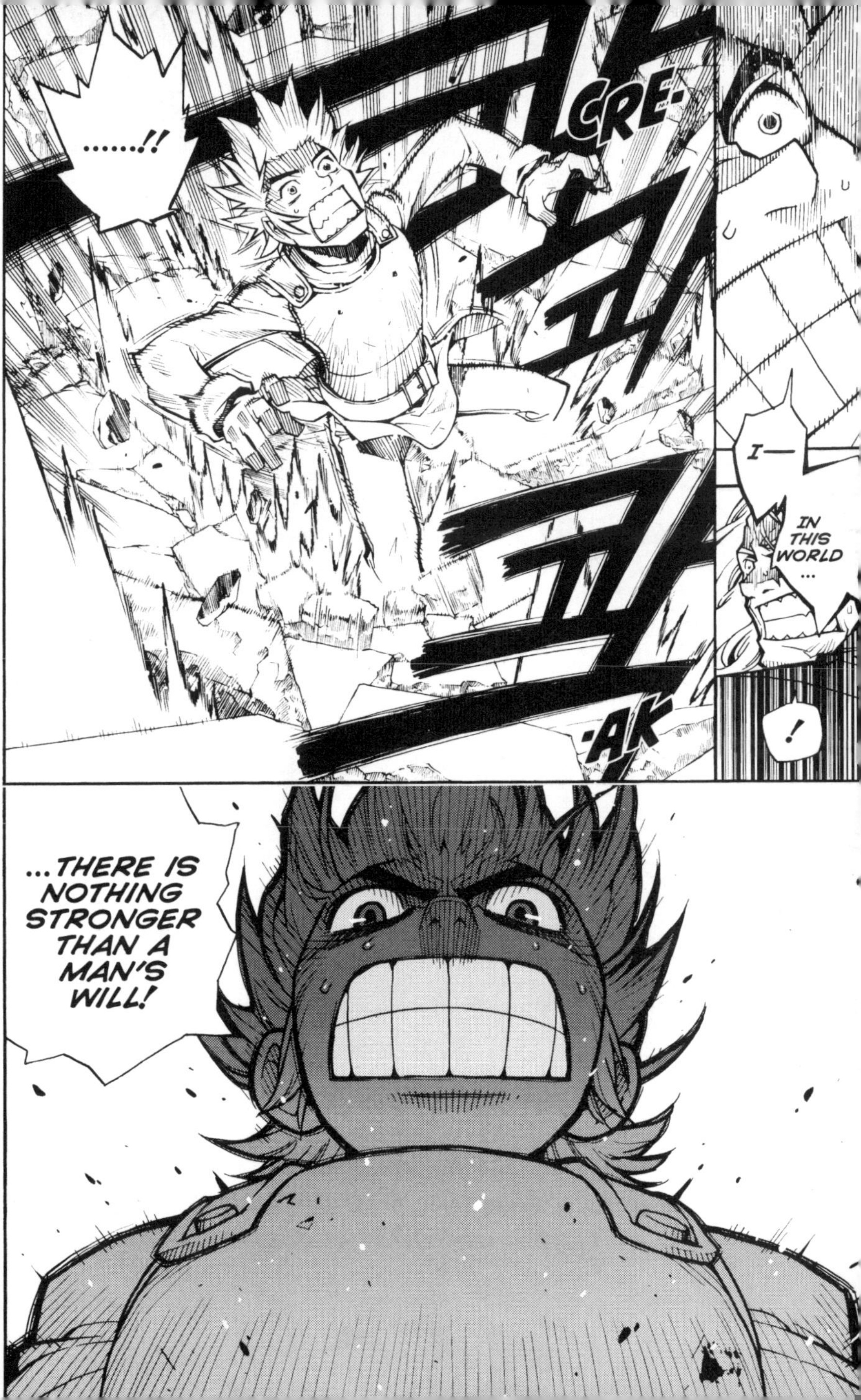

......!!
CRE-
-AK
I—
IN THIS WORLD ...
!
...THERE IS NOTHING STRONGER THAN A MAN'S WILL!

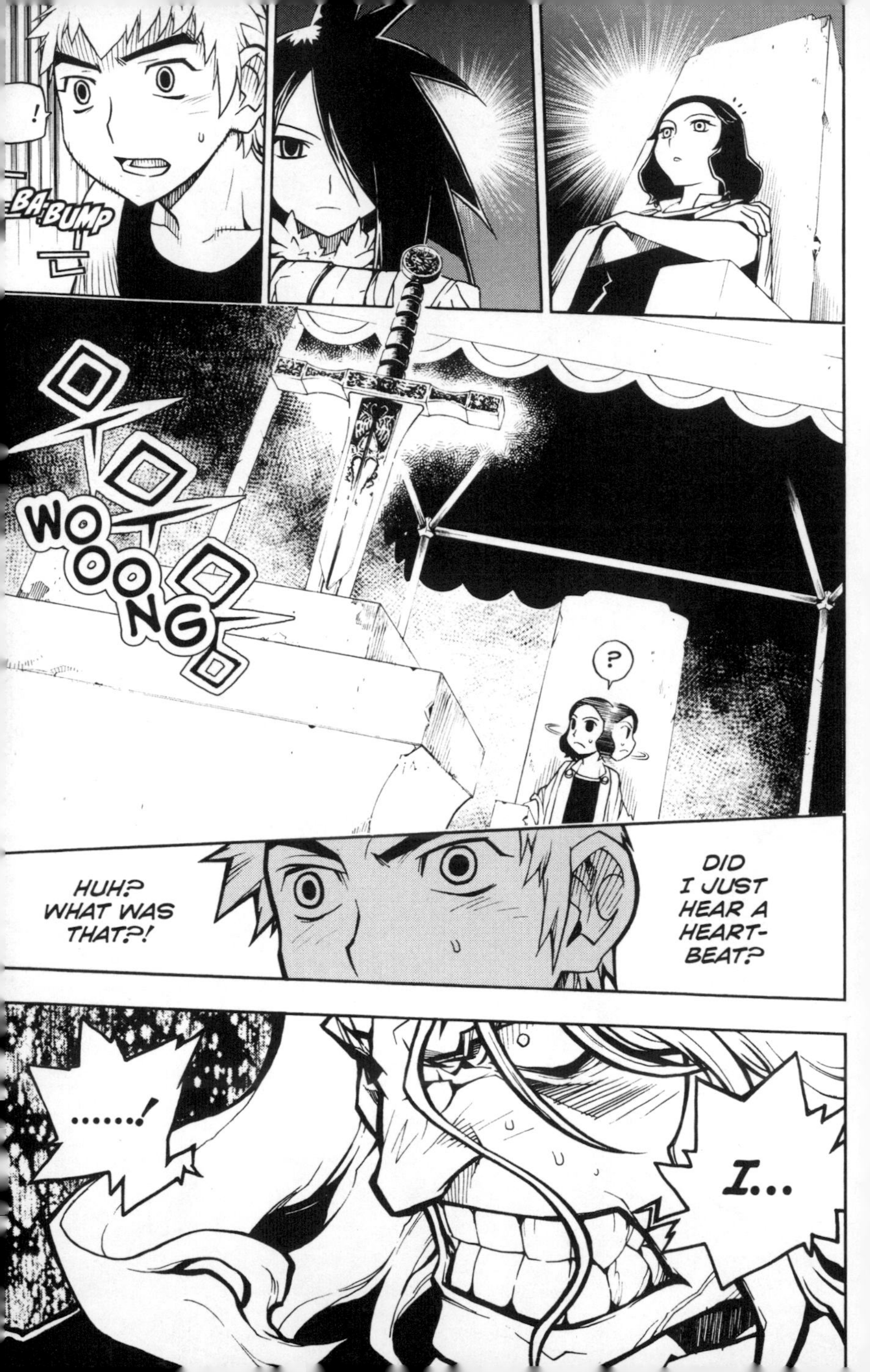
!
BA-BUMP
WOOONG
?
HUH? WHAT WAS THAT?!
DID I JUST HEAR A HEART-BEAT?
......!
I...

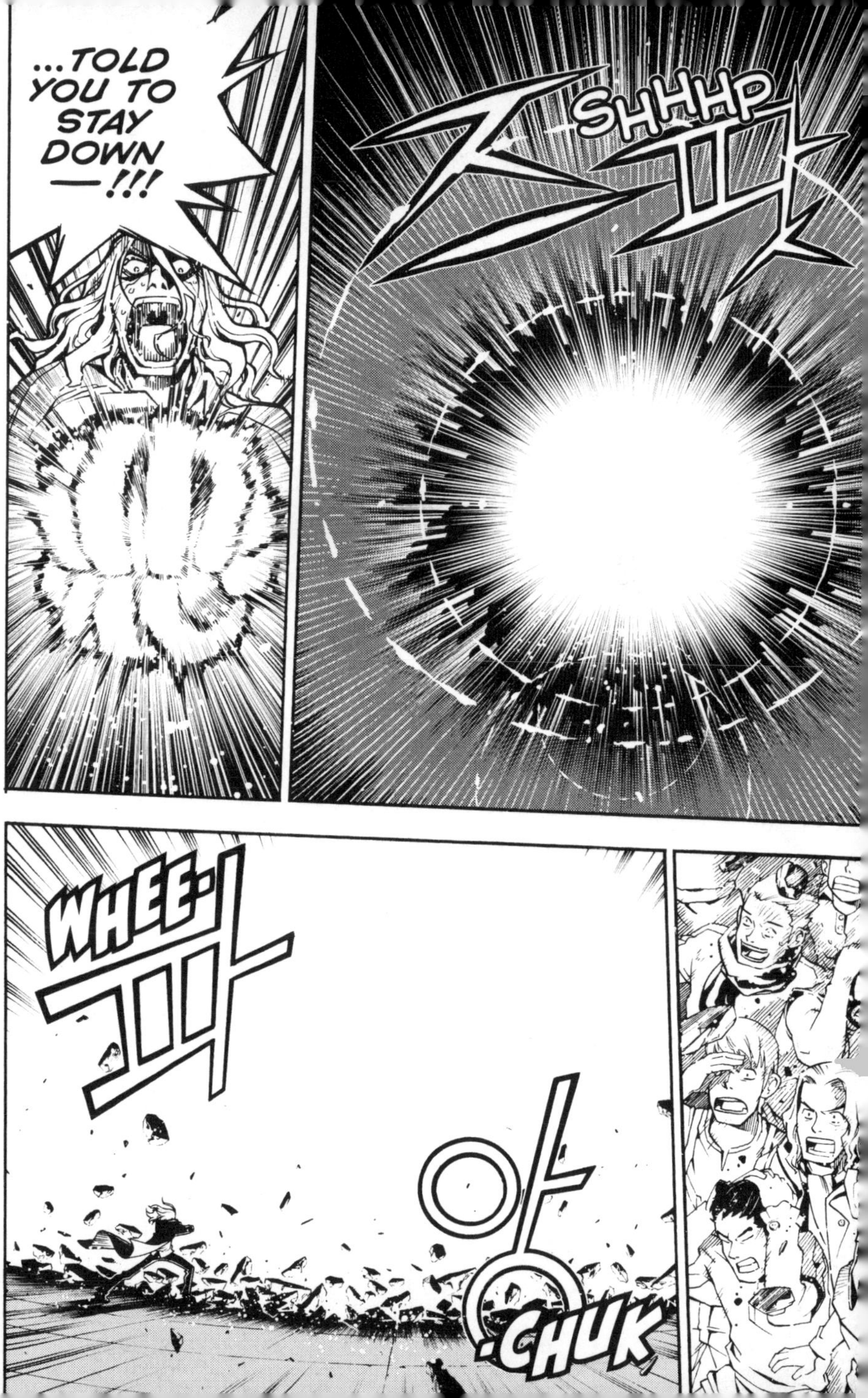
...TOLD YOU TO STAY DOWN—!!!
SHHHP
WHEE-
-CHUK

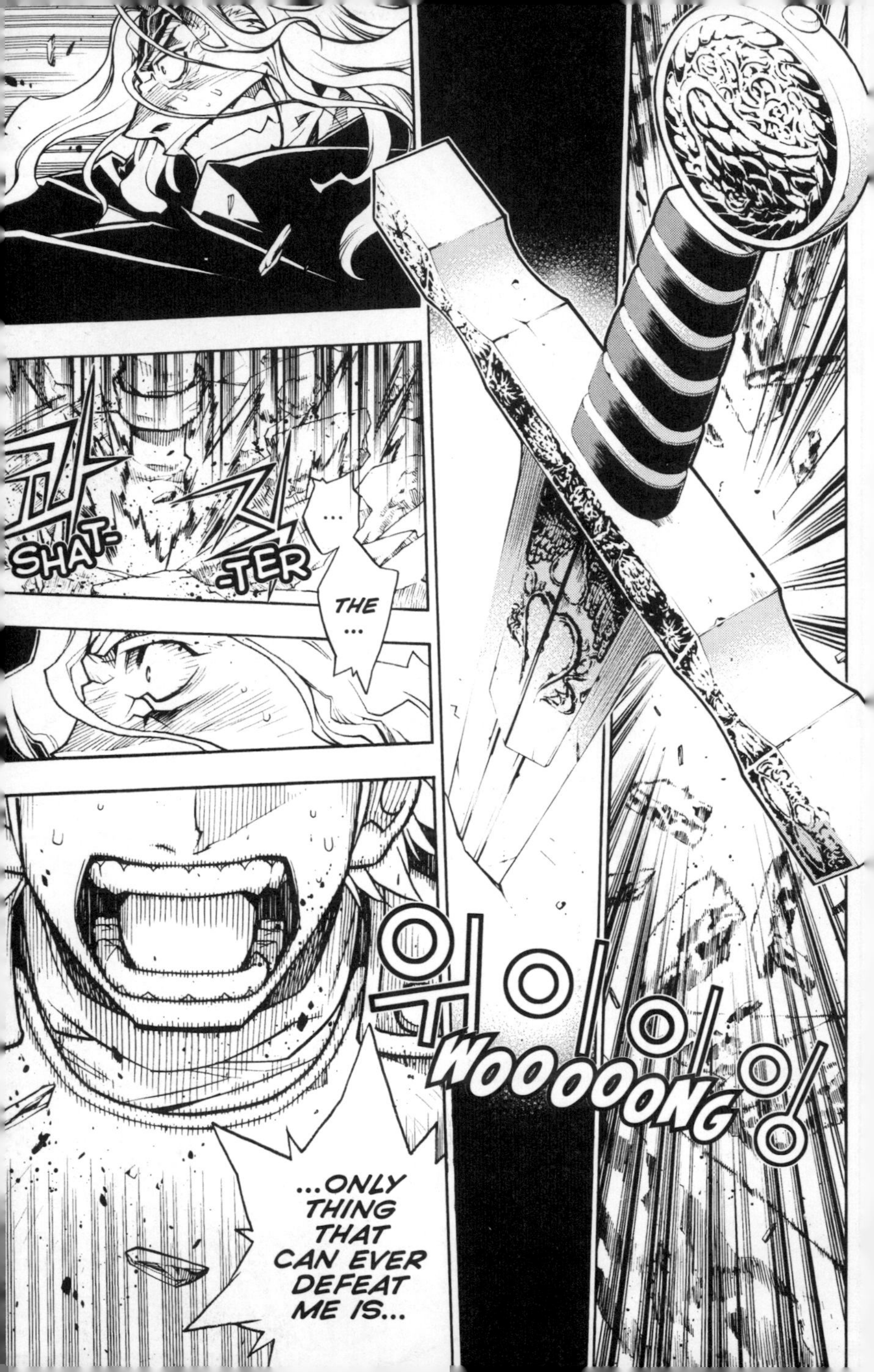
SHAT-
-TER
... THE ...
...ONLY THING THAT CAN EVER DEFEAT ME IS...
WOOOOOONG

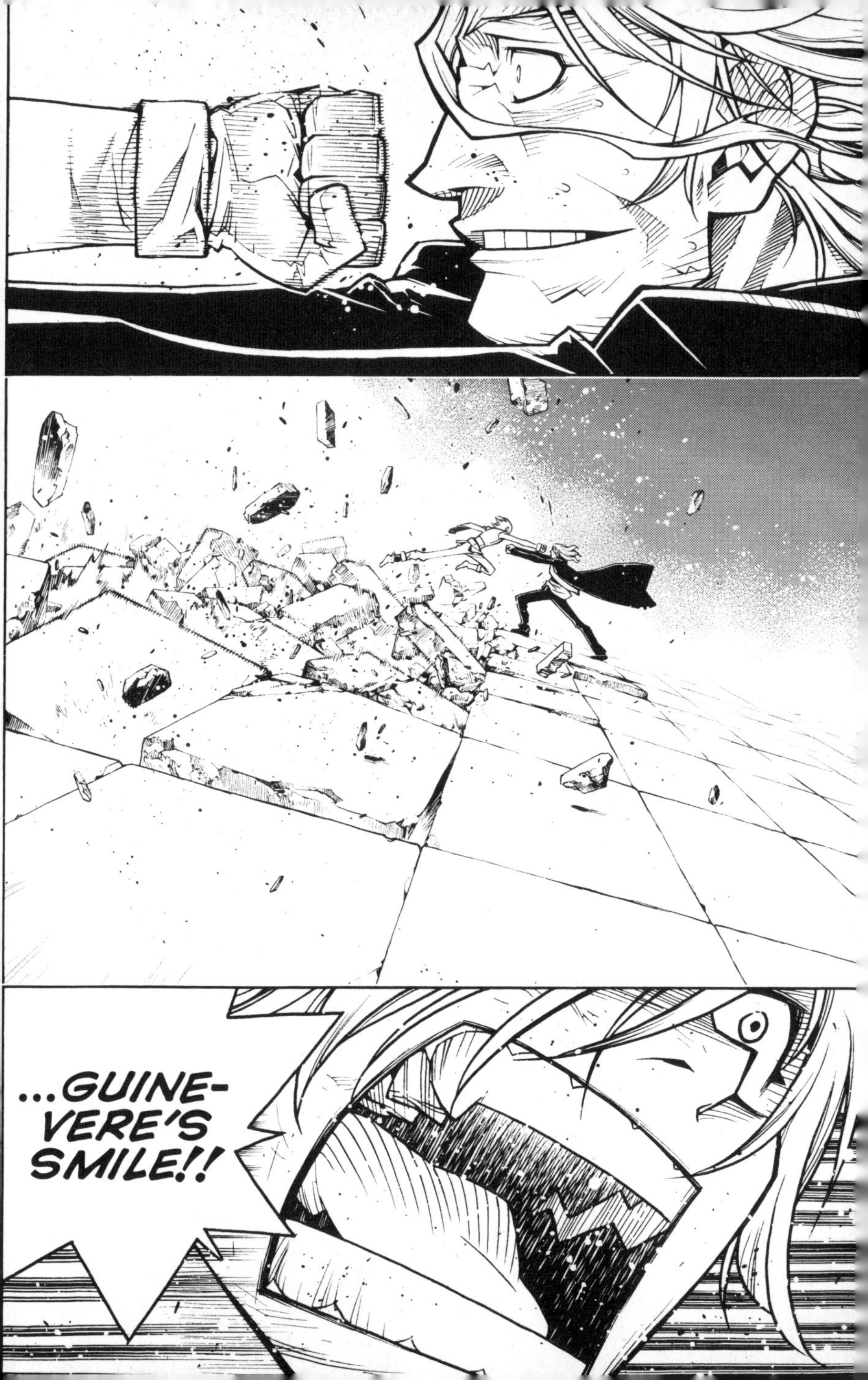
...GUINE-
VERE'S
SMILE!!

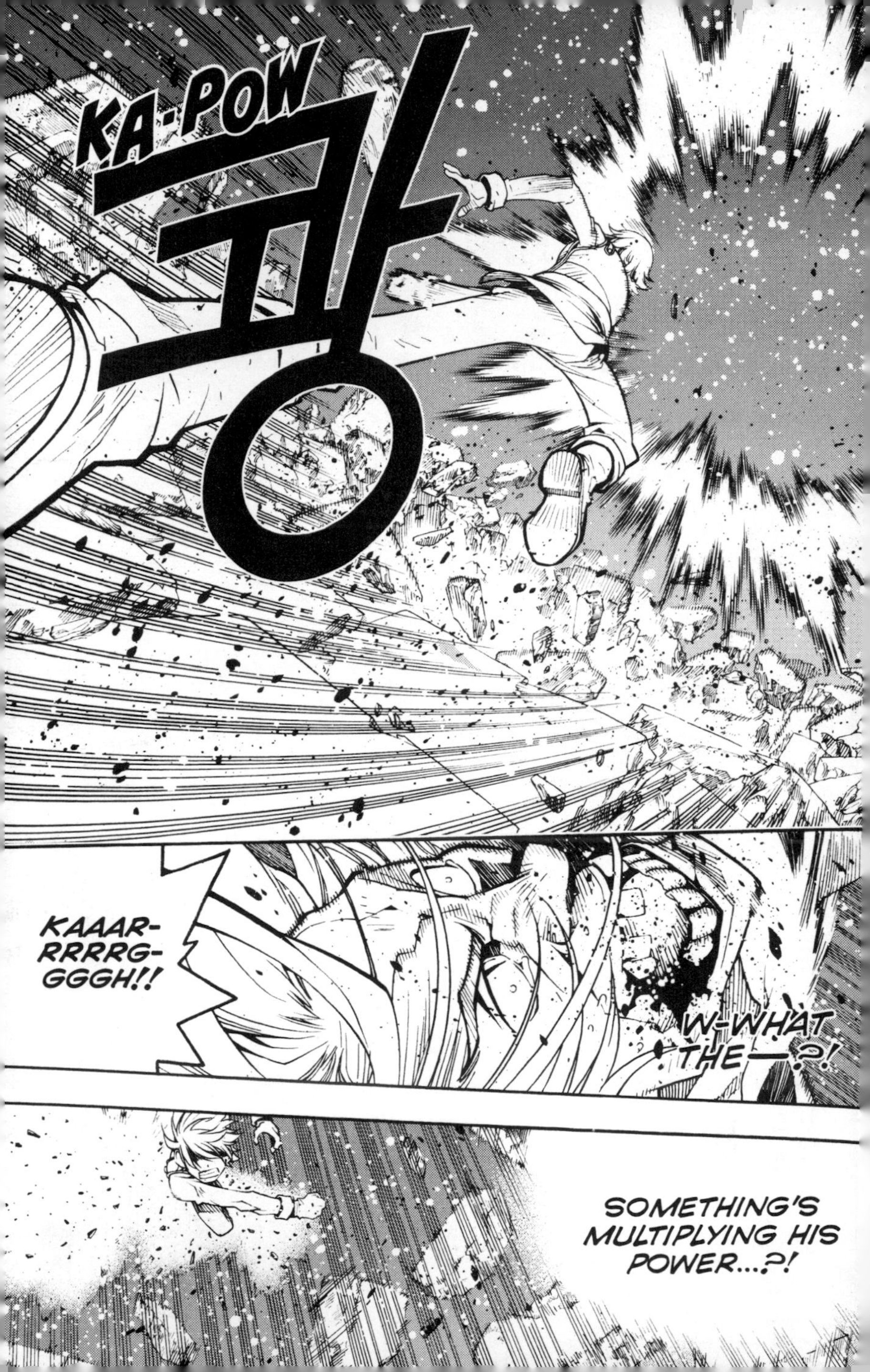
KA-POW
콰앙
KAAAR-RRRRG-GGGH!!
W-WHAT THE—?!
SOMETHING'S MULTIPLYING HIS POWER...?!

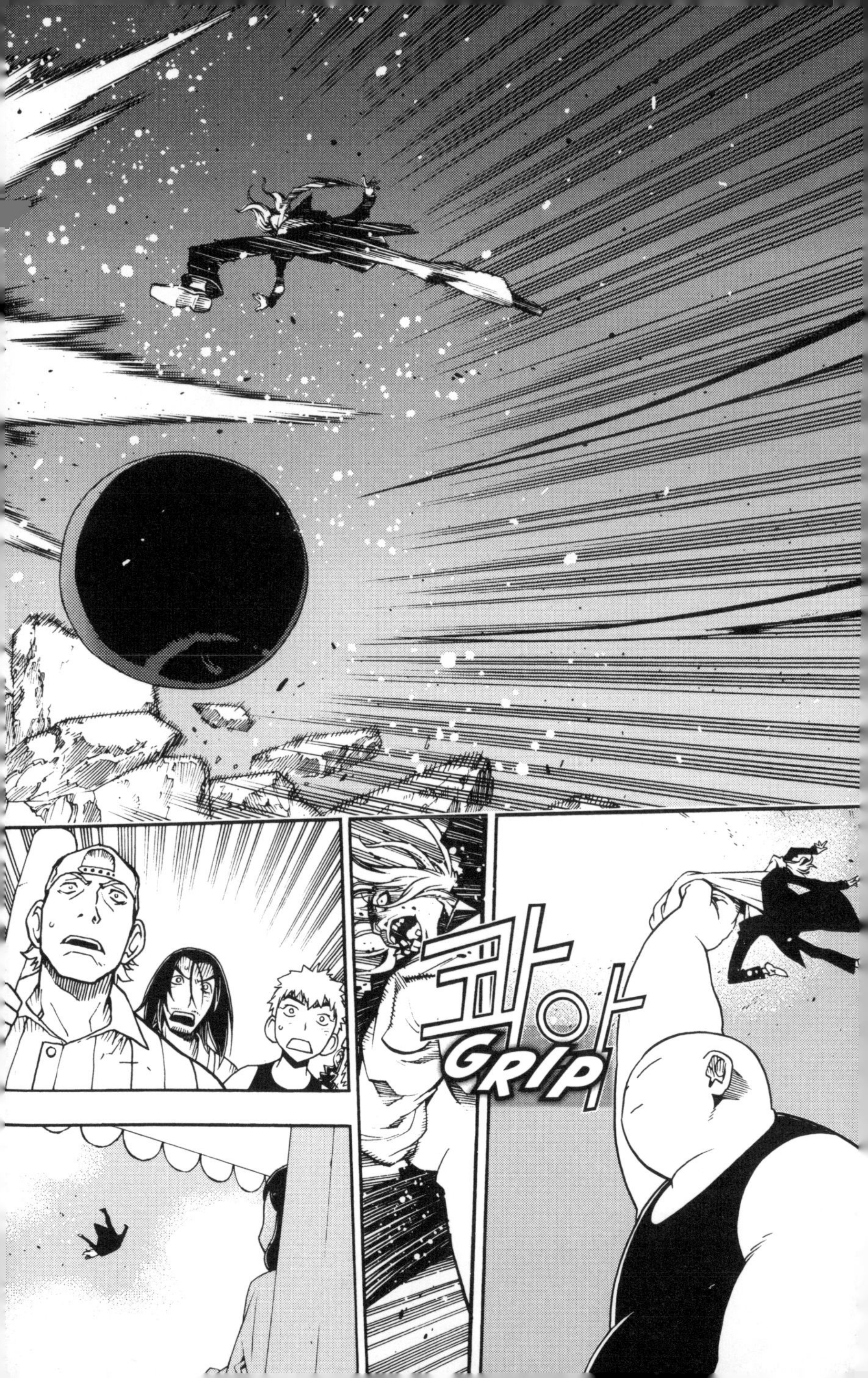
콱아
GRIP

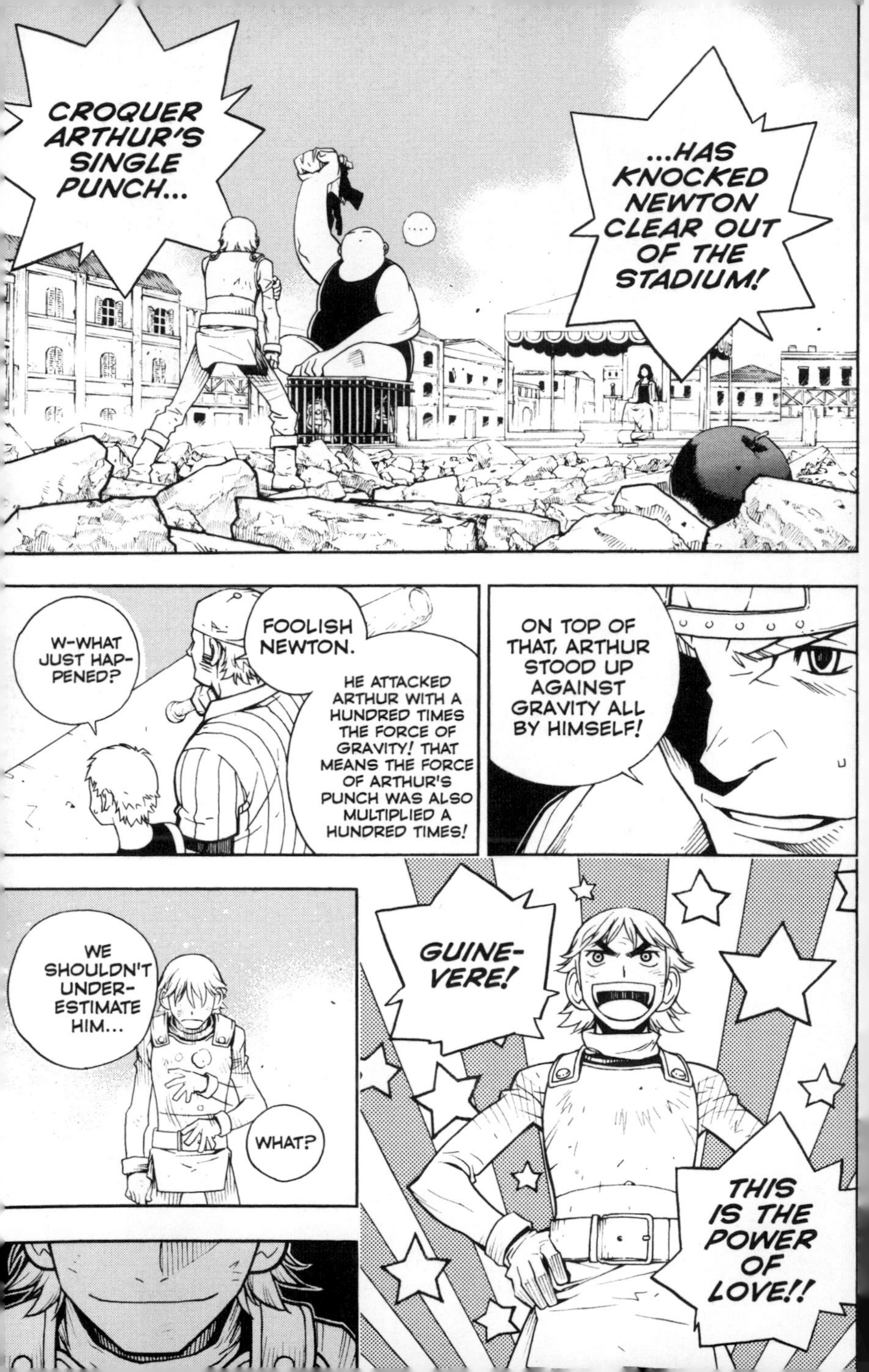
CROQUER ARTHUR'S SINGLE PUNCH...
....
...HAS KNOCKED NEWTON CLEAR OUT OF THE STADIUM!
W-WHAT JUST HAP-PENED?
FOOLISH NEWTON.
HE ATTACKED ARTHUR WITH A HUNDRED TIMES THE FORCE OF GRAVITY! THAT MEANS THE FORCE OF ARTHUR'S PUNCH WAS ALSO MULTIPLIED A HUNDRED TIMES!
ON TOP OF THAT, ARTHUR STOOD UP AGAINST GRAVITY ALL BY HIMSELF!
WE SHOULDN'T UNDER-ESTIMATE HIM...
WHAT?
GUINE-VERE!
THIS IS THE POWER OF LOVE!!

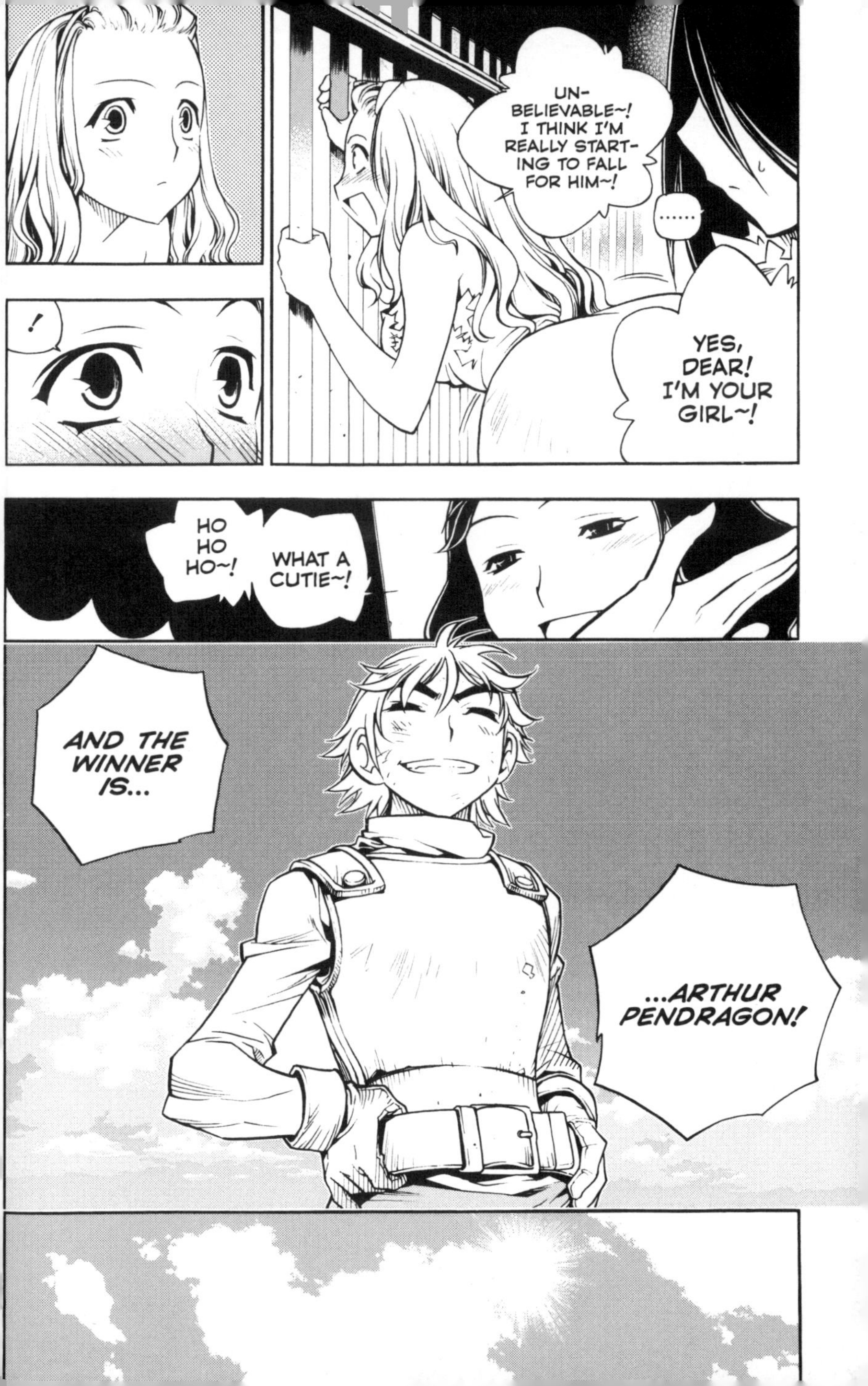
UN-BELIEVABLE~! I THINK I'M REALLY STARTING TO FALL FOR HIM~!
......
!
YES, DEAR! I'M YOUR GIRL~!
HO HO HO~!
WHAT A CUTIE~!
AND THE WINNER IS...
...ARTHUR PENDRAGON!

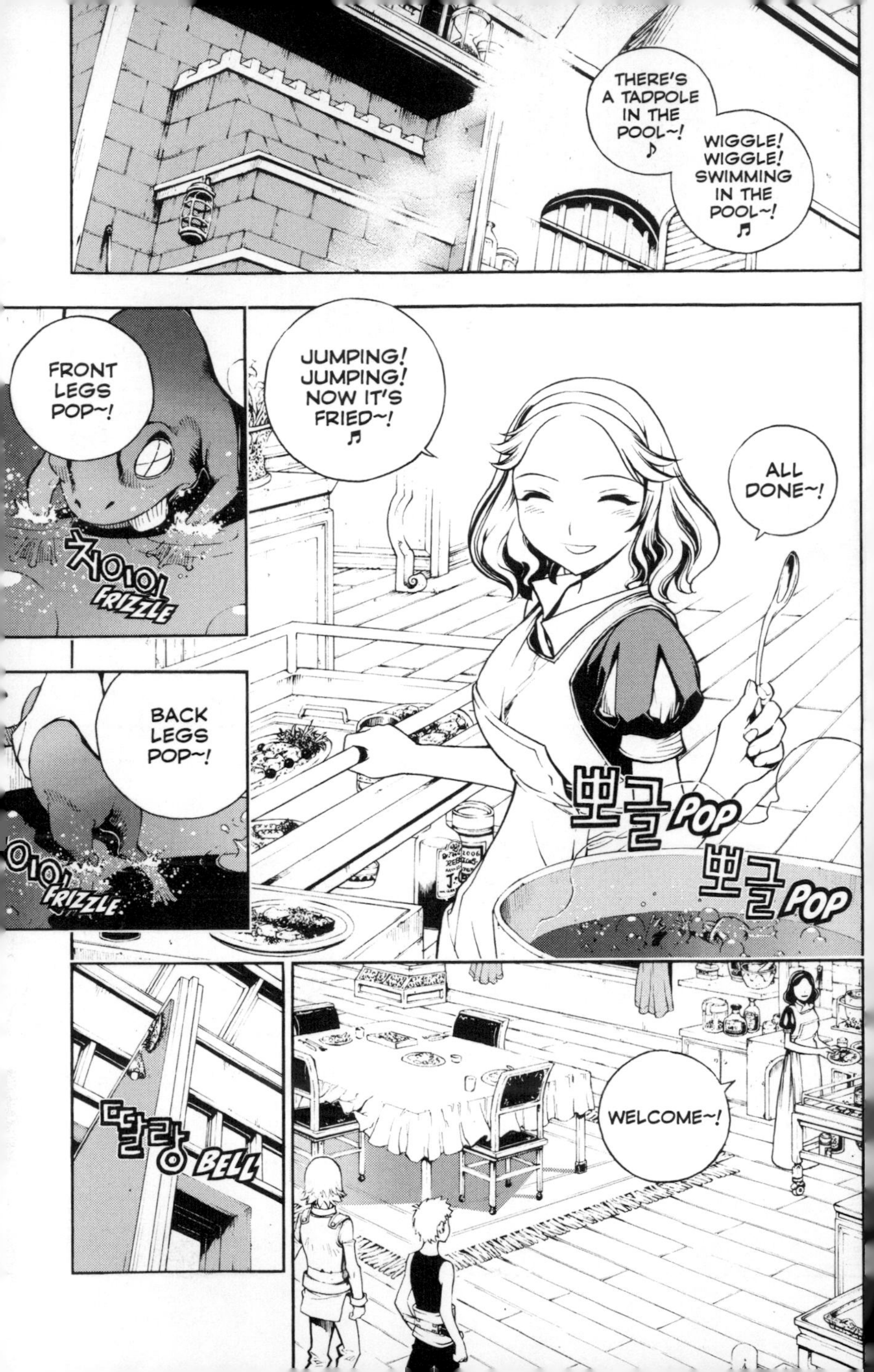
THERE'S A TADPOLE IN THE POOL~! ♪
WIGGLE! WIGGLE! SWIMMING IN THE POOL~! ♬
FRONT LEGS POP~!
치이이 FRIZZLE
BACK LEGS POP~!
이이 FRIZZLE
JUMPING! JUMPING! NOW IT'S FRIED~! ♬
ALL DONE~!
뽀글 POP
뽀글 POP
딸랑 BELL
WELCOME~!

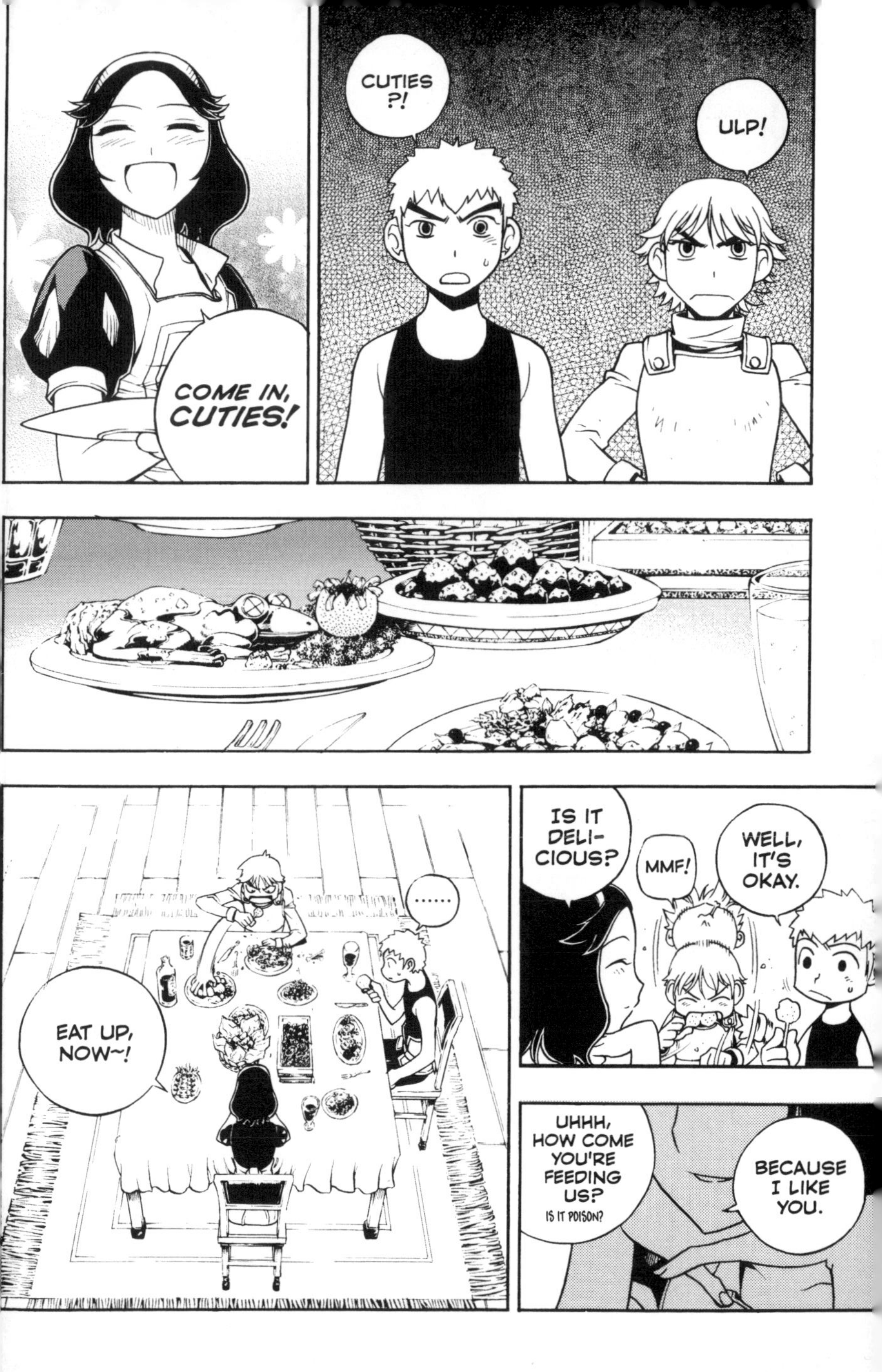
COME IN, CUTIES!
CUTIES ?!
ULP!
EAT UP, NOW~!
......
IS IT DELI- CIOUS?
MMF!
WELL, IT'S OKAY.
UHHH, HOW COME YOU'RE FEEDING US?
IS IT POISON?
BECAUSE I LIKE YOU.

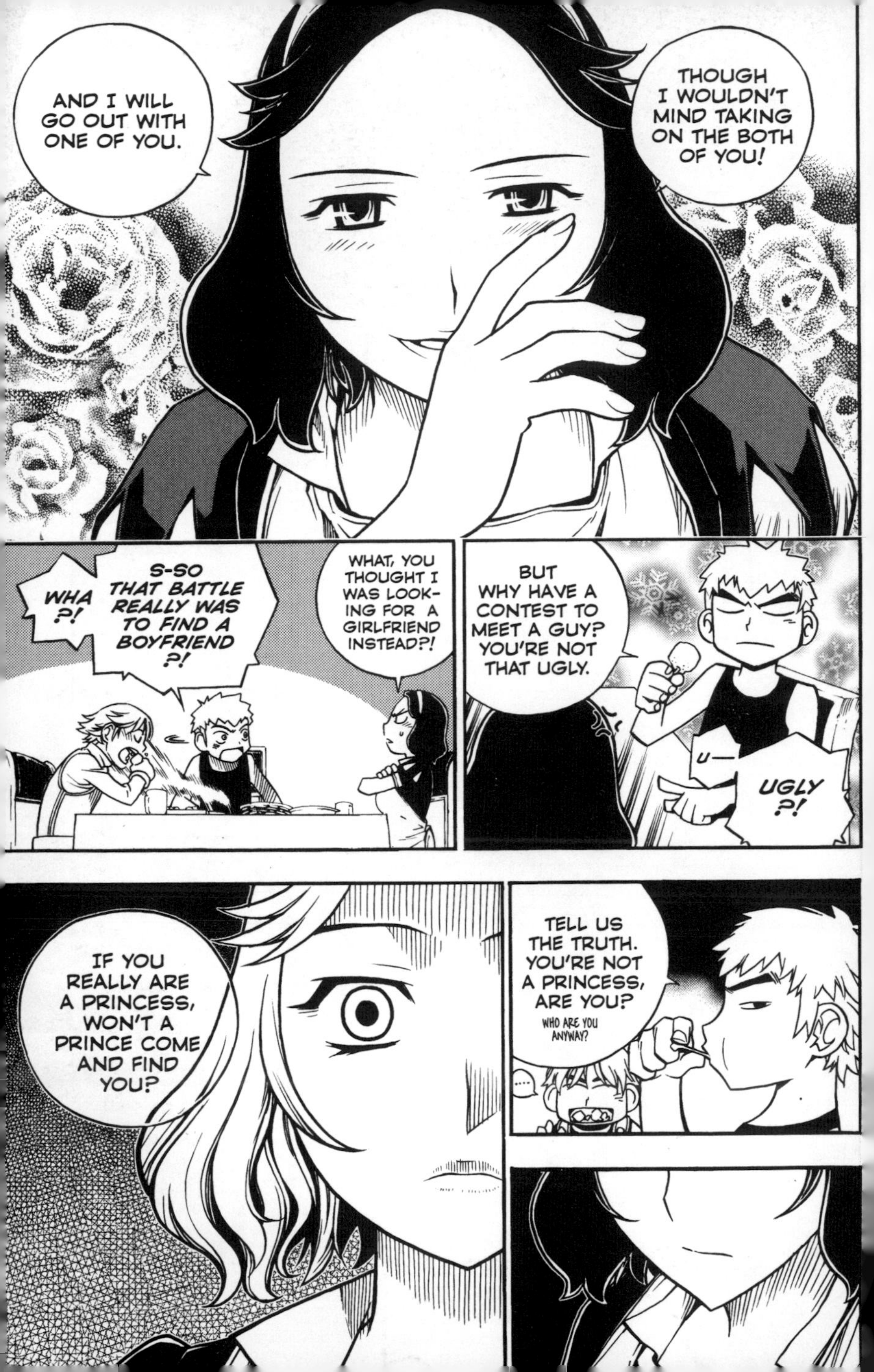
AND I WILL GO OUT WITH ONE OF YOU.
THOUGH I WOULDN'T MIND TAKING ON THE BOTH OF YOU!
WHA ?!
S-SO THAT BATTLE REALLY WAS TO FIND A BOYFRIEND ?!
WHAT, YOU THOUGHT I WAS LOOK-ING FOR A GIRLFRIEND INSTEAD?!
BUT WHY HAVE A CONTEST TO MEET A GUY? YOU'RE NOT THAT UGLY.
U—
UGLY ?!
IF YOU REALLY ARE A PRINCESS, WON'T A PRINCE COME AND FIND YOU?
TELL US THE TRUTH. YOU'RE NOT A PRINCESS, ARE YOU?
WHO ARE YOU ANYWAY?
...

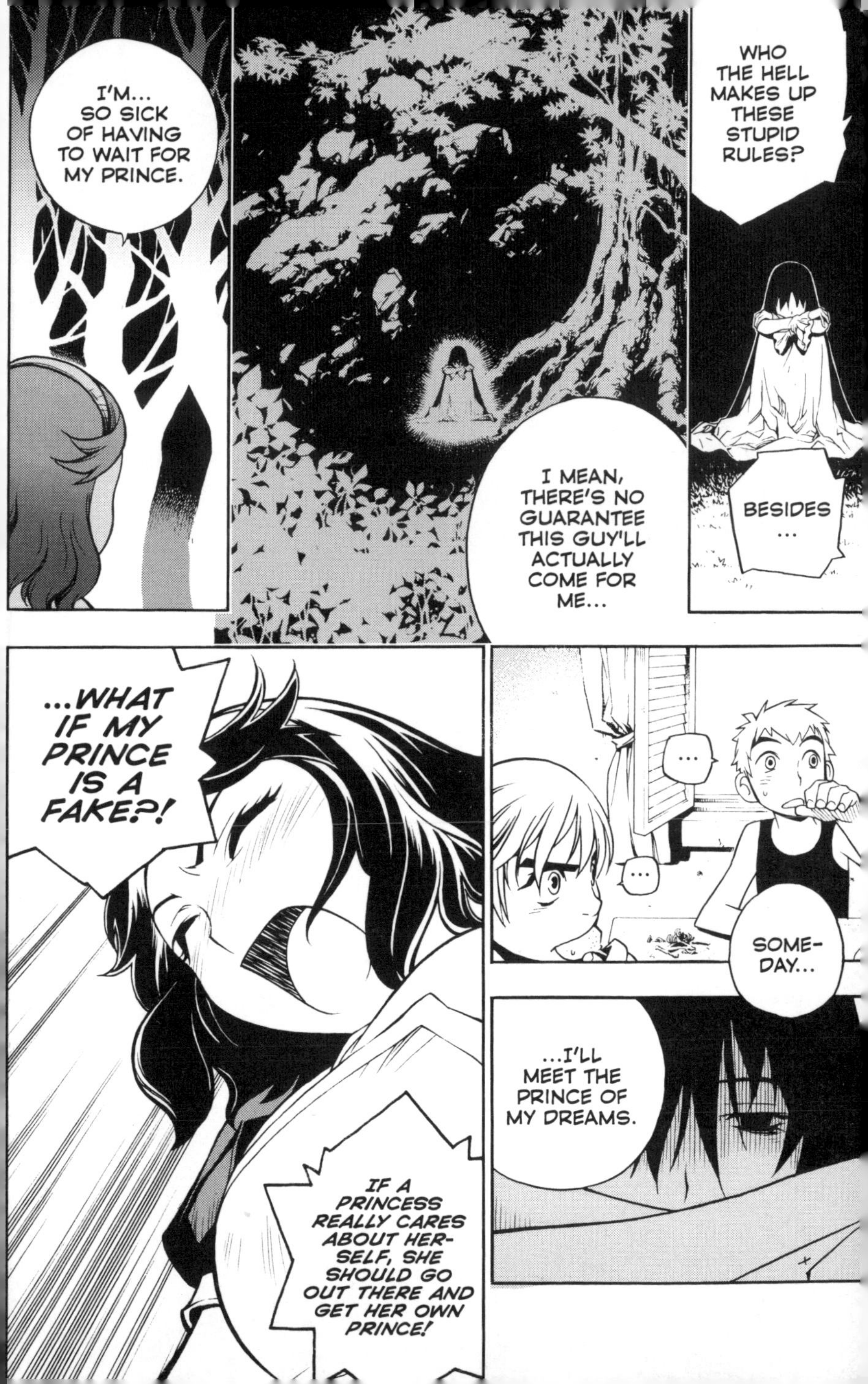
I'M... SO SICK OF HAVING TO WAIT FOR MY PRINCE.
I MEAN, THERE'S NO GUARANTEE THIS GUY'LL ACTUALLY COME FOR ME...
WHO THE HELL MAKES UP THESE STUPID RULES?
BESIDES...
...WHAT IF MY PRINCE IS A FAKE?!
IF A PRINCESS REALLY CARES ABOUT HER-SELF, SHE SHOULD GO OUT THERE AND GET HER OWN PRINCE!
...
...
SOME-DAY...
...I'LL MEET THE PRINCE OF MY DREAMS.

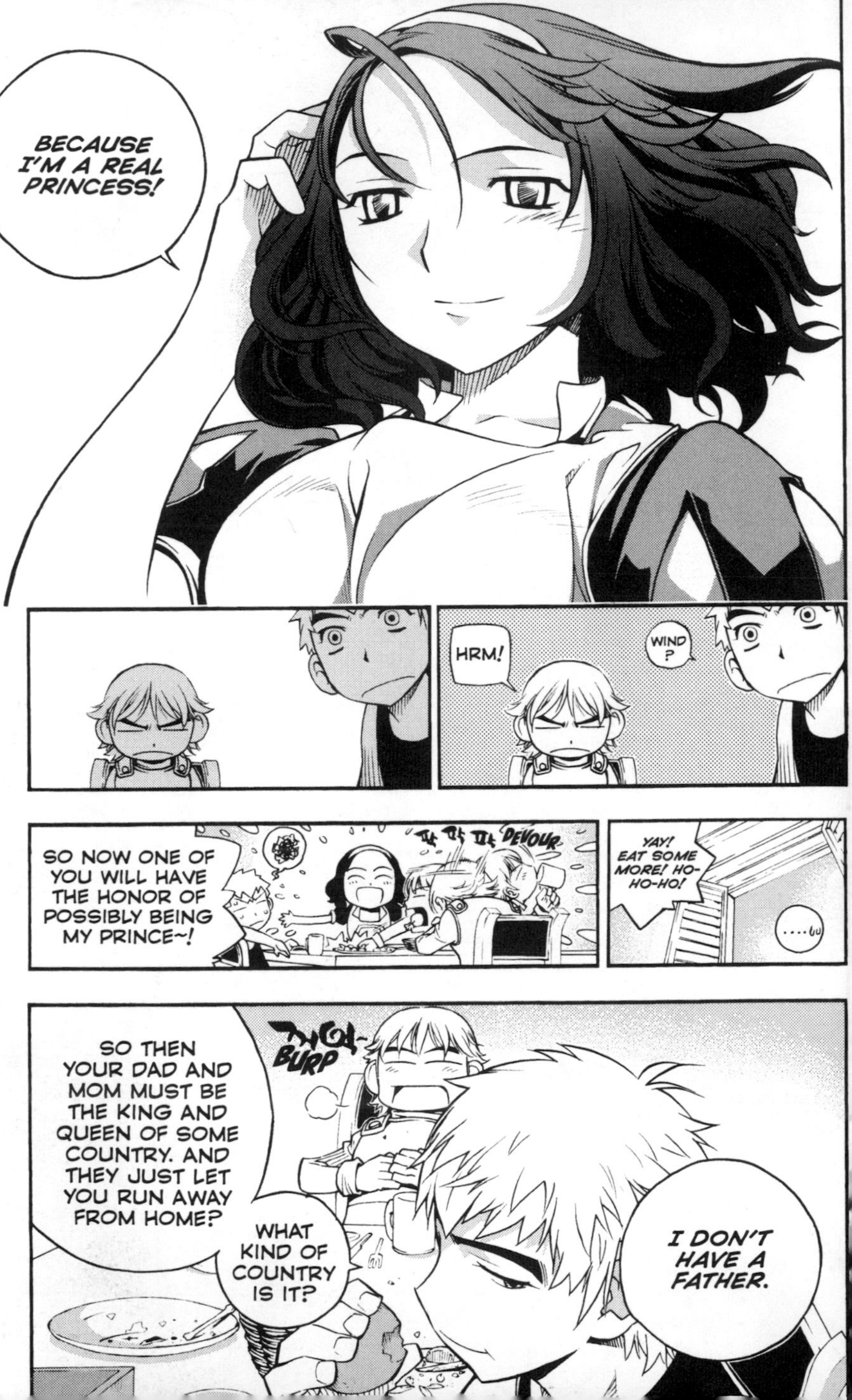

BECAUSE I'M A REAL PRINCESS!
HRM!
WIND?
SO NOW ONE OF YOU WILL HAVE THE HONOR OF POSSIBLY BEING MY PRINCE~!
DEVOUR
YAY! EAT SOME MORE! HO-HO-HO!
....
BURP
SO THEN YOUR DAD AND MOM MUST BE THE KING AND QUEEN OF SOME COUNTRY. AND THEY JUST LET YOU RUN AWAY FROM HOME?
WHAT KIND OF COUNTRY IS IT?
I DON'T HAVE A FATHER.

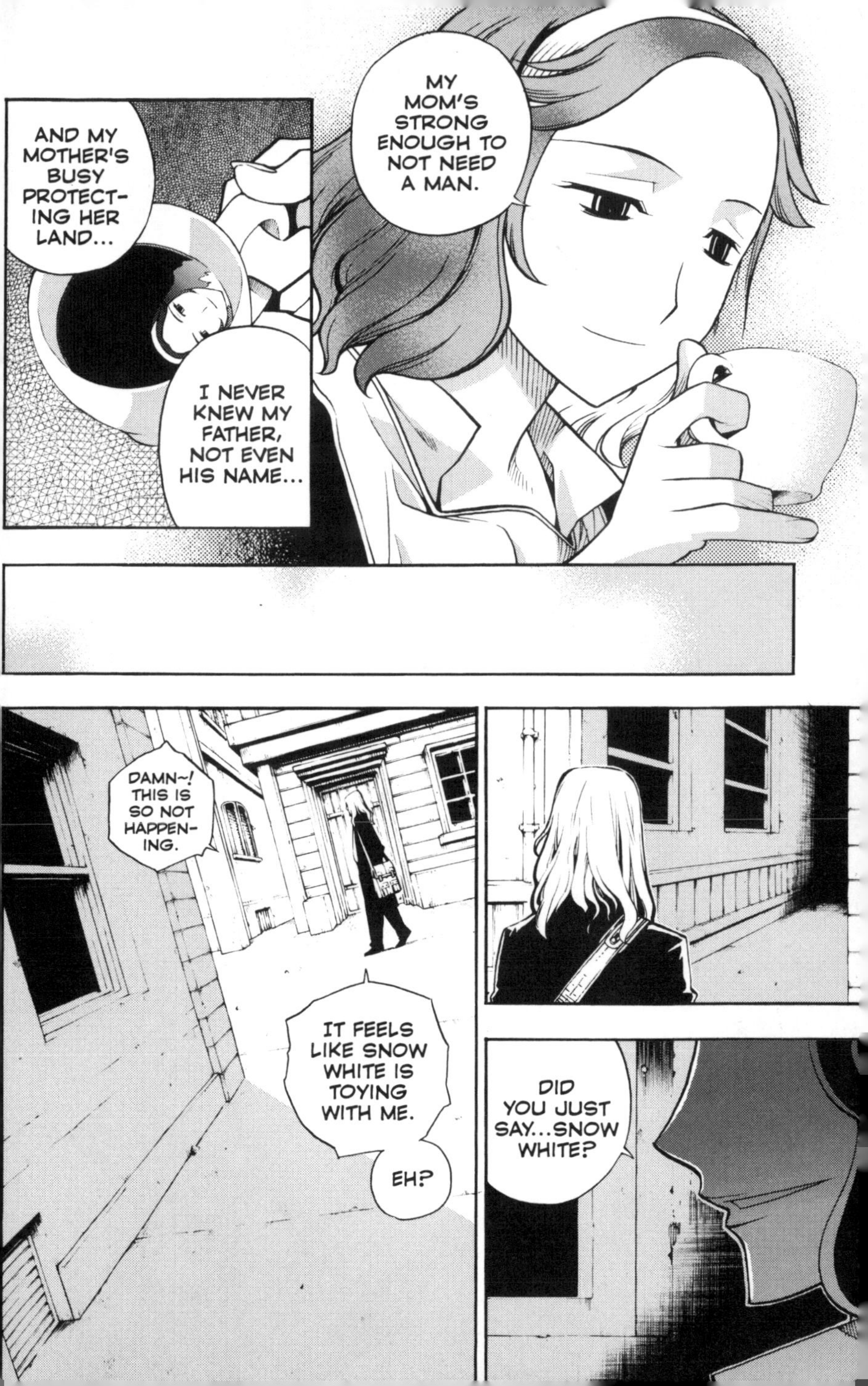
AND MY MOTHER'S BUSY PROTECT-ING HER LAND...
I NEVER KNEW MY FATHER, NOT EVEN HIS NAME...
MY MOM'S STRONG ENOUGH TO NOT NEED A MAN.
DAMN~! THIS IS SO NOT HAPPEN-ING.
IT FEELS LIKE SNOW WHITE IS TOYING WITH ME.
EH?
DID YOU JUST SAY...SNOW WHITE?

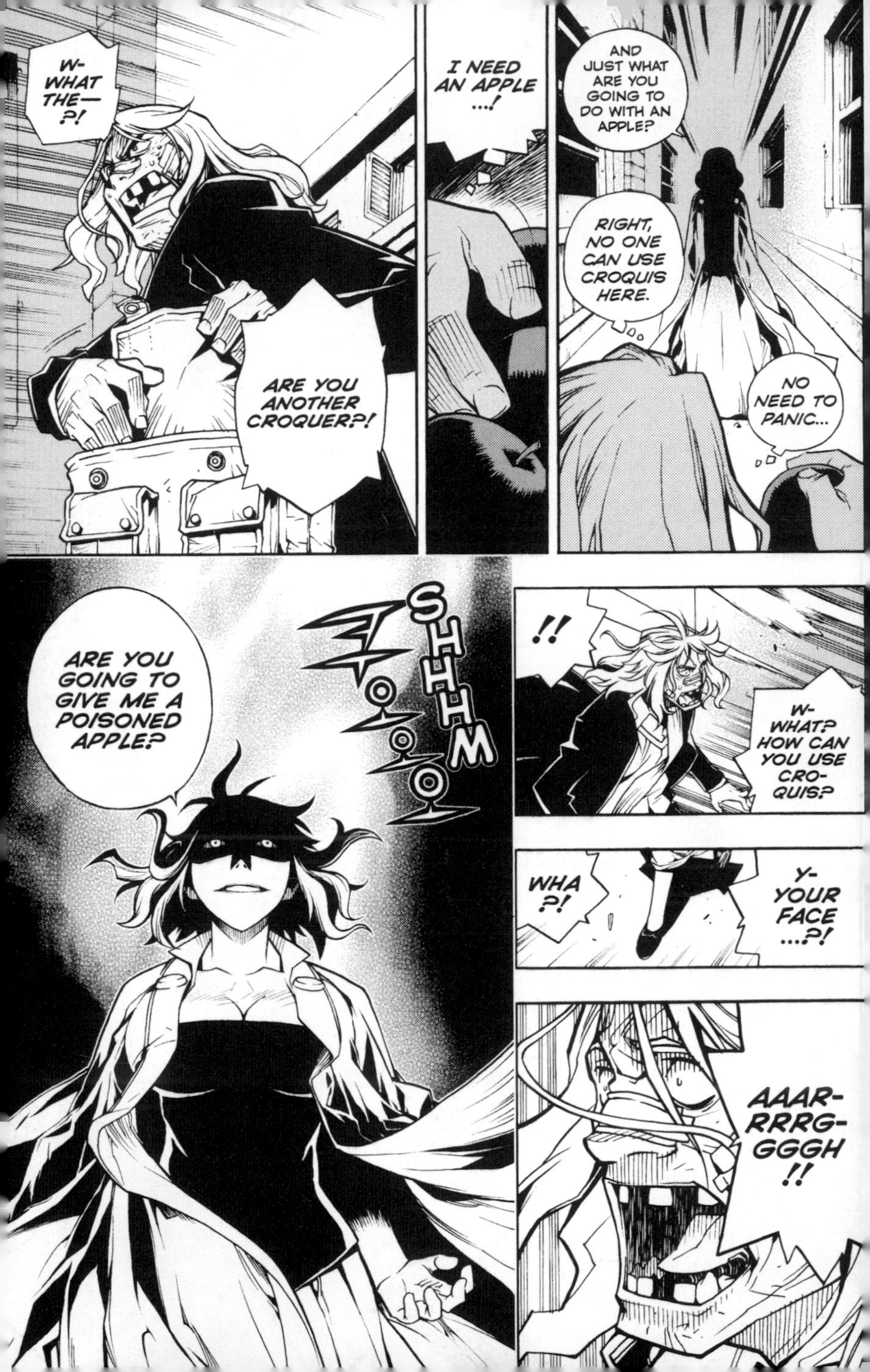
W-WHAT THE—?!
ARE YOU ANOTHER CROQUER?!
I NEED AN APPLE...!
AND JUST WHAT ARE YOU GOING TO DO WITH AN APPLE?
RIGHT, NO ONE CAN USE CROQUIS HERE.
NO NEED TO PANIC...
ARE YOU GOING TO GIVE ME A POISONED APPLE?
SHHHM
!!
W-WHAT? HOW CAN YOU USE CRO-QUIS?
WHA?!
Y-YOUR FACE...?!
AAARRRRGGGGH!!

BITE

SHE'S PLAYING WITH EX-CALIBUR.

THAT'S SOME-THING ONLY SHE WOULD DO.

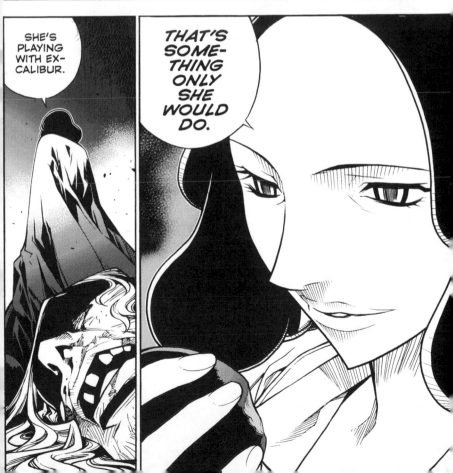

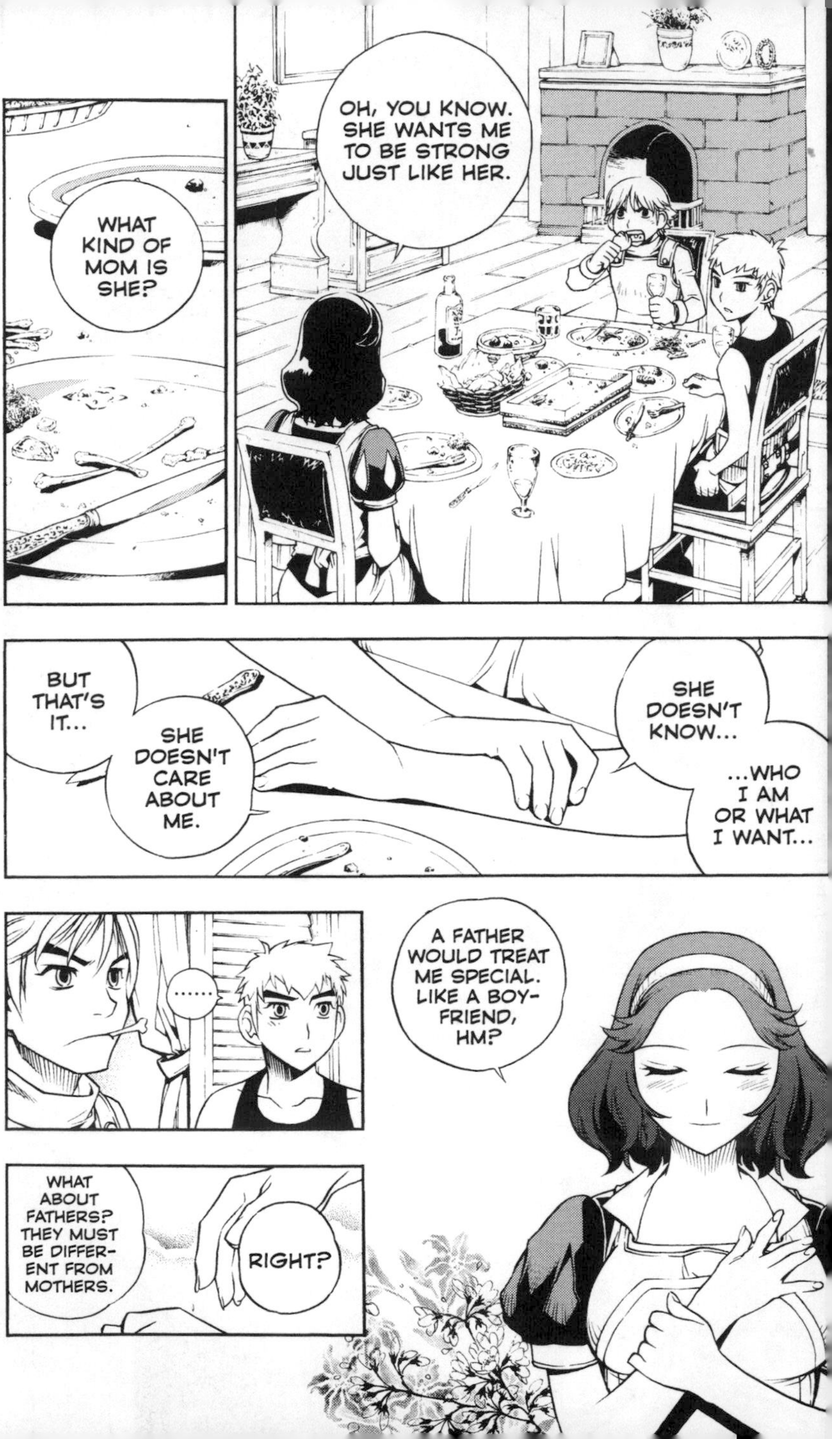
WHAT KIND OF MOM IS SHE?
OH, YOU KNOW. SHE WANTS ME TO BE STRONG JUST LIKE HER.
BUT THAT'S IT...
SHE DOESN'T CARE ABOUT ME.
SHE DOESN'T KNOW...
...WHO I AM OR WHAT I WANT...
......
WHAT ABOUT FATHERS? THEY MUST BE DIFFER-ENT FROM MOTHERS.
RIGHT?
A FATHER WOULD TREAT ME SPECIAL. LIKE A BOY-FRIEND, HM?

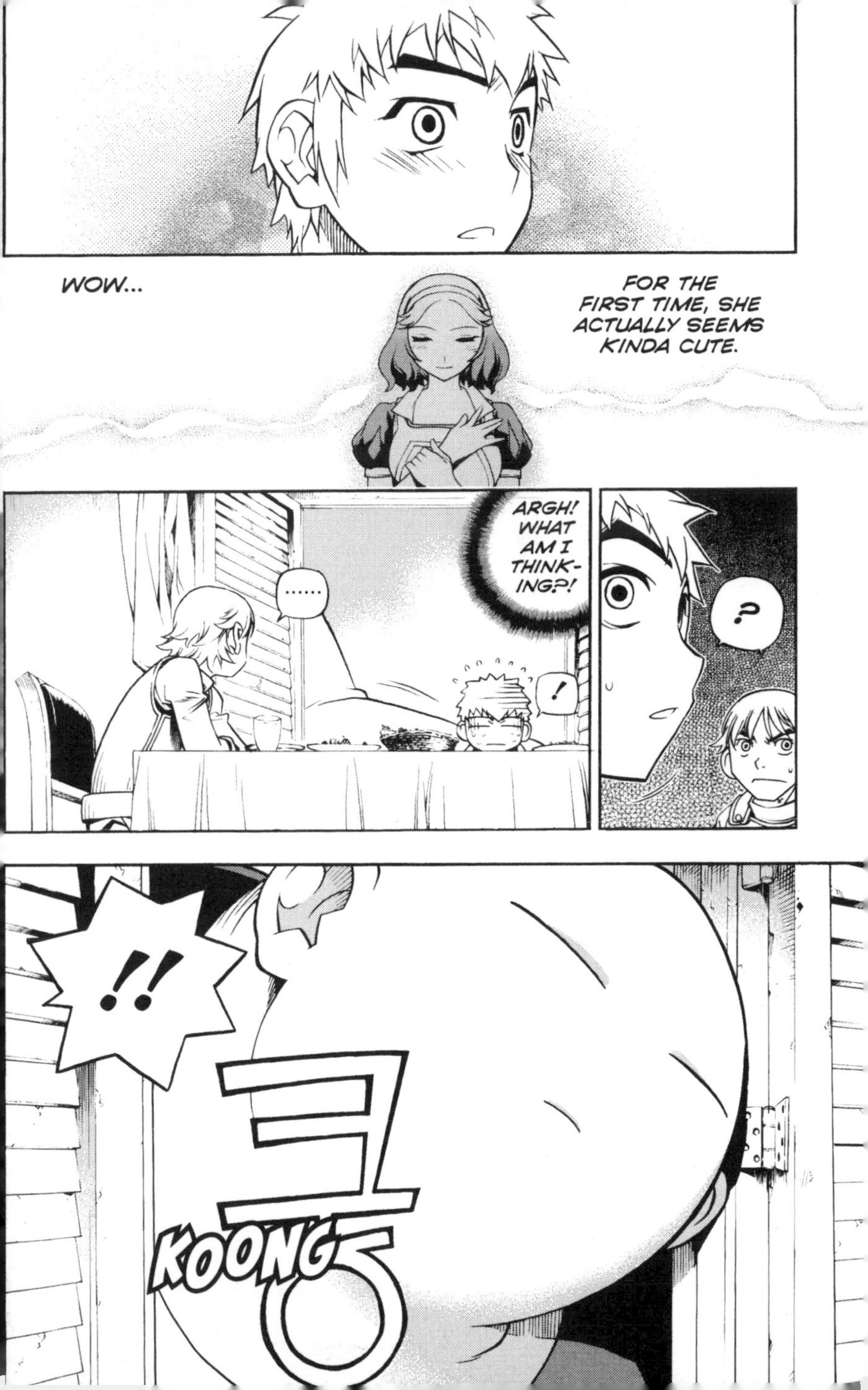
WOW...
FOR THE FIRST TIME, SHE ACTUALLY SEEMS KINDA CUTE.
....
!
ARGH! WHAT AM I THINK-ING?!
?
!!
KOONG

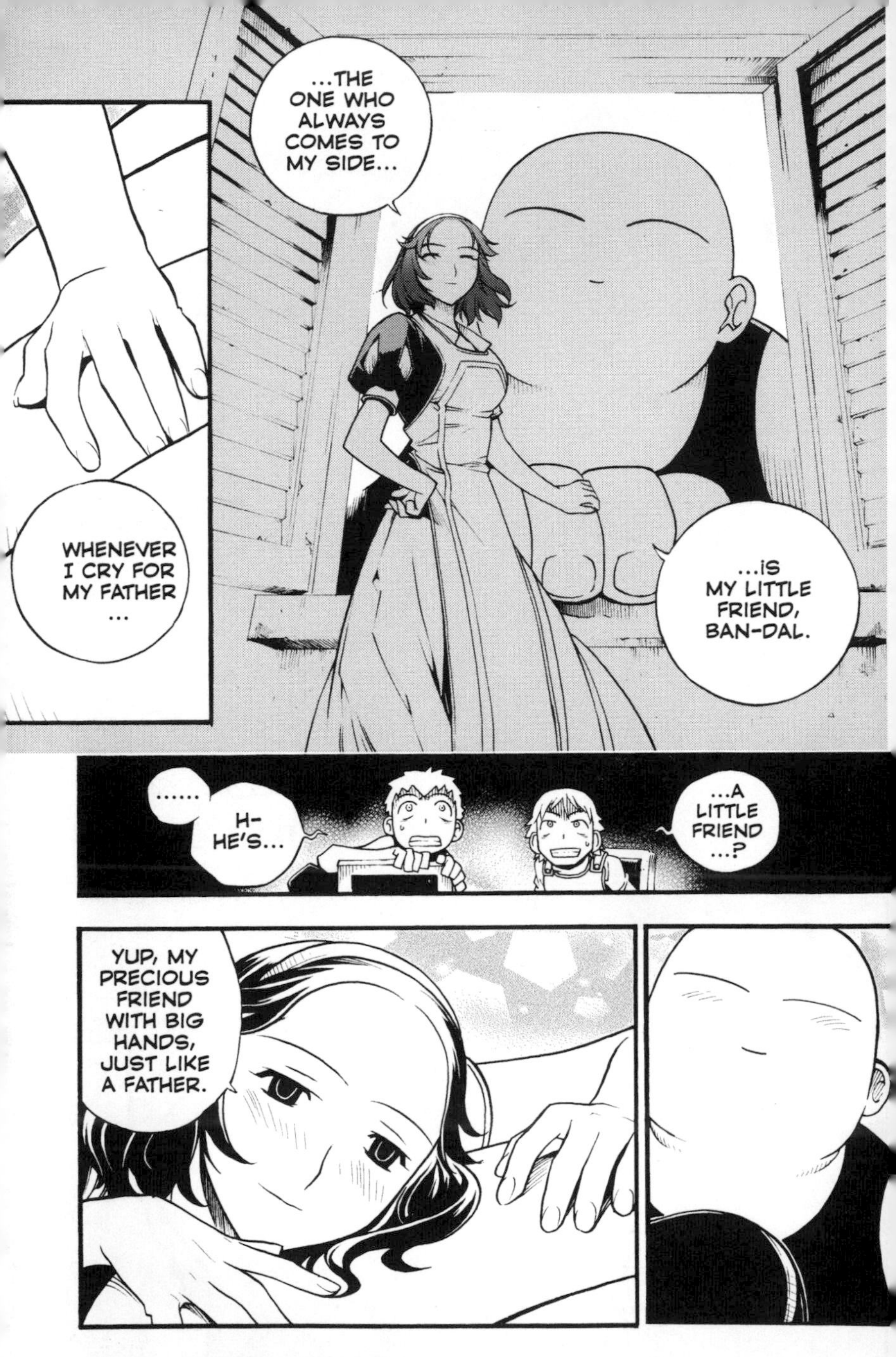
WHENEVER I CRY FOR MY FATHER ...
...THE ONE WHO ALWAYS COMES TO MY SIDE...
...IS MY LITTLE FRIEND, BAN-DAL.
......
H- HE'S...
...A LITTLE FRIEND ...?
YUP, MY PRECIOUS FRIEND WITH BIG HANDS, JUST LIKE A FATHER.

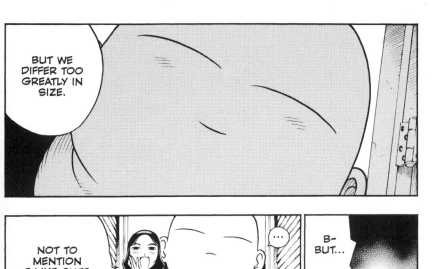

BUT WE DIFFER TOO GREATLY IN SIZE.

NOT TO MENTION I LIKE CUTE AND HANDSOME BOYS.

...

B-BUT...

....

......

SO...

...SHUT UP AND DECIDE!

EVEN IF THERE WERE A HUNDRED OF YOU, I WOULDN'T WANT A SINGLE ONE!

WHAT WAS THAT?

I HAVE GUINEVERE! SHE'S STOLEN MY HEART! I'LL NEVER LEAVE HER!

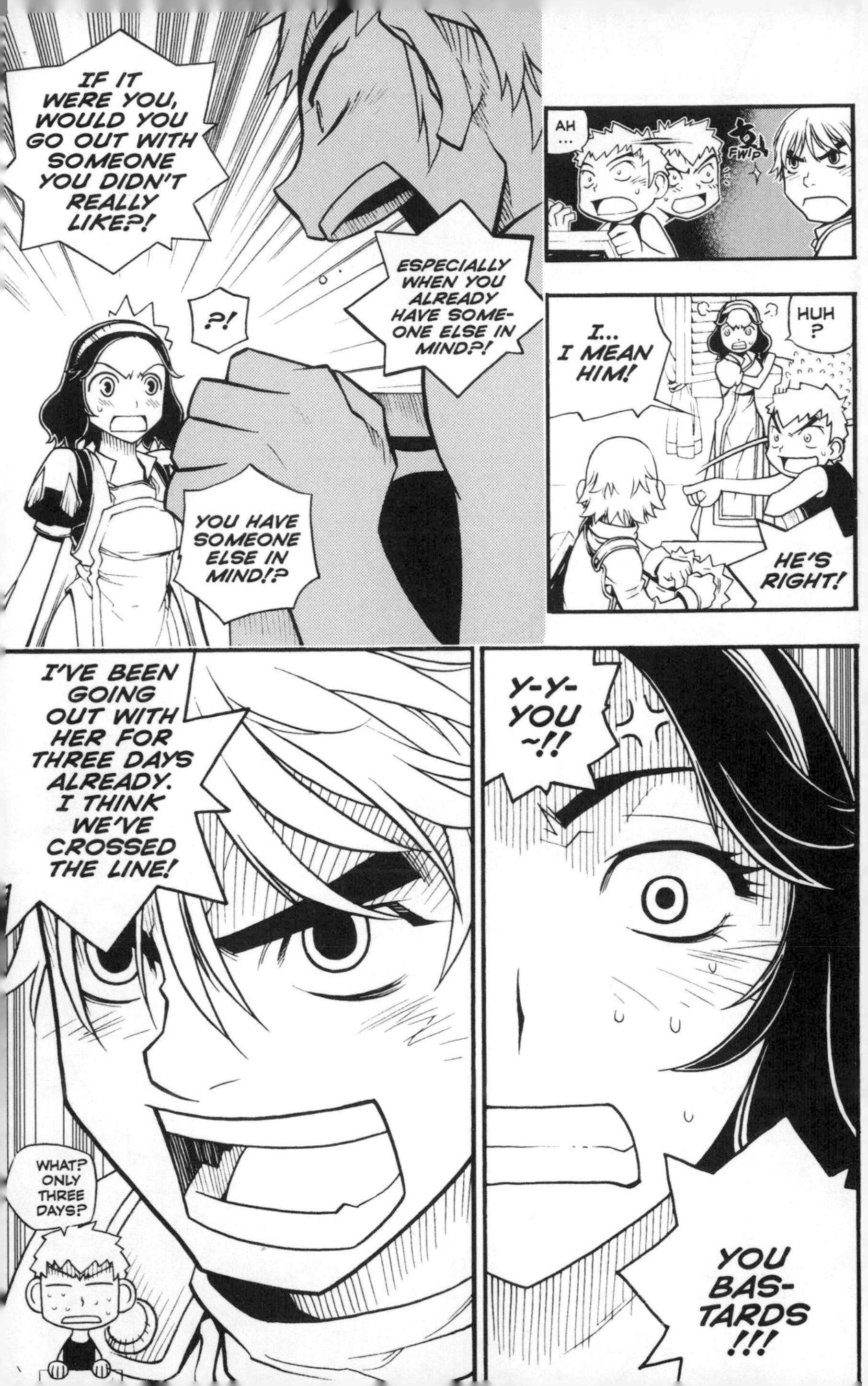
IF IT WERE YOU, WOULD YOU GO OUT WITH SOMEONE YOU DIDN'T REALLY LIKE?!
ESPECIALLY WHEN YOU ALREADY HAVE SOME-ONE ELSE IN MIND?!
?!
YOU HAVE SOMEONE ELSE IN MIND!?
AH ...
FWIP
I... I MEAN HIM!
HUH ?
HE'S RIGHT!
I'VE BEEN GOING OUT WITH HER FOR THREE DAYS ALREADY. I THINK WE'VE CROSSED THE LINE!
WHAT? ONLY THREE DAYS?
Y-Y-YOU ~!!
YOU BAS-TARDS !!!

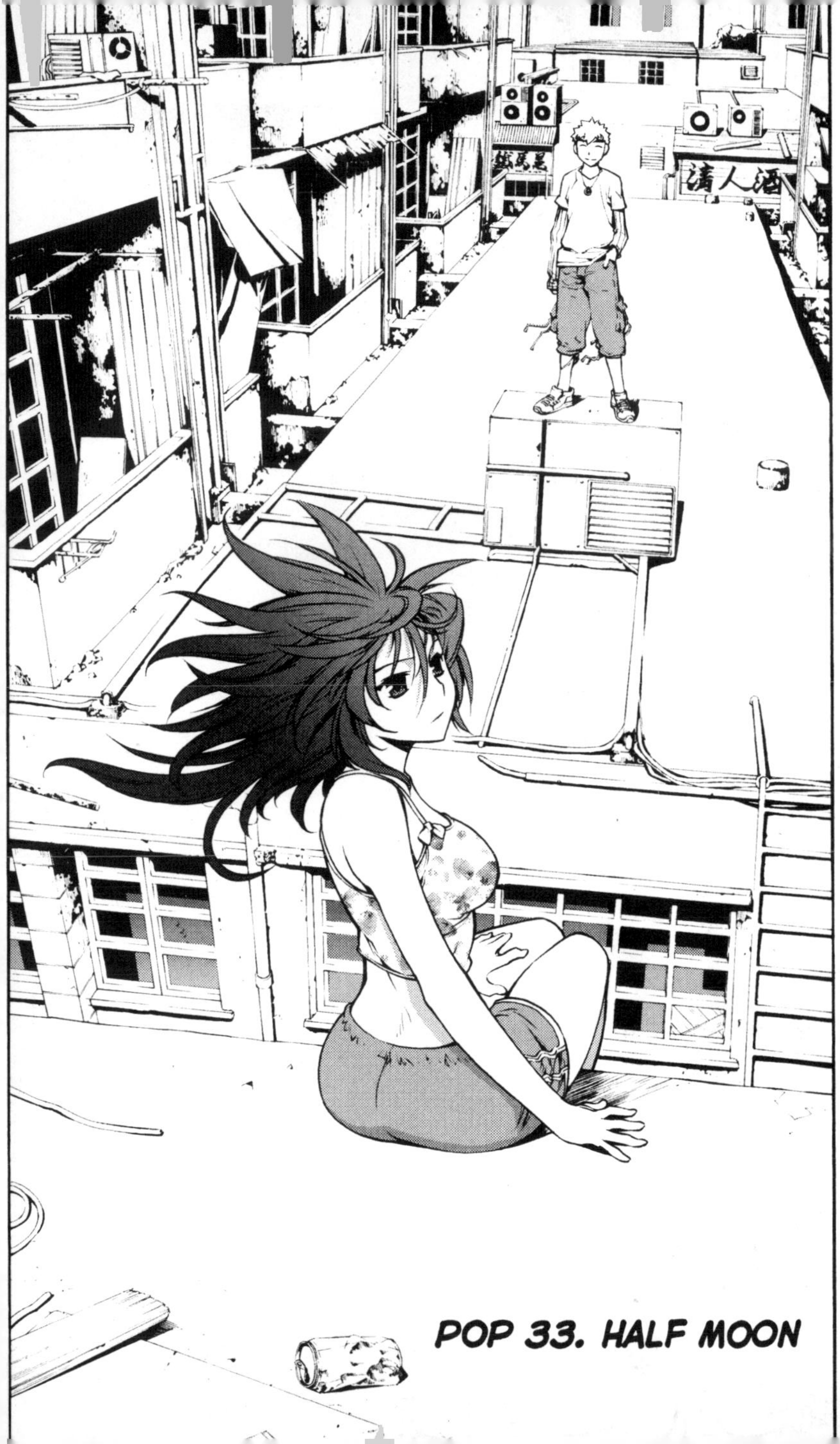

POP 33. HALF MOON

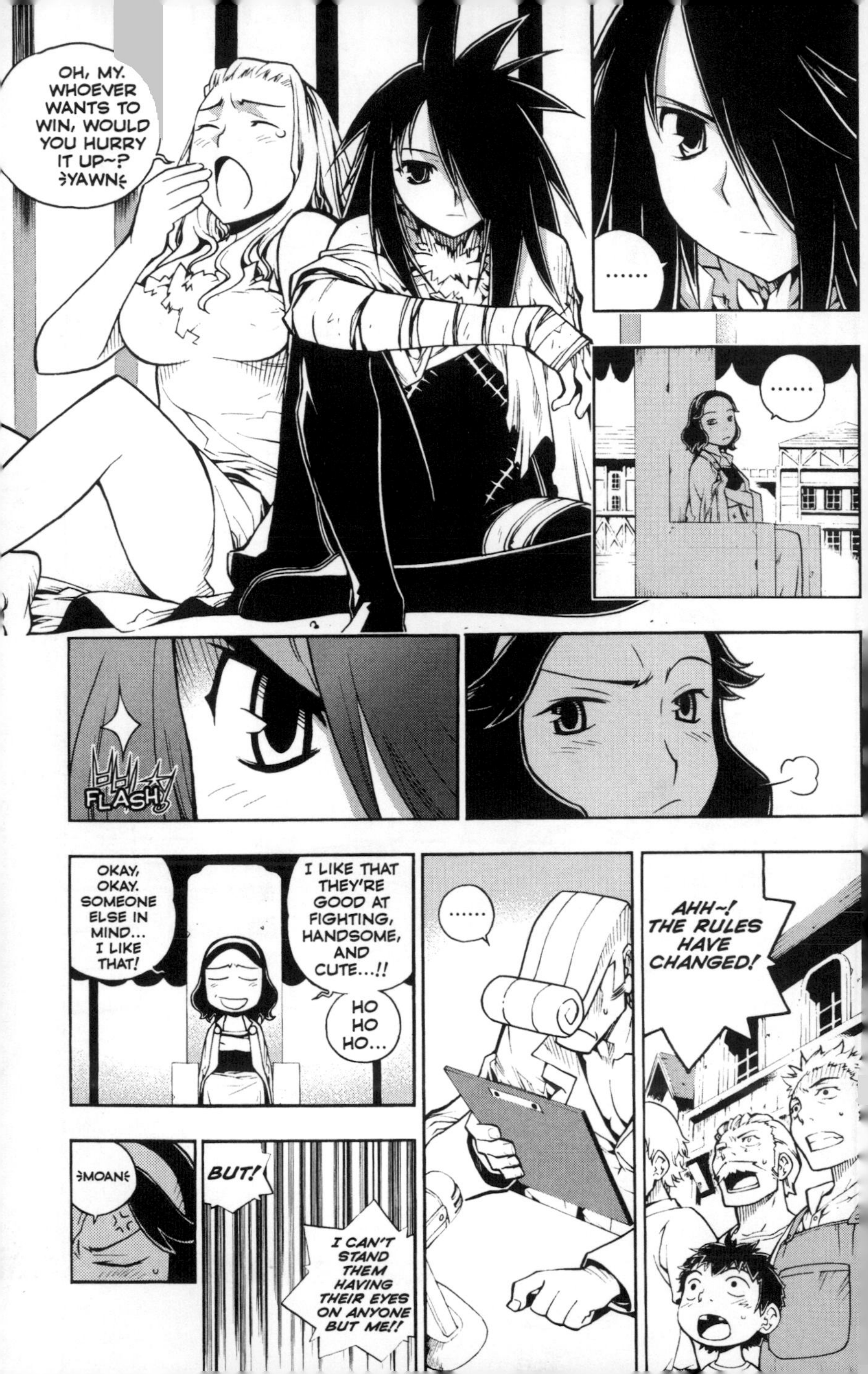
OH, MY. WHOEVER WANTS TO WIN, WOULD YOU HURRY IT UP~? ≯YAWN≮
......
......
FLASH
OKAY, OKAY. SOMEONE ELSE IN MIND... I LIKE THAT!
I LIKE THAT THEY'RE GOOD AT FIGHTING, HANDSOME, AND CUTE...!!
HO HO HO...
≯MOAN≮
BUT!
I CAN'T STAND THEM HAVING THEIR EYES ON ANYONE BUT ME!!
......
AHH~! THE RULES HAVE CHANGED!

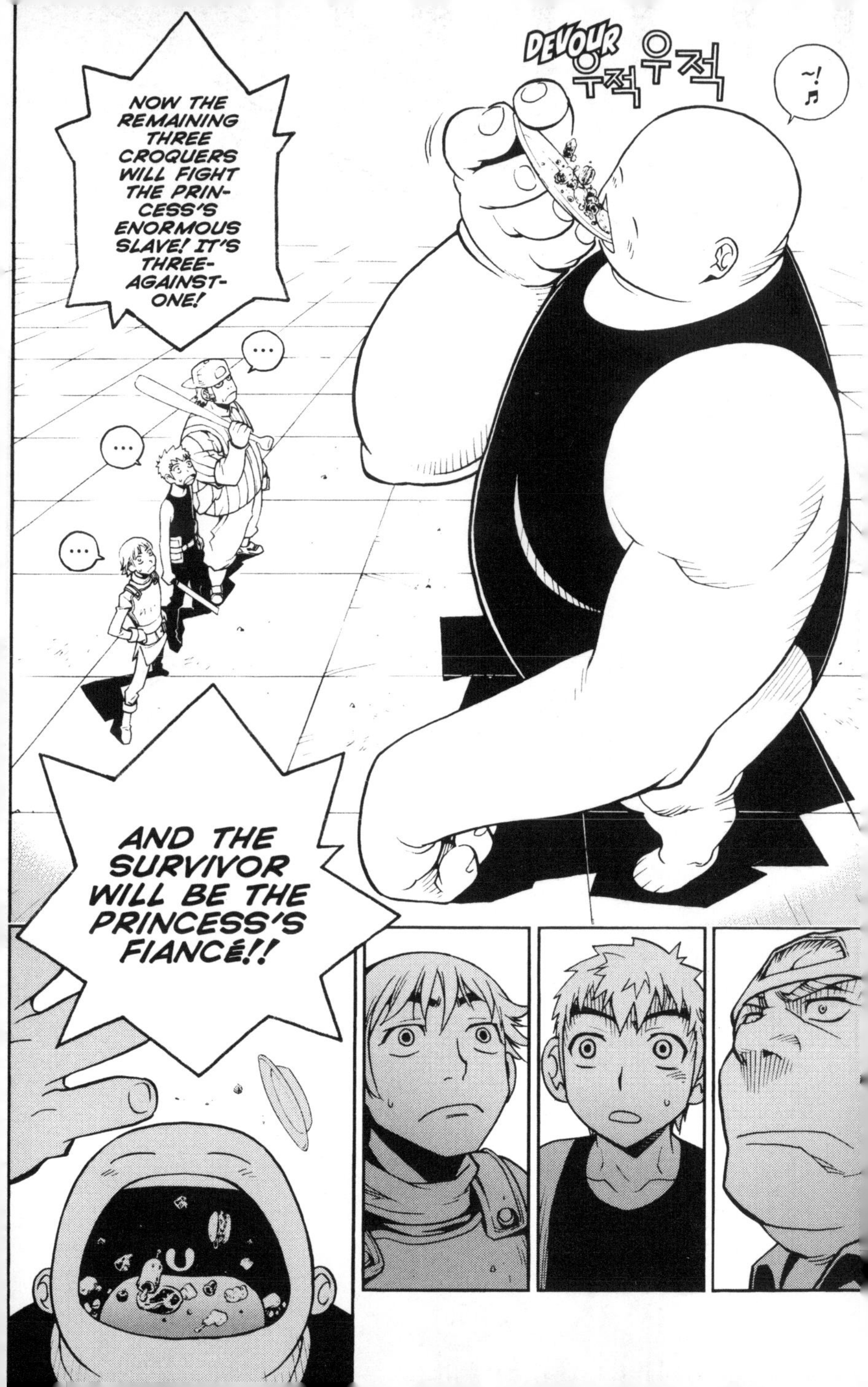
NOW THE REMAINING THREE CROQUERS WILL FIGHT THE PRIN-CESS'S ENORMOUS SLAVE! IT'S THREE-AGAINST-ONE!
DEVOUR 우적우적
~! ♪
...
...
...
AND THE SURVIVOR WILL BE THE PRINCESS'S FIANCÉ!!

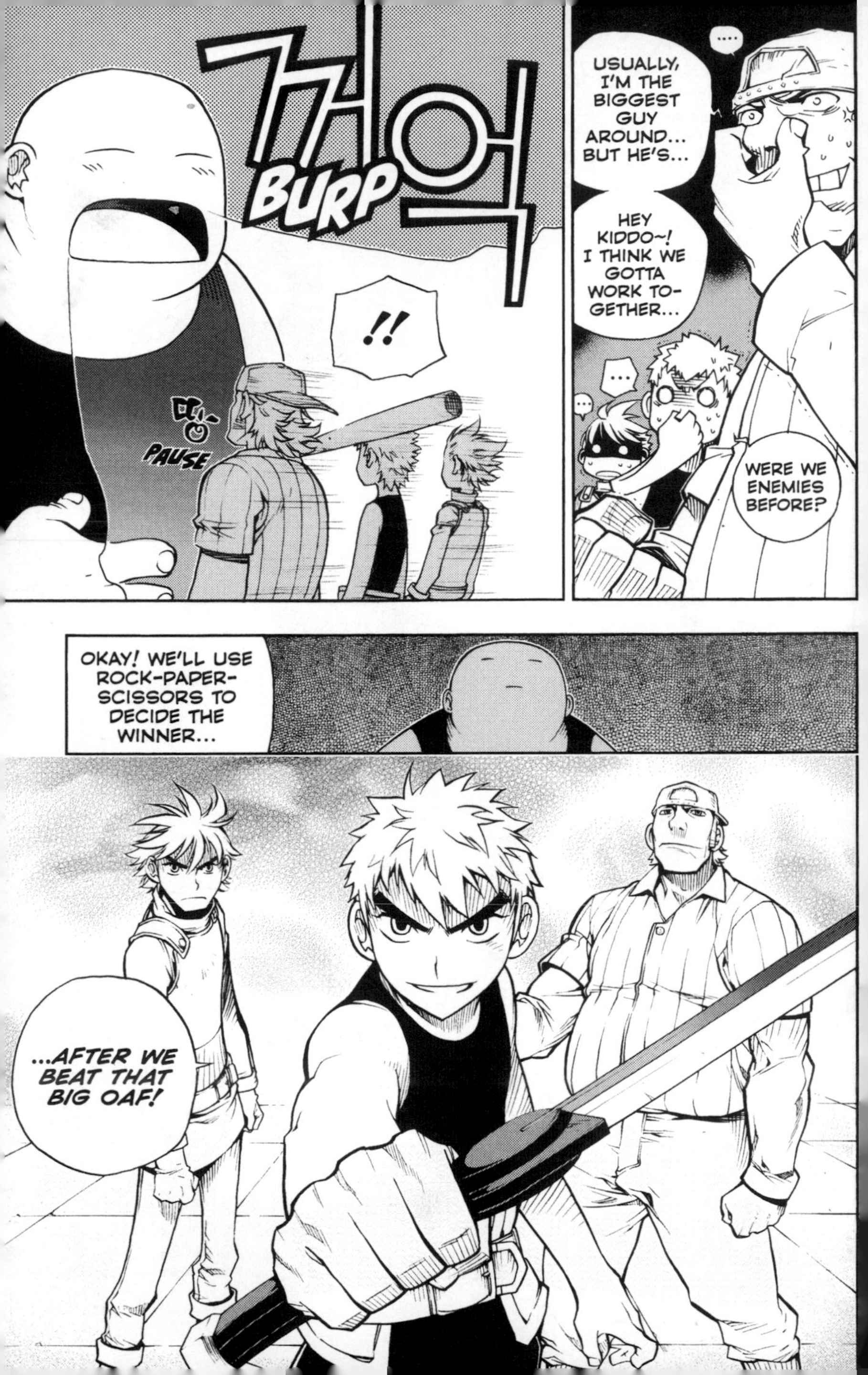
꺼어
BURP
!!
땅
PAUSE
....
USUALLY, I'M THE BIGGEST GUY AROUND... BUT HE'S...
HEY KIDDO~! I THINK WE GOTTA WORK TO-GETHER...
...
...
WERE WE ENEMIES BEFORE?
OKAY! WE'LL USE ROCK-PAPER-SCISSORS TO DECIDE THE WINNER...
...AFTER WE BEAT THAT BIG OAF!

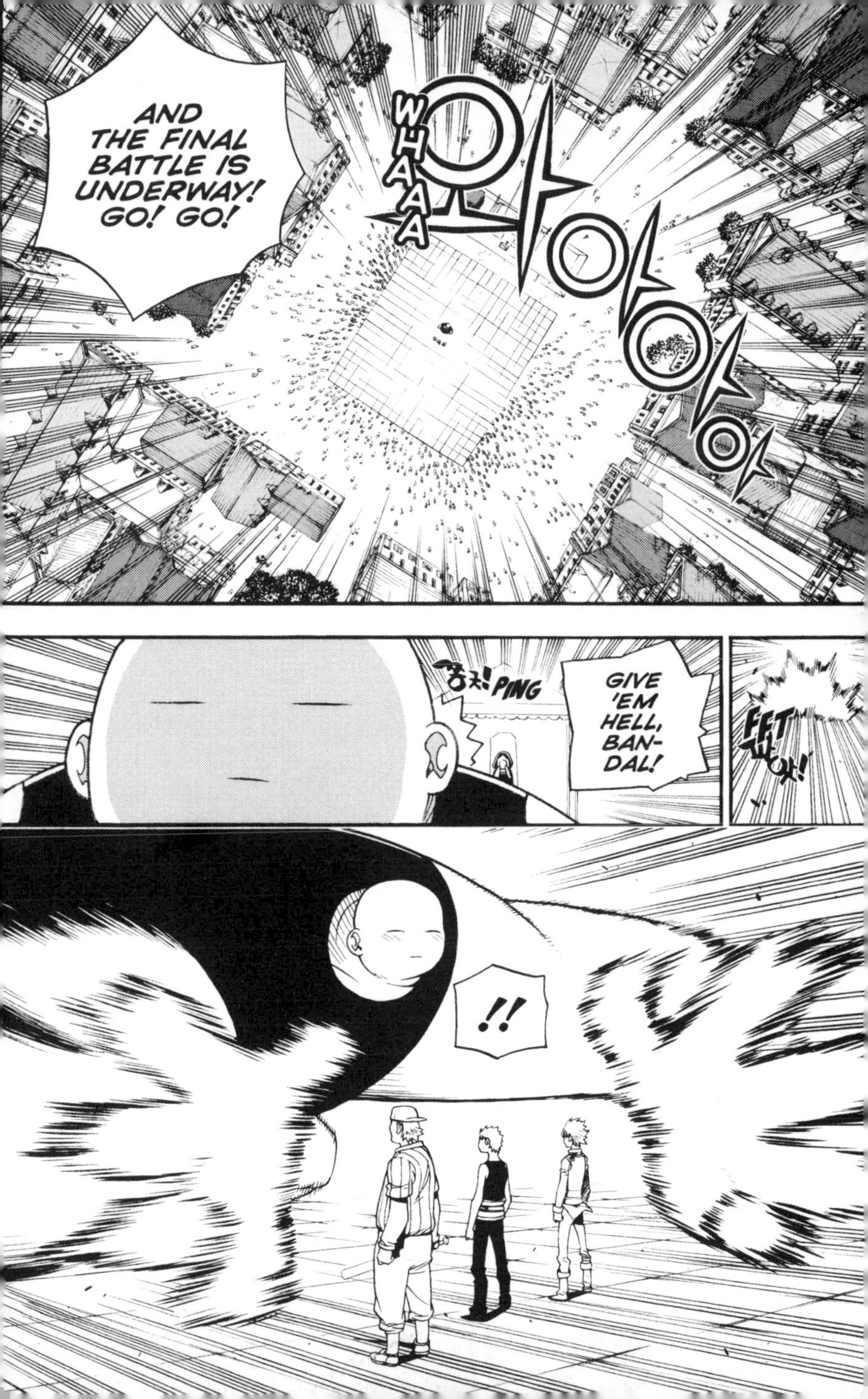
AND THE FINAL BATTLE IS UNDERWAY! GO! GO!
WHAAA
PING
GIVE 'EM HELL, BAN-DAL!
FFT
!!

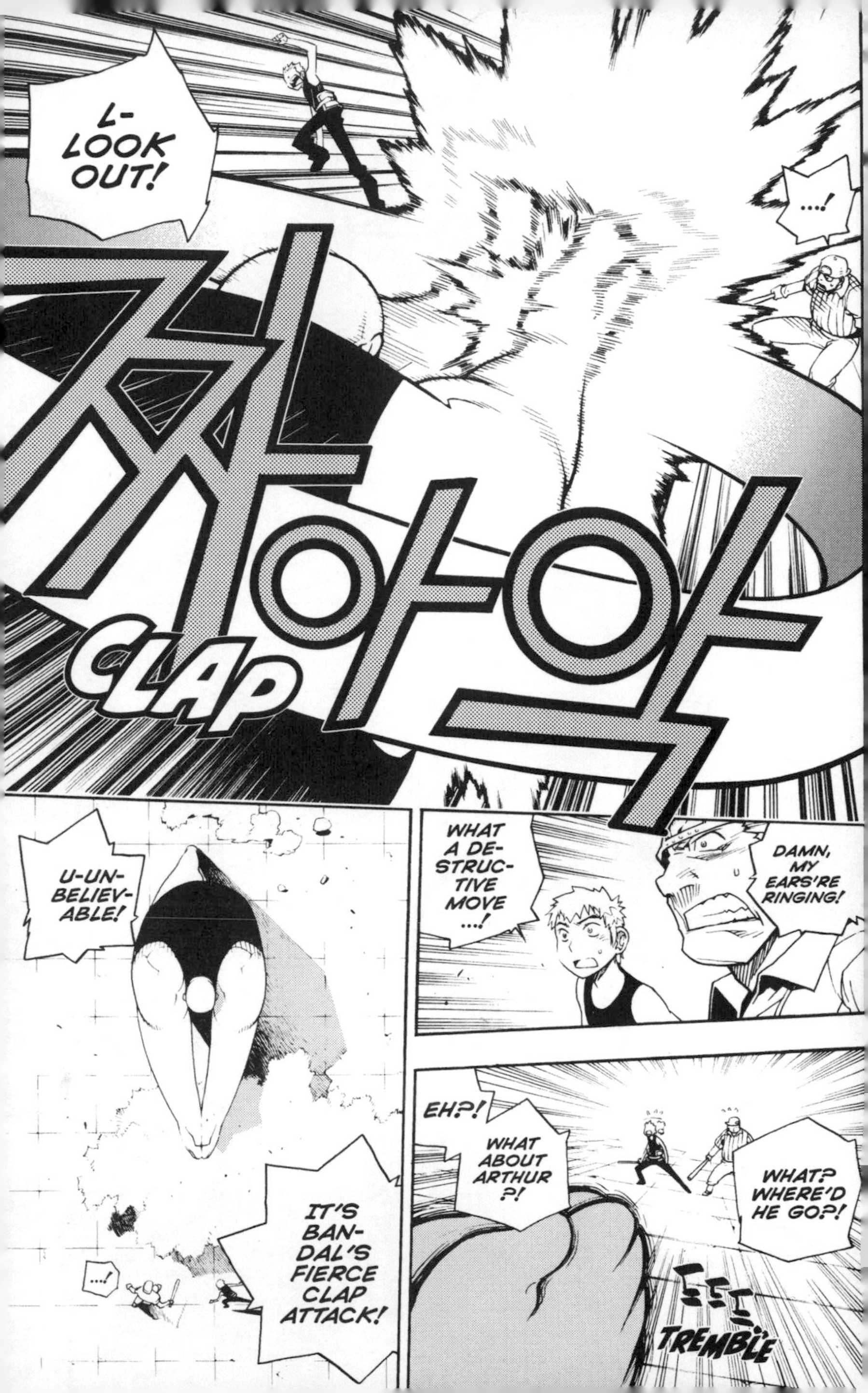
L- LOOK OUT!
...!
CLAP
U-UN-BELIEV-ABLE!
...!
IT'S BAN-DAL'S FIERCE CLAP ATTACK!
WHAT A DE-STRUC-TIVE MOVE ...!
DAMN, MY EARS'RE RINGING!
EH?!
WHAT ABOUT ARTHUR ?!
WHAT? WHERE'D HE GO?!
TREMBLE

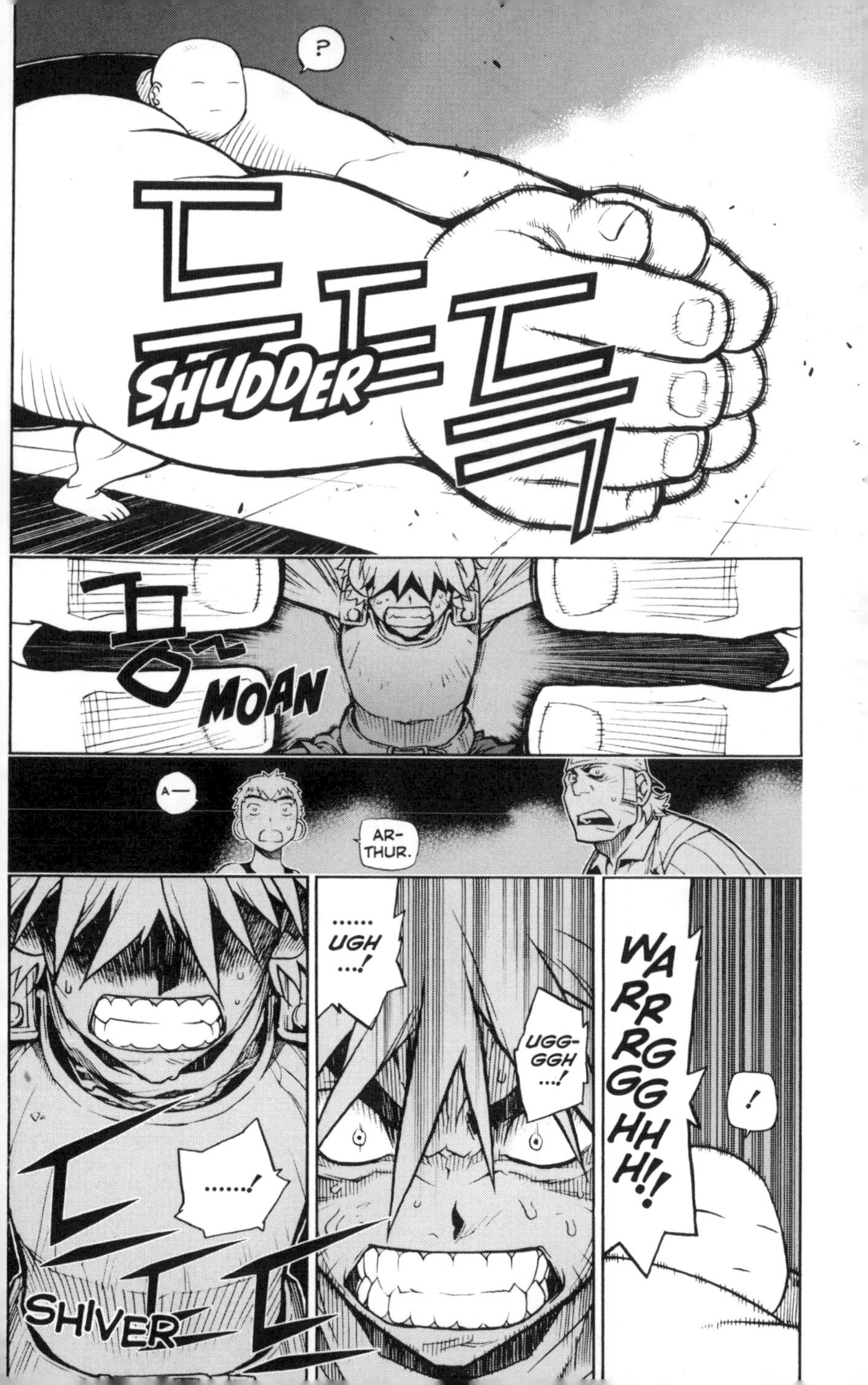
?
SHUDDER
MOAN
A—
AR-
THUR.
....
UGH
...!
UGG-
GGH
...!
WARRRRGGGHHH!!
!
.......!
SHIVER

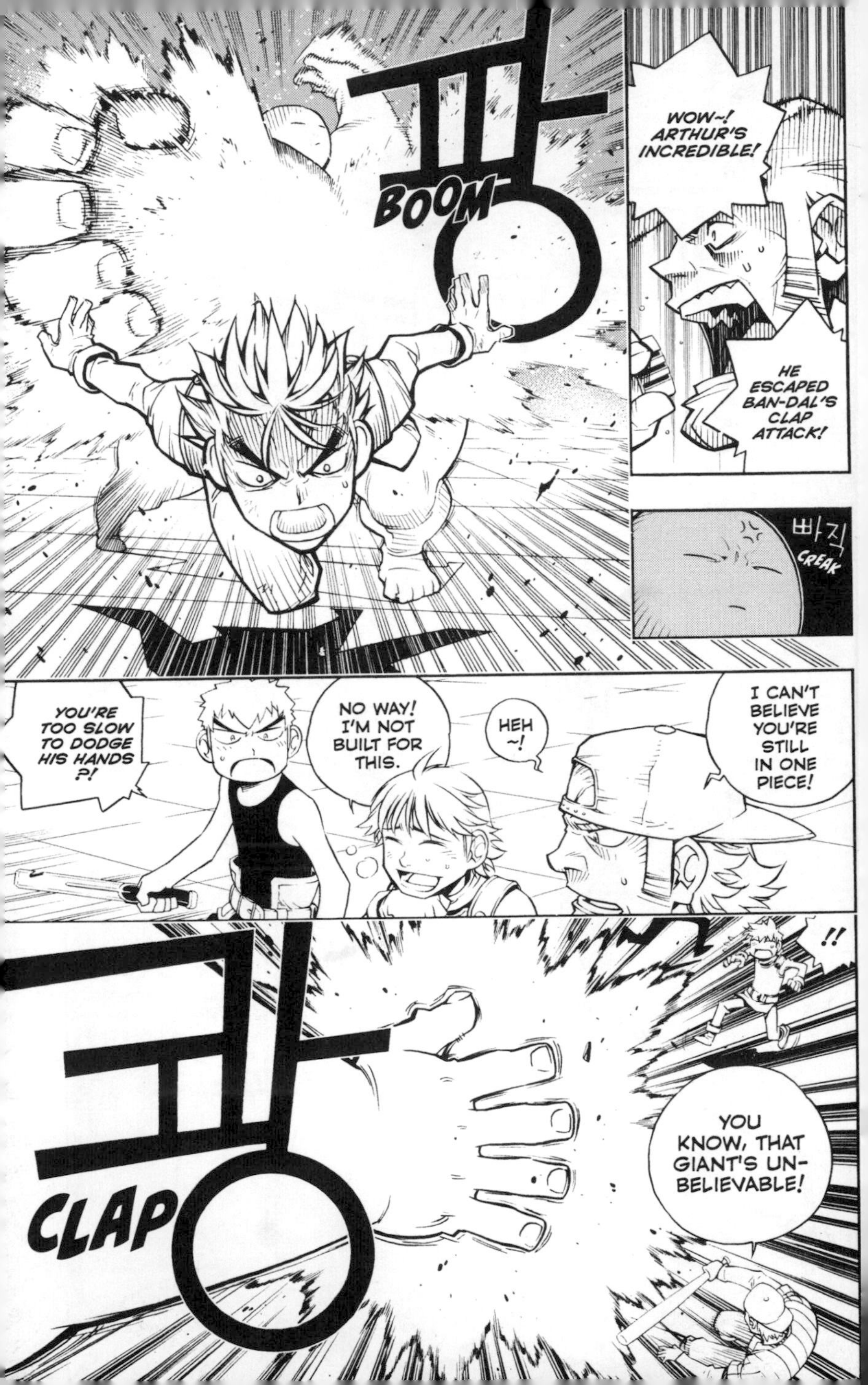

팡
BOOM
WOW~! ARTHUR'S INCREDIBLE!
HE ESCAPED BAN-DAL'S CLAP ATTACK!
빠직
CREAK
YOU'RE TOO SLOW TO DODGE HIS HANDS ?!
NO WAY! I'M NOT BUILT FOR THIS.
HEH ~!
I CAN'T BELIEVE YOU'RE STILL IN ONE PIECE!
콰
CLAP
!!
YOU KNOW, THAT GIANT'S UN-BELIEVABLE!

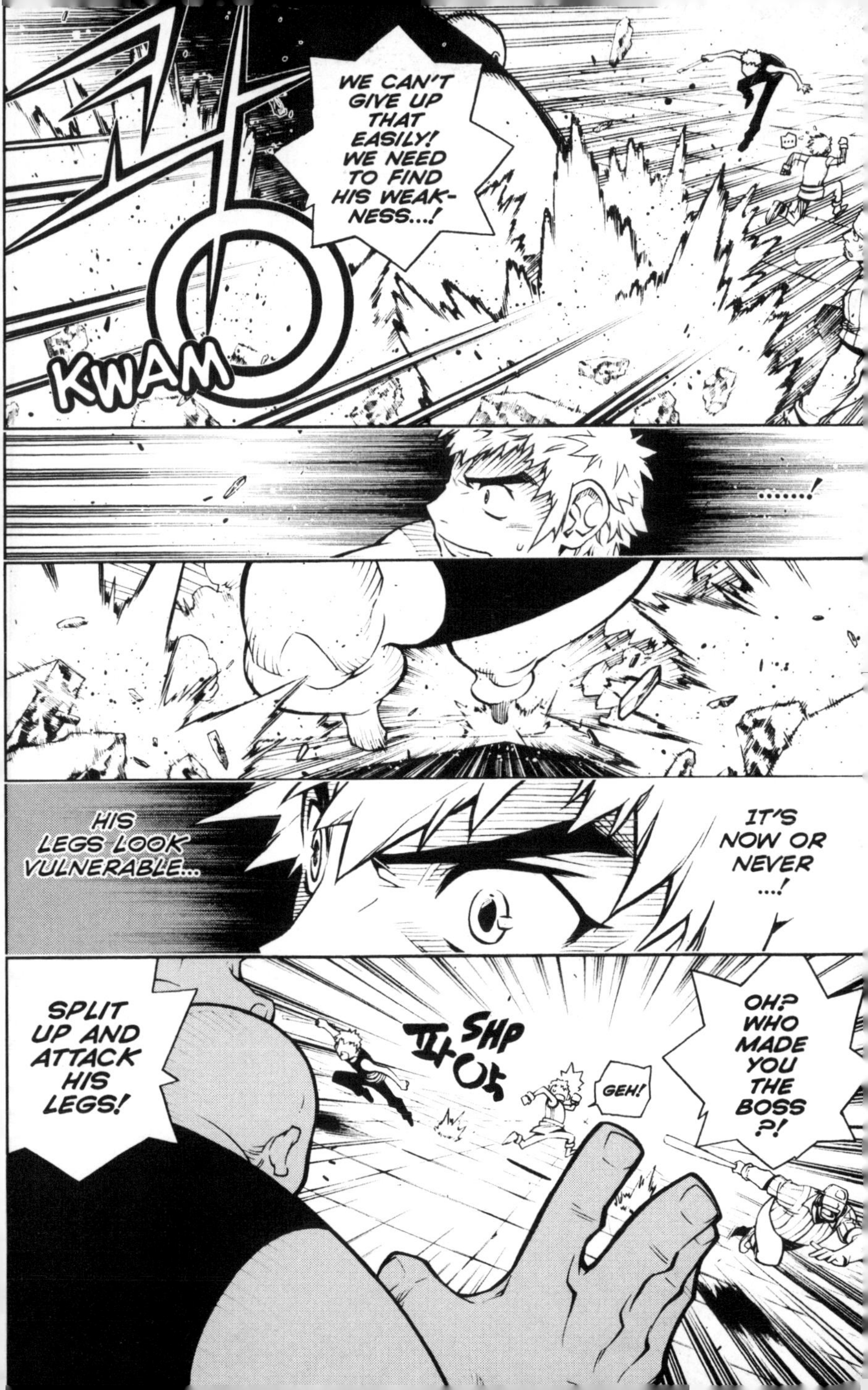
WE CAN'T GIVE UP THAT EASILY! WE NEED TO FIND HIS WEAK-NESS...!
KWAM
.......!
HIS LEGS LOOK VULNERABLE...
IT'S NOW OR NEVER ...!
SPLIT UP AND ATTACK HIS LEGS!
SHP
GEH!
OH? WHO MADE YOU THE BOSS ?!

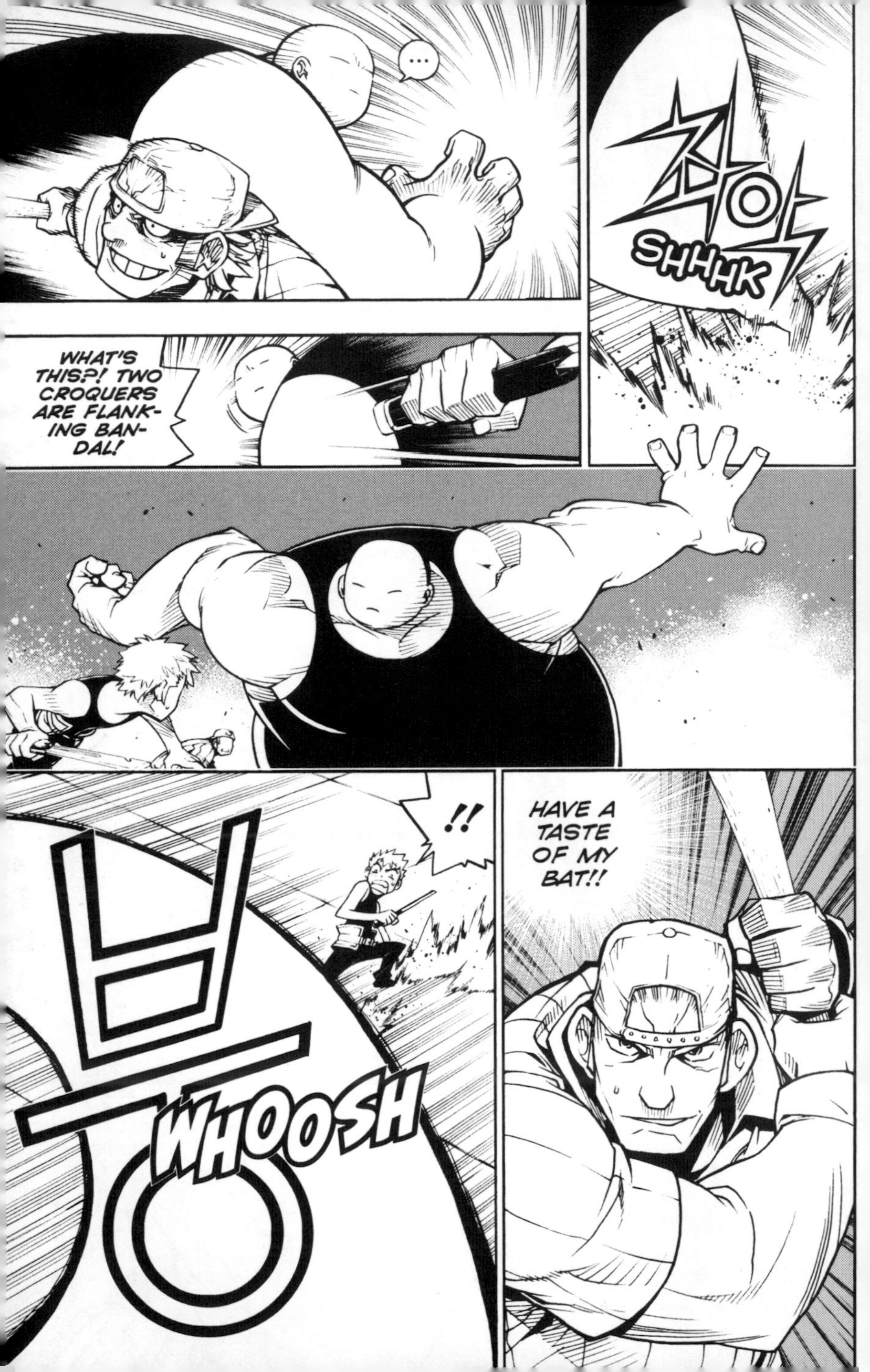
...
SHHHK
WHAT'S THIS?! TWO CROQUERS ARE FLANK-ING BAN-DAL!
WHOOSH
!!
HAVE A TASTE OF MY BAT!!

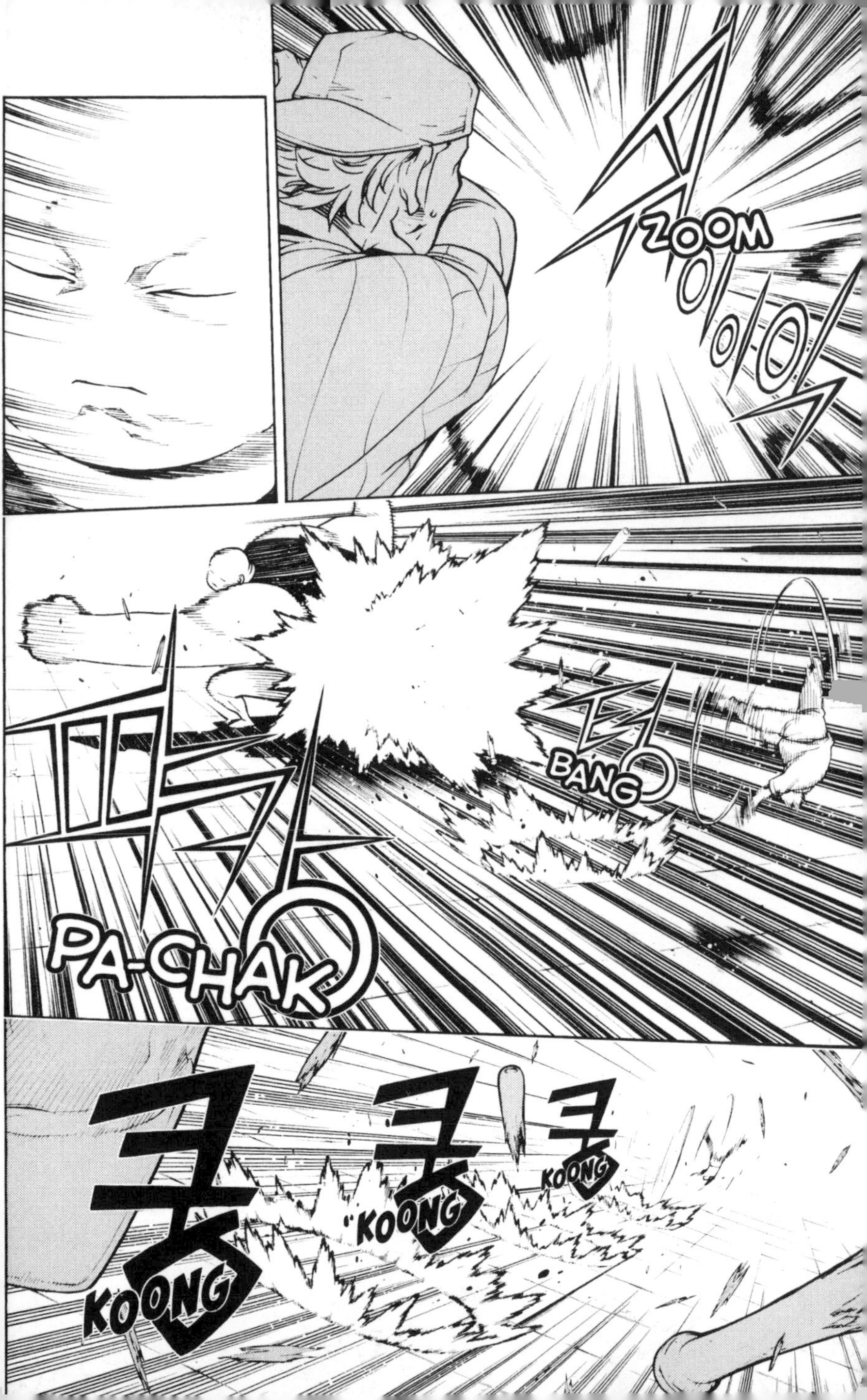

ZOOM
PA-CHAK
BANG
쿵
KOONG
쿵
KOONG
쿵
KOONG

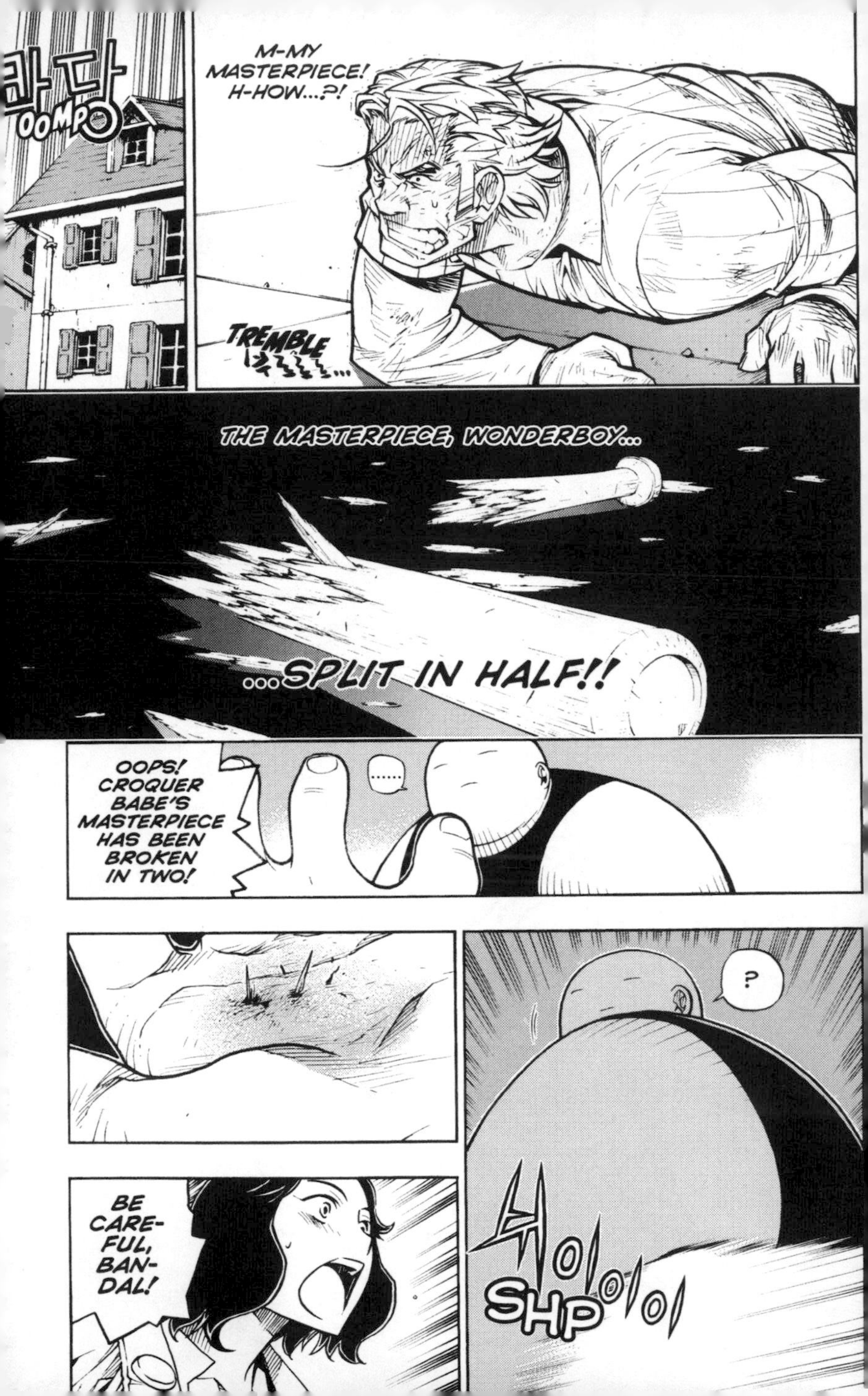
OOMP
M-MY MASTERPIECE! H-HOW...?!
TREMBLE
THE MASTERPIECE, WONDERBOY...
...SPLIT IN HALF!!
OOPS! CROQUER BABE'S MASTERPIECE HAS BEEN BROKEN IN TWO!
......
BE CARE-FUL, BAN-DAL!
?
SHP

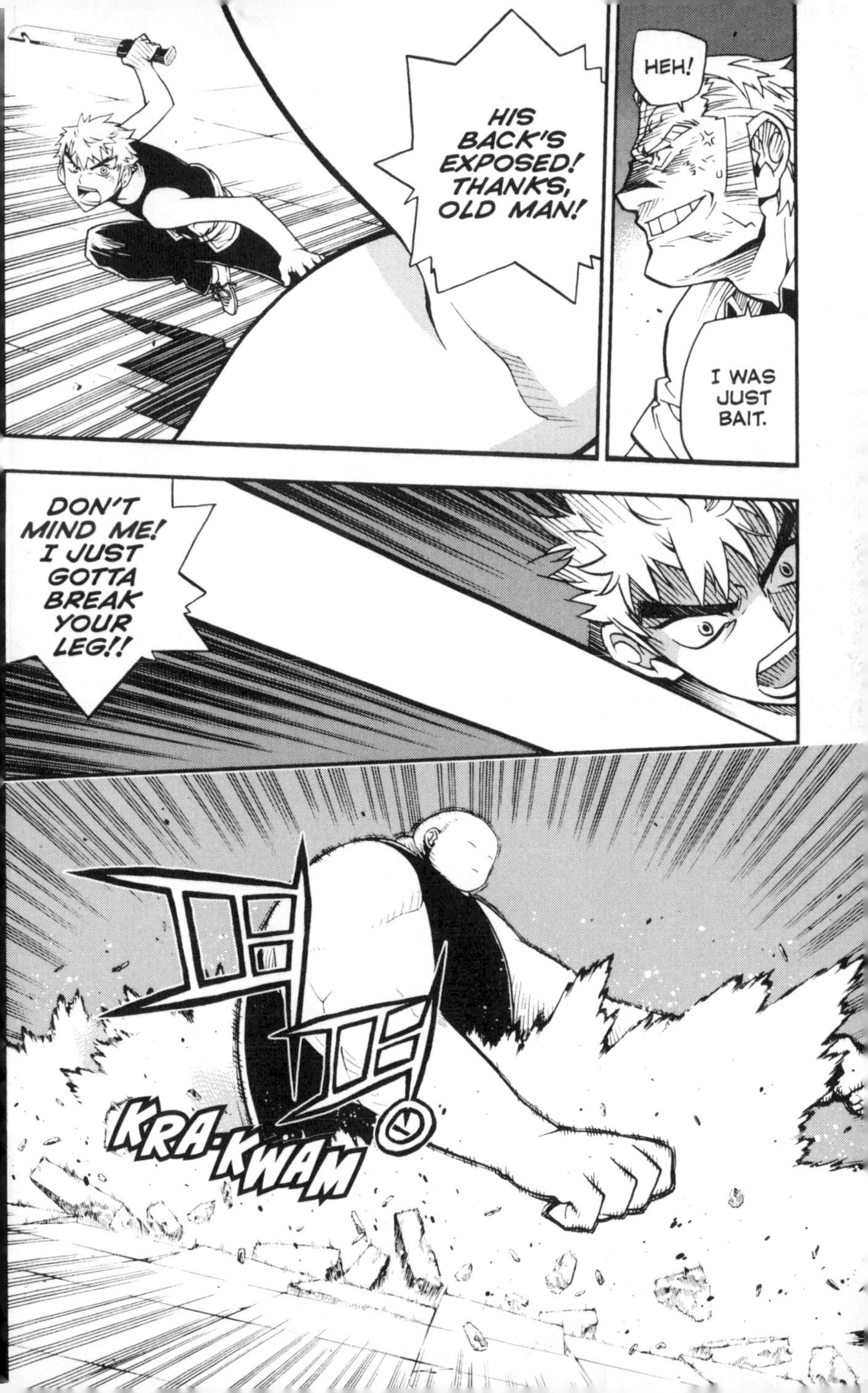
HIS BACK'S EXPOSED! THANKS, OLD MAN!
HEH!
I WAS JUST BAIT.
DON'T MIND ME! I JUST GOTTA BREAK YOUR LEG!!
KRA-KWAM

CROQUER DA-IL'S EXECUTING HIS SPECIAL ATTACK!

......

SHOOOM ㅠ으읏...

THIS COULD ACTUALLY HURT BAN-DAL, STRONG AS HE MIGHT BE....!

AH....

EH?

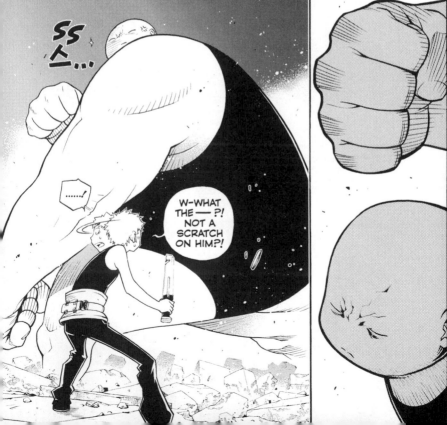

SS ᄉ一...

......!

W-WHAT THE ── ?! NOT A SCRATCH ON HIM?!

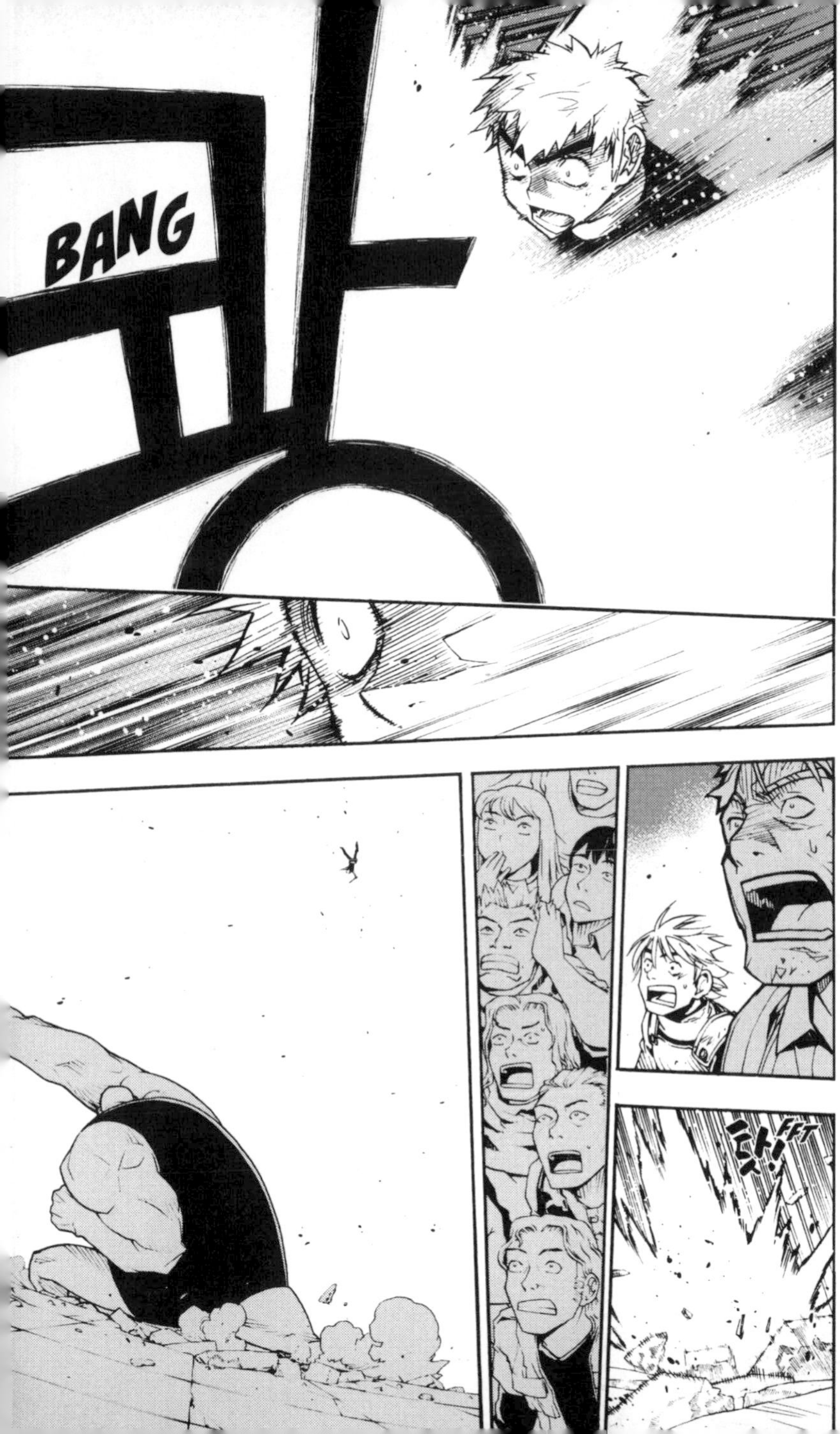
BANG
FFT

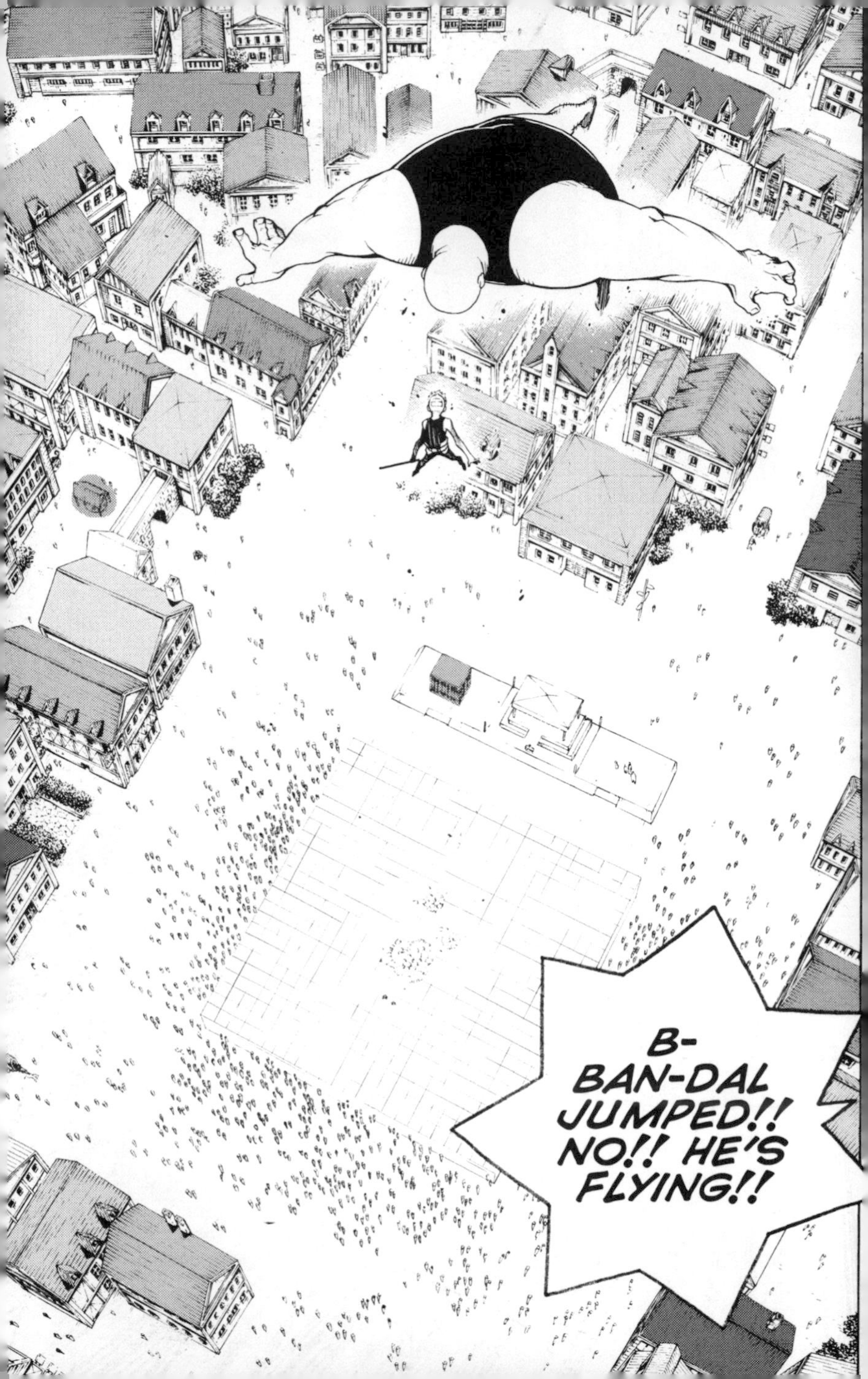
B-BAN-DAL JUMPED!! NO!! HE'S FLYING!!

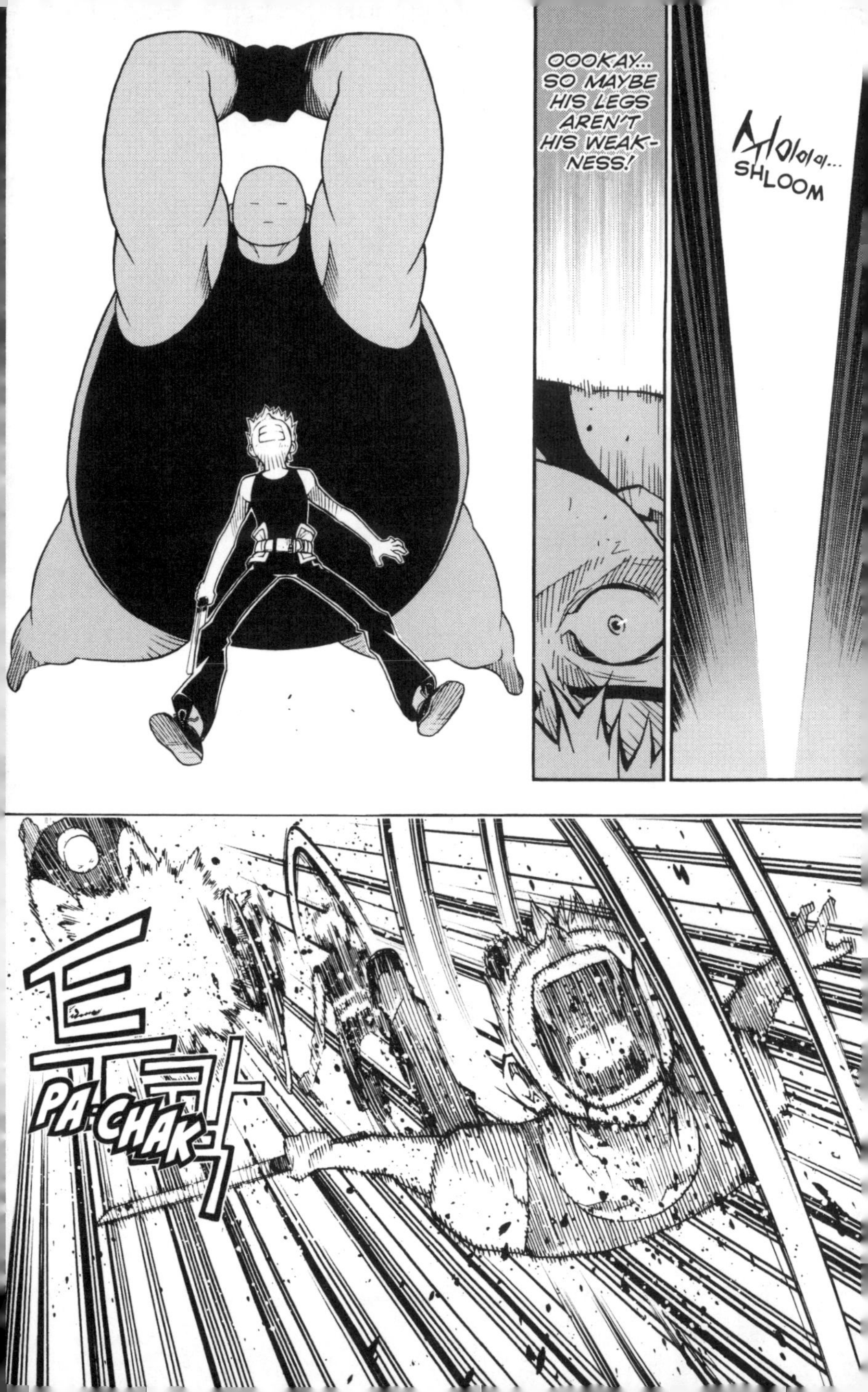
OOOKAY... SO MAYBE HIS LEGS AREN'T HIS WEAK-NESS!
SHLOOM
PA-CHAK

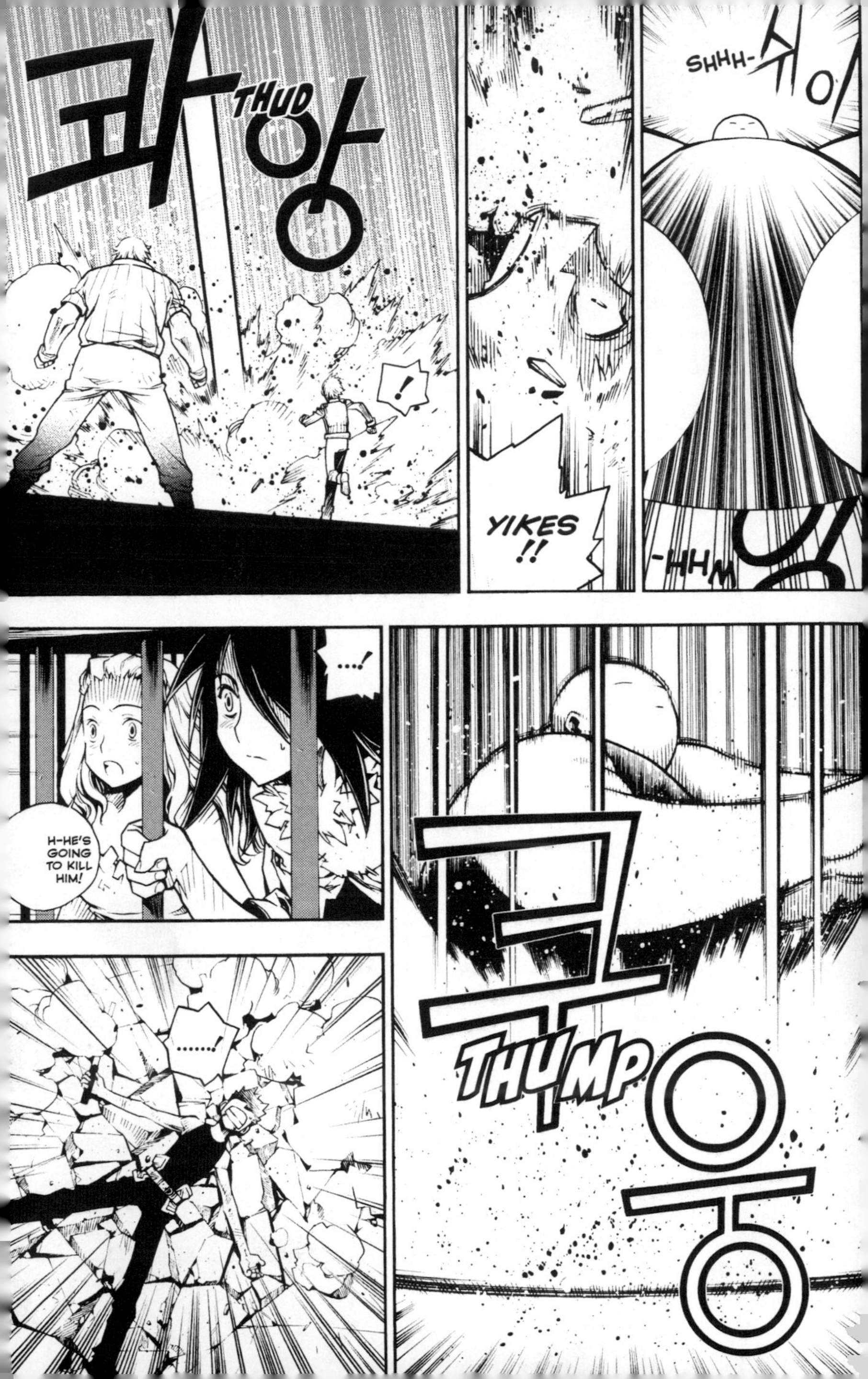

콰앙
THUD
!
YIKES!!
SHHH-
-HHM
...!
H-HE'S GOING TO KILL HIM!
......!
THUMP

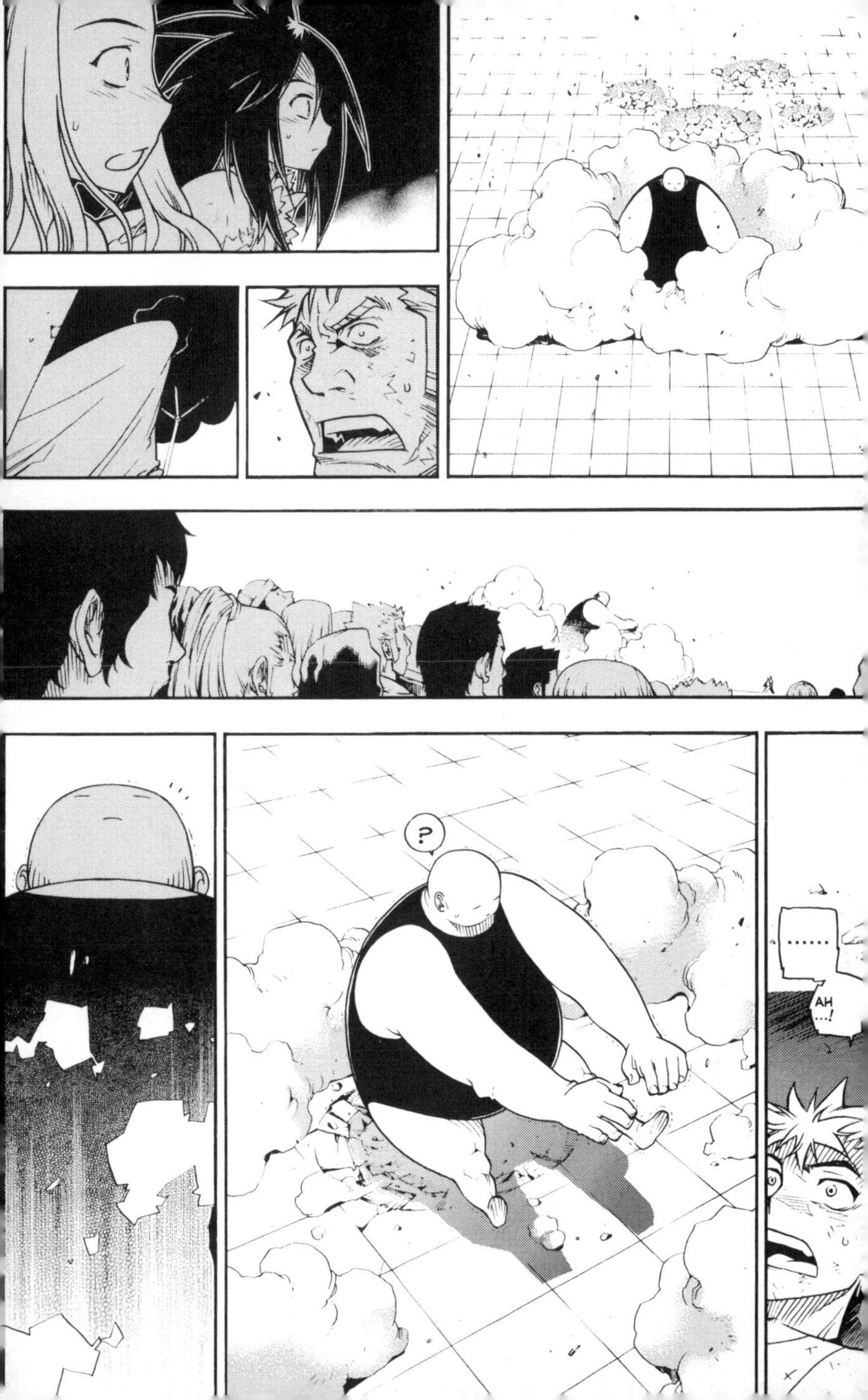
?
......
AH ...!

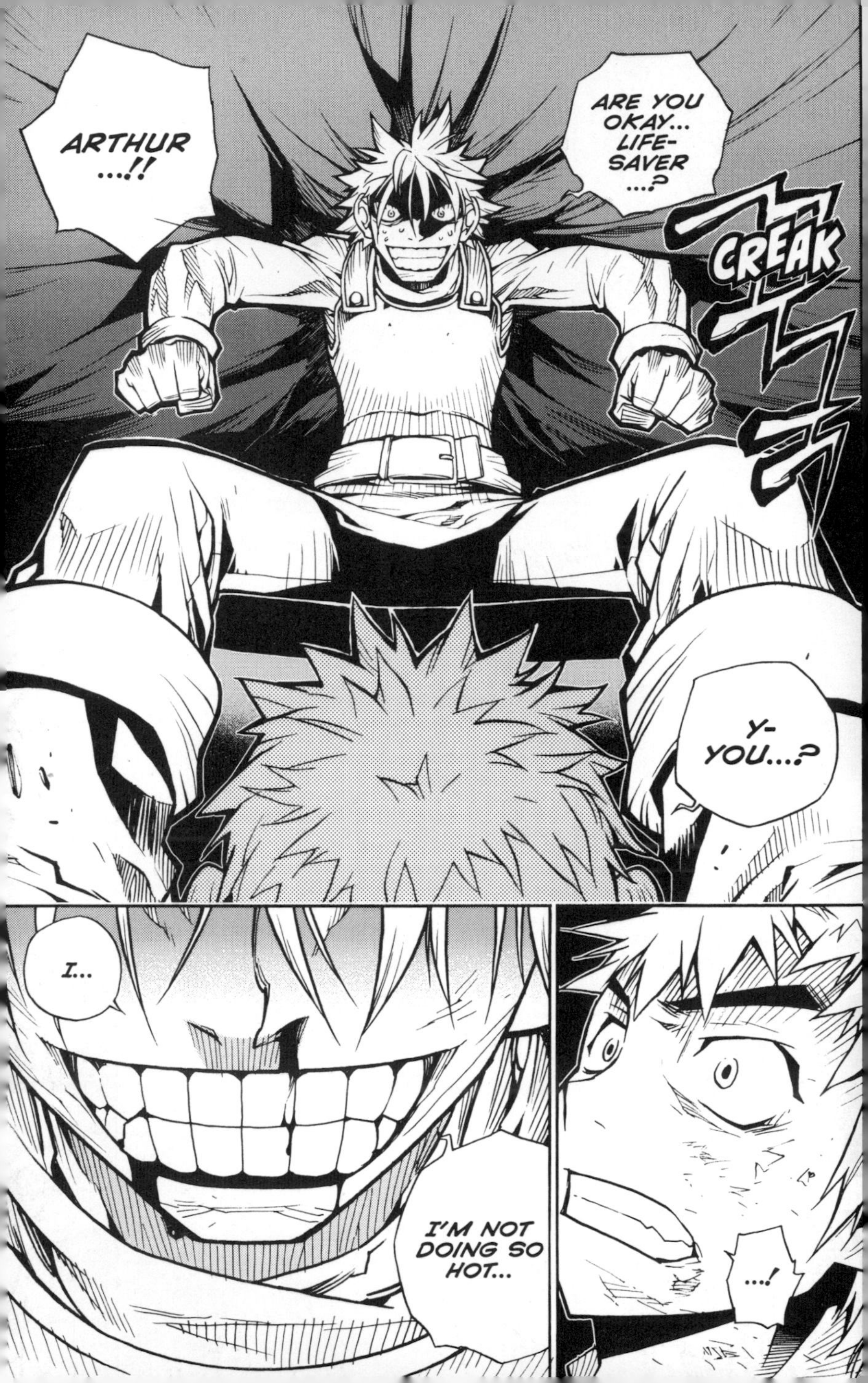
ARTHUR ...!!
ARE YOU OKAY... LIFE-SAVER ...?
CREAK
Y-YOU...?
I...
I'M NOT DOING SO HOT...
...!

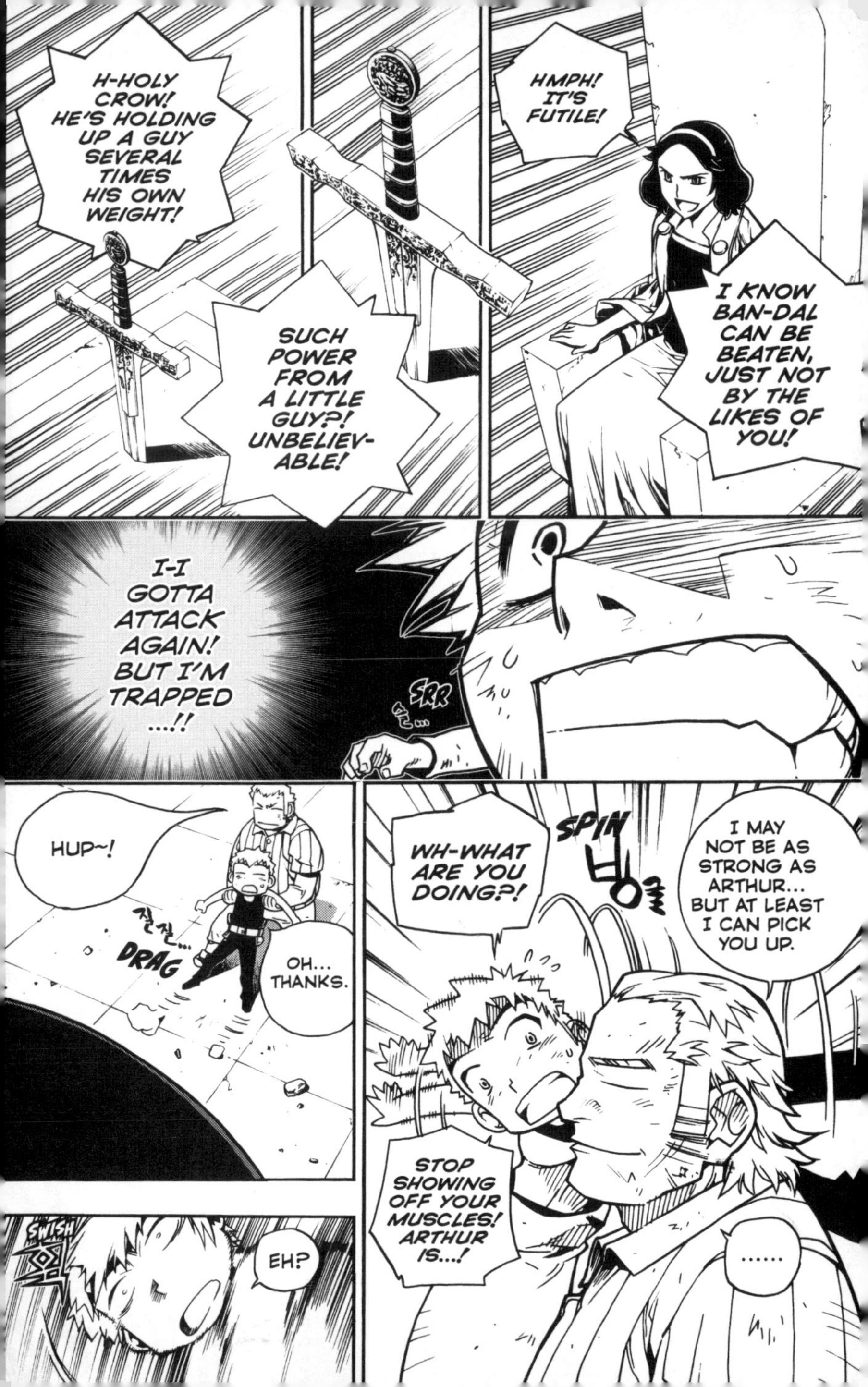
H-HOLY CROW! HE'S HOLDING UP A GUY SEVERAL TIMES HIS OWN WEIGHT!
SUCH POWER FROM A LITTLE GUY?! UNBELIEV-ABLE!
HMPH! IT'S FUTILE!
I KNOW BAN-DAL CAN BE BEATEN, JUST NOT BY THE LIKES OF YOU!
I-I GOTTA ATTACK AGAIN! BUT I'M TRAPPED ...!!
SRR
HUP~!
질질...
DRAG
OH... THANKS.
SWISH
EH?
WH-WHAT ARE YOU DOING?!
SPIN
I MAY NOT BE AS STRONG AS ARTHUR... BUT AT LEAST I CAN PICK YOU UP.
STOP SHOWING OFF YOUR MUSCLES! ARTHUR IS...!
......

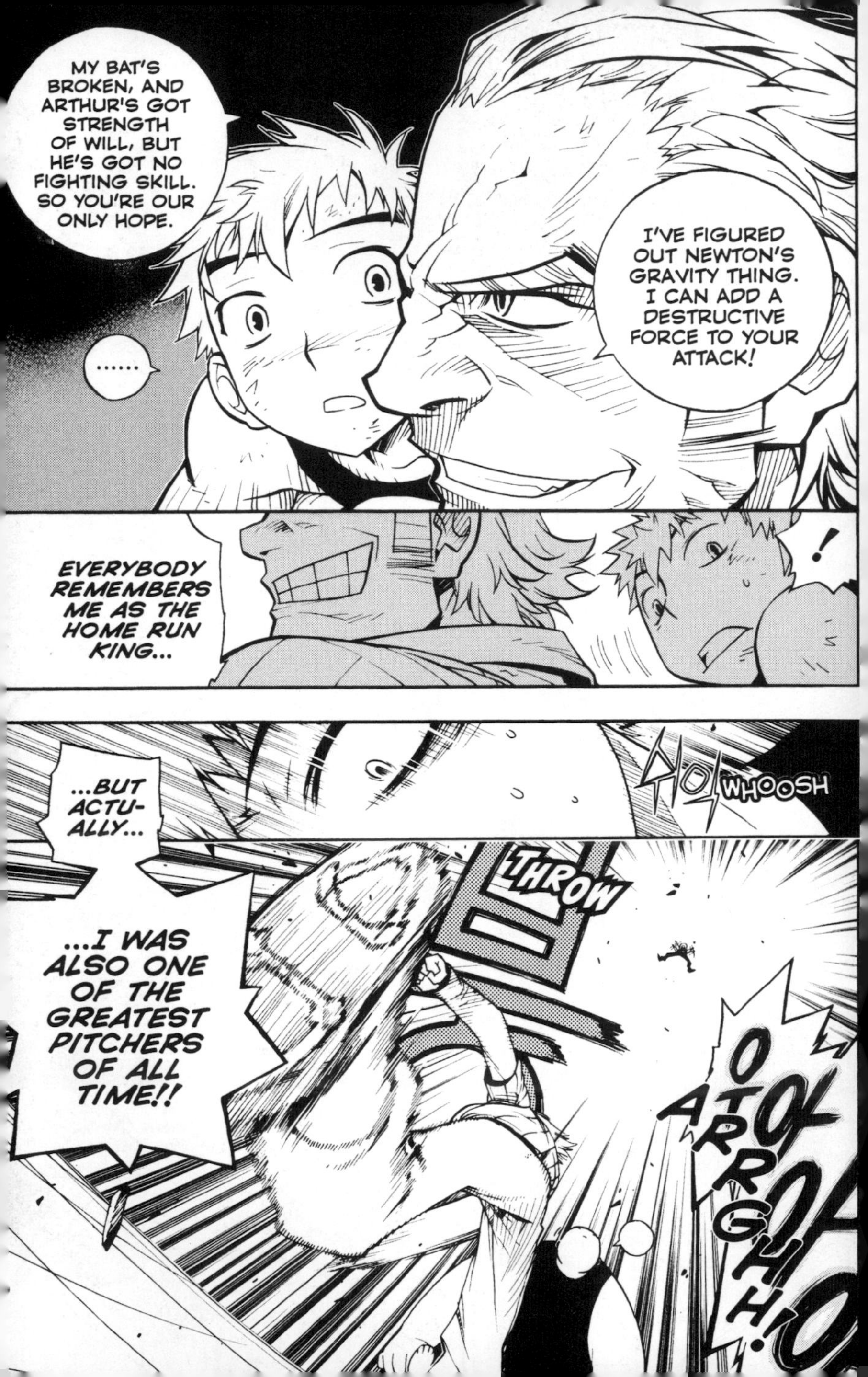

MY BAT'S BROKEN, AND ARTHUR'S GOT STRENGTH OF WILL, BUT HE'S GOT NO FIGHTING SKILL. SO YOU'RE OUR ONLY HOPE.
I'VE FIGURED OUT NEWTON'S GRAVITY THING. I CAN ADD A DESTRUCTIVE FORCE TO YOUR ATTACK!
......
EVERYBODY REMEMBERS ME AS THE HOME RUN KING...
!
...BUT ACTU-ALLY...
WHOOSH
THROW
...I WAS ALSO ONE OF THE GREATEST PITCHERS OF ALL TIME!!
ARRGHH!

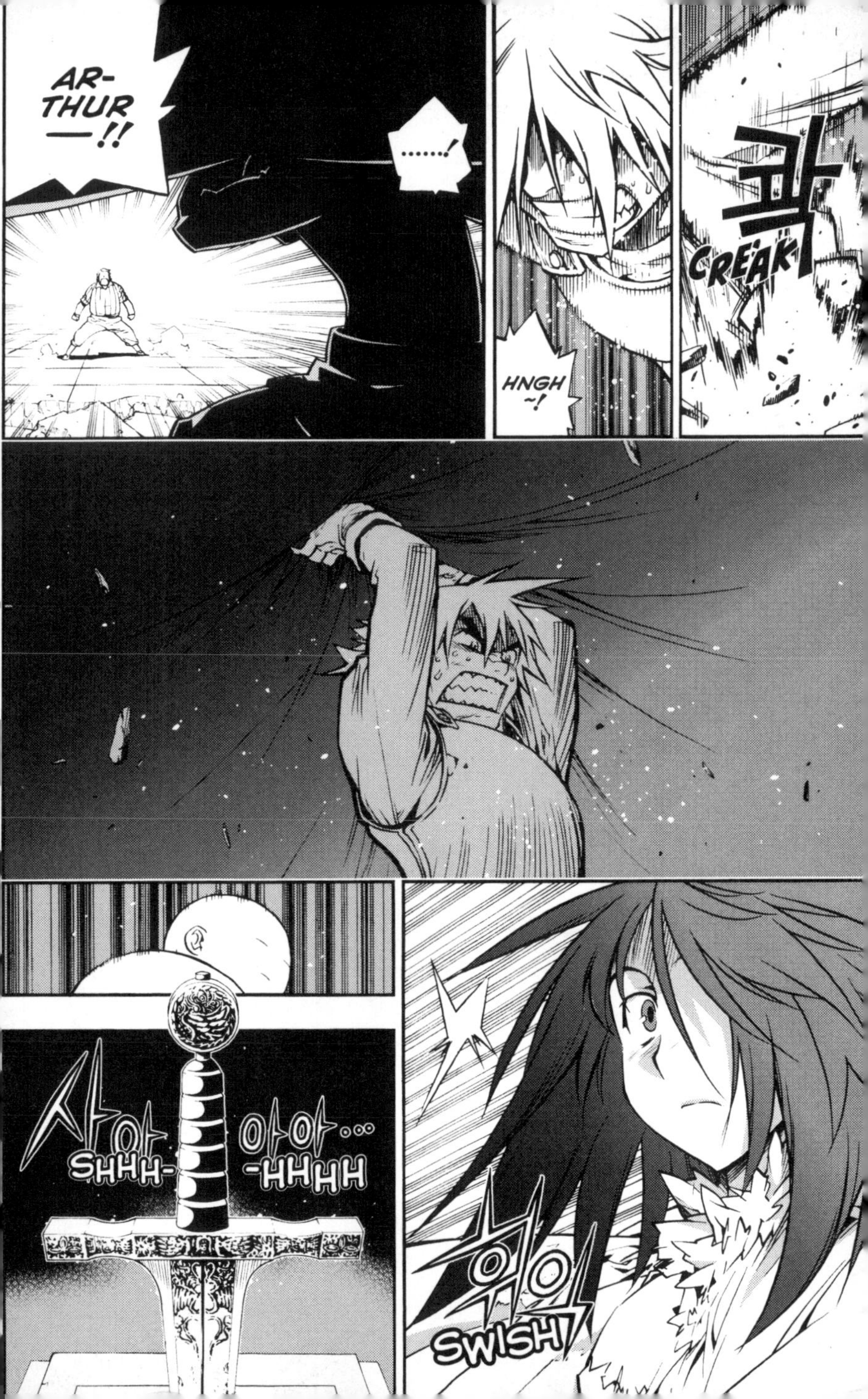

AR-THUR—!!
......!
HNGH~!
콱
CREAK
샤아
SHHH-
아아아...
-HHHH
SWISH

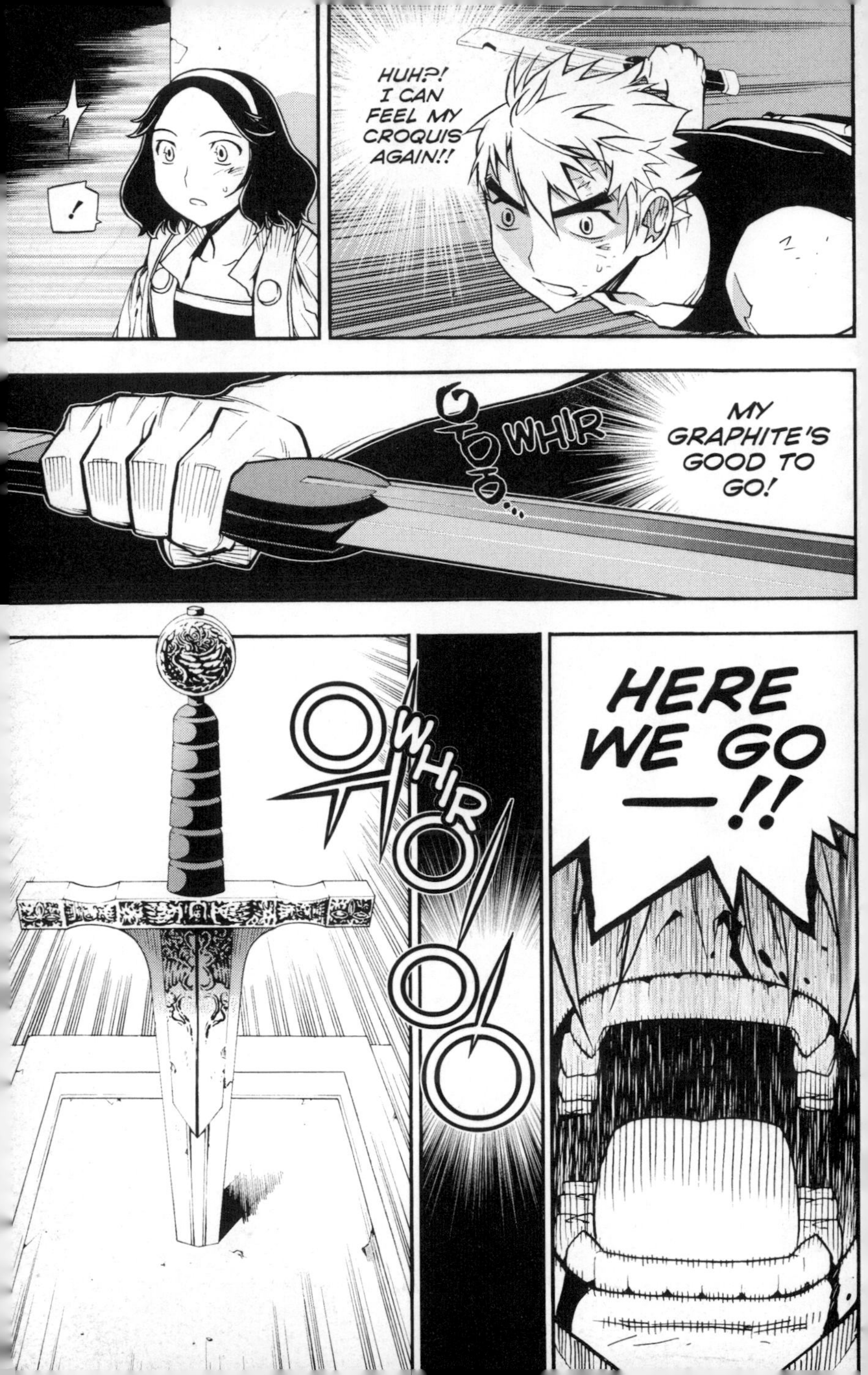
!
HUH?! I CAN FEEL MY CROQUIS AGAIN!!
WHIR
MY GRAPHITE'S GOOD TO GO!
WHIR
HERE WE GO—!!

POP 34. FLY OUT!

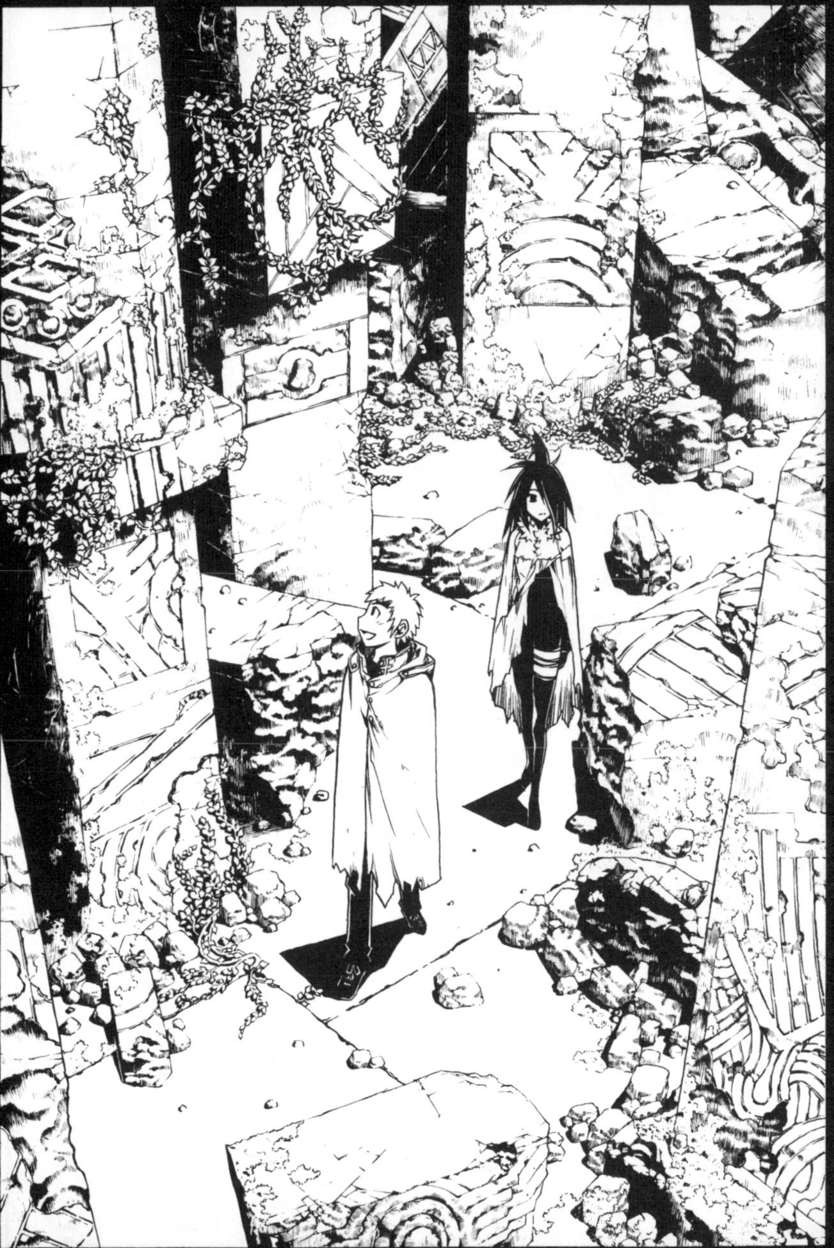

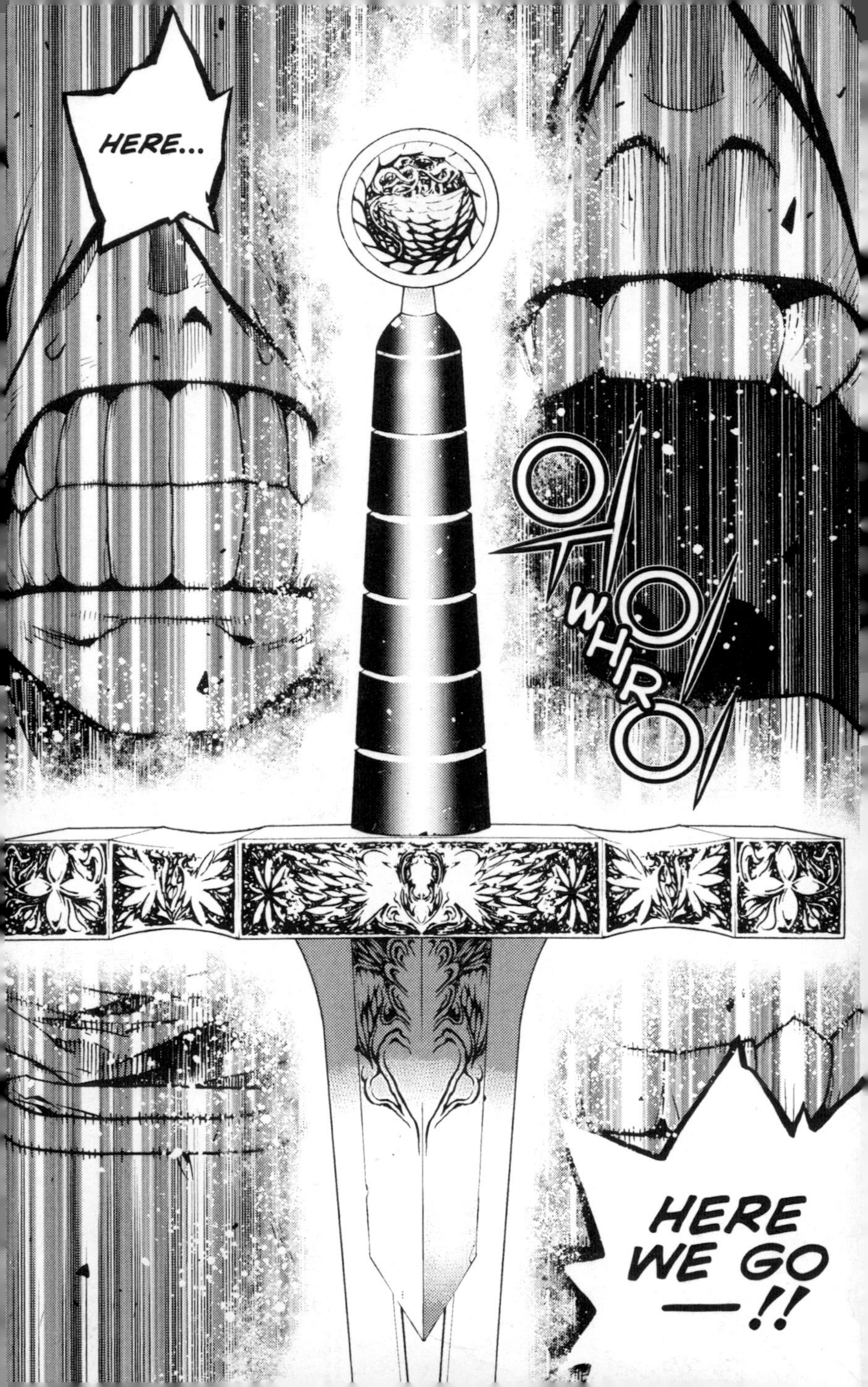
HERE...
WHIRR
HERE WE GO —!!

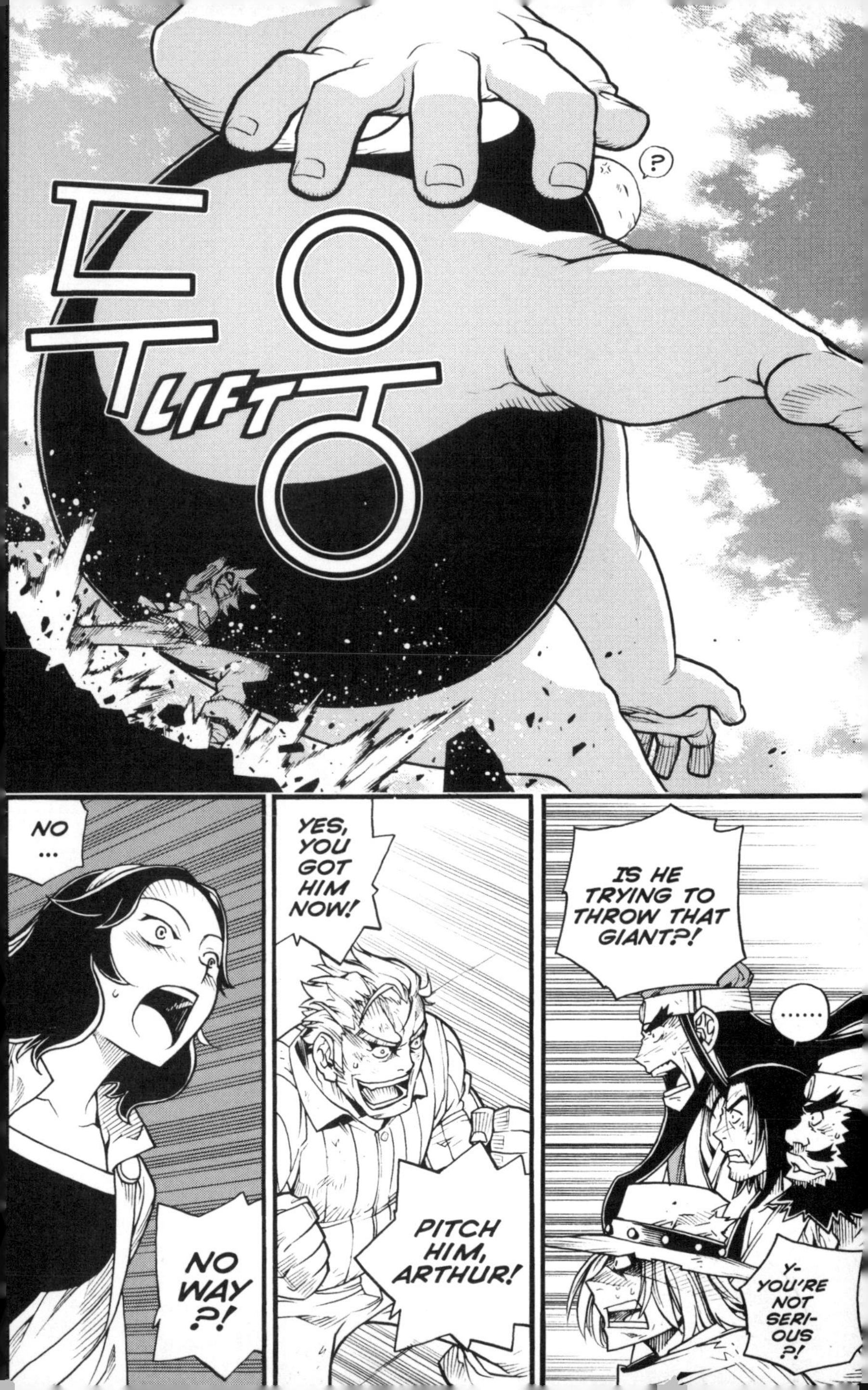
?
LIFT
NO ...
NO WAY ?!
YES, YOU GOT HIM NOW!
PITCH HIM, ARTHUR!
IS HE TRYING TO THROW THAT GIANT?!
....
Y-YOU'RE NOT SERI-OUS ?!

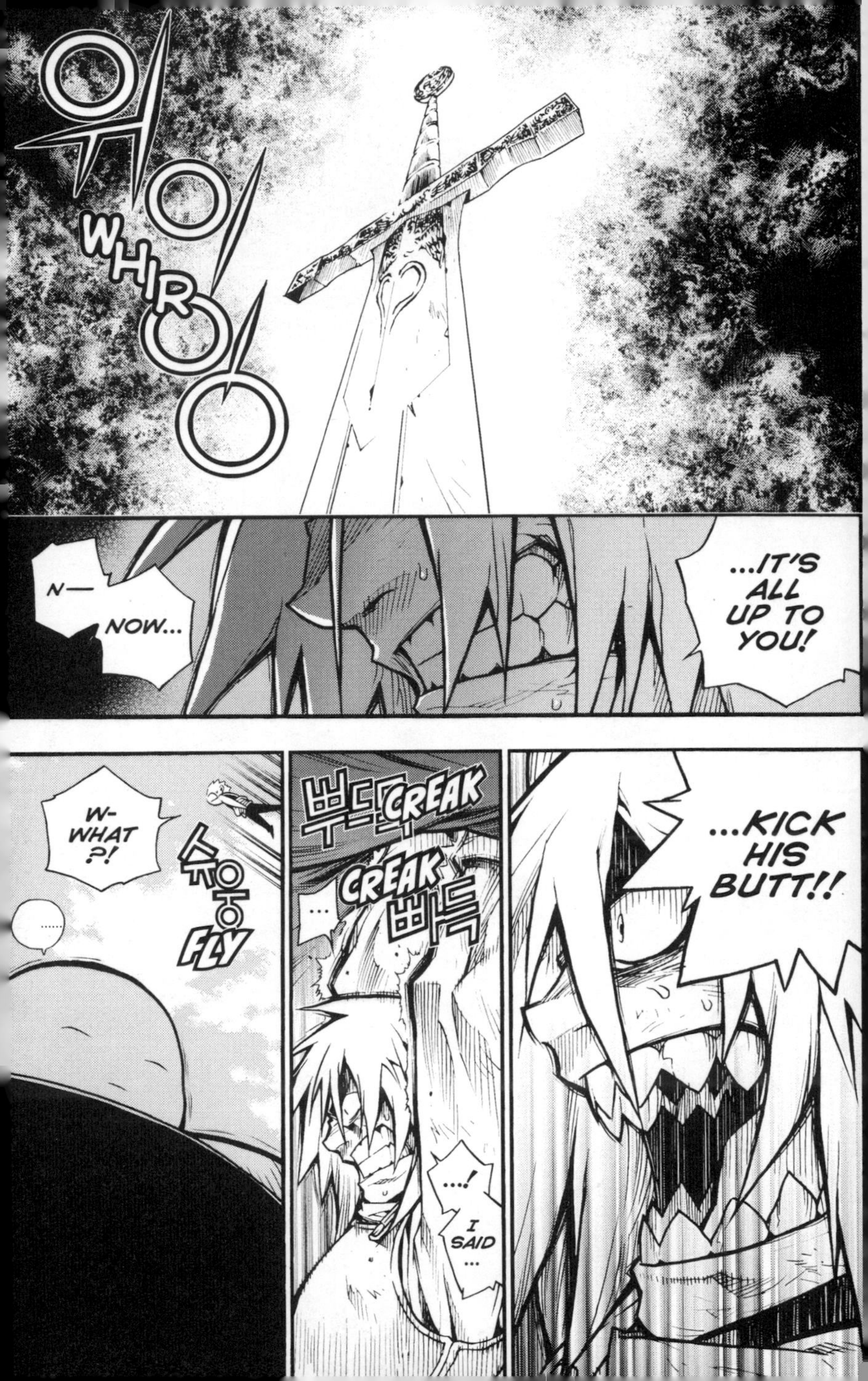
WHIR
N— NOW...
...IT'S ALL UP TO YOU!
W- WHAT?!
......
FLY
CREAK
CREAK
...
...!
I SAID ...
...KICK HIS BUTT!!

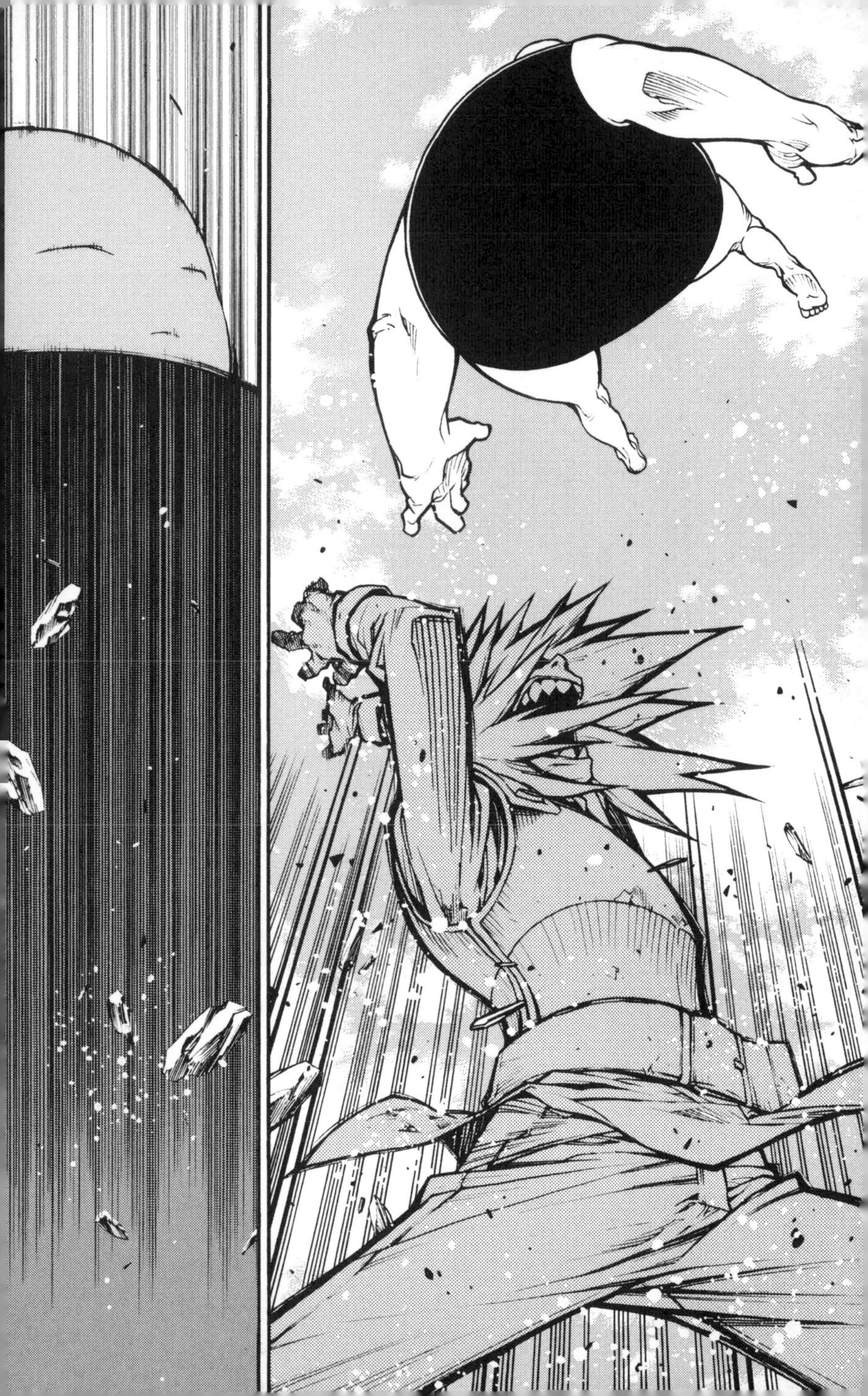

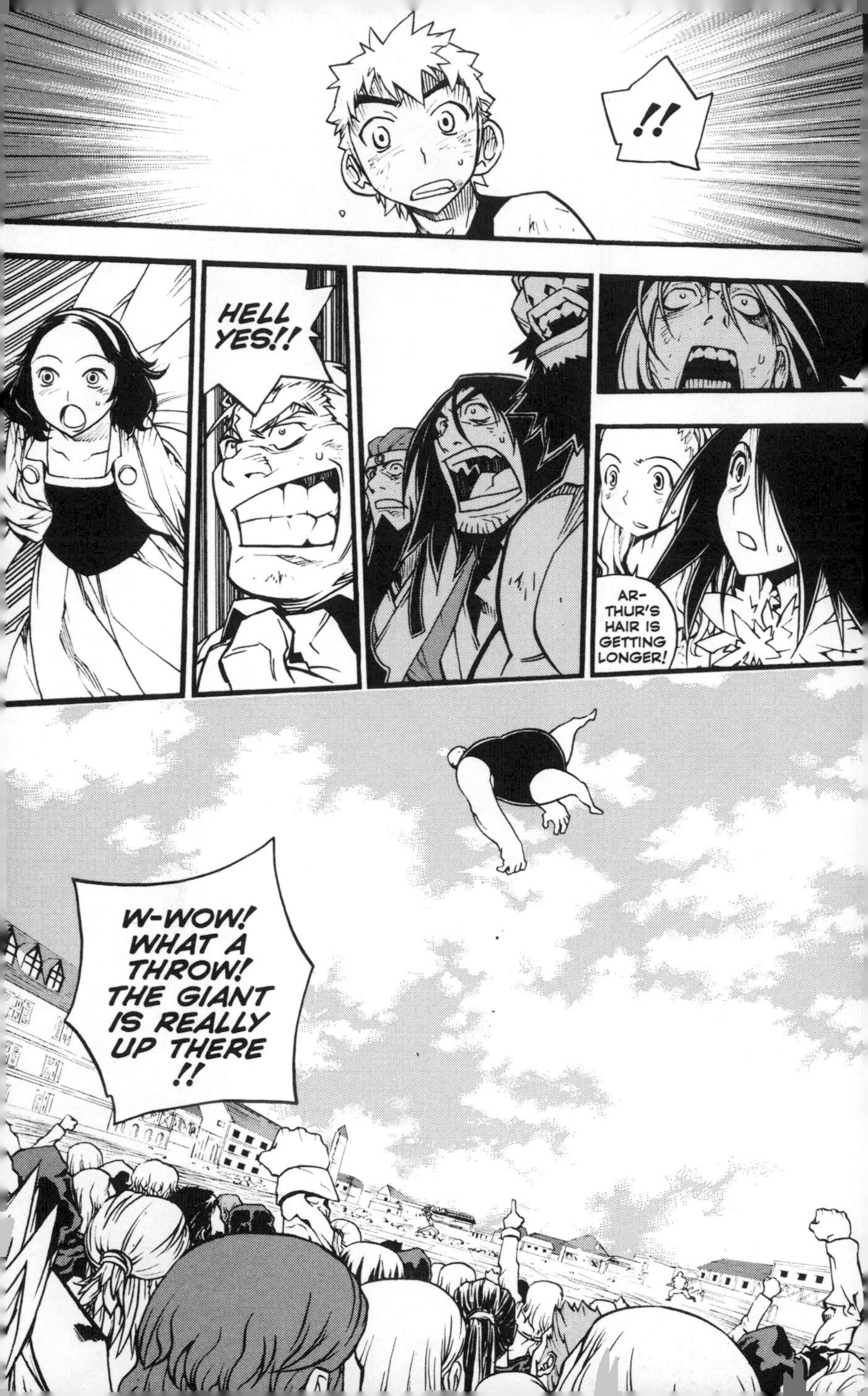
!!
HELL YES!!
AR-THUR'S HAIR IS GETTING LONGER!
W-WOW! WHAT A THROW! THE GIANT IS REALLY UP THERE !!

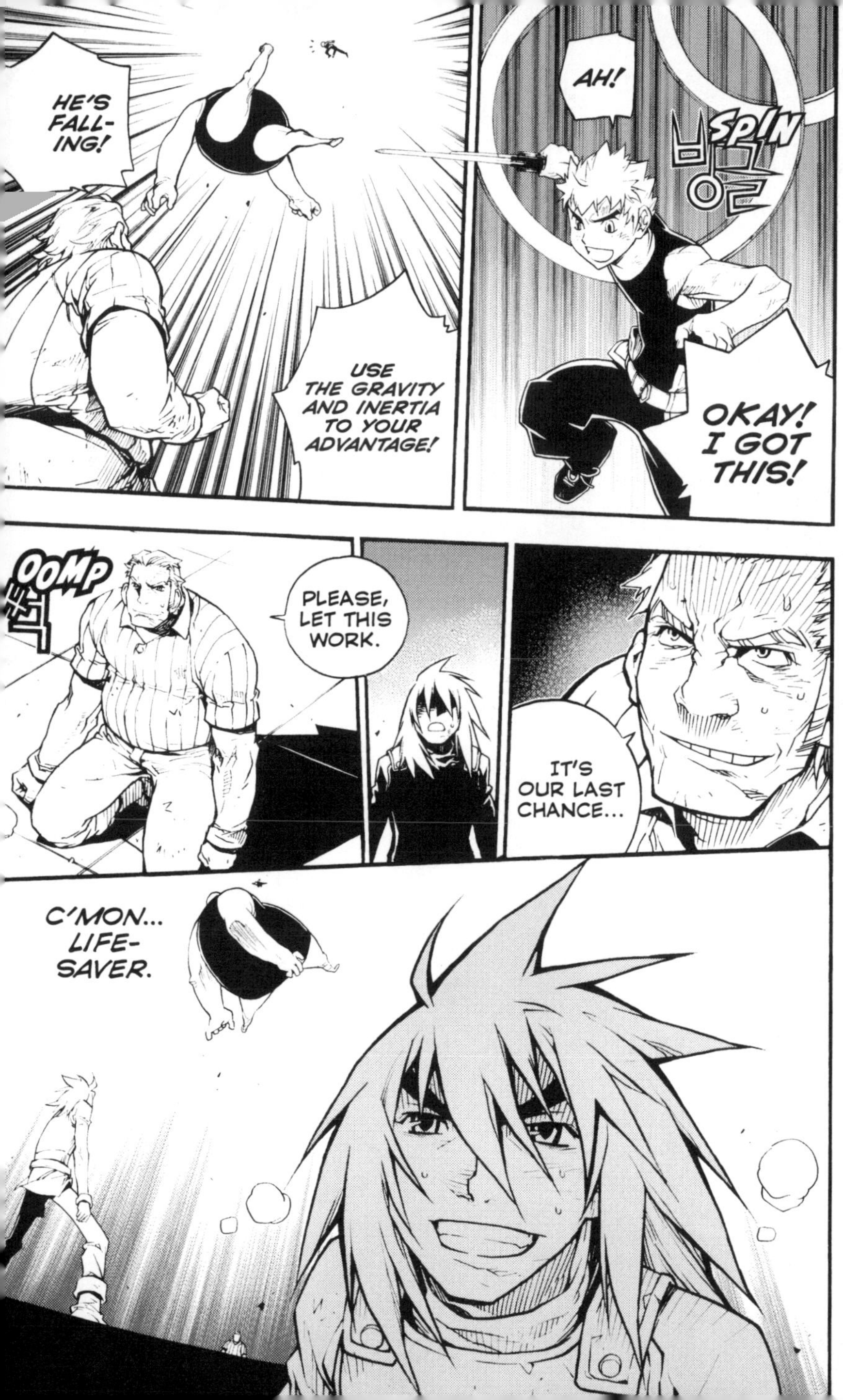
HE'S FALLING!
USE THE GRAVITY AND INERTIA TO YOUR ADVANTAGE!
AH!
SPIN
OKAY! I GOT THIS!
OOMP
PLEASE, LET THIS WORK.
IT'S OUR LAST CHANCE...
C'MON... LIFE-SAVER.

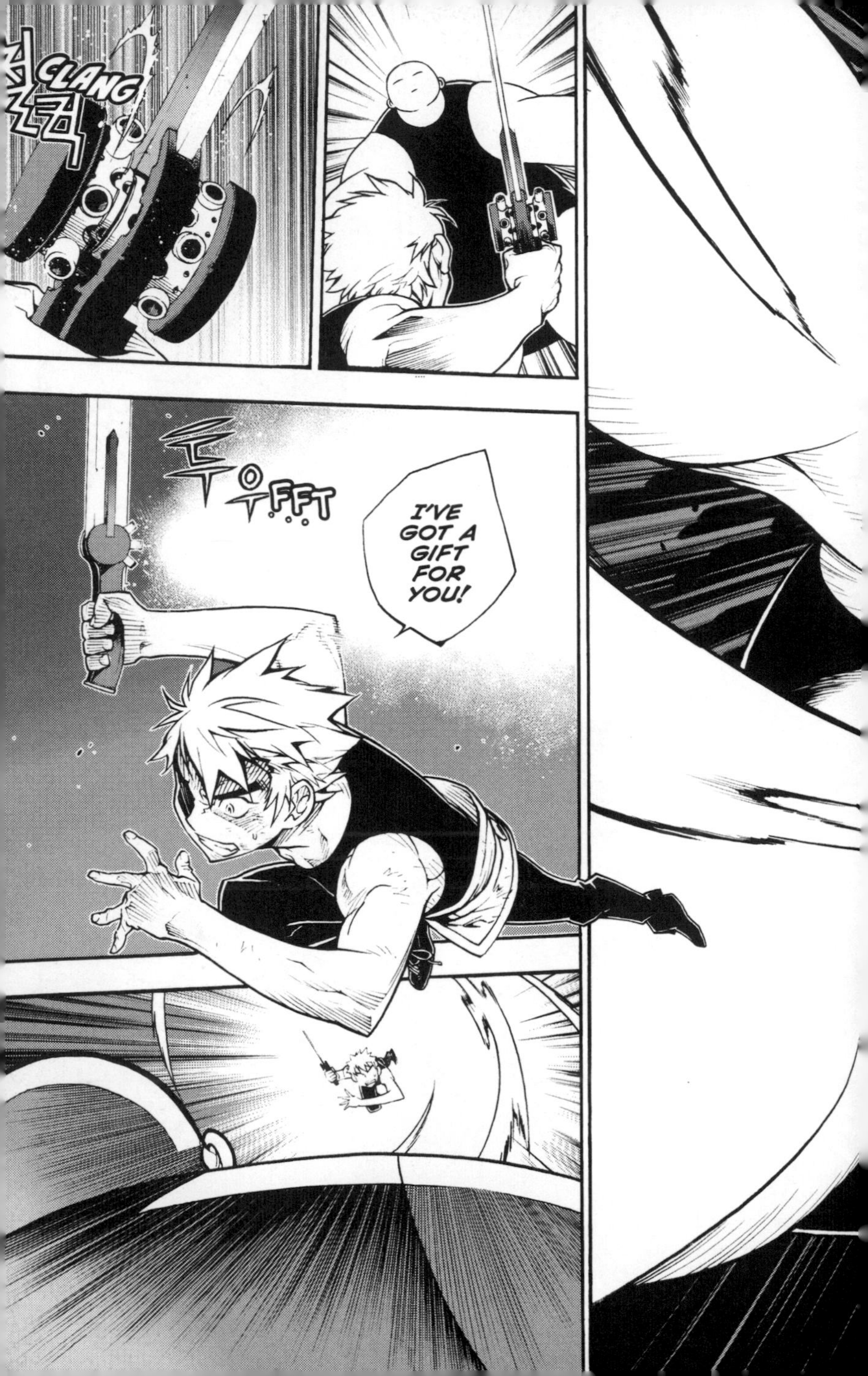
CLANG
FFT
I'VE GOT A GIFT FOR YOU!

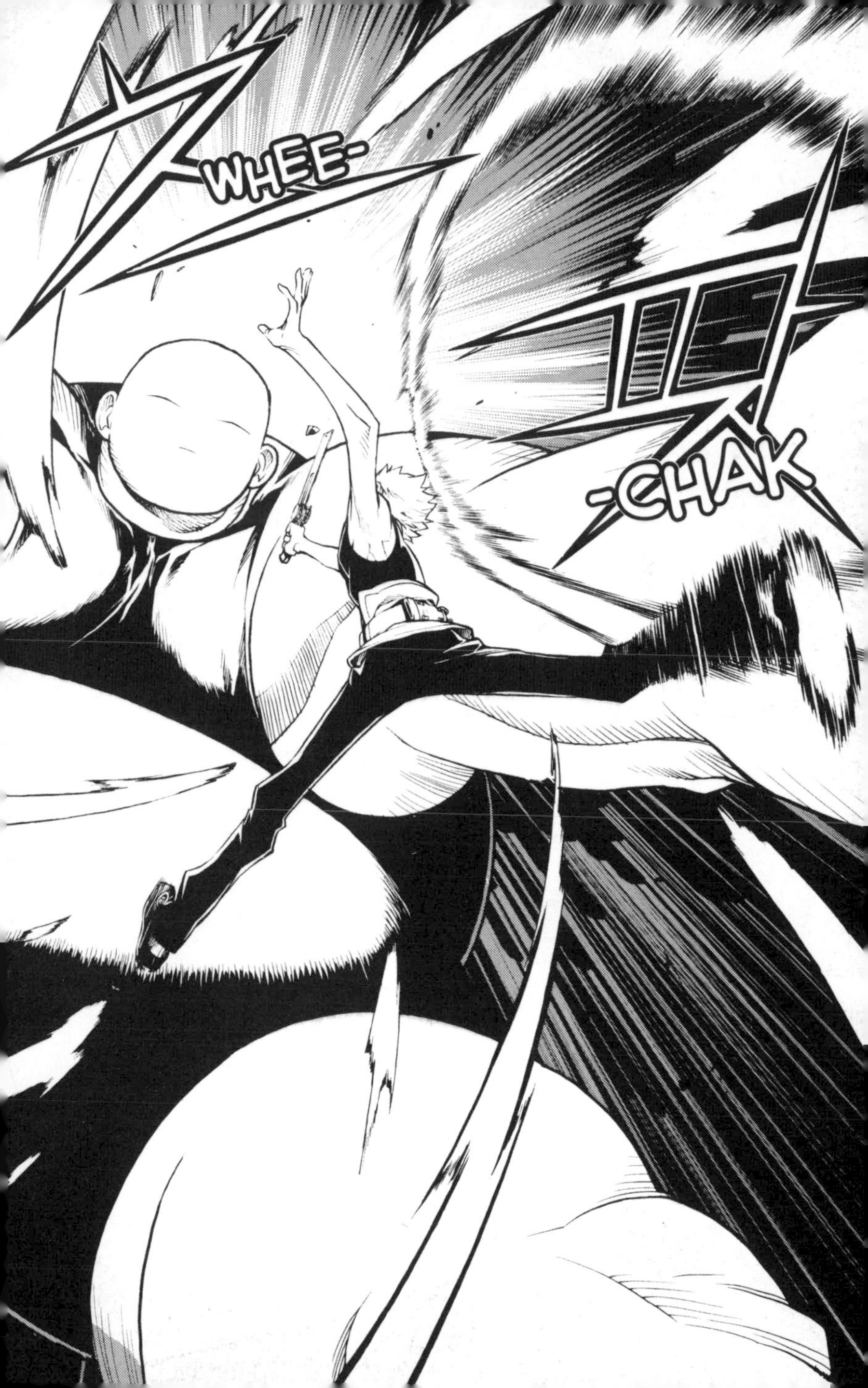
WHEE-
-CHAK

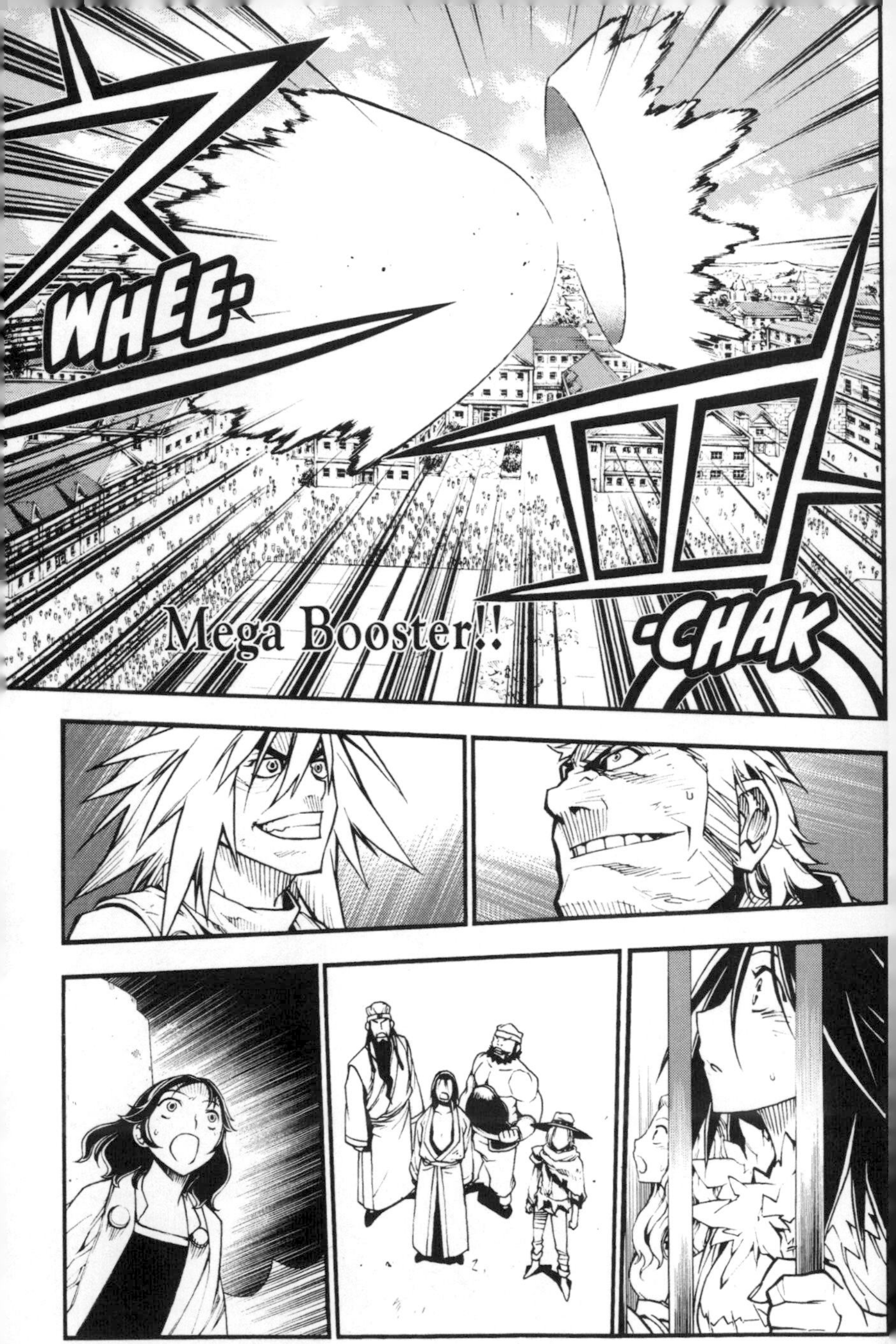
WHEE-
Mega Booster!!
-CHAK

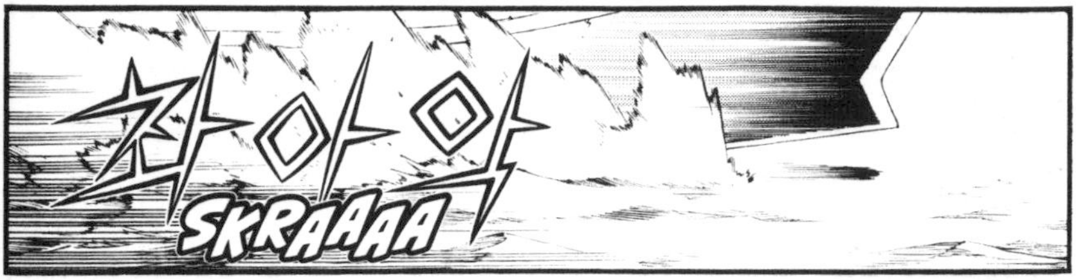
SKRAAAA
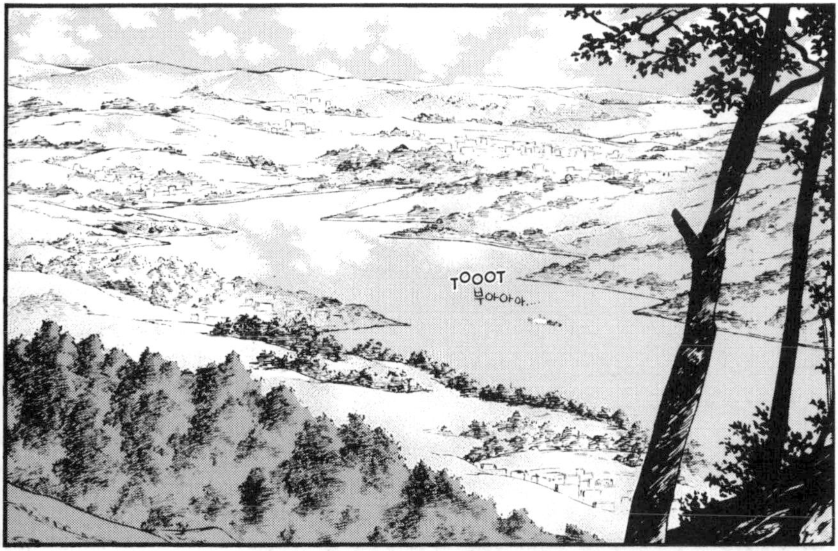
TOOOT
부아아아...
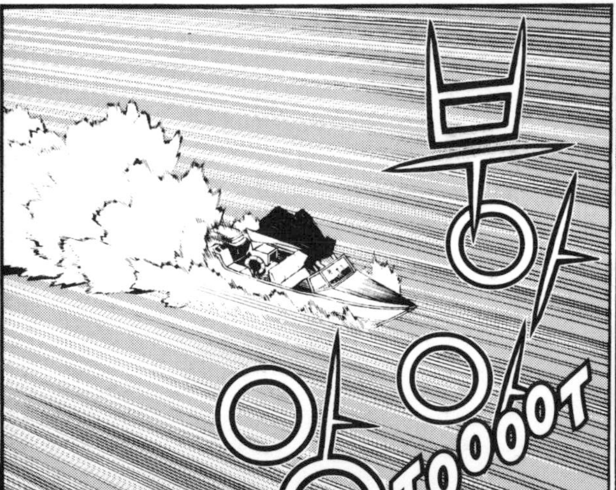
TOOOOT
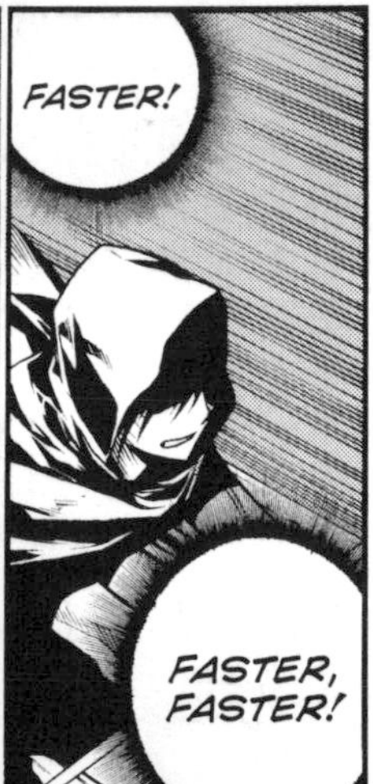
FASTER!
FASTER, FASTER!

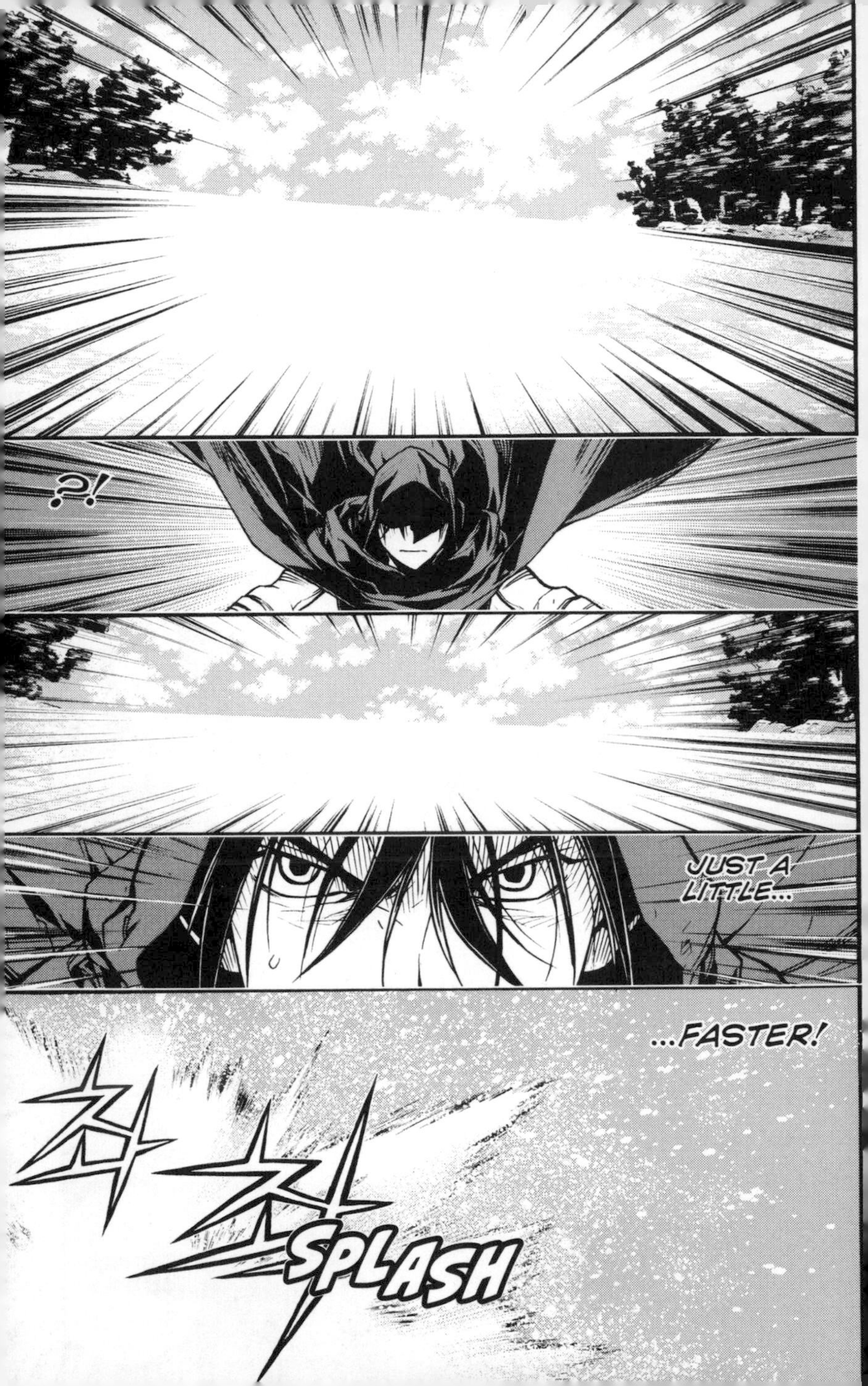
?!
JUST A LITTLE...
...FASTER!
SPLASH

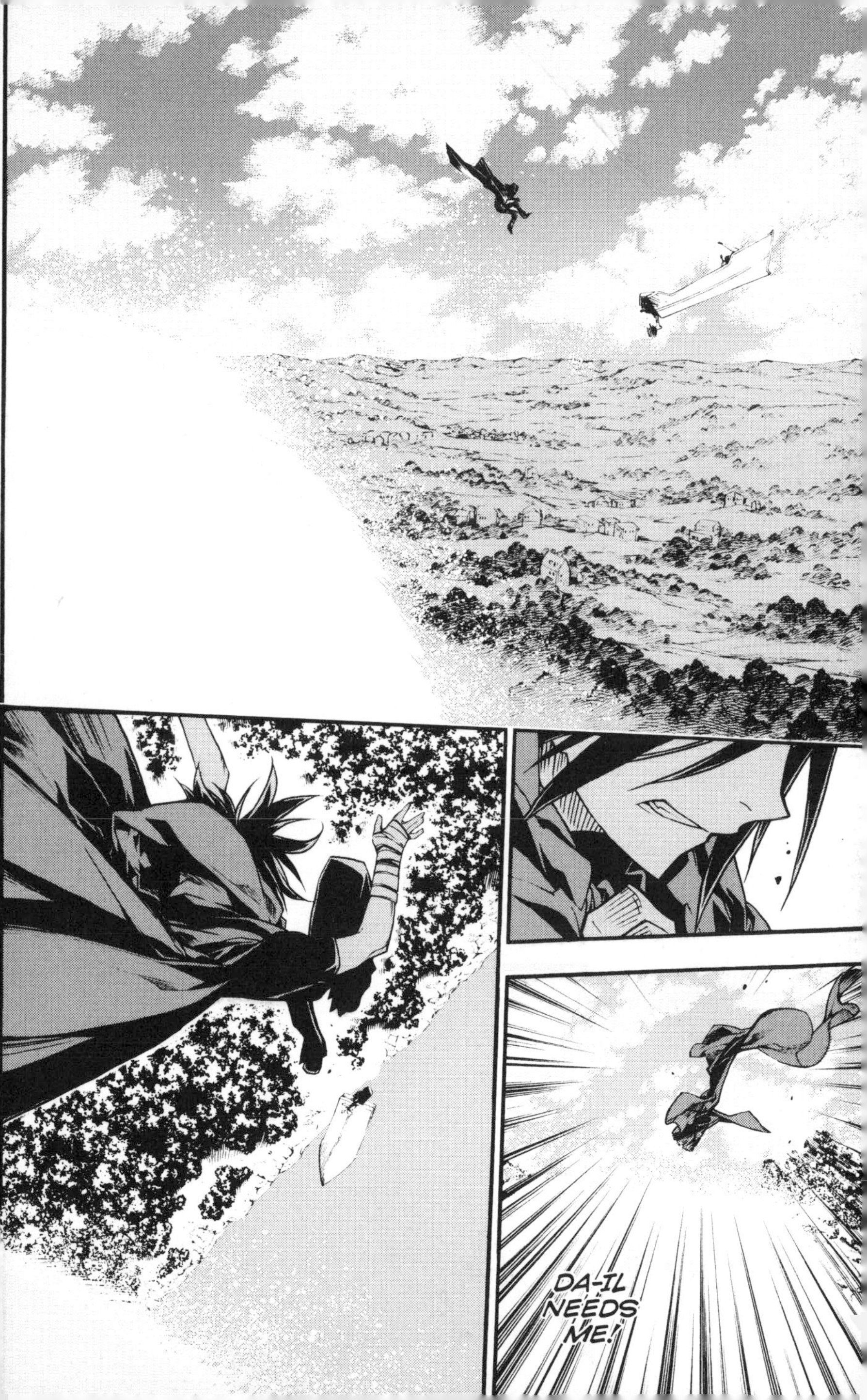
DA-IL NEEDS ME!

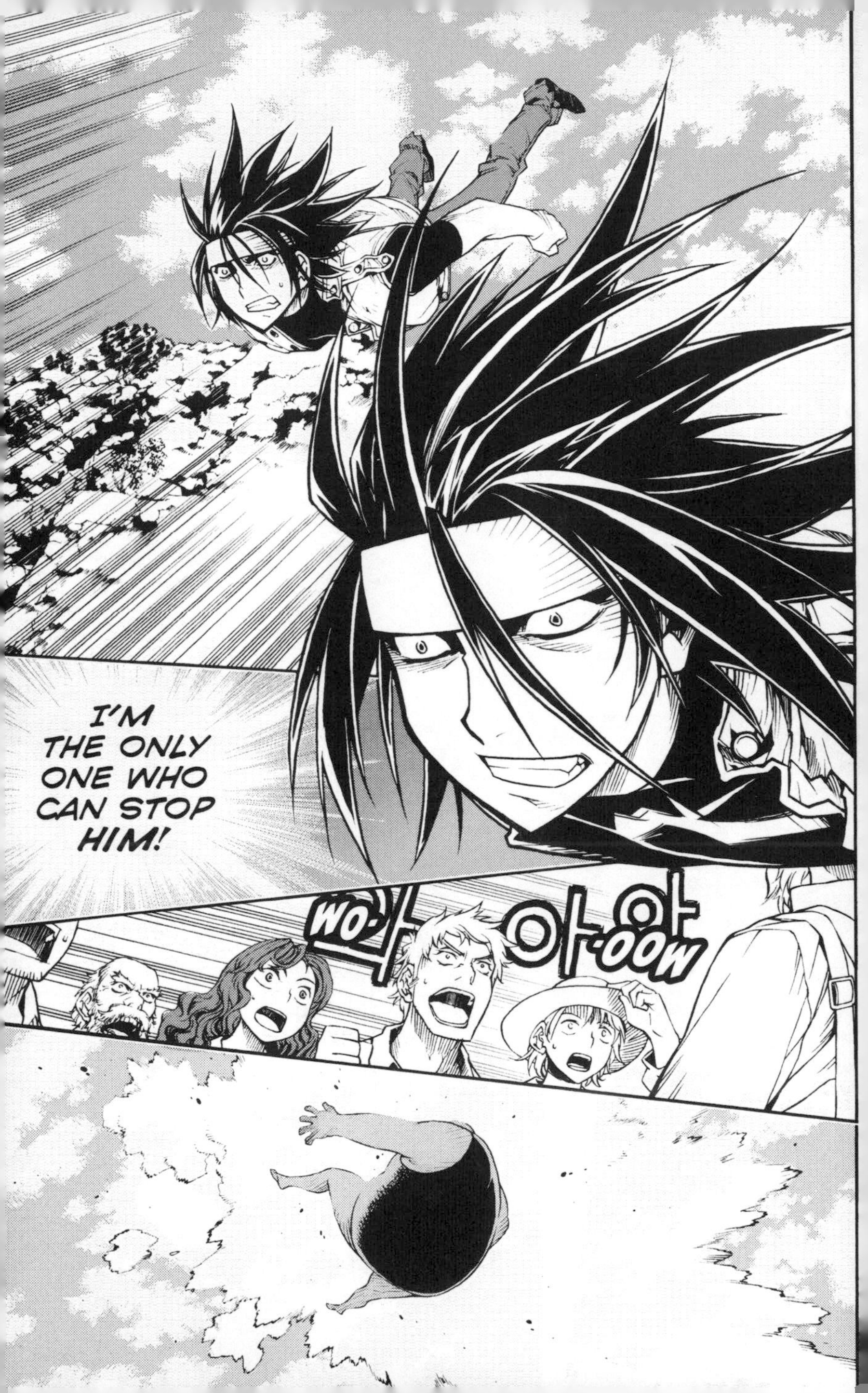
I'M THE ONLY ONE WHO CAN STOP HIM!
WO-아아아-OOW

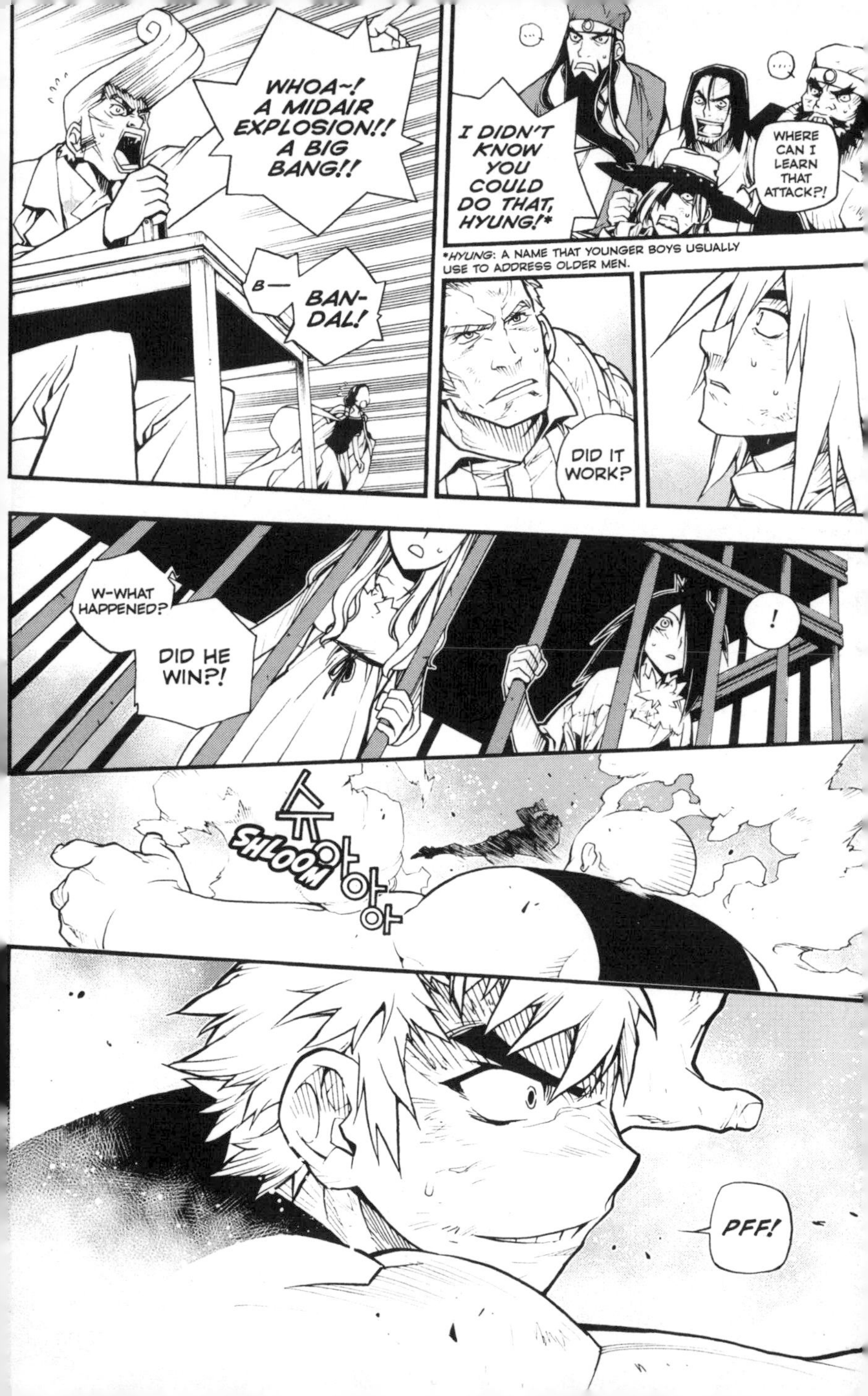
WHOA~! A MIDAIR EXPLOSION!! A BIG BANG!!
B—
BAN-DAL!
I DIDN'T KNOW YOU COULD DO THAT, HYUNG!*
WHERE CAN I LEARN THAT ATTACK?!
*HYUNG: A NAME THAT YOUNGER BOYS USUALLY USE TO ADDRESS OLDER MEN.
DID IT WORK?
W-WHAT HAPPENED?
DID HE WIN?!
!
슈아아
SHLOOM
PFF!

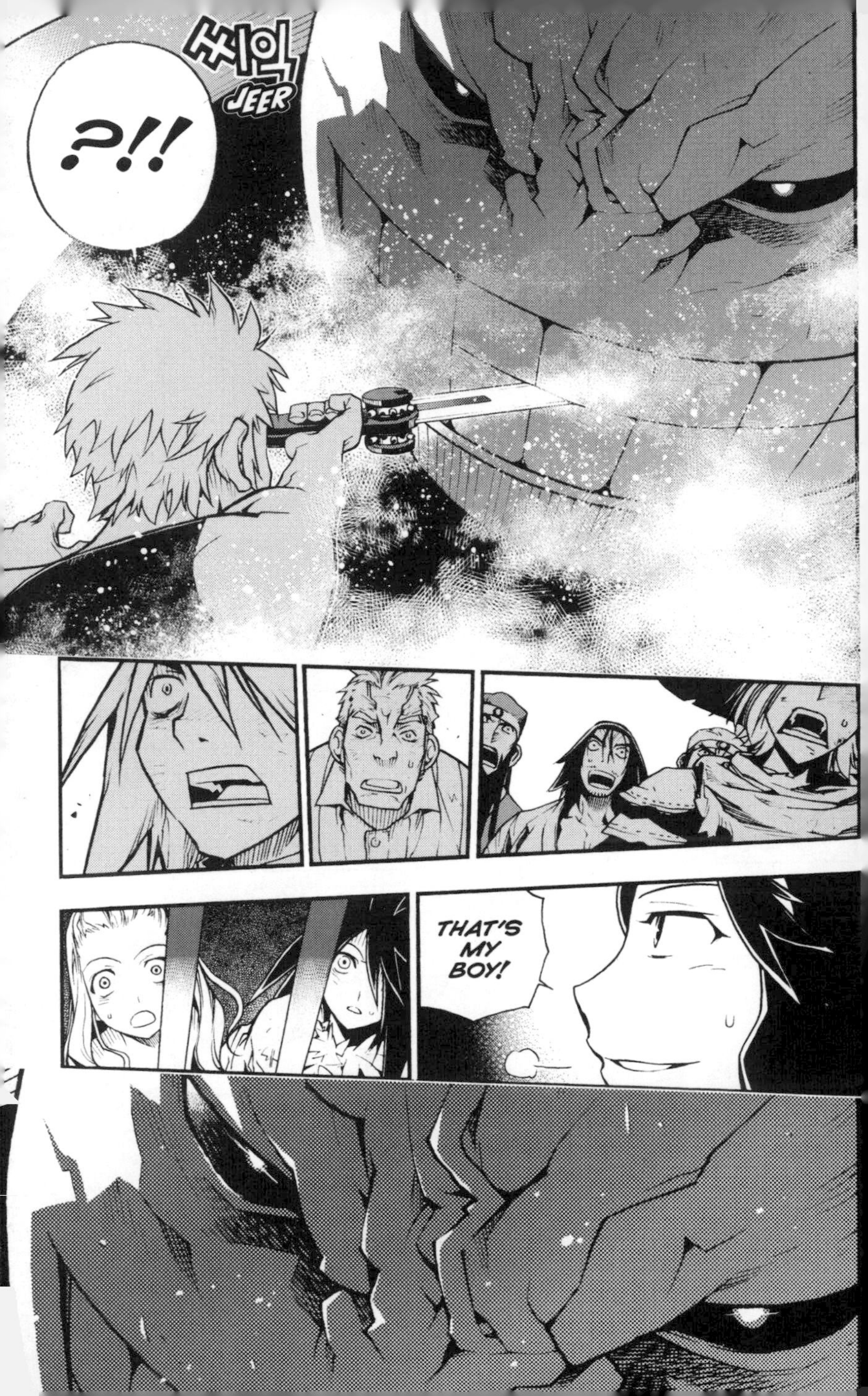
?!!
쓰익
JEER
THAT'S MY BOY!

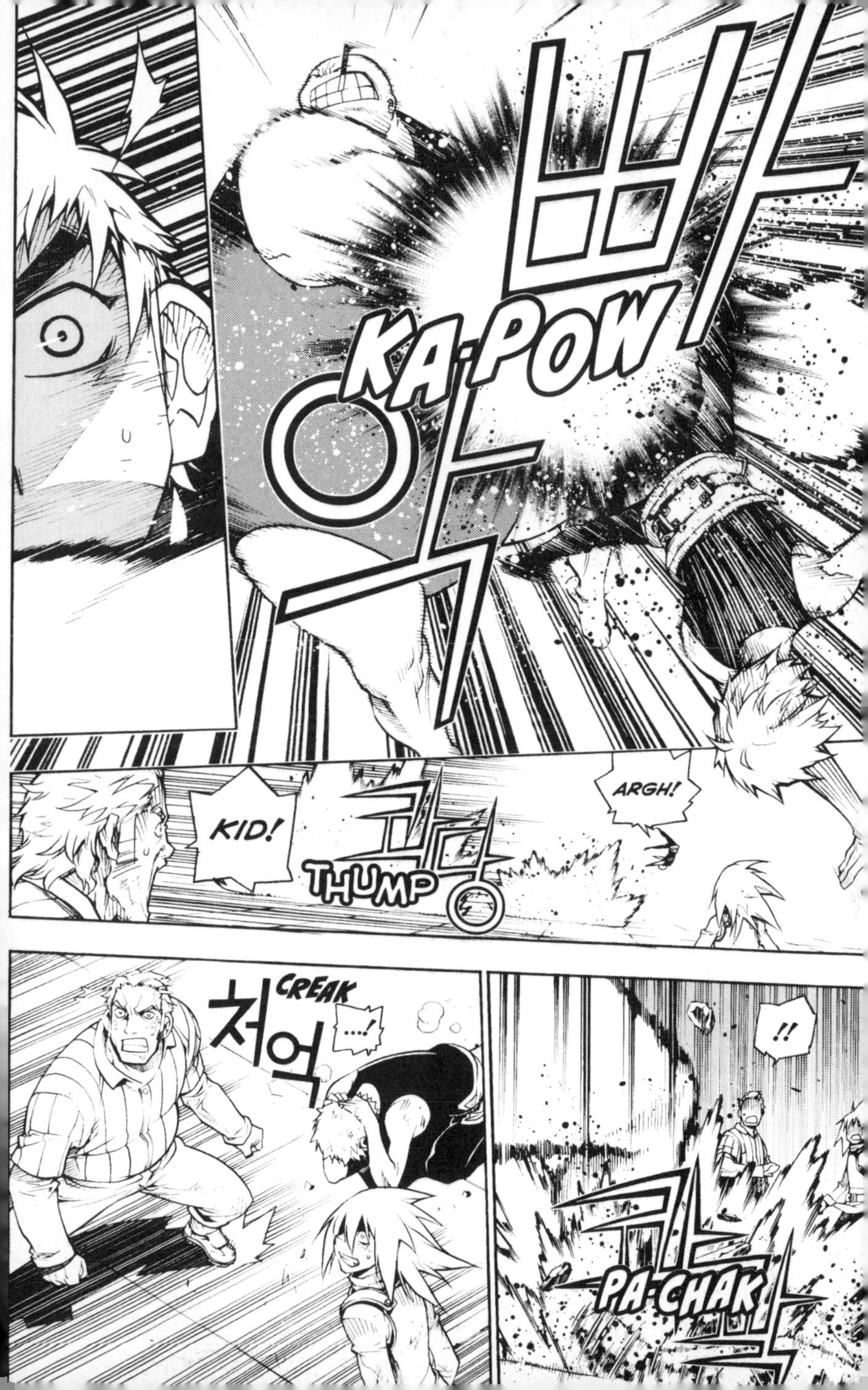
빠악
KA-POW
KID!
THUMP
ARGH!
처억
CREAK
....!
!!
PA-CHAK

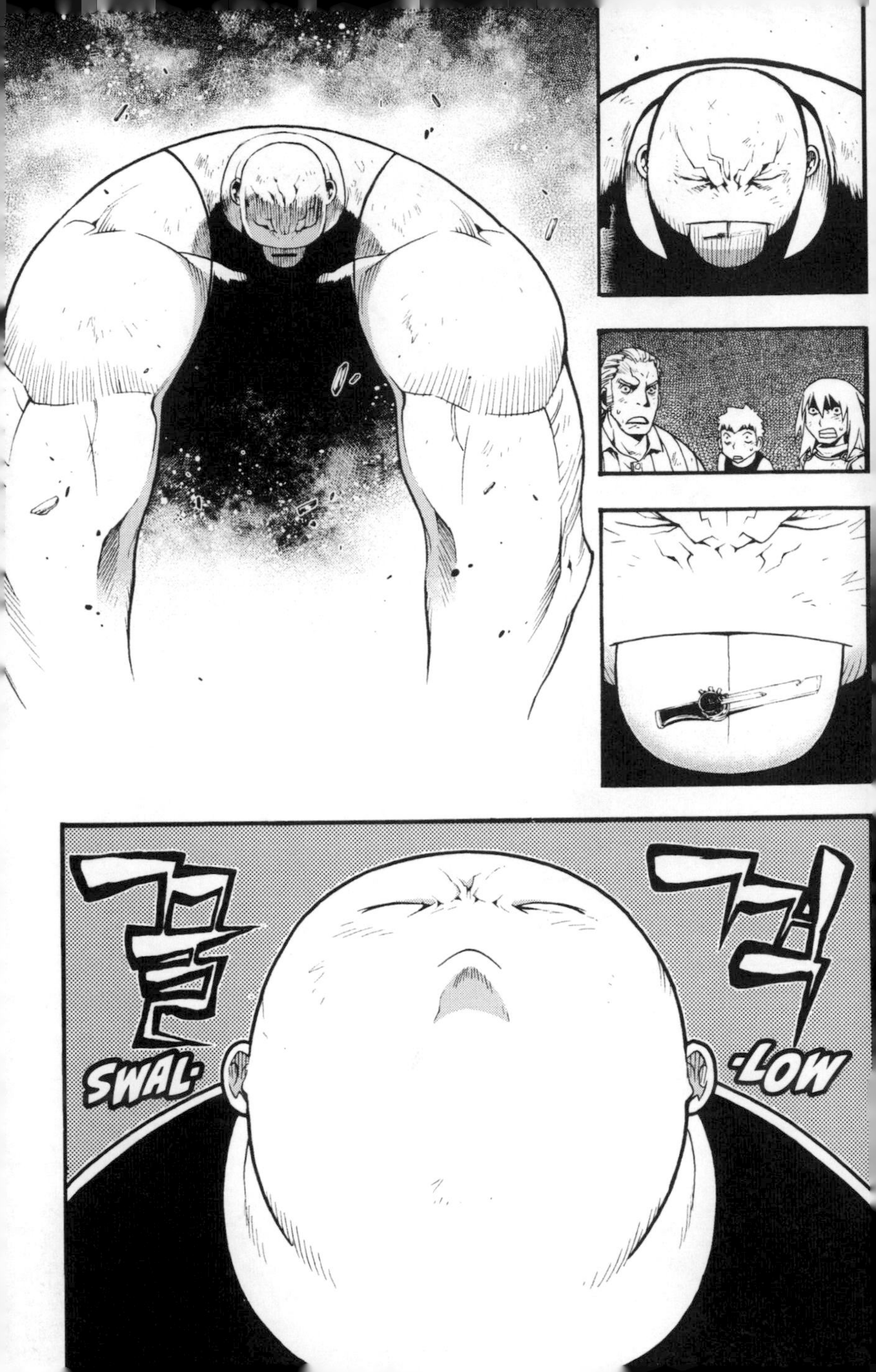
SWAL-
-LOW

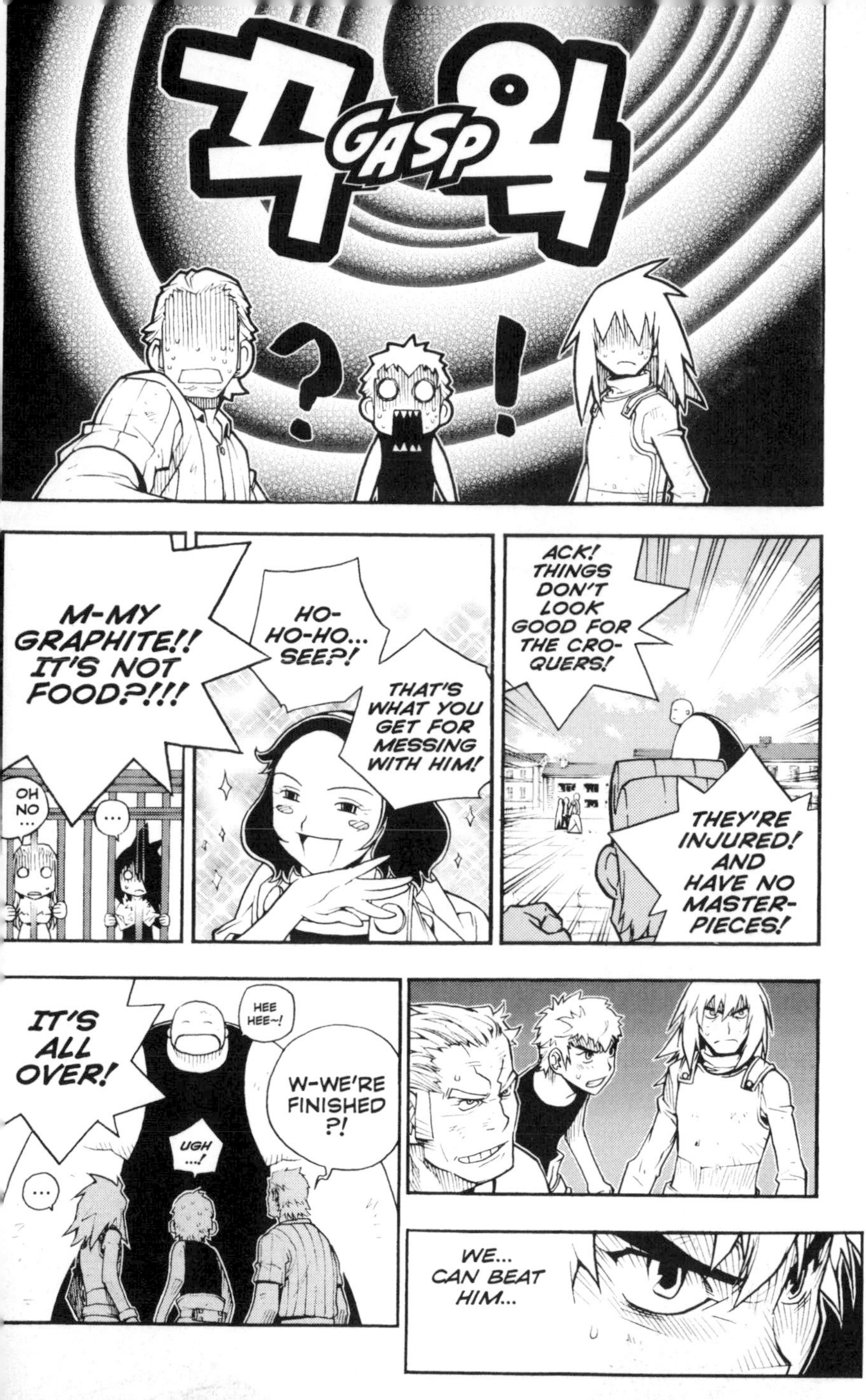
GASP
M-MY GRAPHITE!! IT'S NOT FOOD?!!!
OH NO ...
...
HO-HO-HO... SEE?!
THAT'S WHAT YOU GET FOR MESSING WITH HIM!
ACK! THINGS DON'T LOOK GOOD FOR THE CRO-QUERS!
THEY'RE INJURED! AND HAVE NO MASTER-PIECES!
IT'S ALL OVER!
HEE HEE~!
W-WE'RE FINISHED ?!
UGH ...!
...
WE... CAN BEAT HIM...

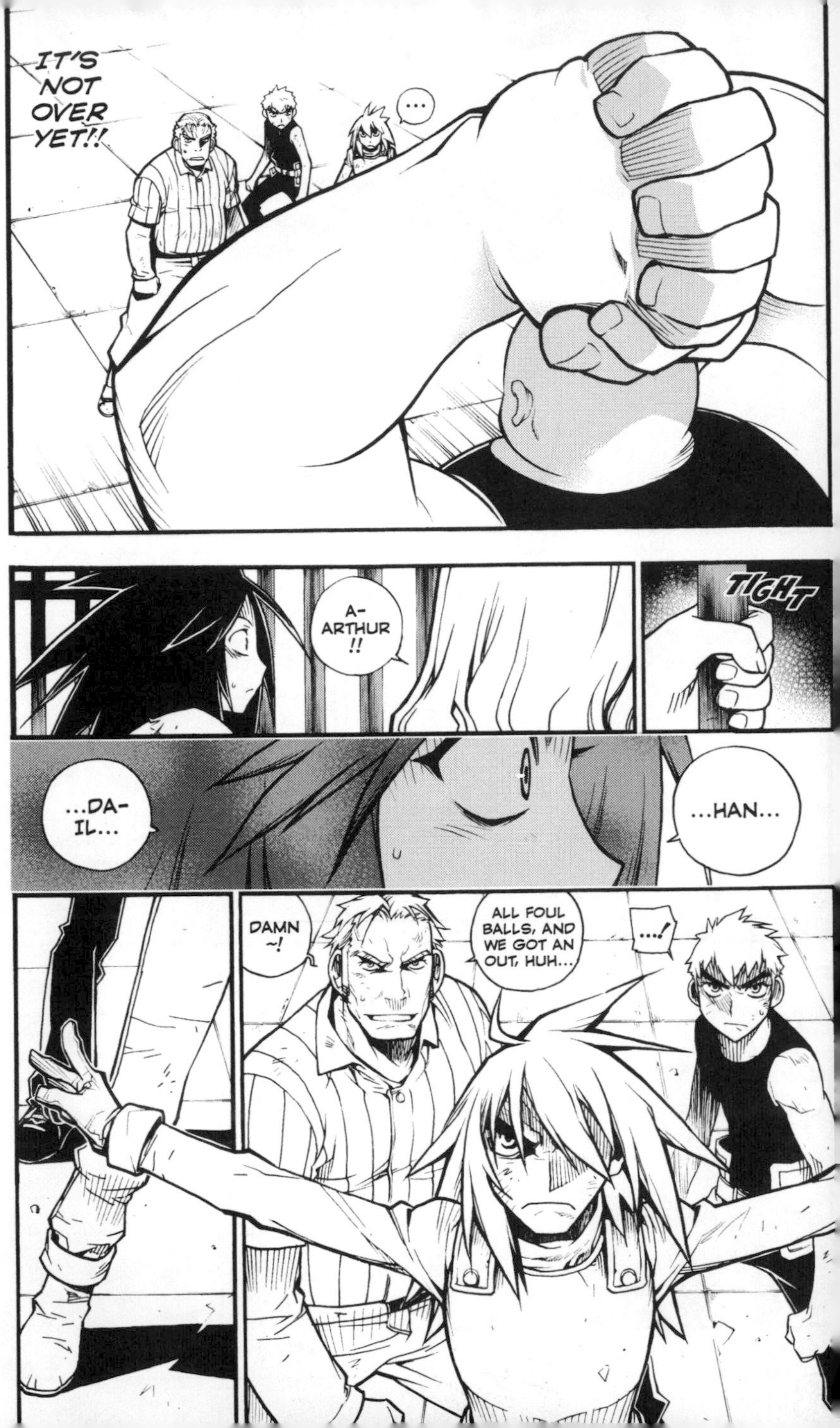
IT'S NOT OVER YET!!
...
A-ARTHUR!!
TIGHT
...DA-IL...
...HAN...
DAMN~!
ALL FOUL BALLS, AND WE GOT AN OUT, HUH...
...!

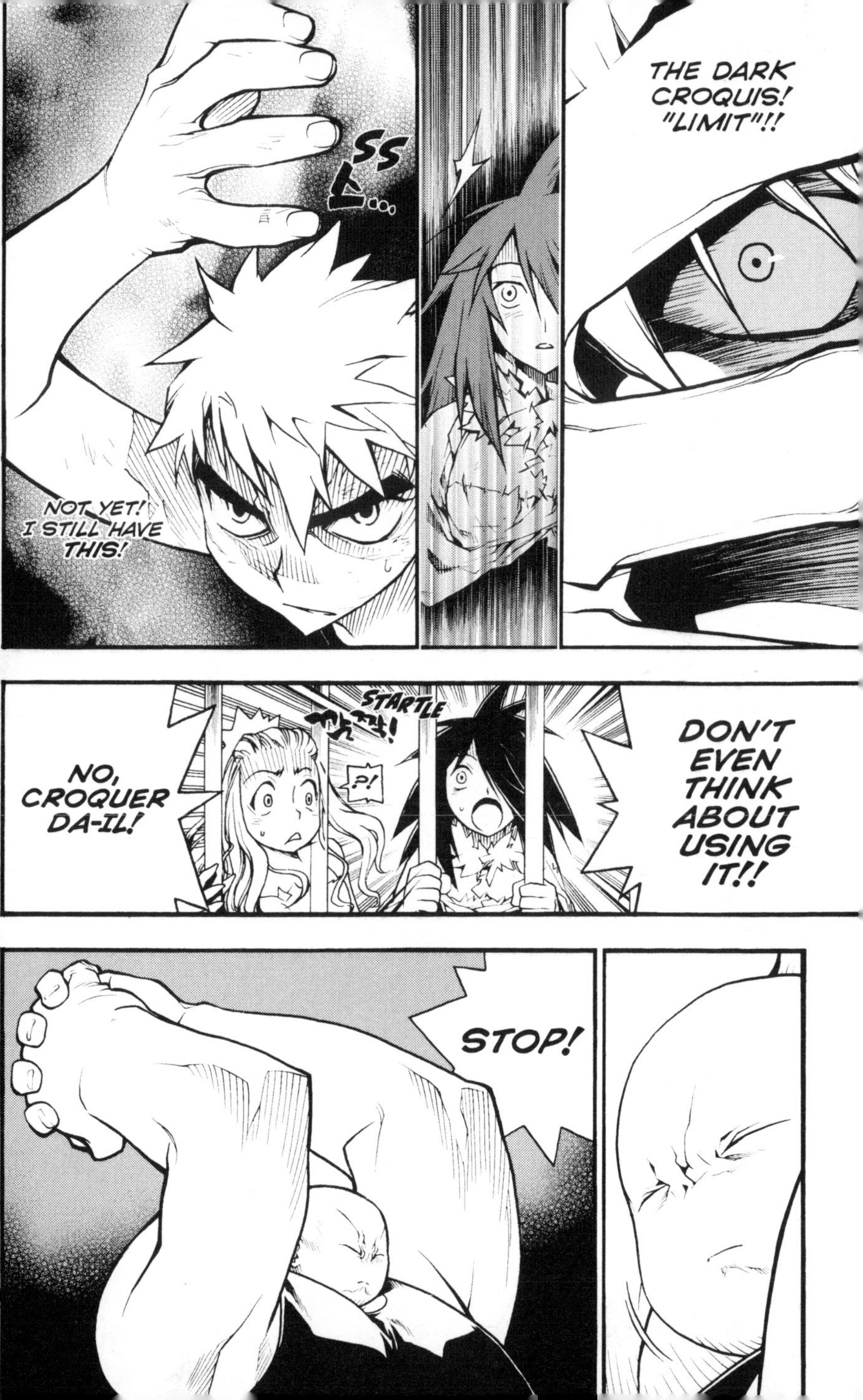
NOT YET! I STILL HAVE THIS!
THE DARK CROQUIS! "LIMIT"!!
NO, CROQUER DA-IL!
STARTLE
?!
DON'T EVEN THINK ABOUT USING IT!!
STOP!

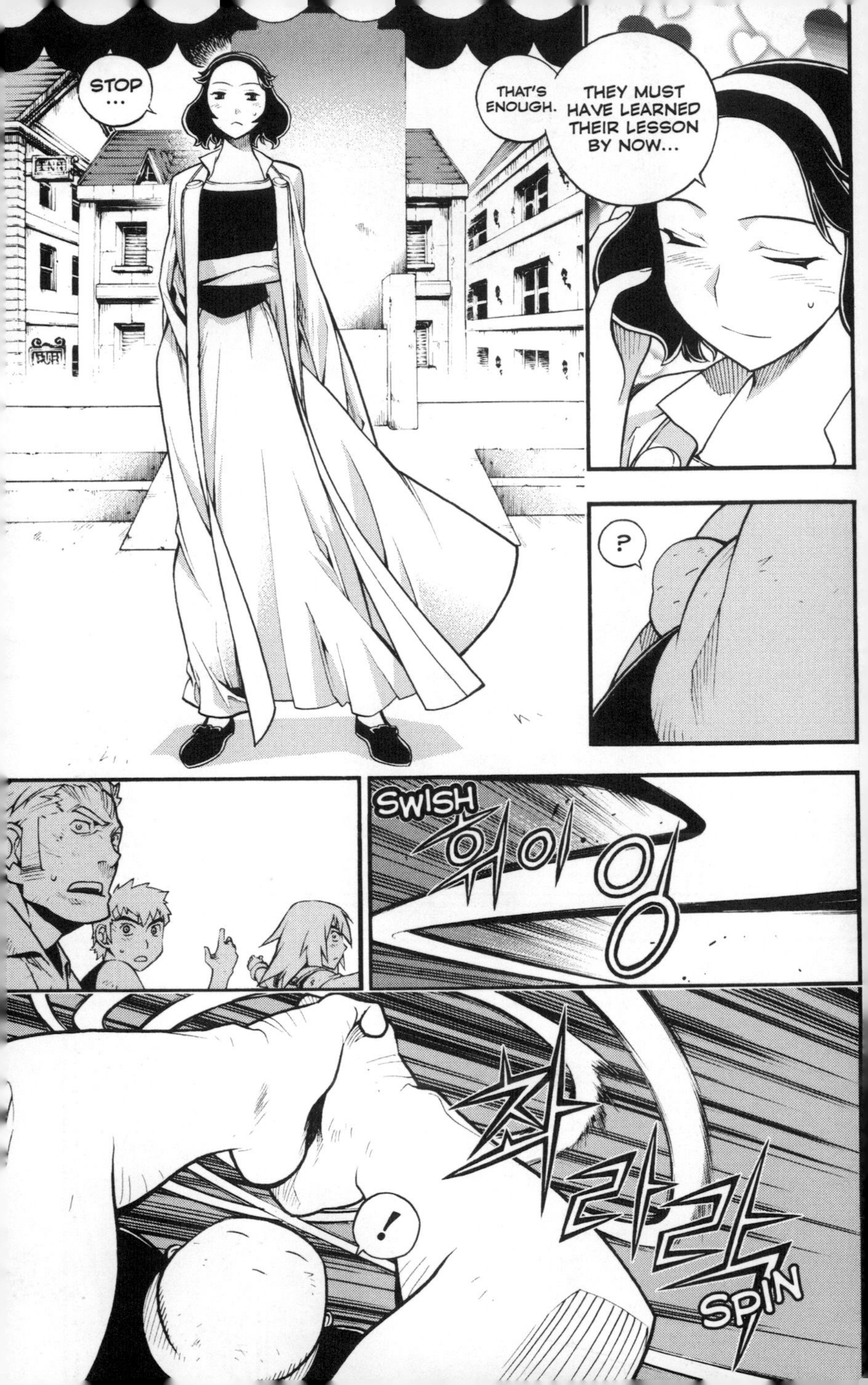
STOP ...
THAT'S ENOUGH.
THEY MUST HAVE LEARNED THEIR LESSON BY NOW...
?
SWISH
화이이잉
착
!
SPIN

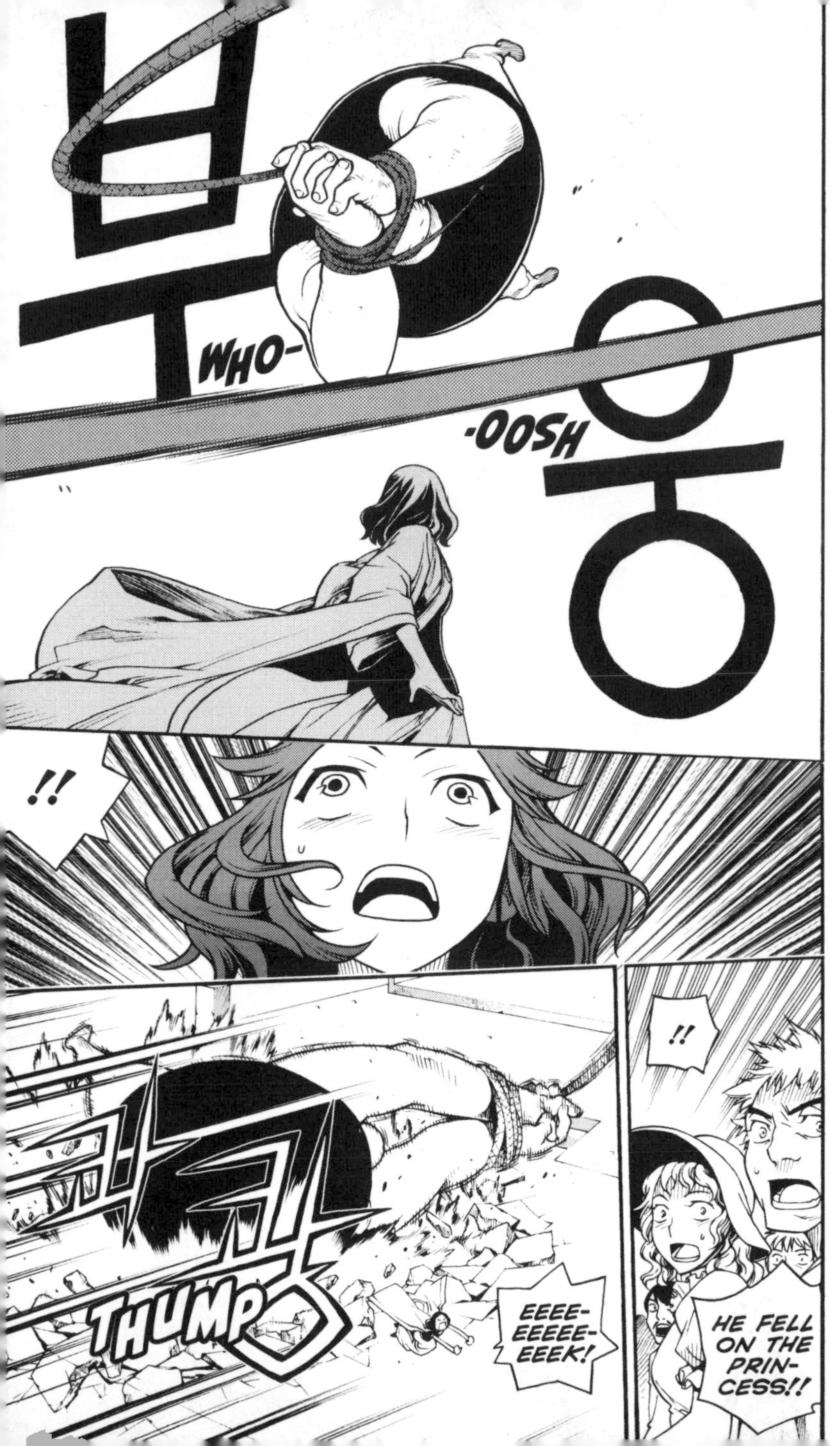

부웅
WHO-
-OOSH
!!
THUMP
EEEE-
EEEEE-
EEEK!
!!
HE FELL
ON THE
PRIN-
CESS!!

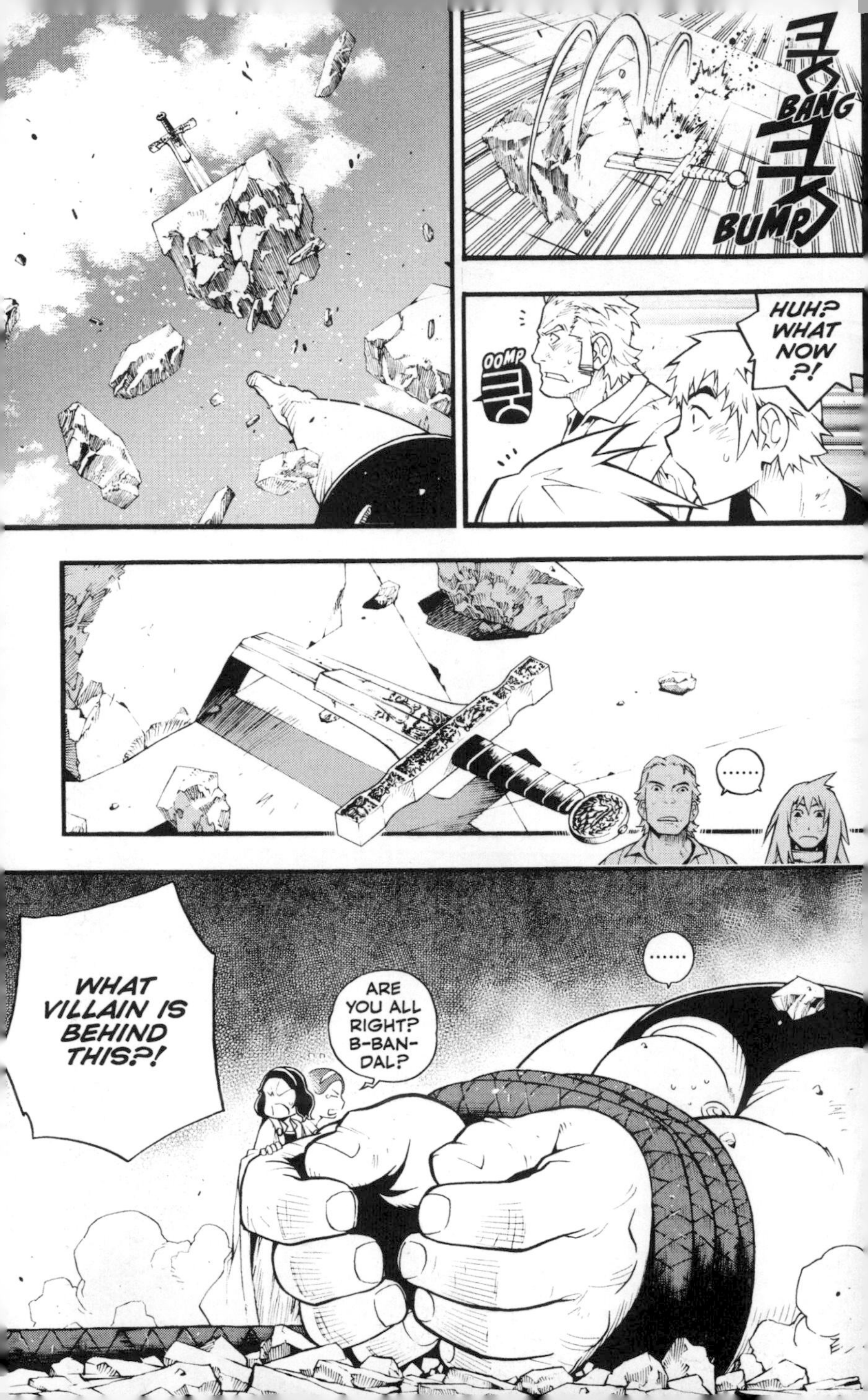
BANG
BUMP
OOMP
HUH? WHAT NOW?!
......
WHAT VILLAIN IS BEHIND THIS?!
ARE YOU ALL RIGHT? B-BANDAL?
......

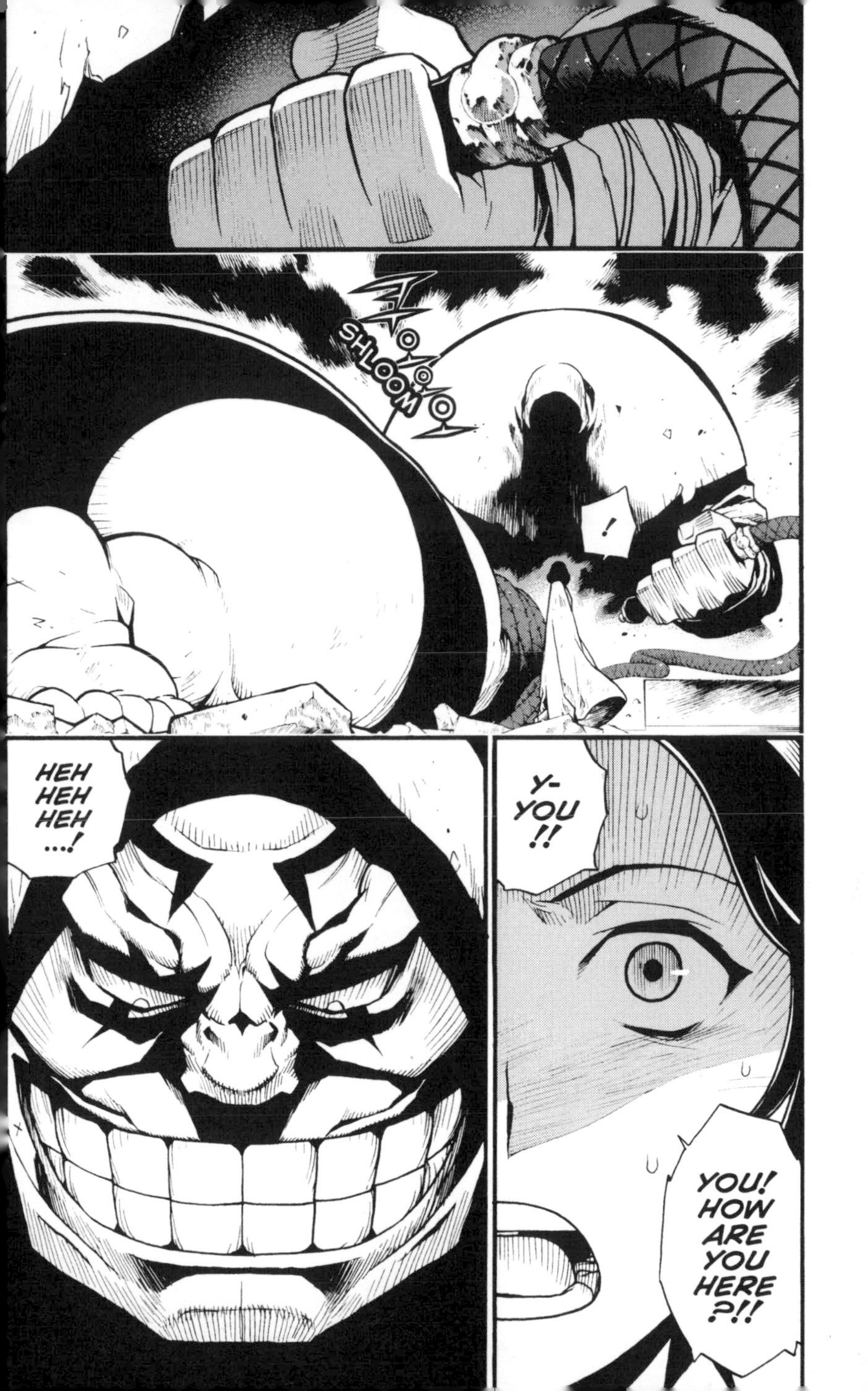
SHLOOM
!
HEH HEH HEH ...!
Y- YOU !!
YOU! HOW ARE YOU HERE ?!!

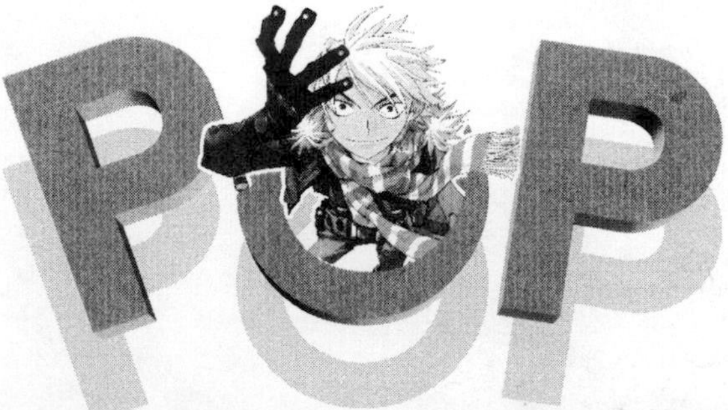
POP

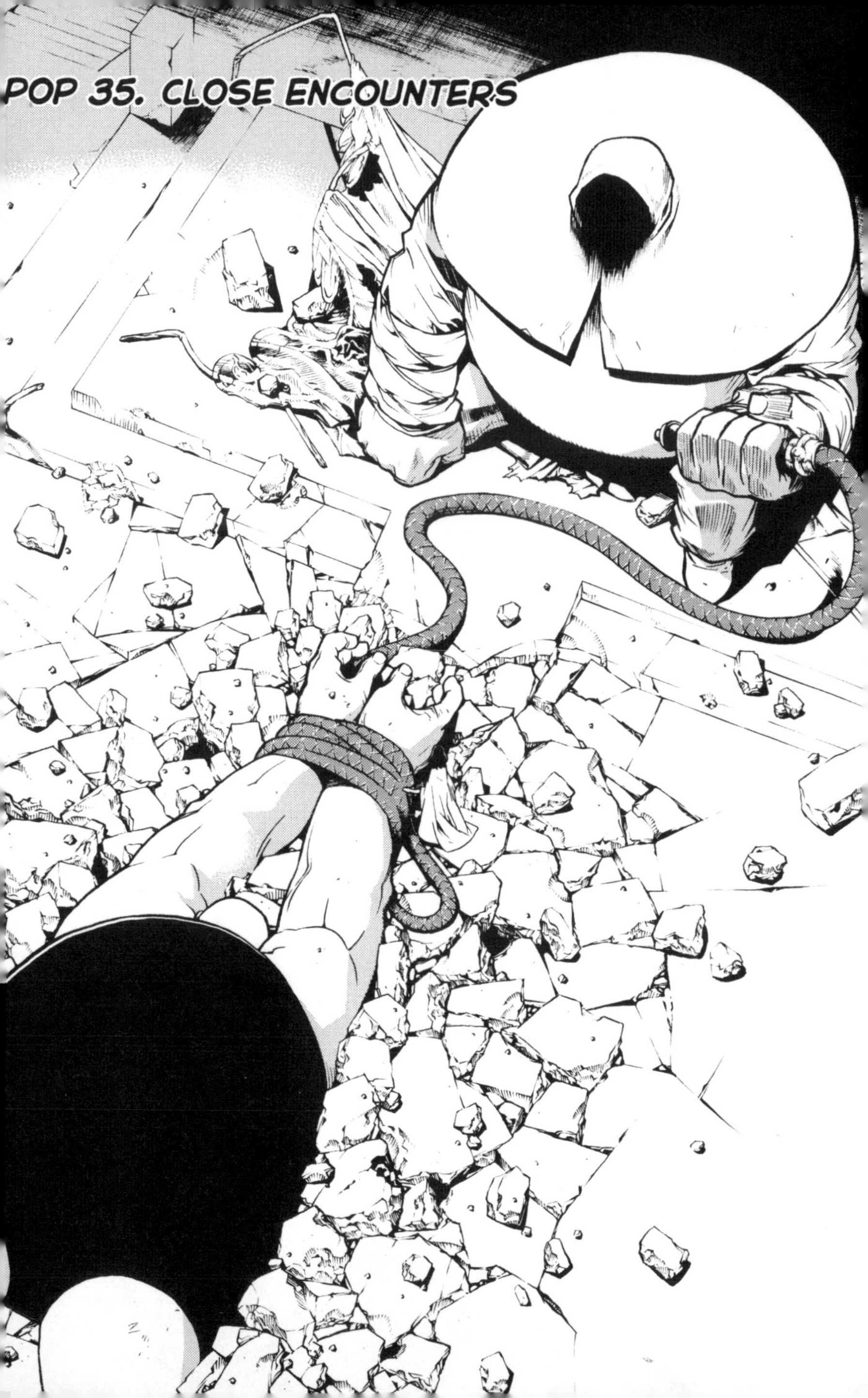
POP 35. CLOSE ENCOUNTERS

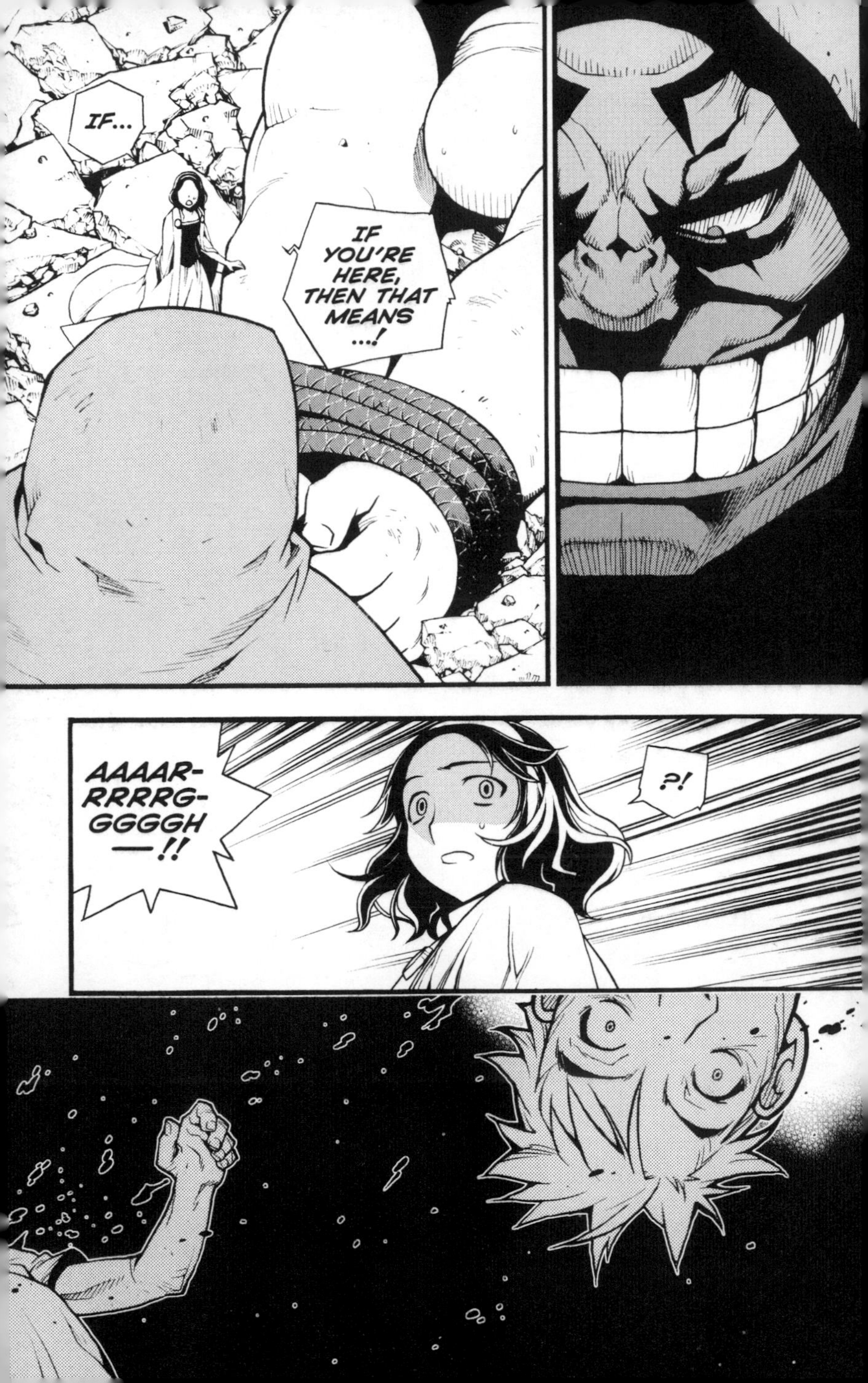
IF...
IF YOU'RE HERE, THEN THAT MEANS ...!
AAAAR-RRRRG-GGGGH—!!
?!

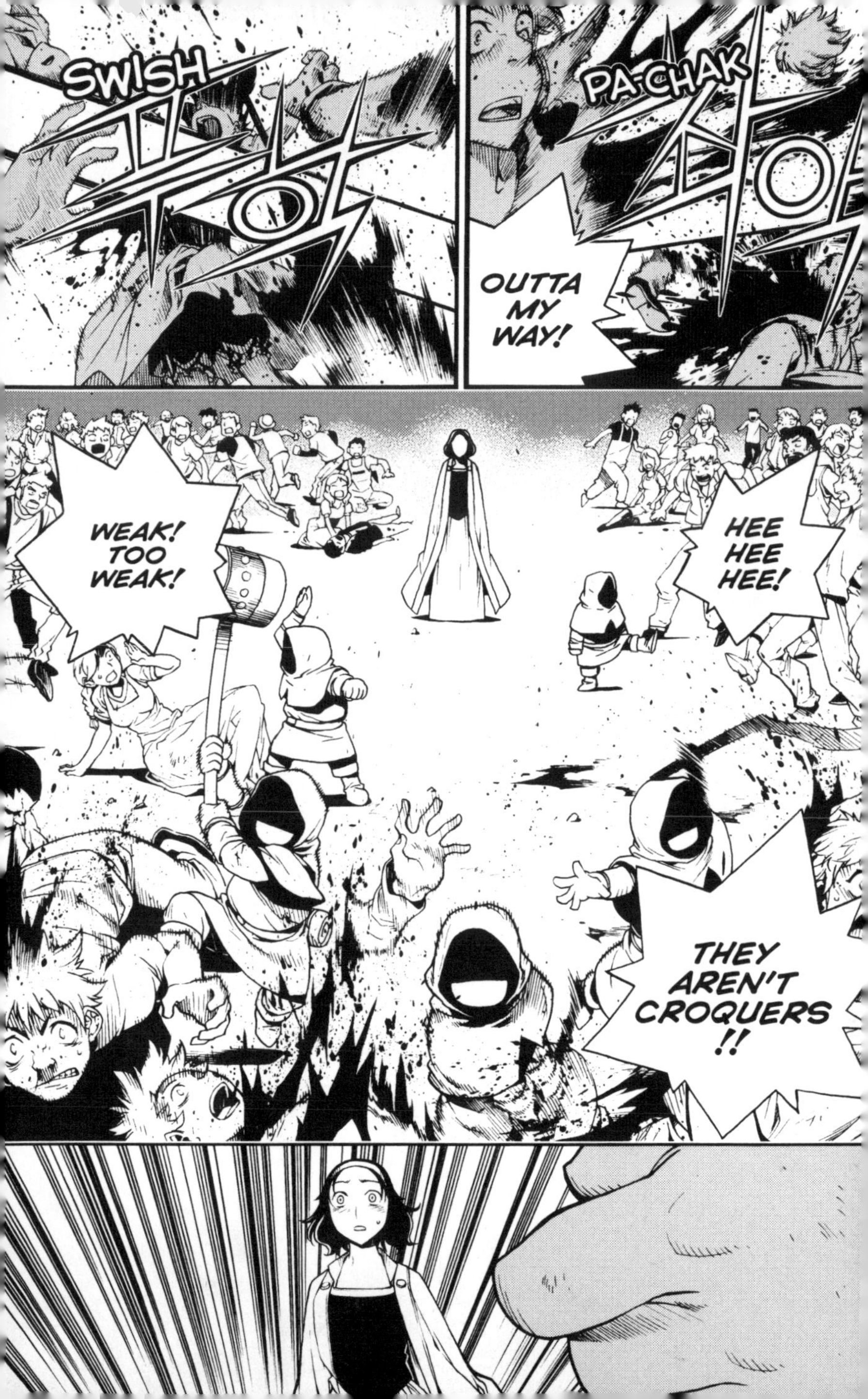
SWISH
PA-CHAK
OUTTA MY WAY!
WEAK! TOO WEAK!
HEE HEE HEE!
THEY AREN'T CROQUERS!!

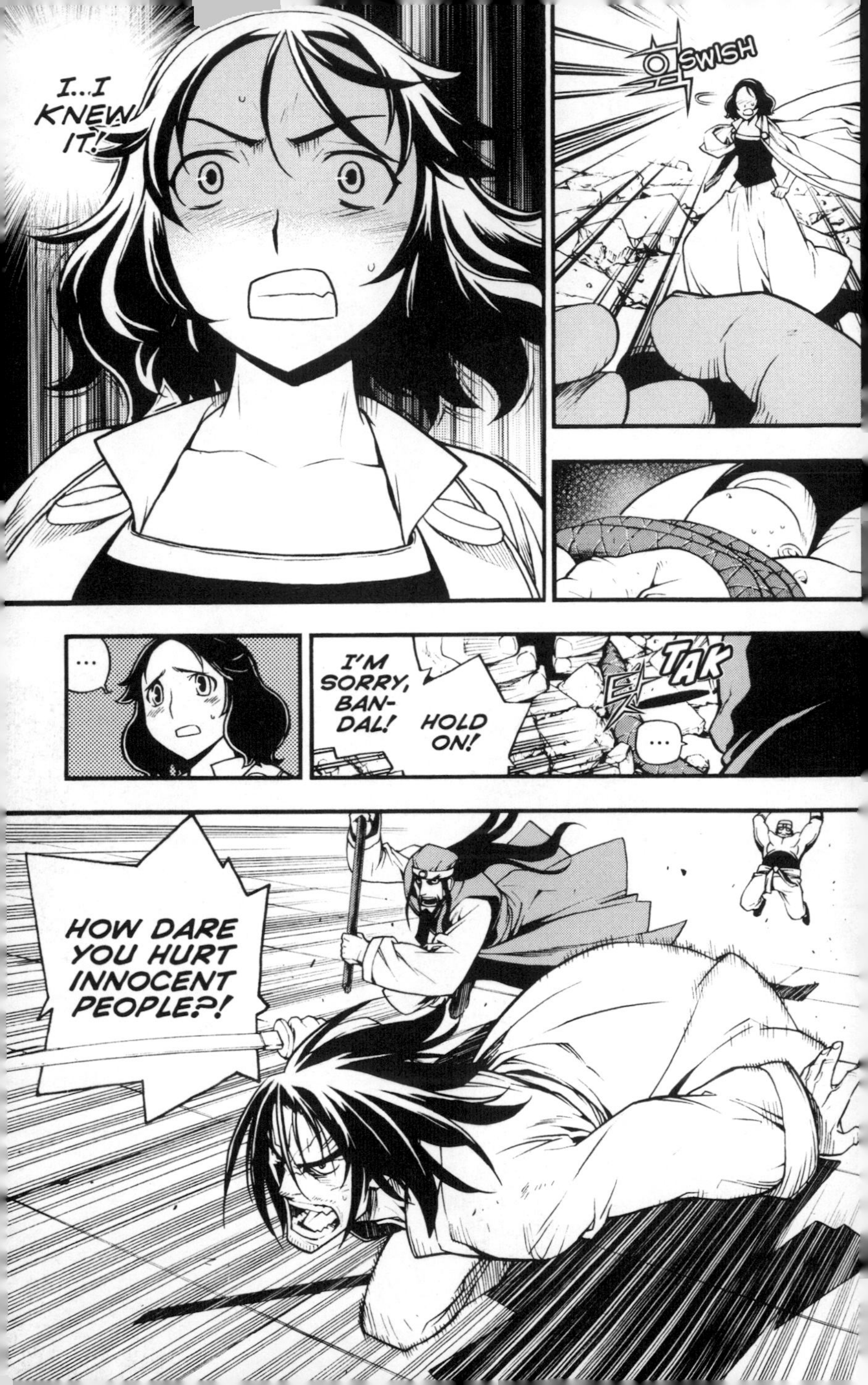
I...I KNEW IT!
SWISH
...
I'M SORRY, BAN-DAL!
HOLD ON!
TAK
...
HOW DARE YOU HURT INNOCENT PEOPLE?!

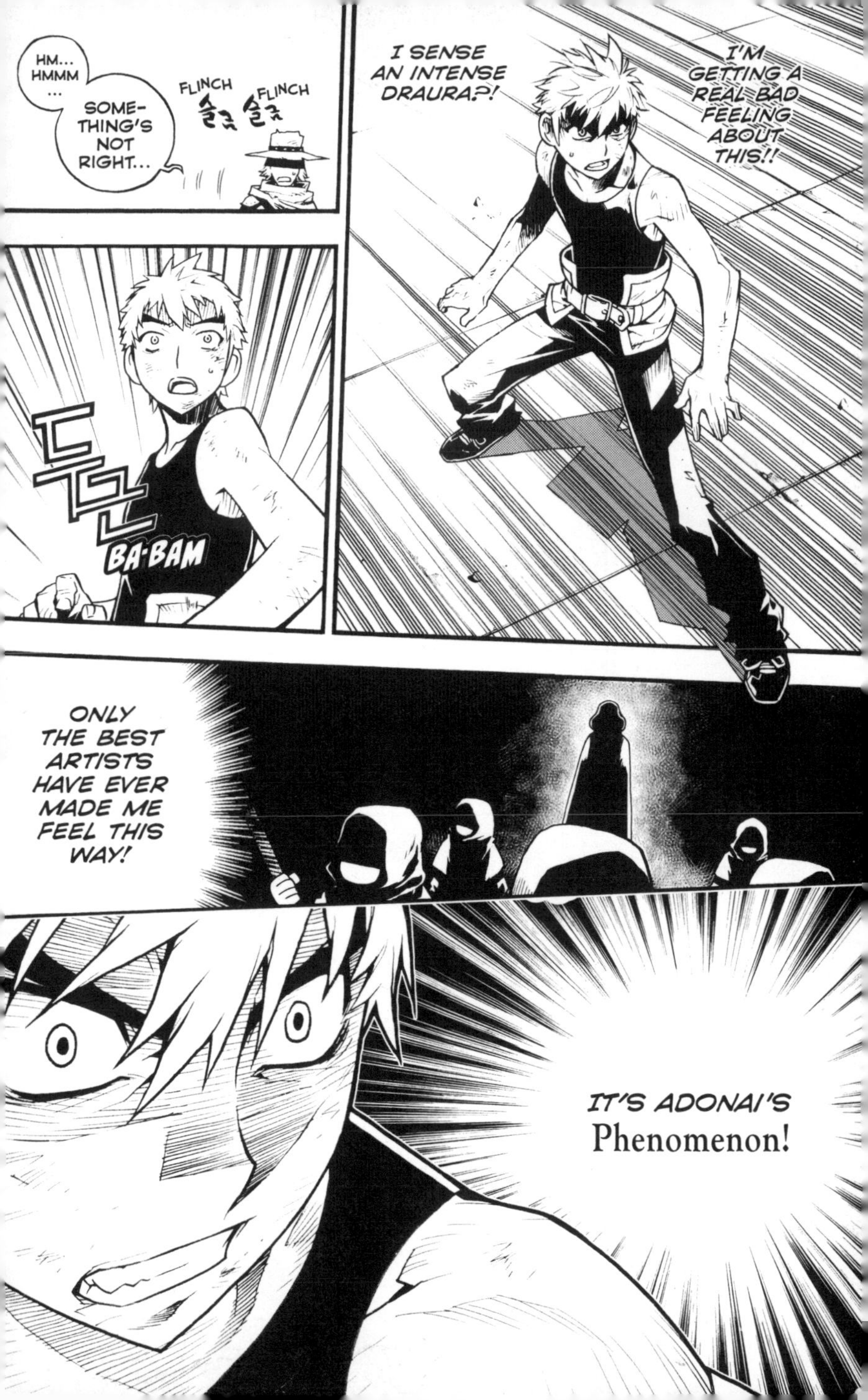
HM... HMMM ...
SOME-THING'S NOT RIGHT...
FLINCH
FLINCH
슬금 슬금
BA-BAM
I SENSE AN INTENSE DRAURA?!
I'M GETTING A REAL BAD FEELING ABOUT THIS!!
ONLY THE BEST ARTISTS HAVE EVER MADE ME FEEL THIS WAY!
IT'S ADONAI'S Phenomenon!

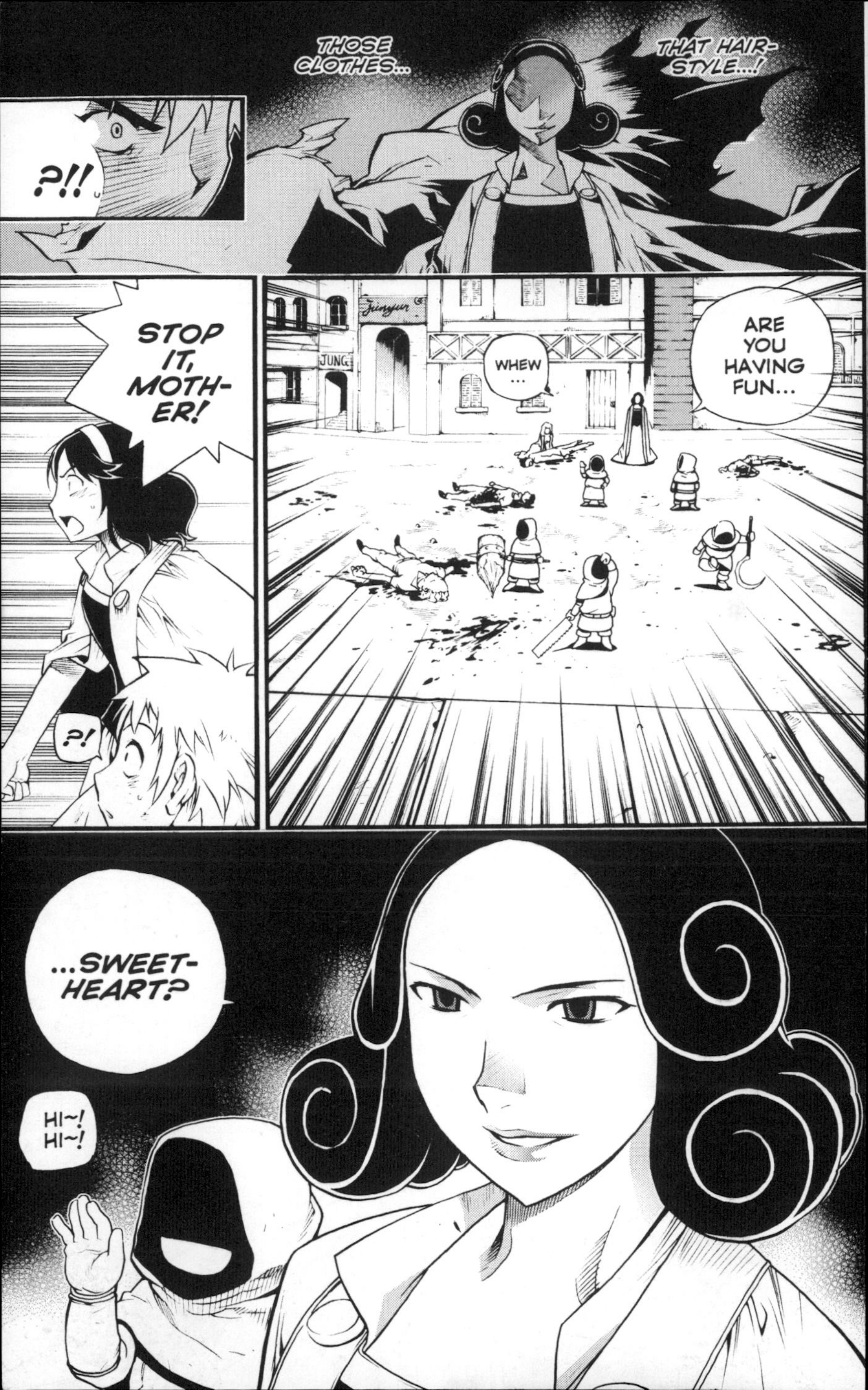
?!!
THOSE CLOTHES...
THAT HAIR-STYLE...!
STOP IT, MOTH-ER!
?!
WHEW ...
ARE YOU HAVING FUN...
...SWEET-HEART?
HI~! HI~!

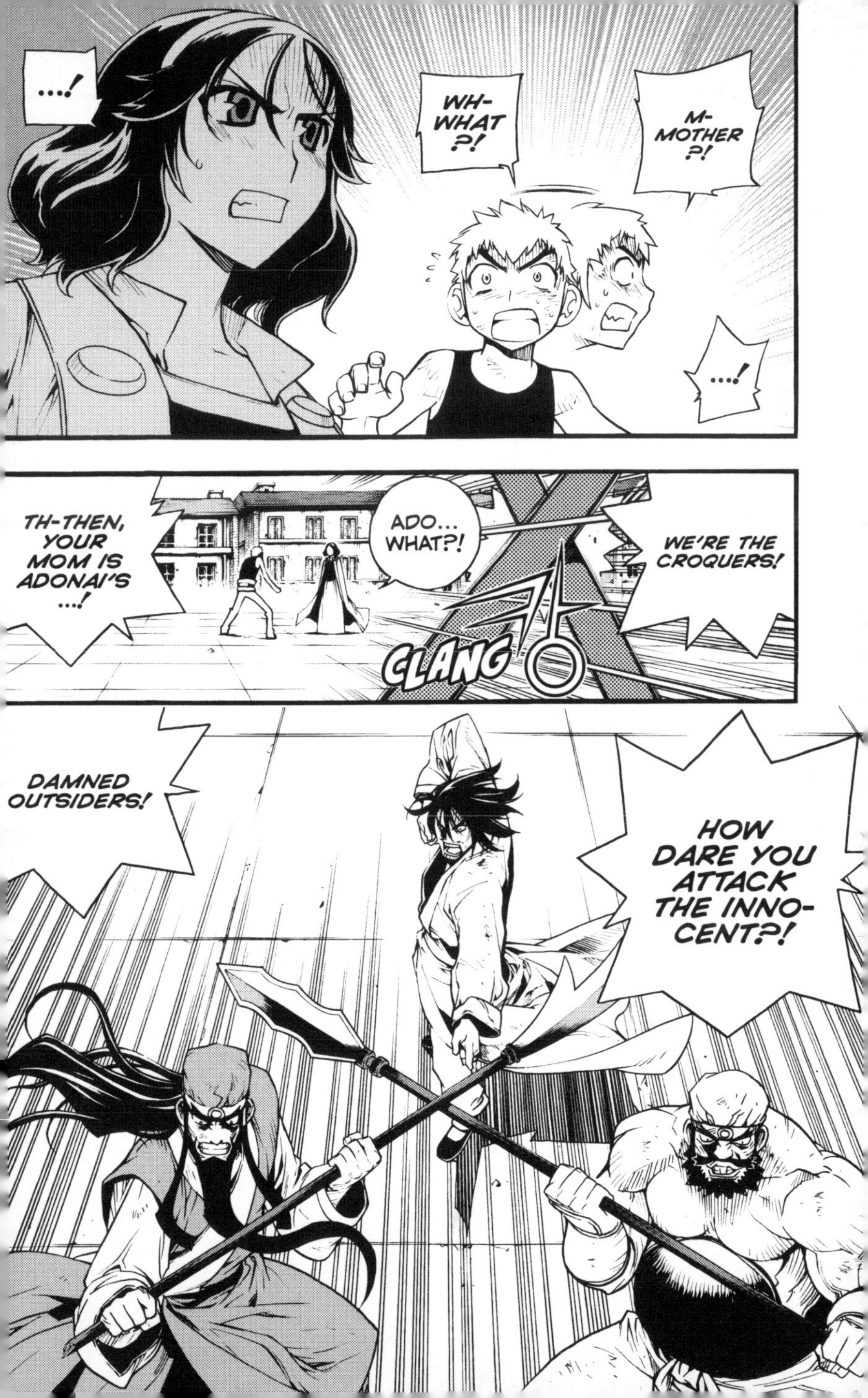
...!
WH-WHAT?!
M-MOTHER?!
...!
TH-THEN, YOUR MOM IS ADONAI'S ...!
ADO... WHAT?!
WE'RE THE CROQUERS!
CLANG
DAMNED OUTSIDERS!
HOW DARE YOU ATTACK THE INNO-CENT?!

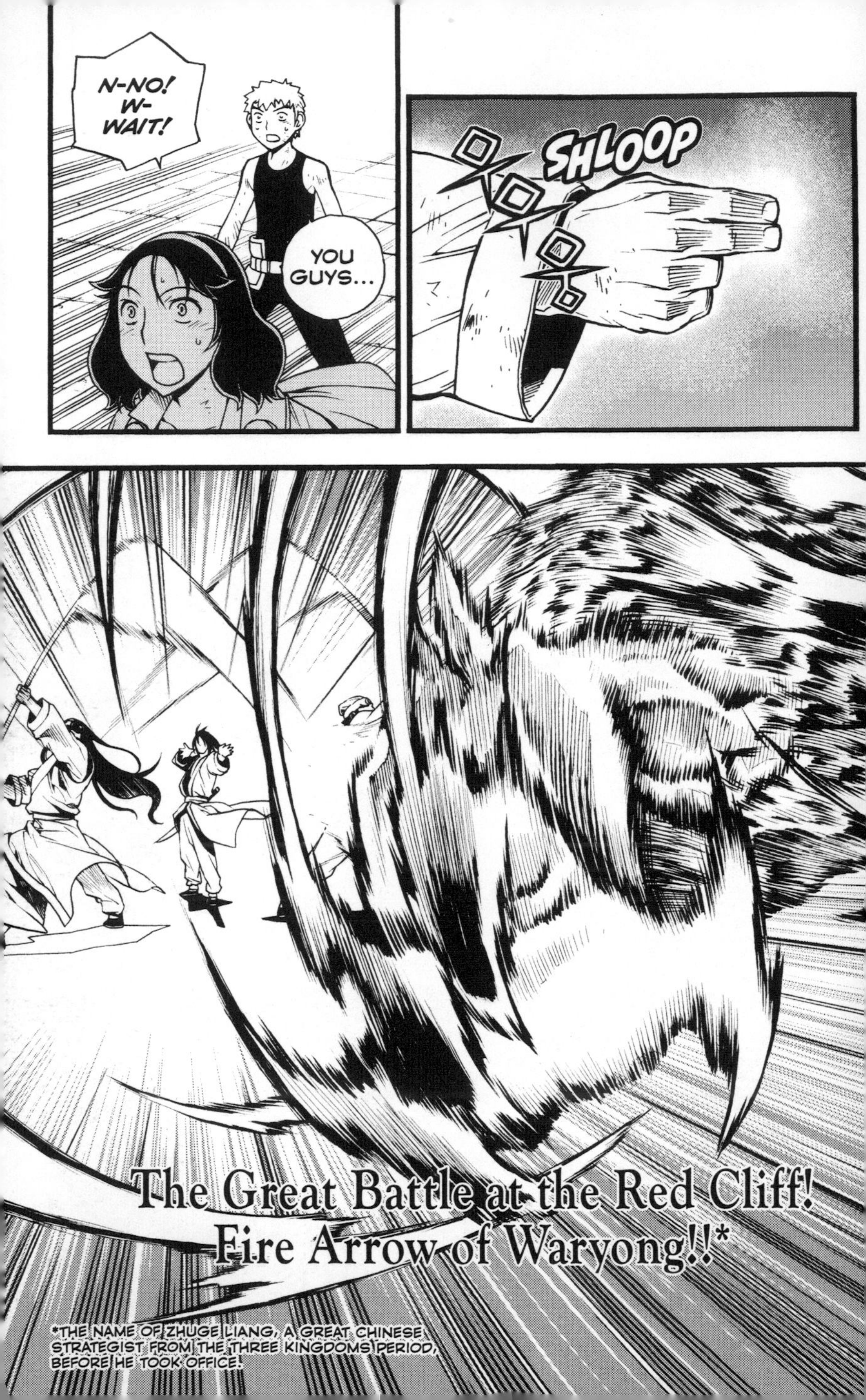
N-NO! W-WAIT!
YOU GUYS...
SHLOOP
The Great Battle at the Red Cliff! Fire Arrow of Waryong!!*
*THE NAME OF ZHUGE LIANG, A GREAT CHINESE STRATEGIST FROM THE THREE KINGDOMS PERIOD, BEFORE HE TOOK OFFICE.

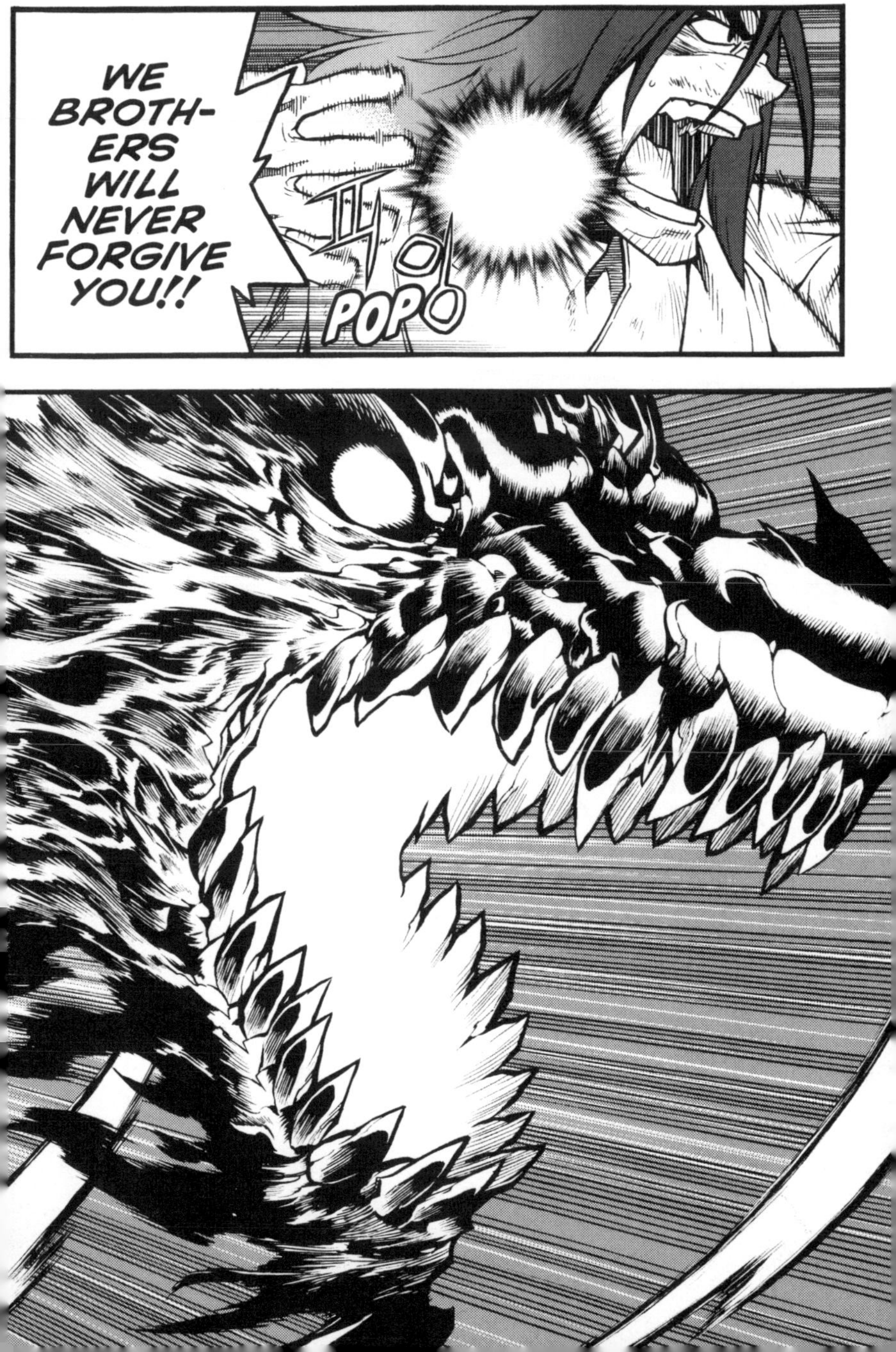
WE BROTH-ERS WILL NEVER FORGIVE YOU!!
POP

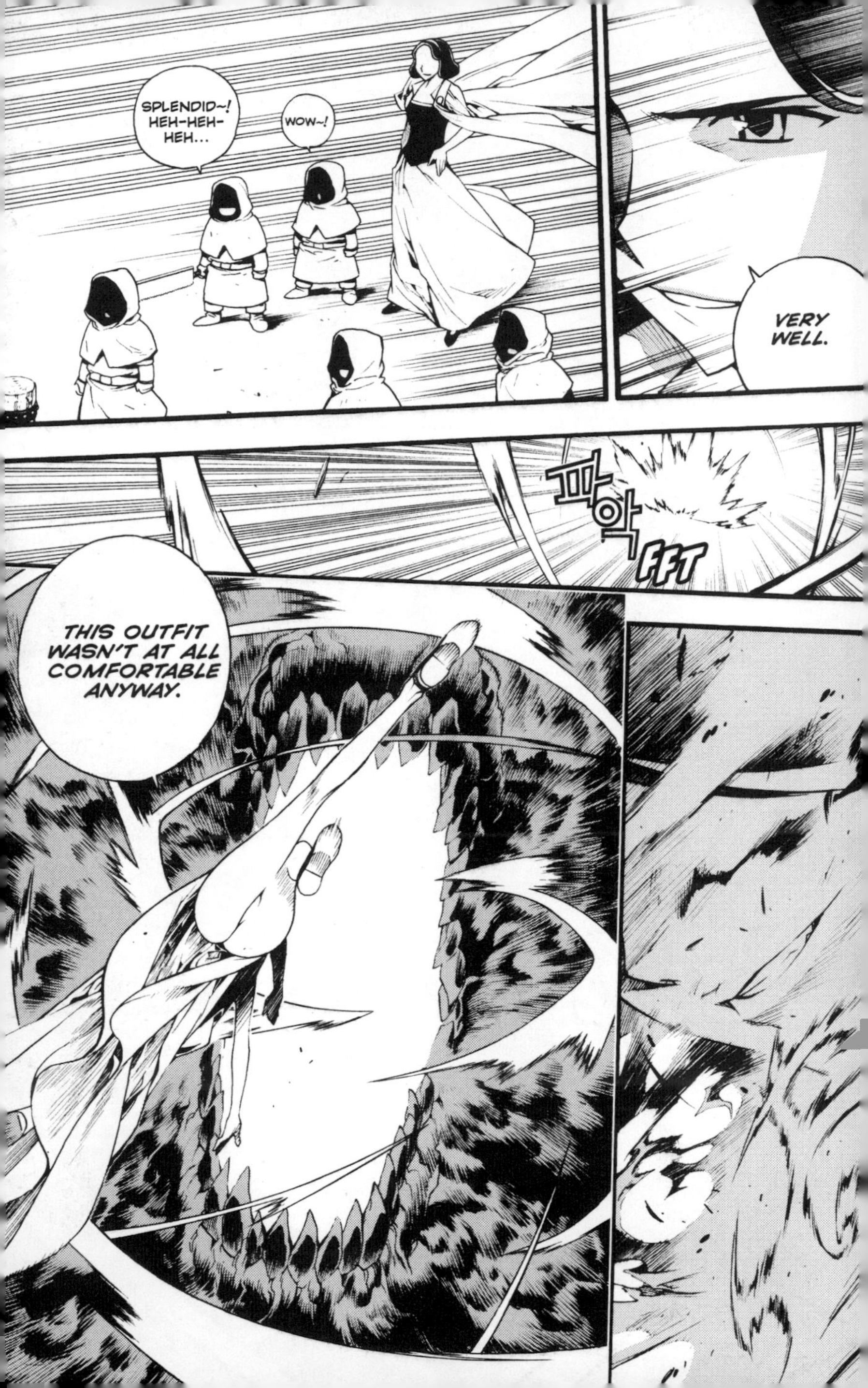
VERY WELL.
SPLENDID~! HEH-HEH-HEH...
WOW~!
파악
FFT
THIS OUTFIT WASN'T AT ALL COMFORTABLE ANYWAY.

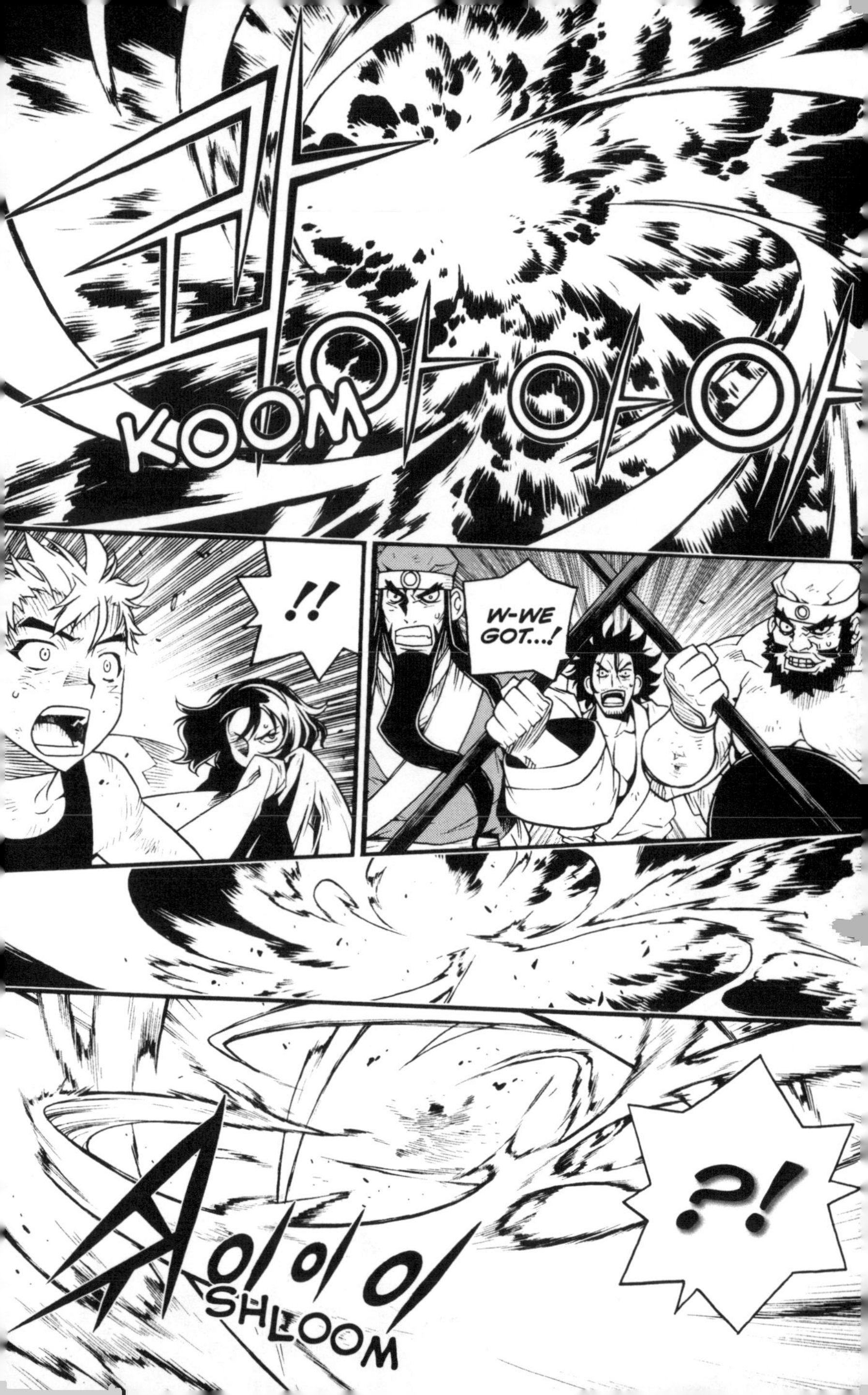

KOOM
!!
W-WE GOT...!
SHLOOM
?!

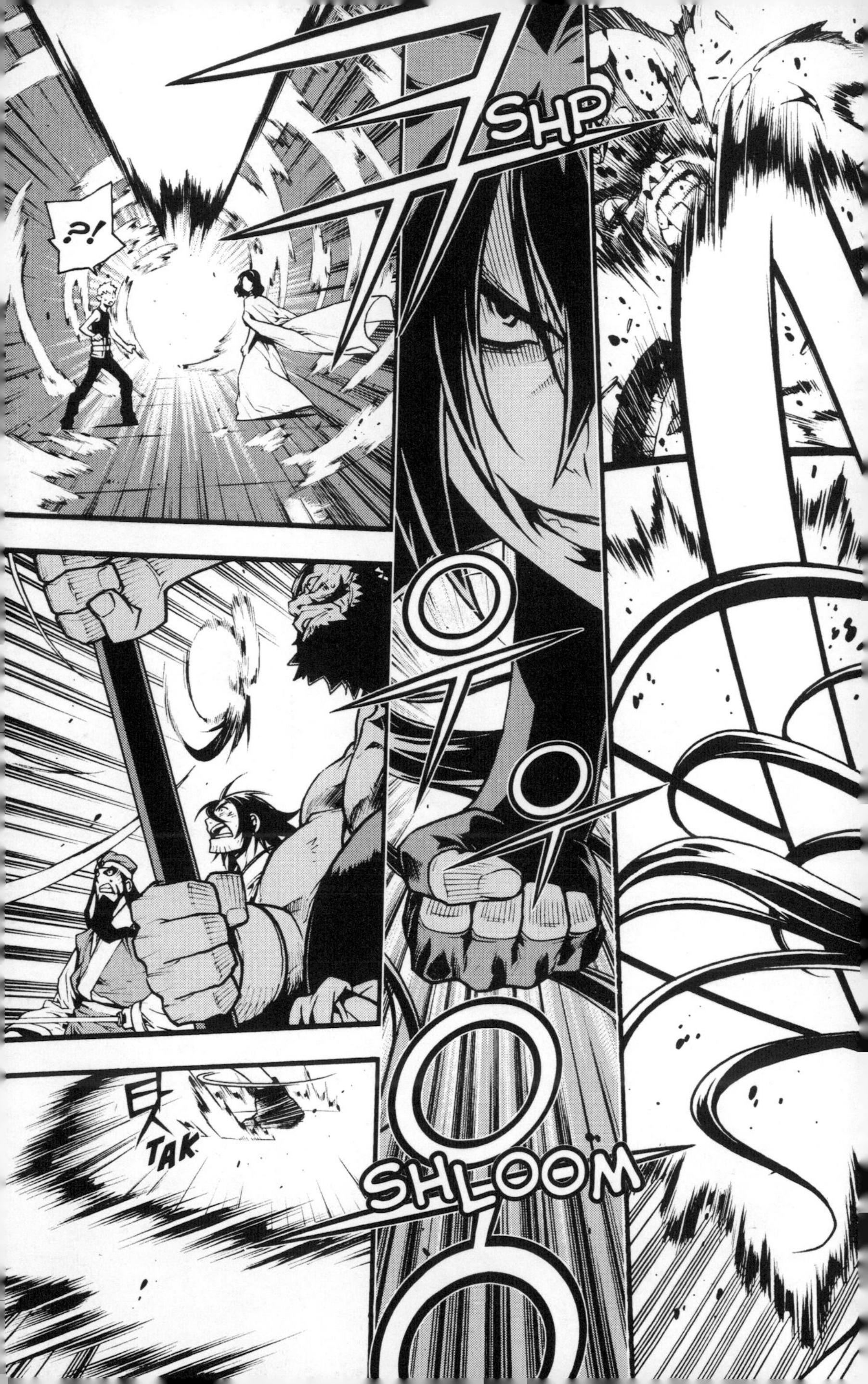

?!
SHP
TAK
SHLOOM

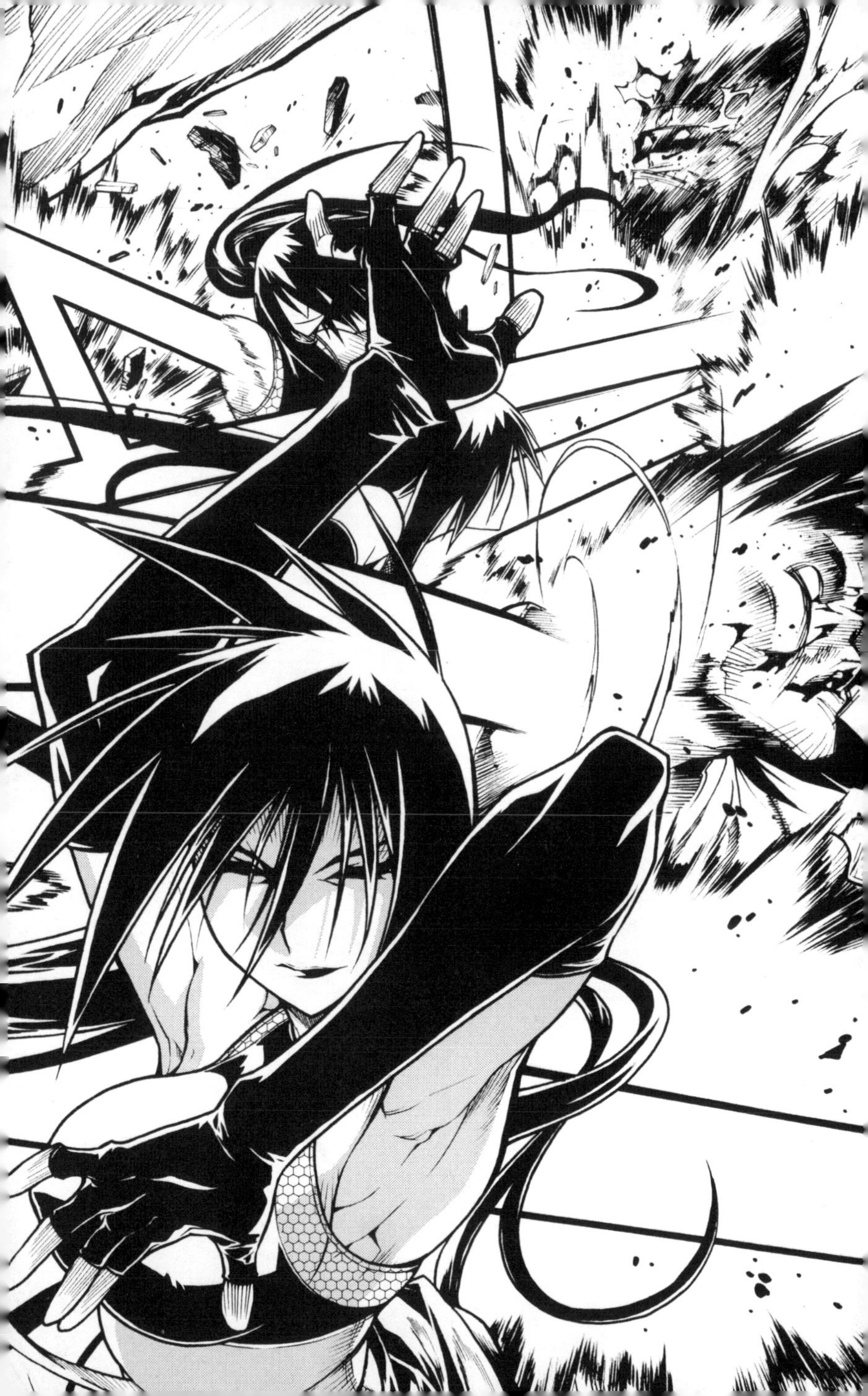

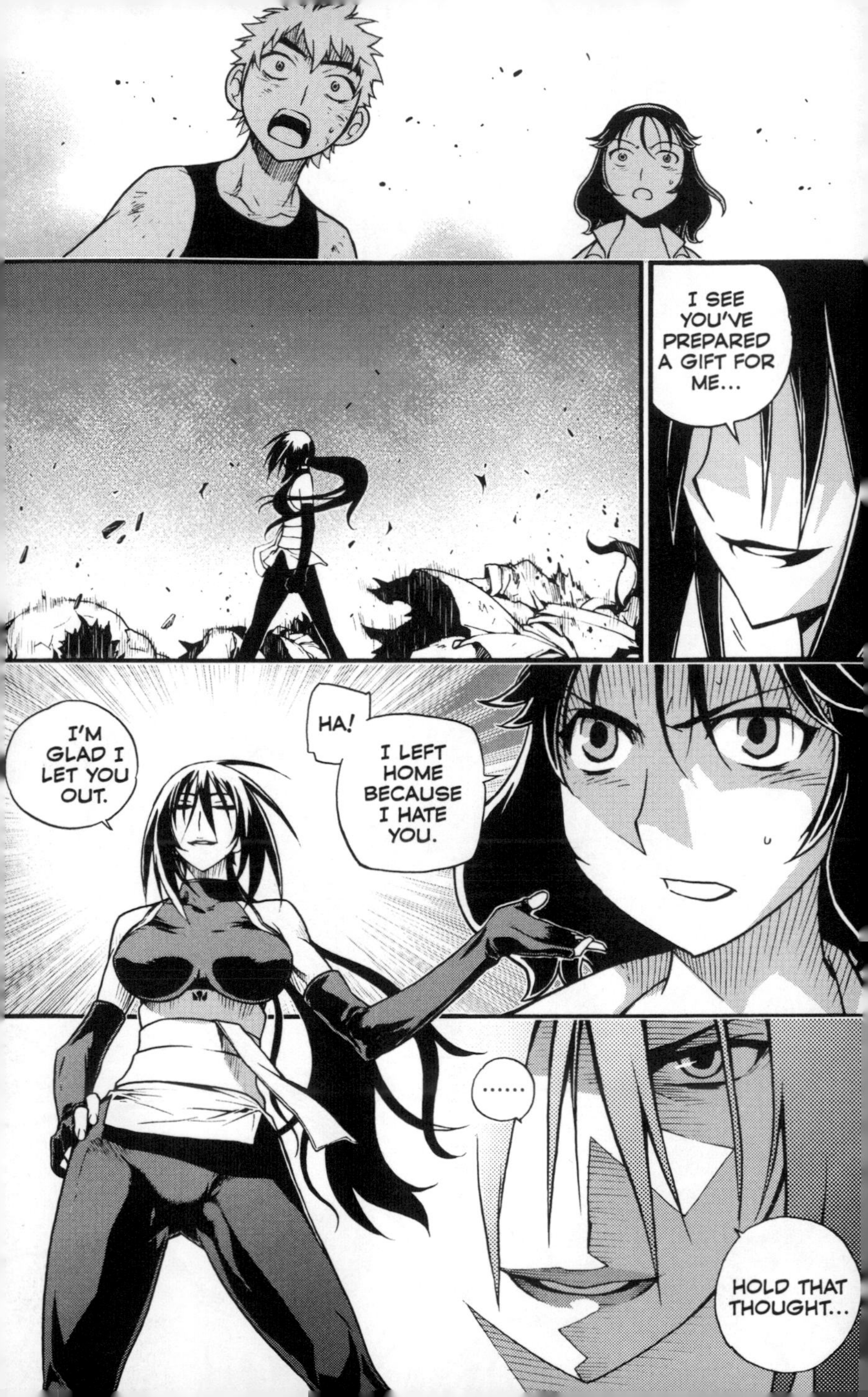
I SEE YOU'VE PREPARED A GIFT FOR ME...
I'M GLAD I LET YOU OUT.
HA!
I LEFT HOME BECAUSE I HATE YOU.
......
HOLD THAT THOUGHT...

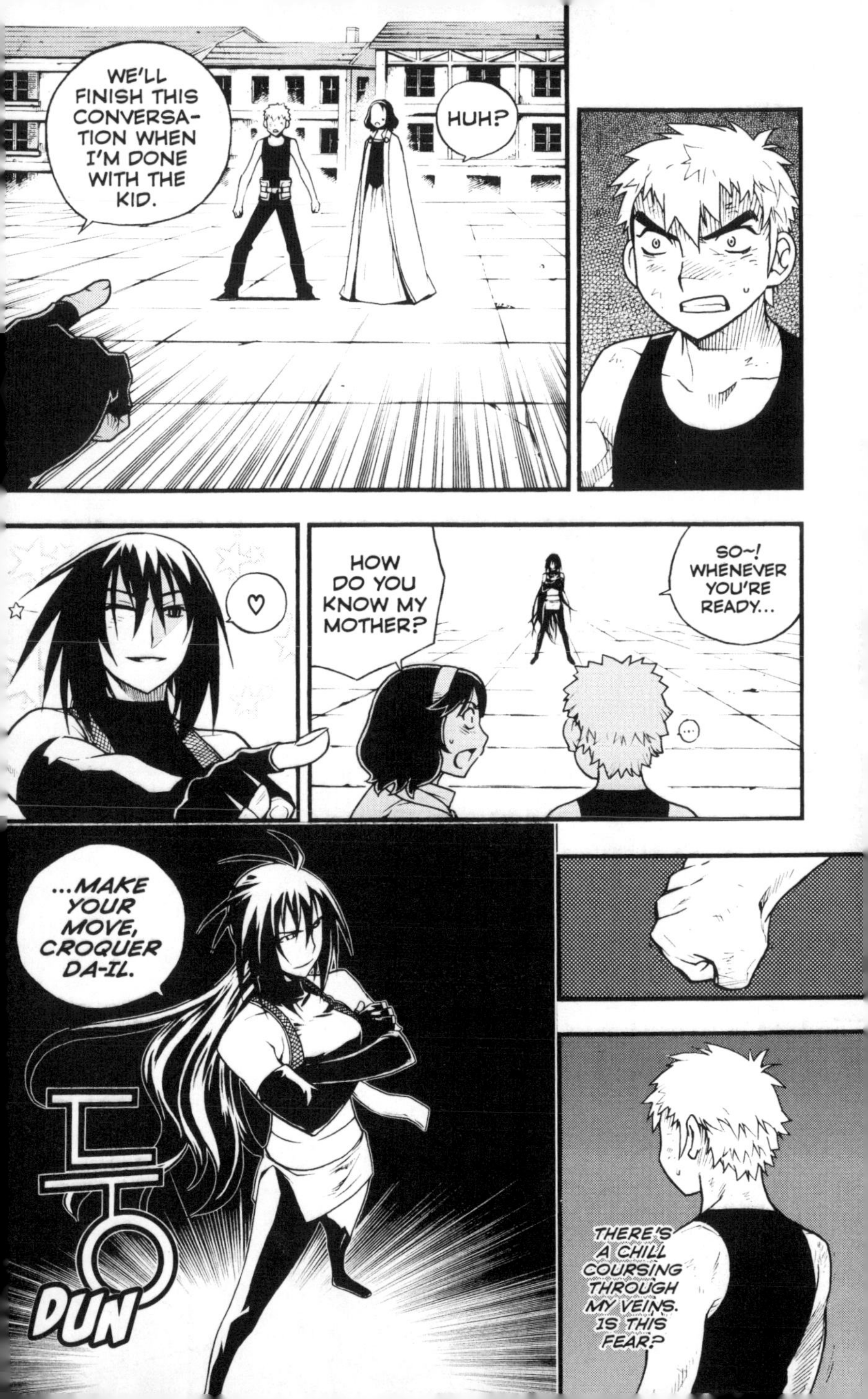
WE'LL FINISH THIS CONVERSA-TION WHEN I'M DONE WITH THE KID.
HUH?
♡
HOW DO YOU KNOW MY MOTHER?
SO~! WHENEVER YOU'RE READY...
...
...MAKE YOUR MOVE, CROQUER DA-IL.
DUN
THERE'S A CHILL COURSING THROUGH MY VEINS. IS THIS FEAR?

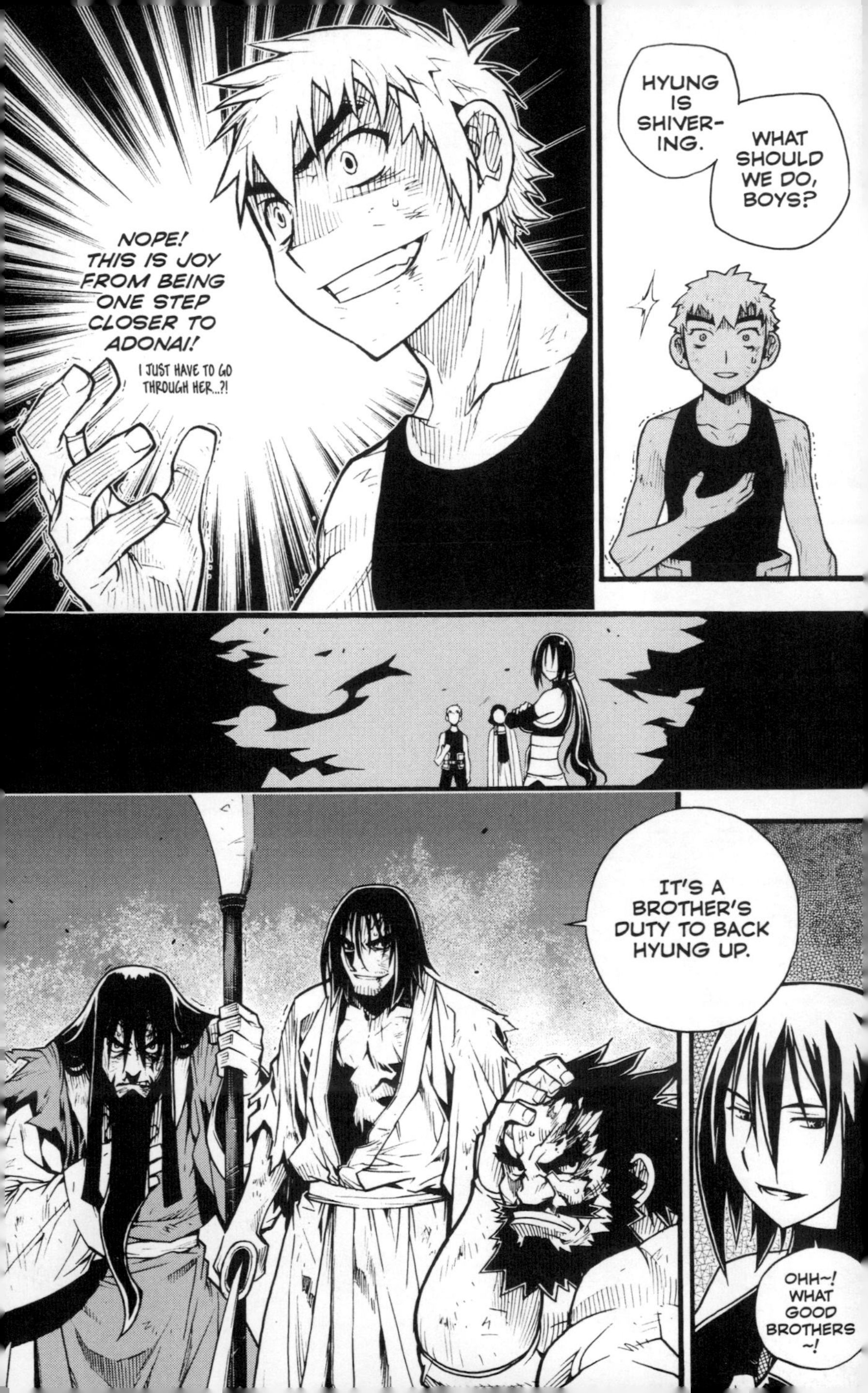
NOPE! THIS IS JOY FROM BEING ONE STEP CLOSER TO ADONAI!
I JUST HAVE TO GO THROUGH HER...?!
HYUNG IS SHIVER-ING.
WHAT SHOULD WE DO, BOYS?
IT'S A BROTHER'S DUTY TO BACK HYUNG UP.
OHH~! WHAT GOOD BROTHERS ~!

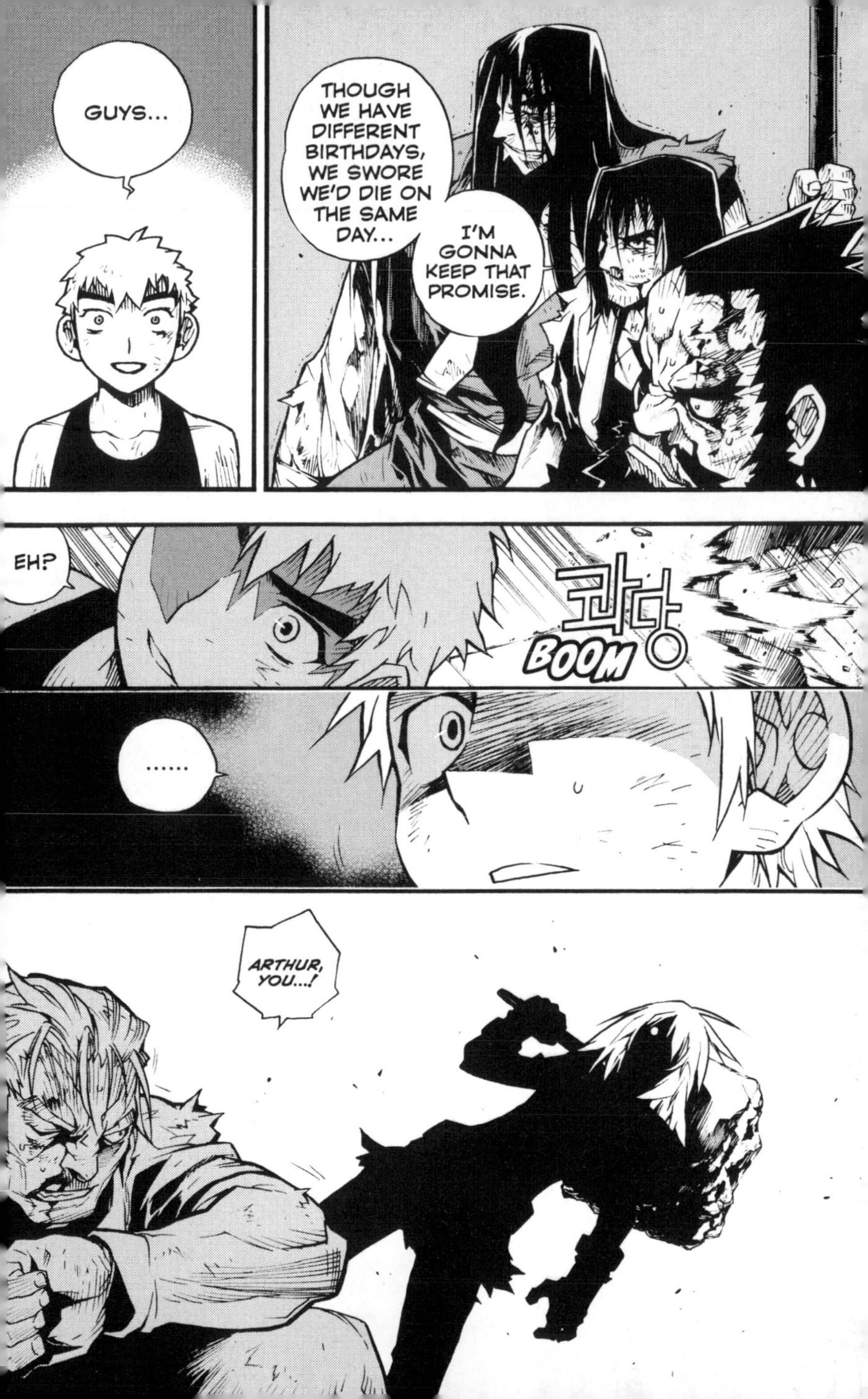
GUYS...
THOUGH WE HAVE DIFFERENT BIRTHDAYS, WE SWORE WE'D DIE ON THE SAME DAY...
I'M GONNA KEEP THAT PROMISE.
EH?
콰당
BOOM
......
ARTHUR, YOU...!

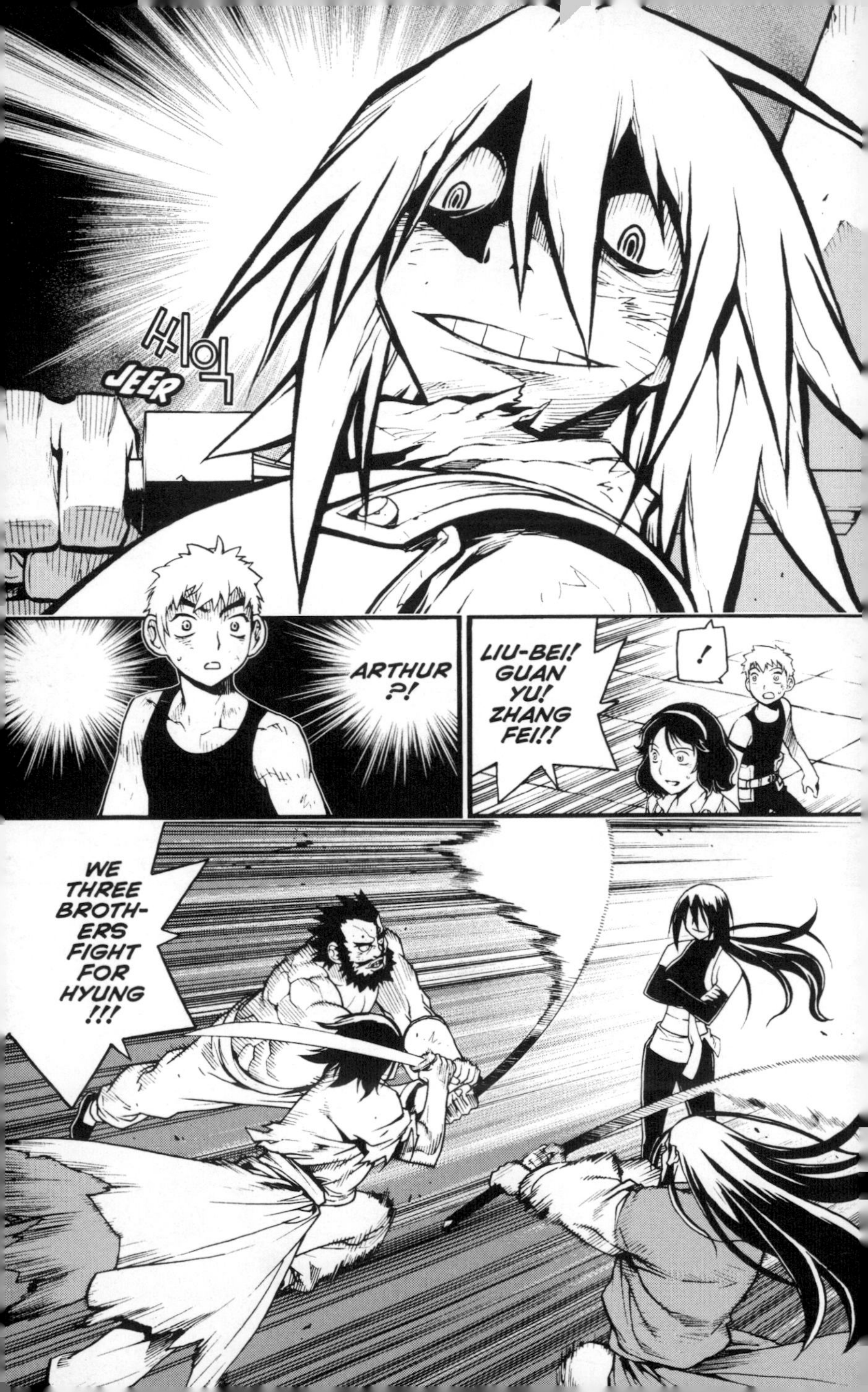
씨익
JEER
ARTHUR ?!
LIU-BEI! GUAN YU! ZHANG FEI!!
!
WE THREE BROTHERS FIGHT FOR HYUNG !!!

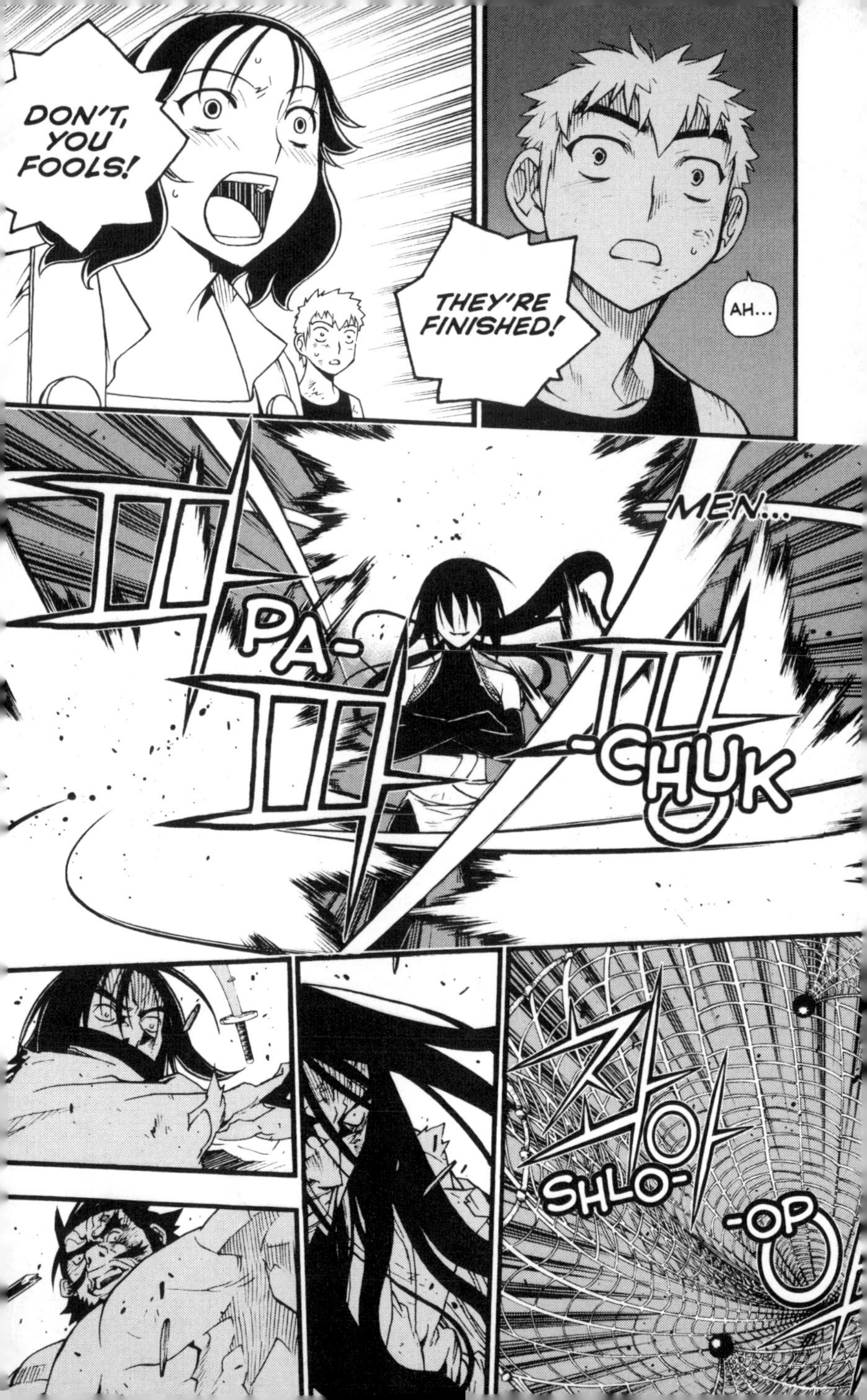
DON'T, YOU FOOLS!
THEY'RE FINISHED!
AH...
MEN...
PA-
-CHUK
SHLO-
-OP

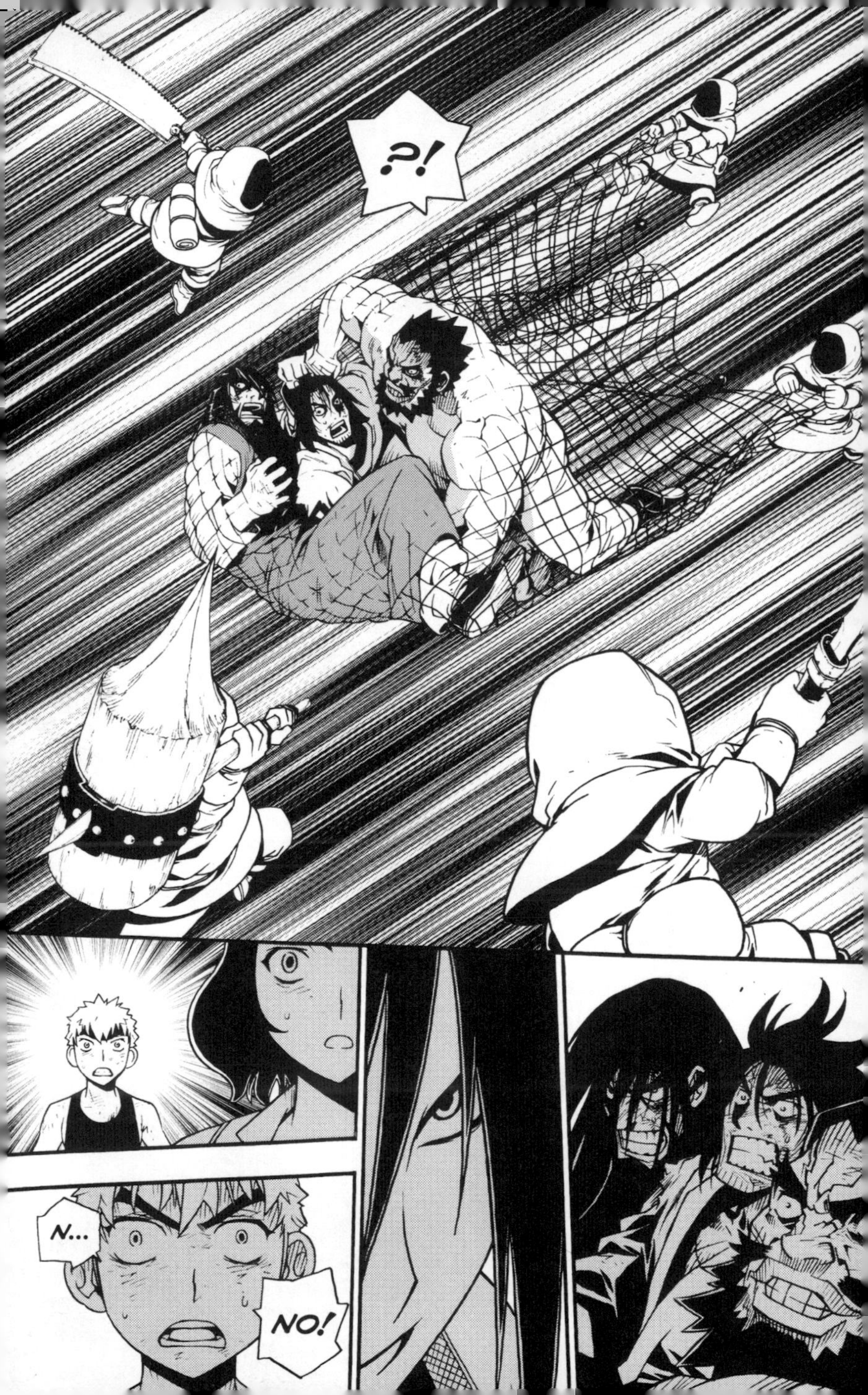
?!
N...
NO!

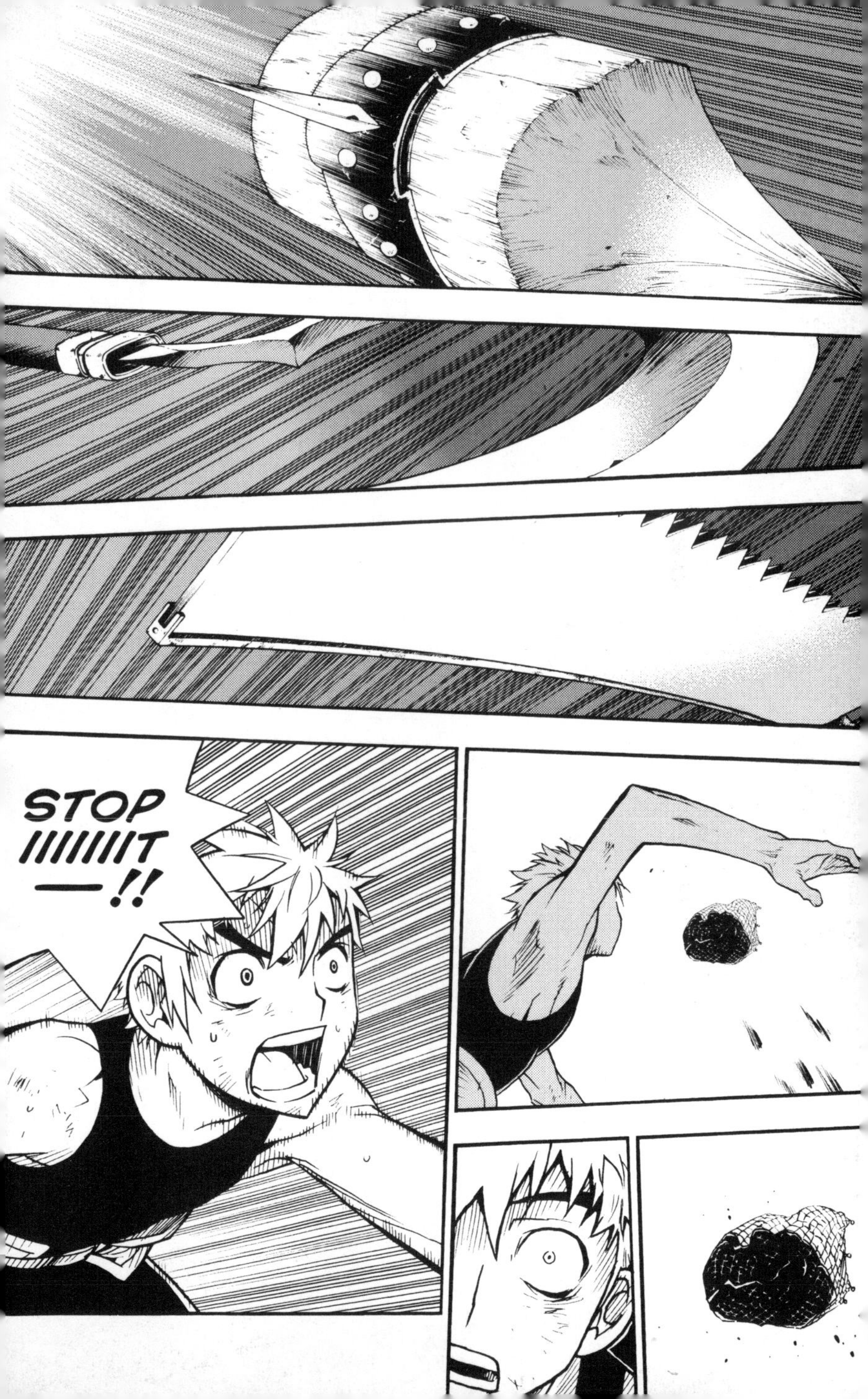
STOP IIIIIIIT —!!

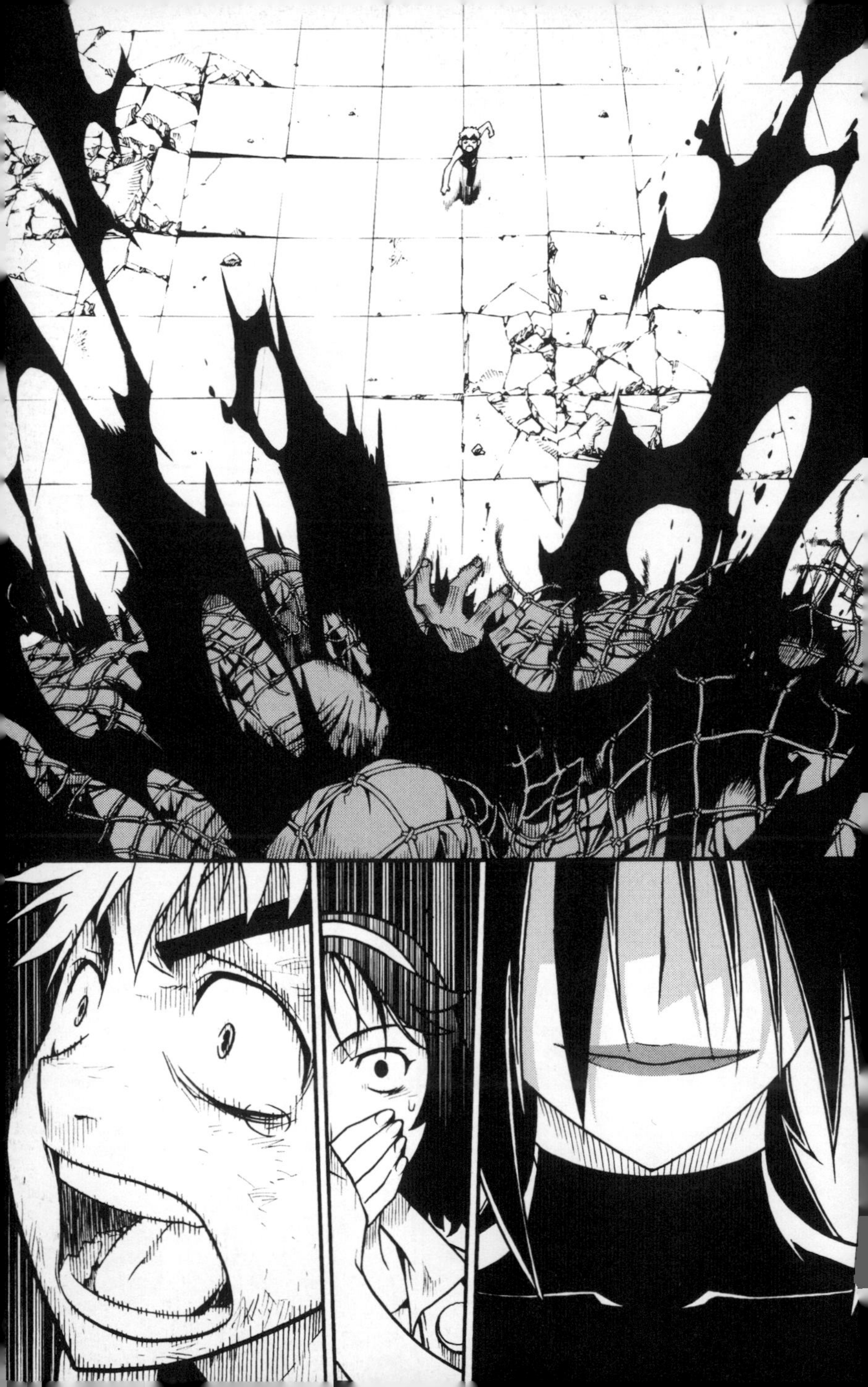

POP 36. PHENOMENON

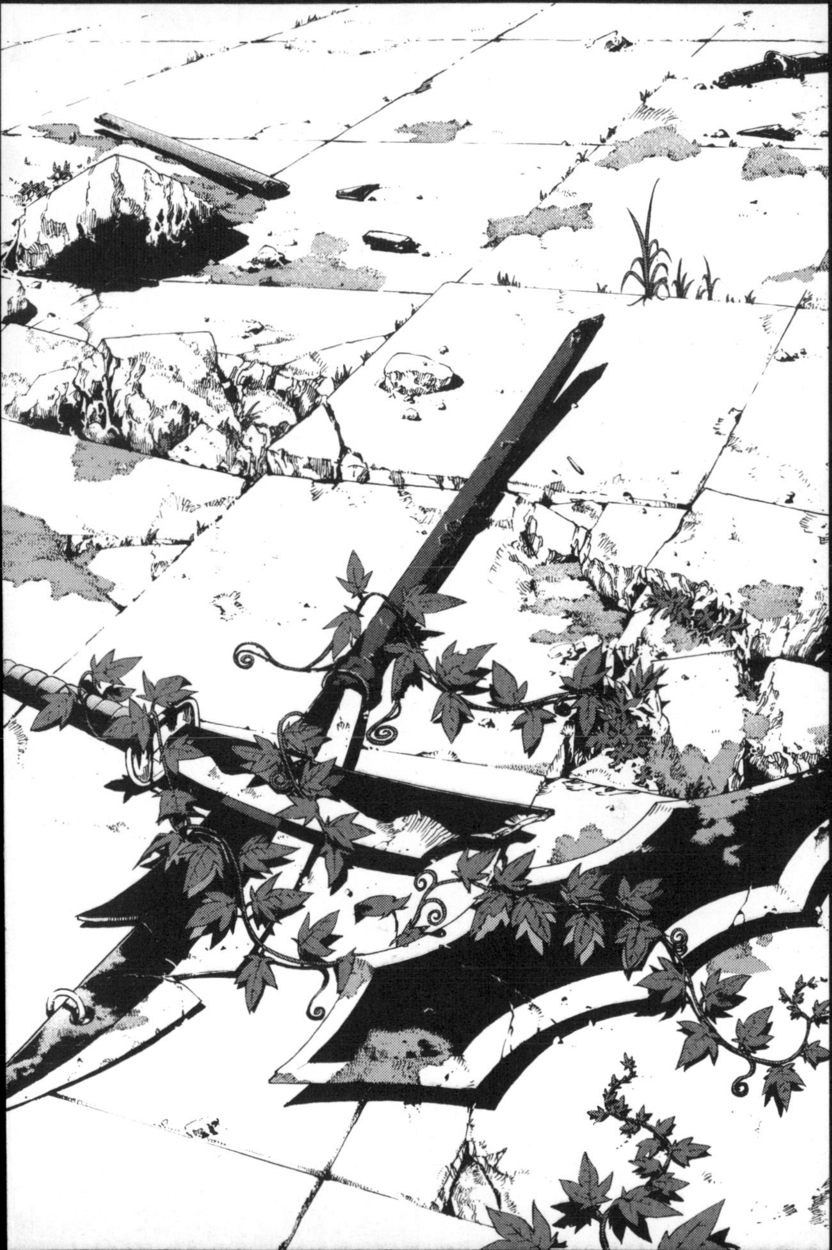

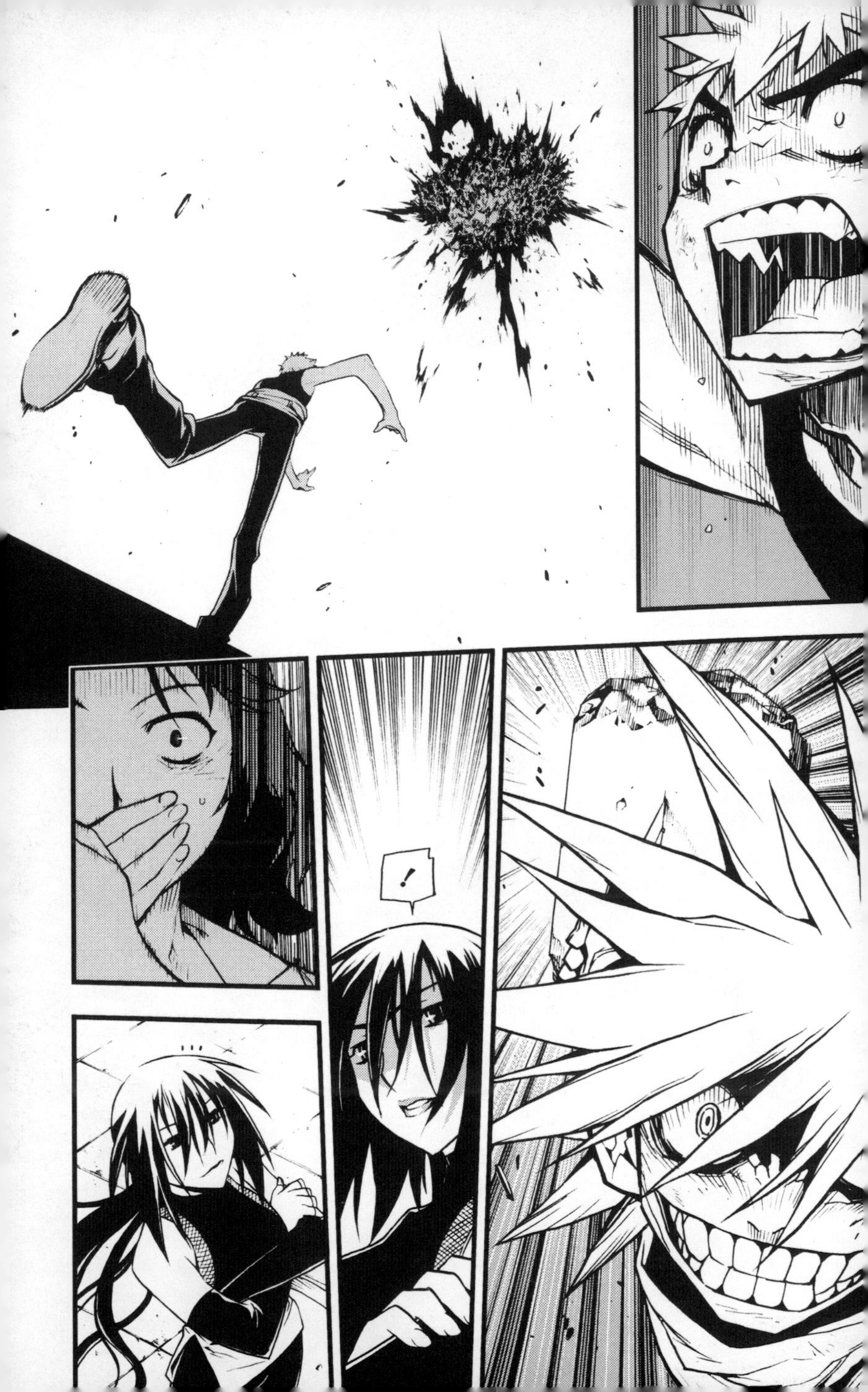
!

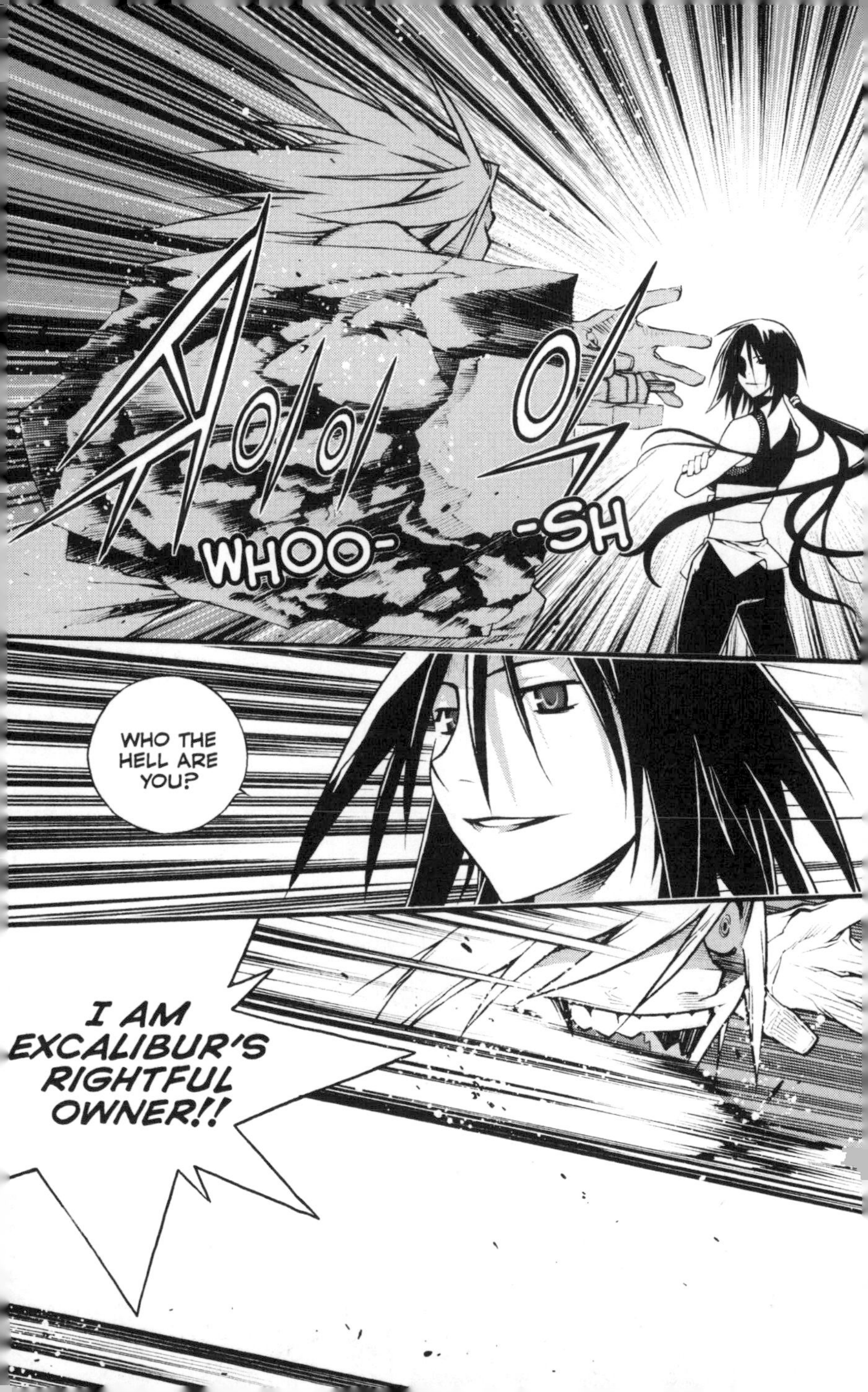
WHOO-
-SH
WHO THE HELL ARE YOU?
I AM EXCALIBUR'S RIGHTFUL OWNER!!

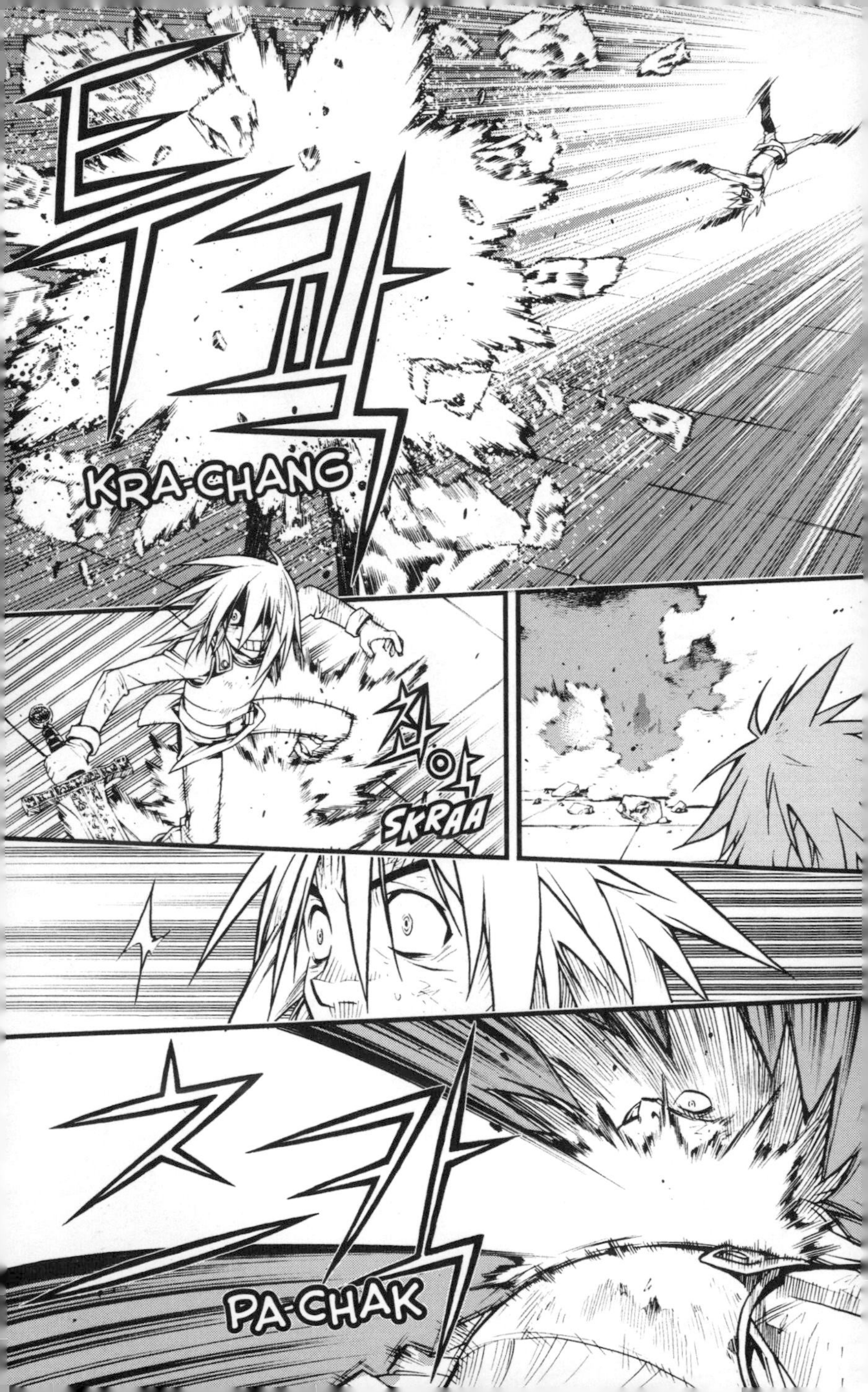
KRA-CHANG
SKRAA
PA-CHAK

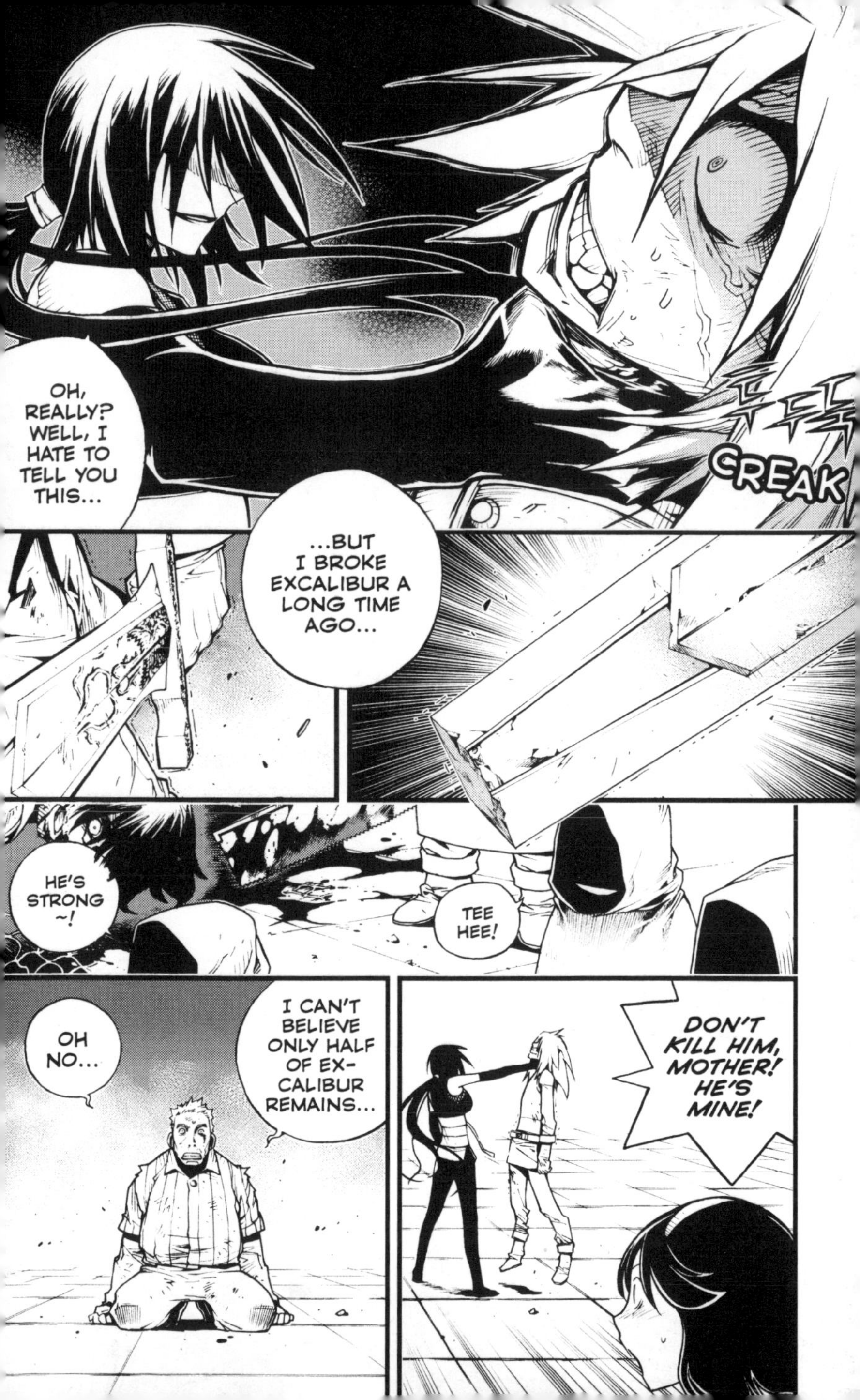
OH, REALLY? WELL, I HATE TO TELL YOU THIS...
CREAK
...BUT I BROKE EXCALIBUR A LONG TIME AGO...
HE'S STRONG ~!
TEE HEE!
OH NO...
I CAN'T BELIEVE ONLY HALF OF EX-CALIBUR REMAINS...
DON'T KILL HIM, MOTHER! HE'S MINE!

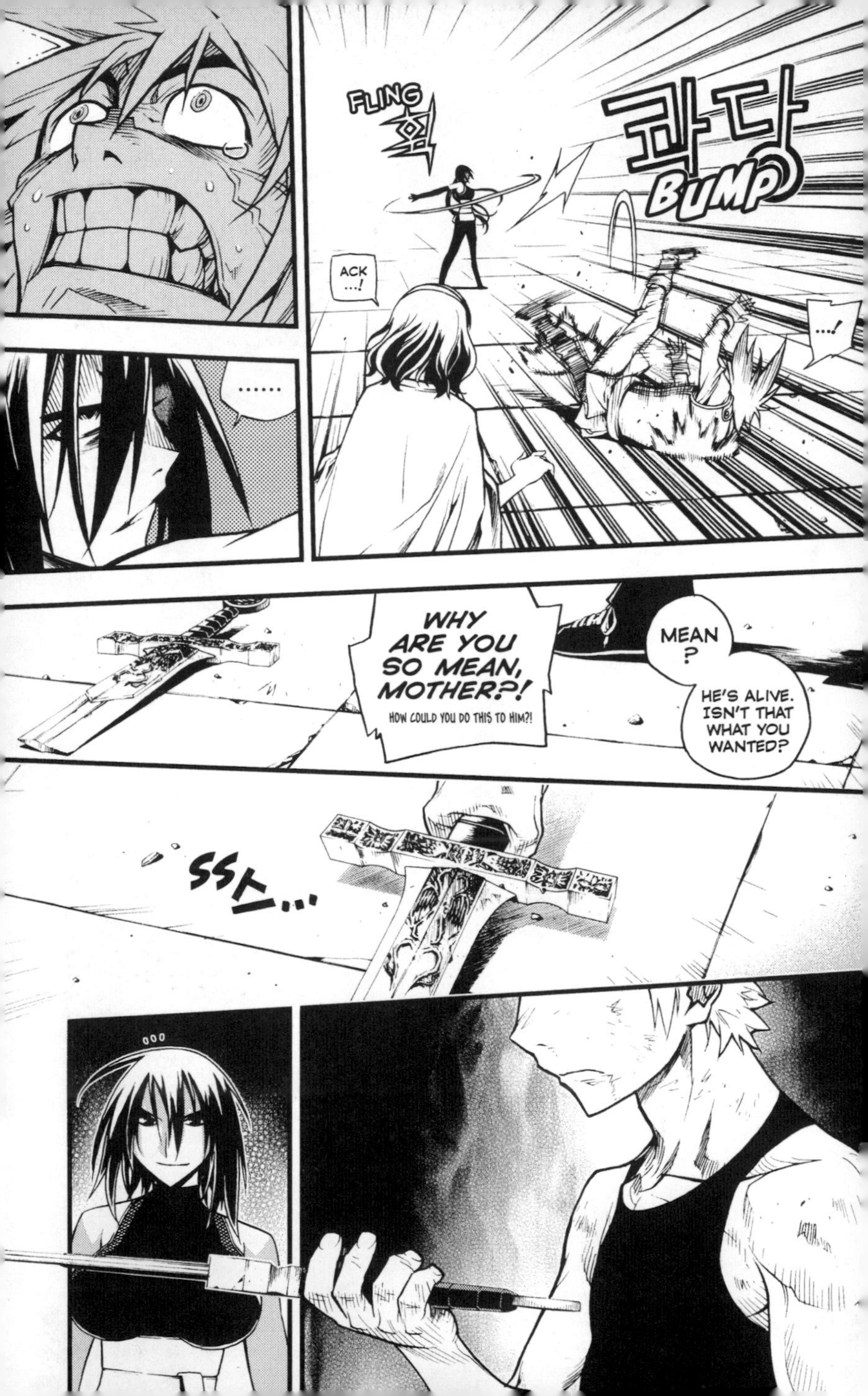
......
FLING
콰당
BUMP
ACK ...!
...!
WHY ARE YOU SO MEAN, MOTHER?!
HOW COULD YOU DO THIS TO HIM?!
MEAN?
HE'S ALIVE. ISN'T THAT WHAT YOU WANTED?
SSt...
ooo

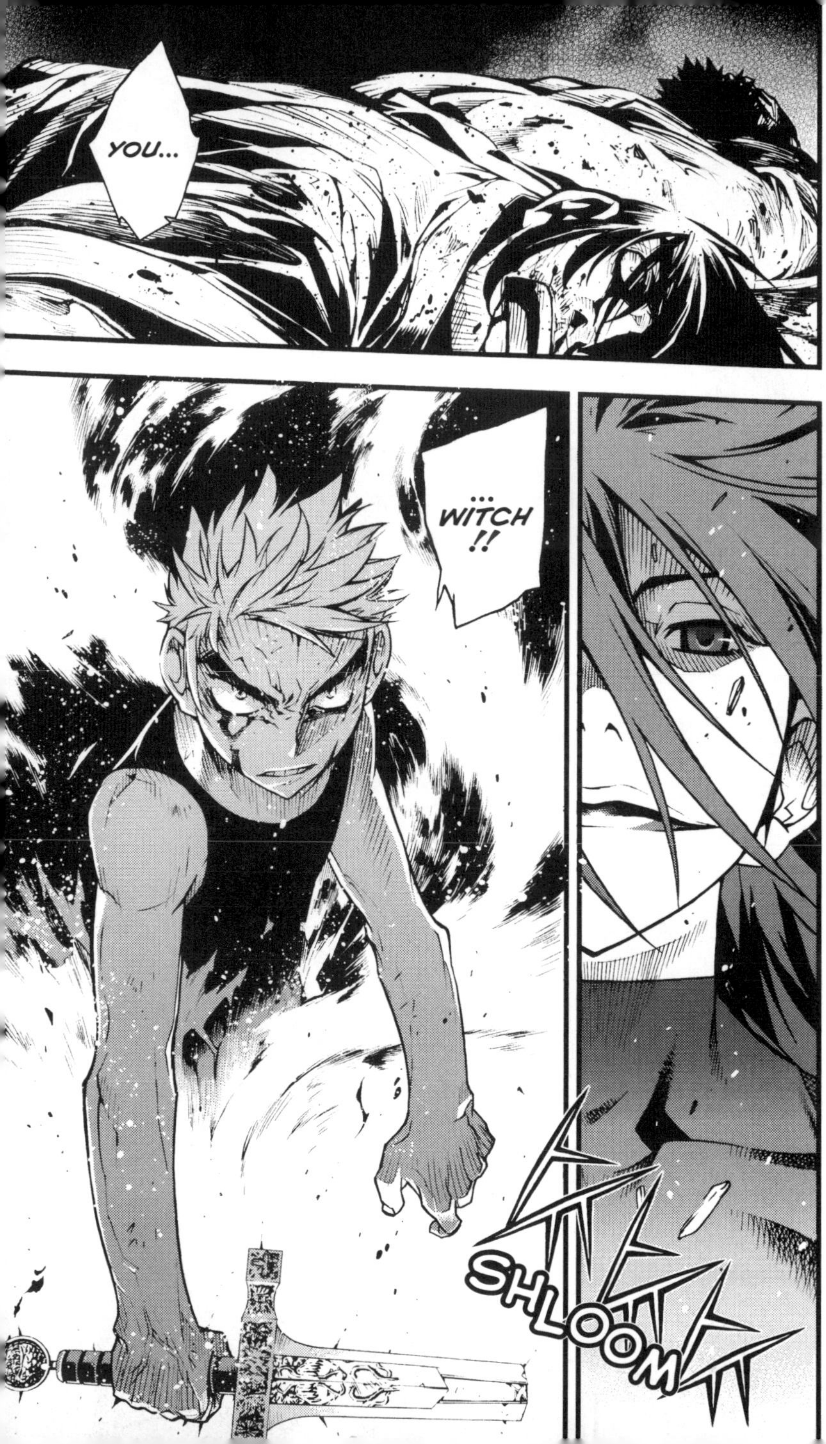
YOU...
...WITCH !!
SHLOOM

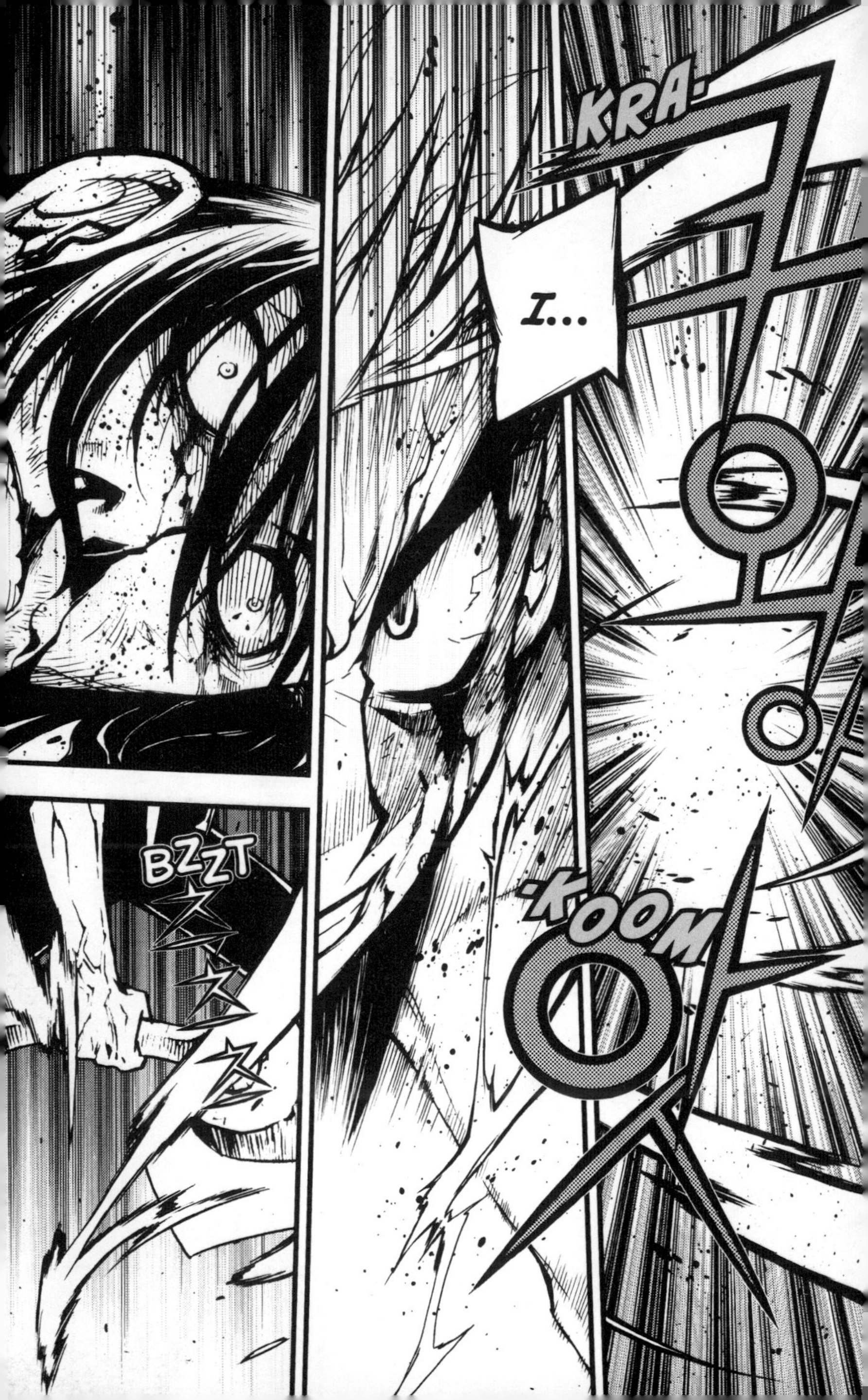
BZZT
KRA-
I...
-KOOM

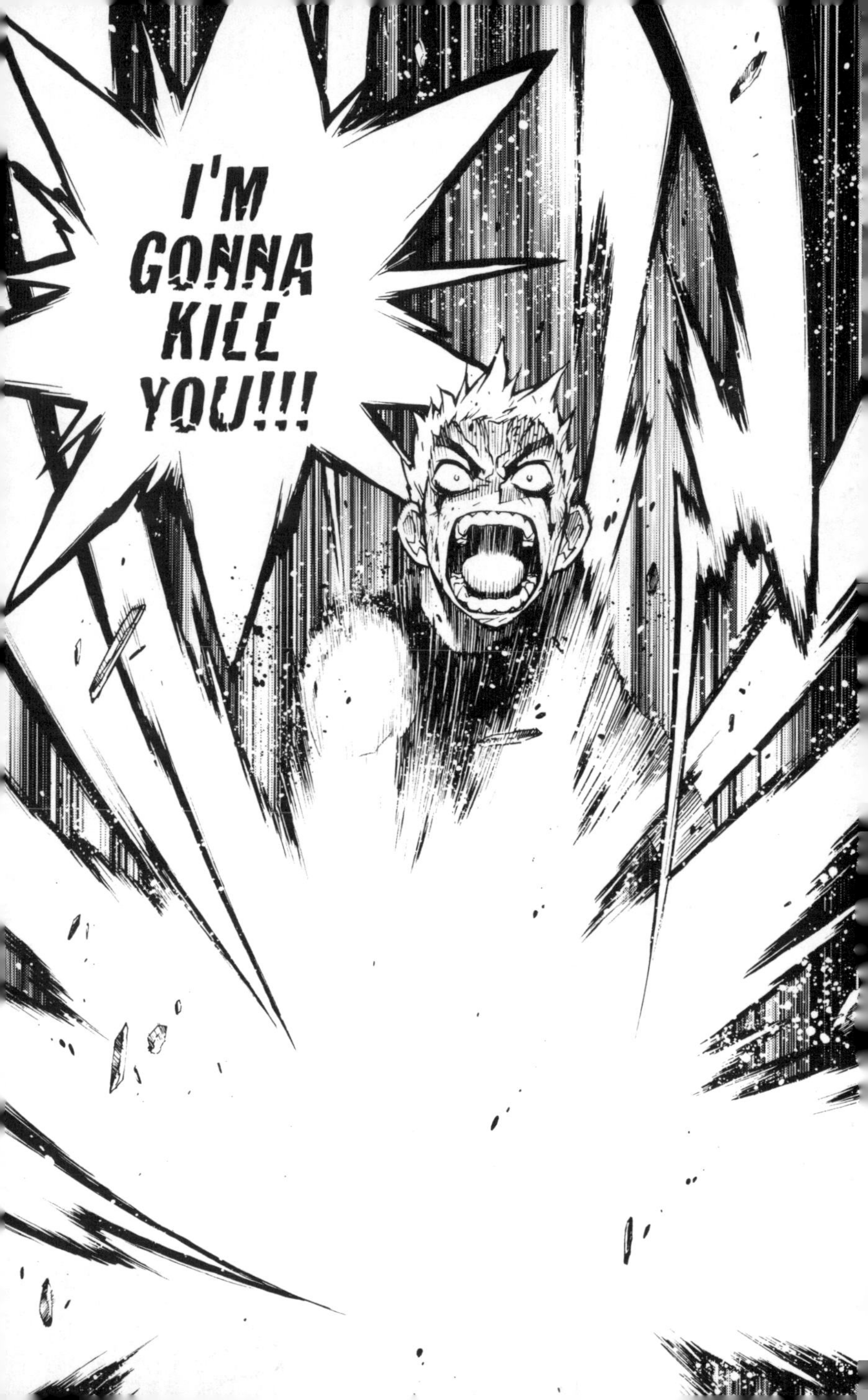
I'M GONNA KILL YOU!!!

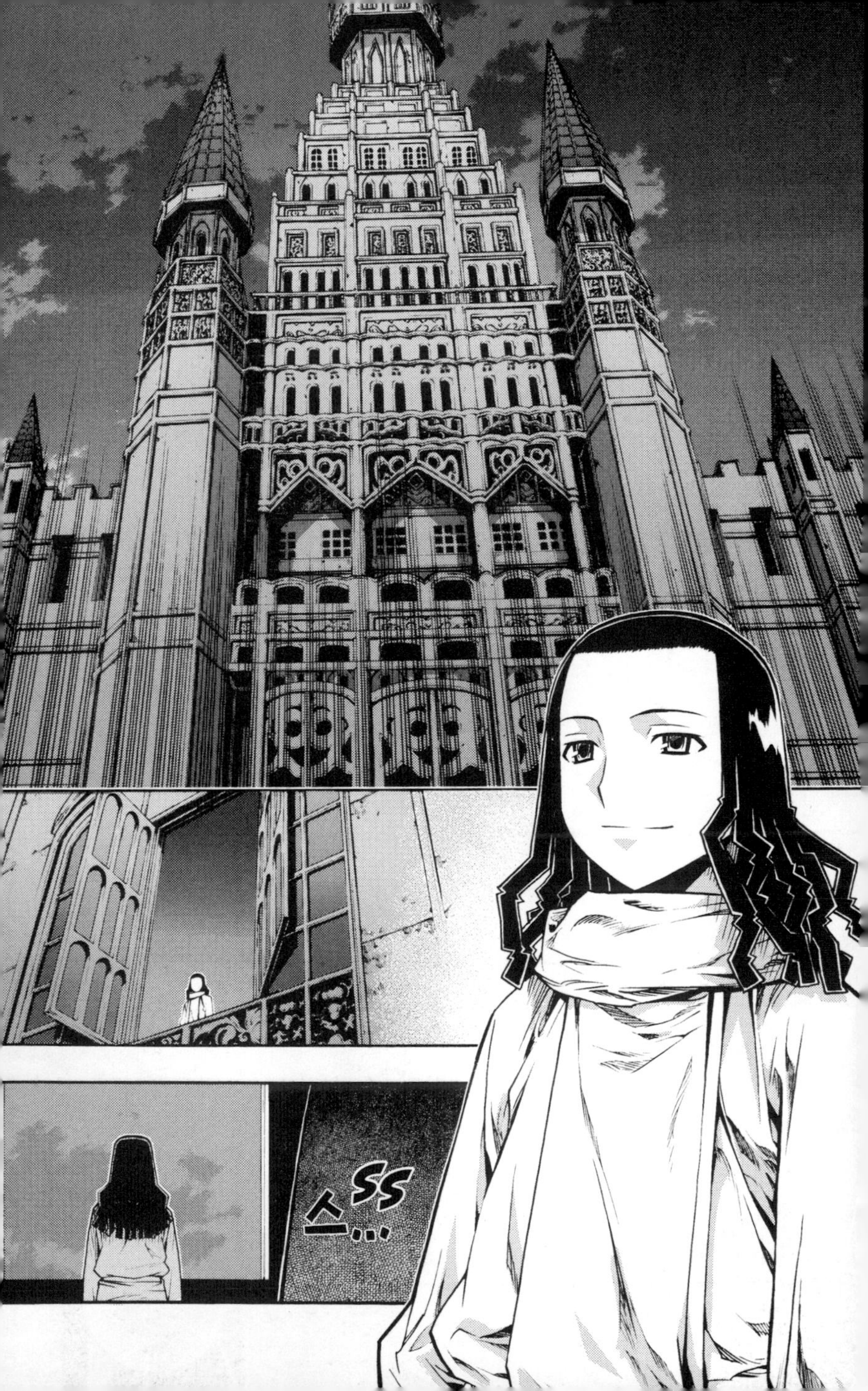
SS
스...

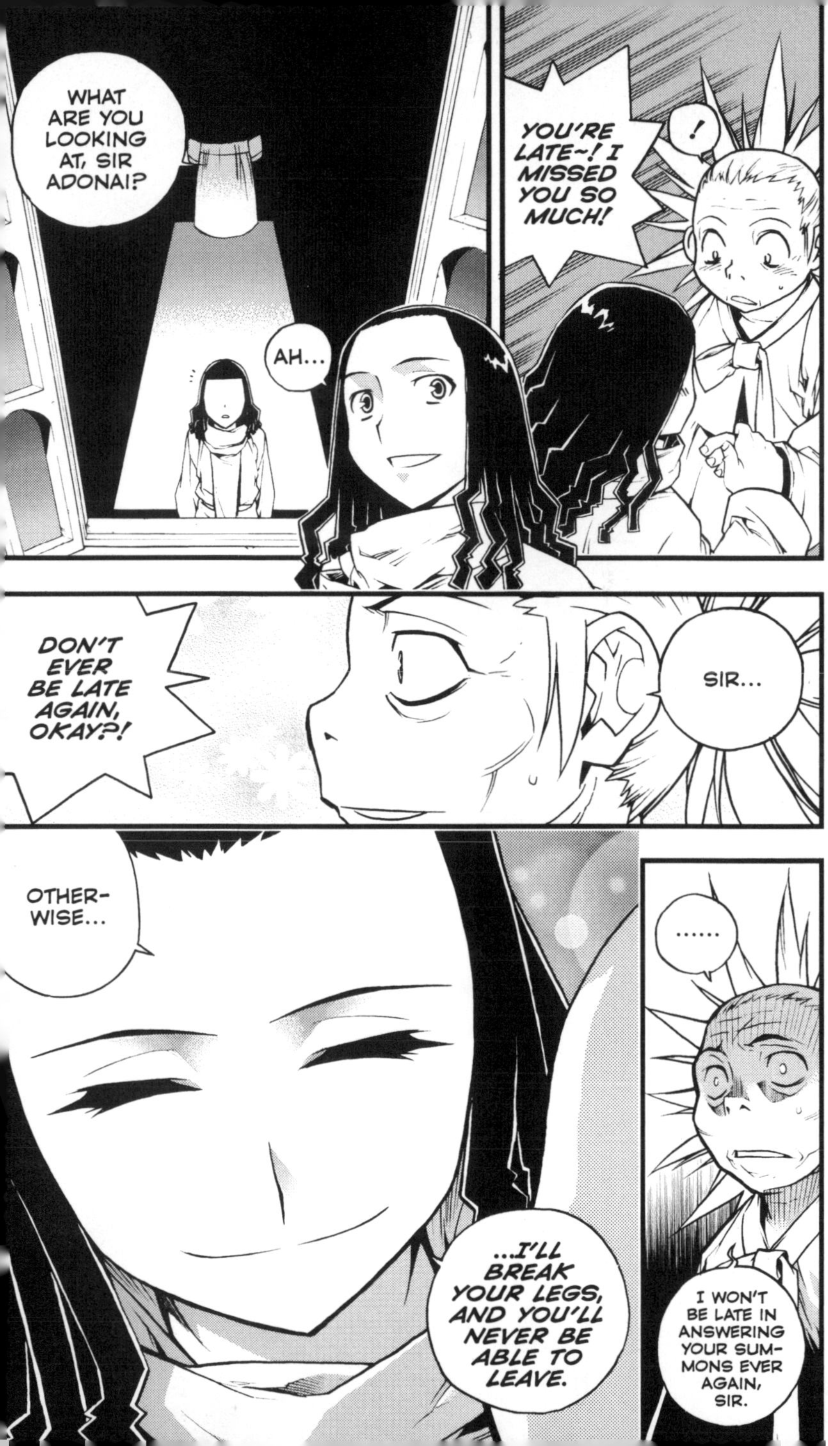
WHAT ARE YOU LOOKING AT, SIR ADONAI?
AH...
YOU'RE LATE~! I MISSED YOU SO MUCH!
!
DON'T EVER BE LATE AGAIN, OKAY?!
SIR...
OTHER-WISE...
...I'LL BREAK YOUR LEGS, AND YOU'LL NEVER BE ABLE TO LEAVE.
......
I WON'T BE LATE IN ANSWERING YOUR SUM-MONS EVER AGAIN, SIR.

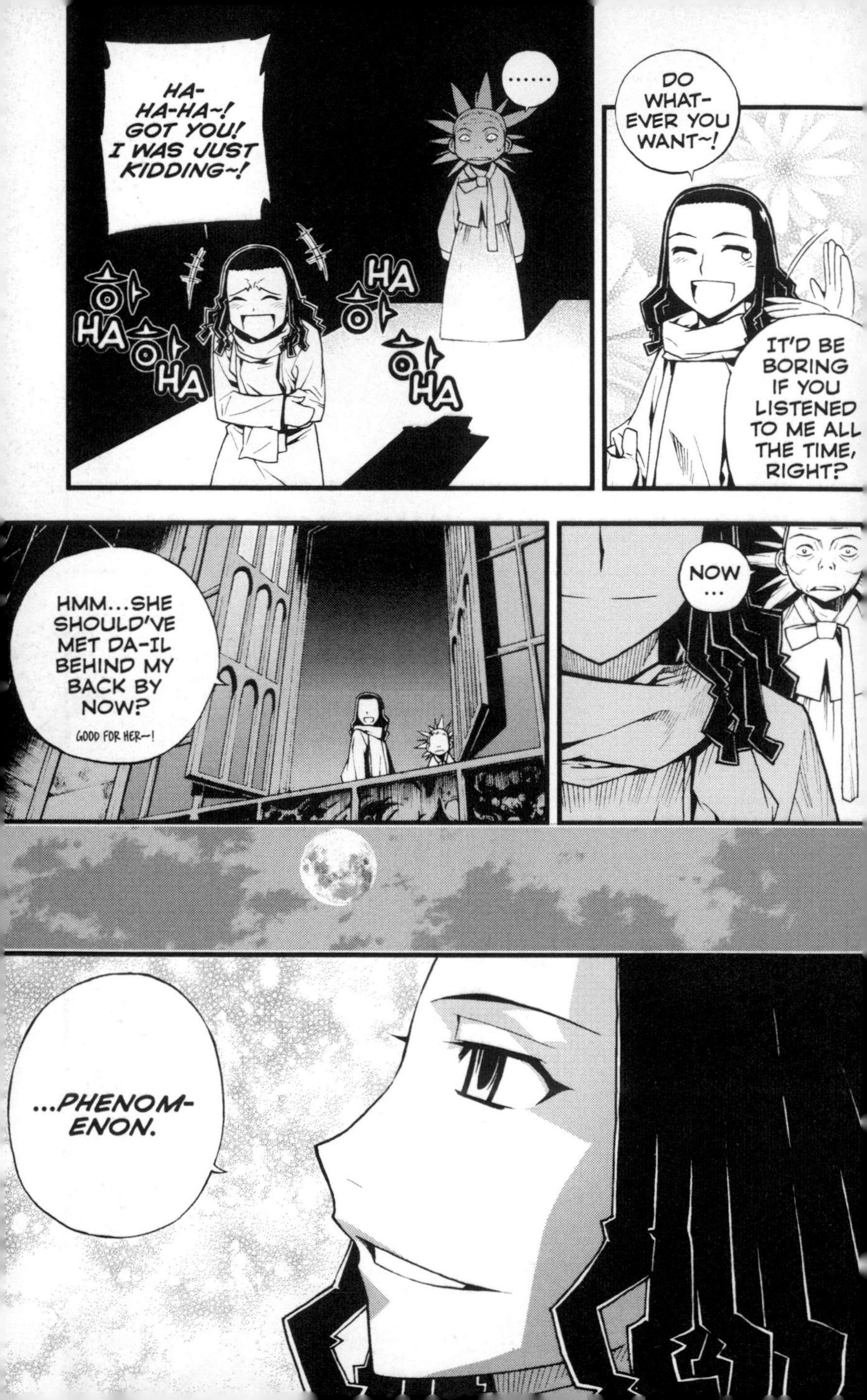
HA-HA-HA~! GOT YOU! I WAS JUST KIDDING~!
......
하 HA 하 HA
HA 하 하 HA
DO WHAT-EVER YOU WANT~!
IT'D BE BORING IF YOU LISTENED TO ME ALL THE TIME, RIGHT?
HMM...SHE SHOULD'VE MET DA-IL BEHIND MY BACK BY NOW?
GOOD FOR HER~!
NOW...
...PHENOM-ENON.

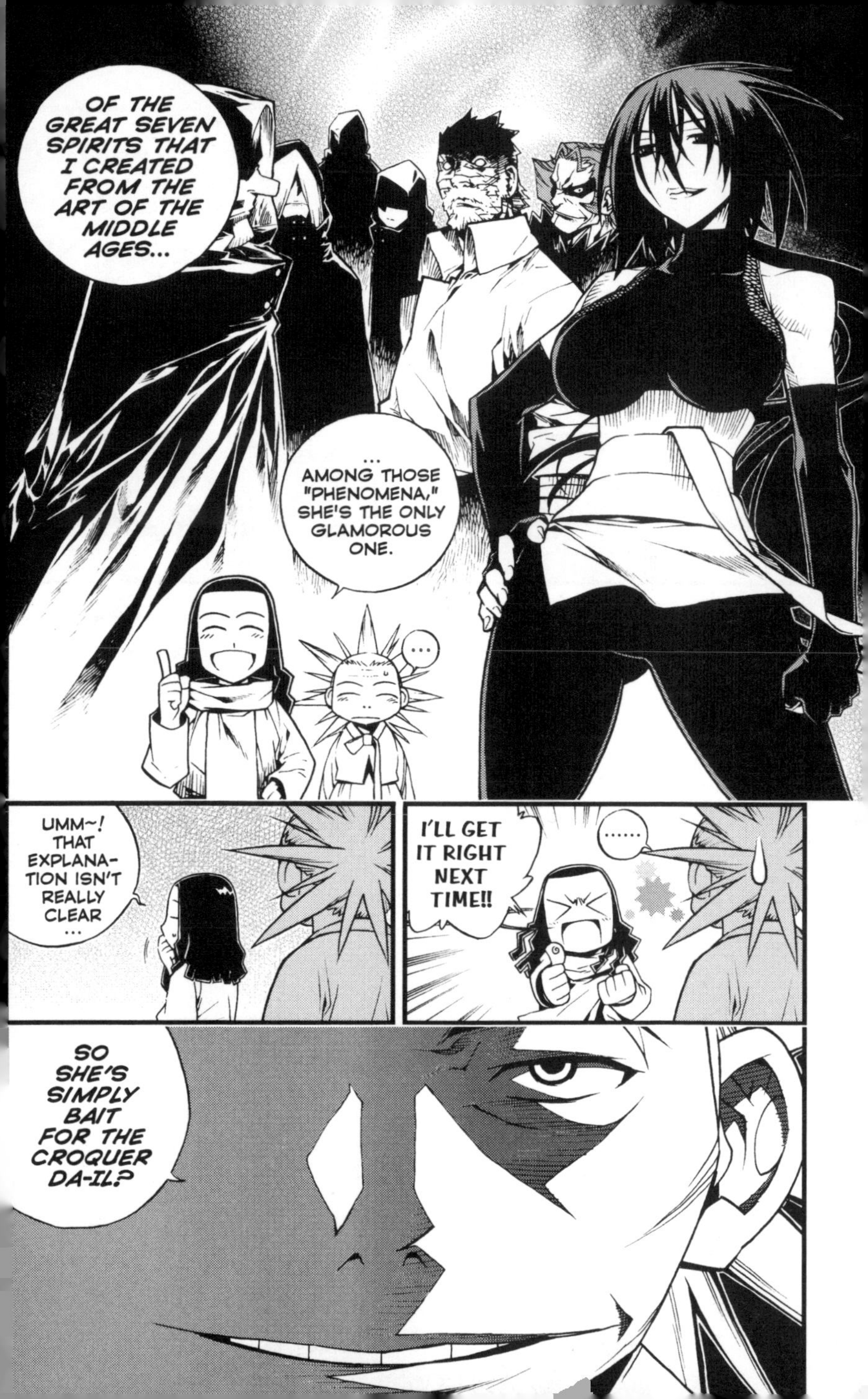
OF THE GREAT SEVEN SPIRITS THAT I CREATED FROM THE ART OF THE MIDDLE AGES...
... AMONG THOSE "PHENOMENA," SHE'S THE ONLY GLAMOROUS ONE.
...
UMM~! THAT EXPLANATION ISN'T REALLY CLEAR ...
I'LL GET IT RIGHT NEXT TIME!!
....
SO SHE'S SIMPLY BAIT FOR THE CROQUER DA-IL?

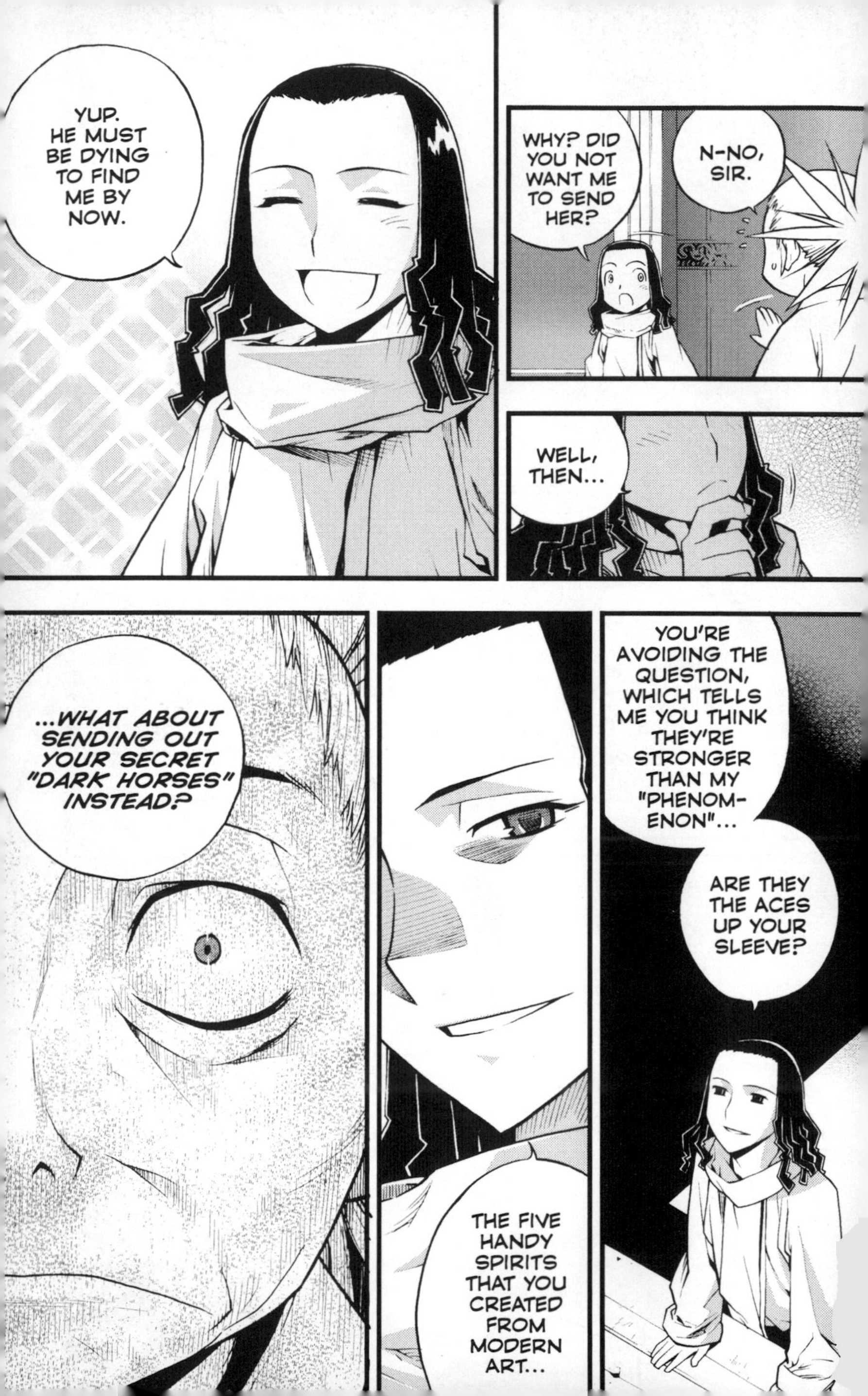
YUP. HE MUST BE DYING TO FIND ME BY NOW.
WHY? DID YOU NOT WANT ME TO SEND HER?
N-NO, SIR.
WELL, THEN...
...WHAT ABOUT SENDING OUT YOUR SECRET "DARK HORSES" INSTEAD?
THE FIVE HANDY SPIRITS THAT YOU CREATED FROM MODERN ART...
YOU'RE AVOIDING THE QUESTION, WHICH TELLS ME YOU THINK THEY'RE STRONGER THAN MY "PHENOM-ENON"...
ARE THEY THE ACES UP YOUR SLEEVE?

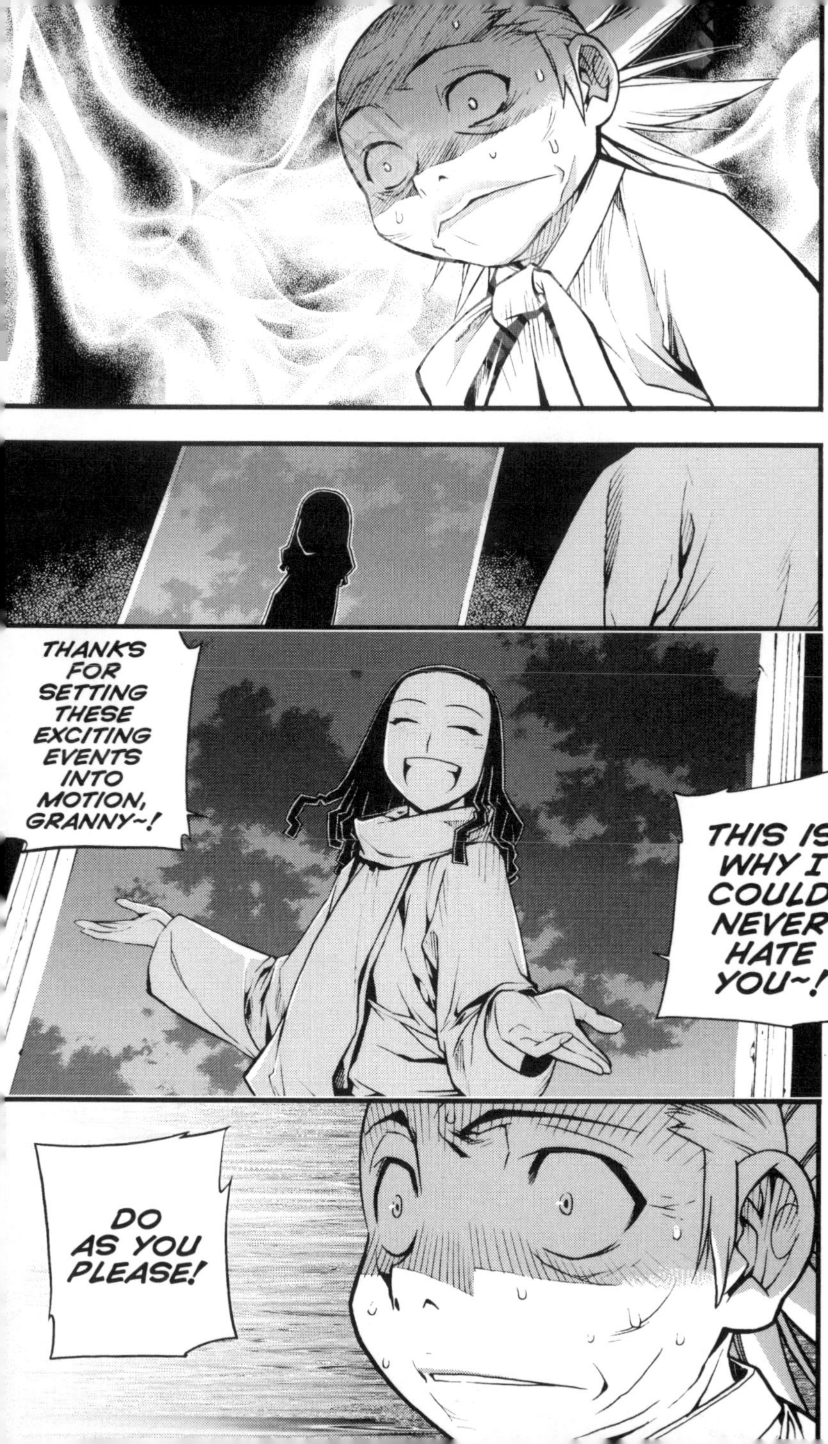
THANKS FOR SETTING THESE EXCITING EVENTS INTO MOTION, GRANNY~!
THIS IS WHY I COULD NEVER HATE YOU~!
DO AS YOU PLEASE!

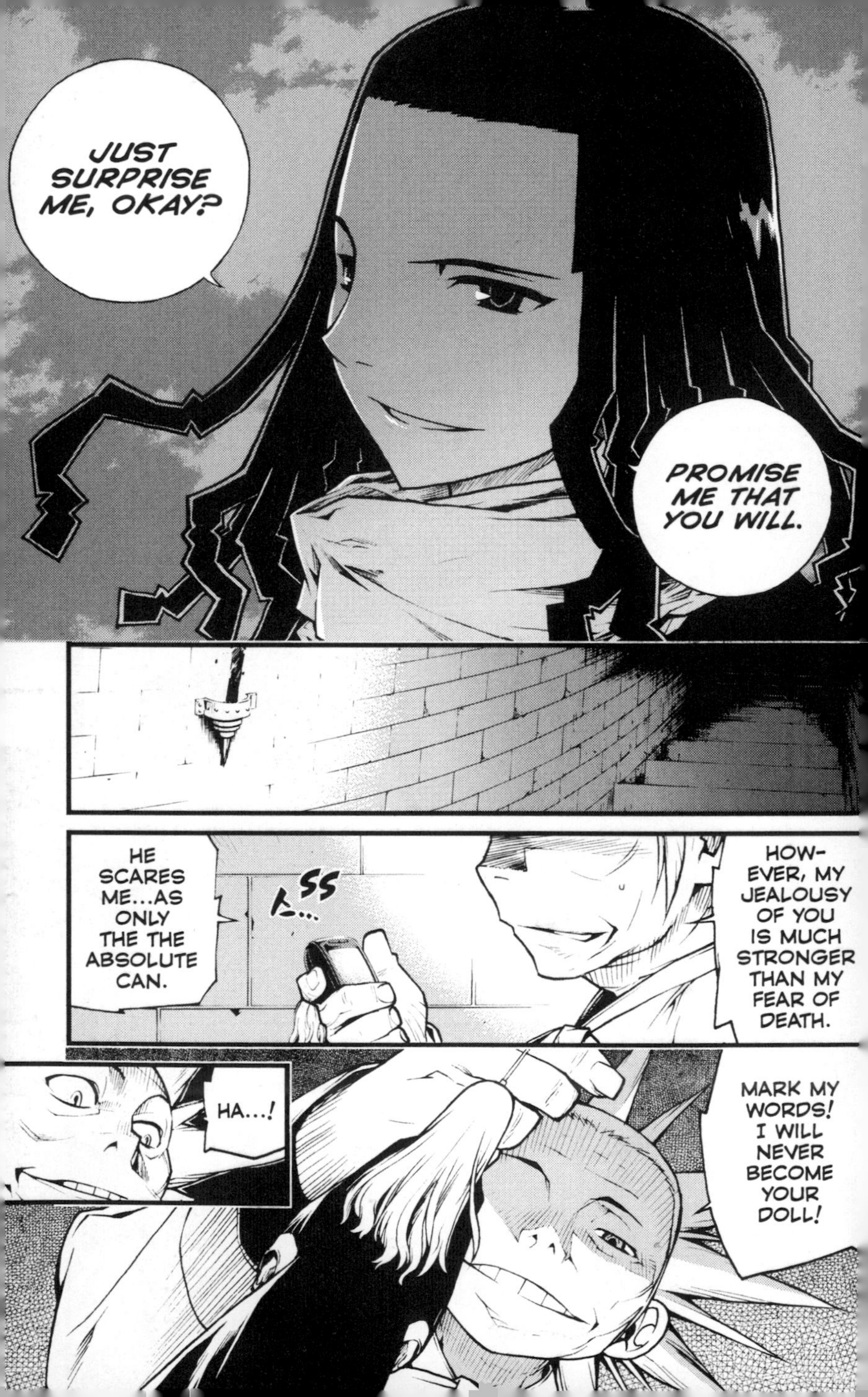
JUST SURPRISE ME, OKAY?
PROMISE ME THAT YOU WILL.
HE SCARES ME...AS ONLY THE THE ABSOLUTE CAN.
SS
HOW-EVER, MY JEALOUSY OF YOU IS MUCH STRONGER THAN MY FEAR OF DEATH.
HA...!
MARK MY WORDS! I WILL NEVER BECOME YOUR DOLL!

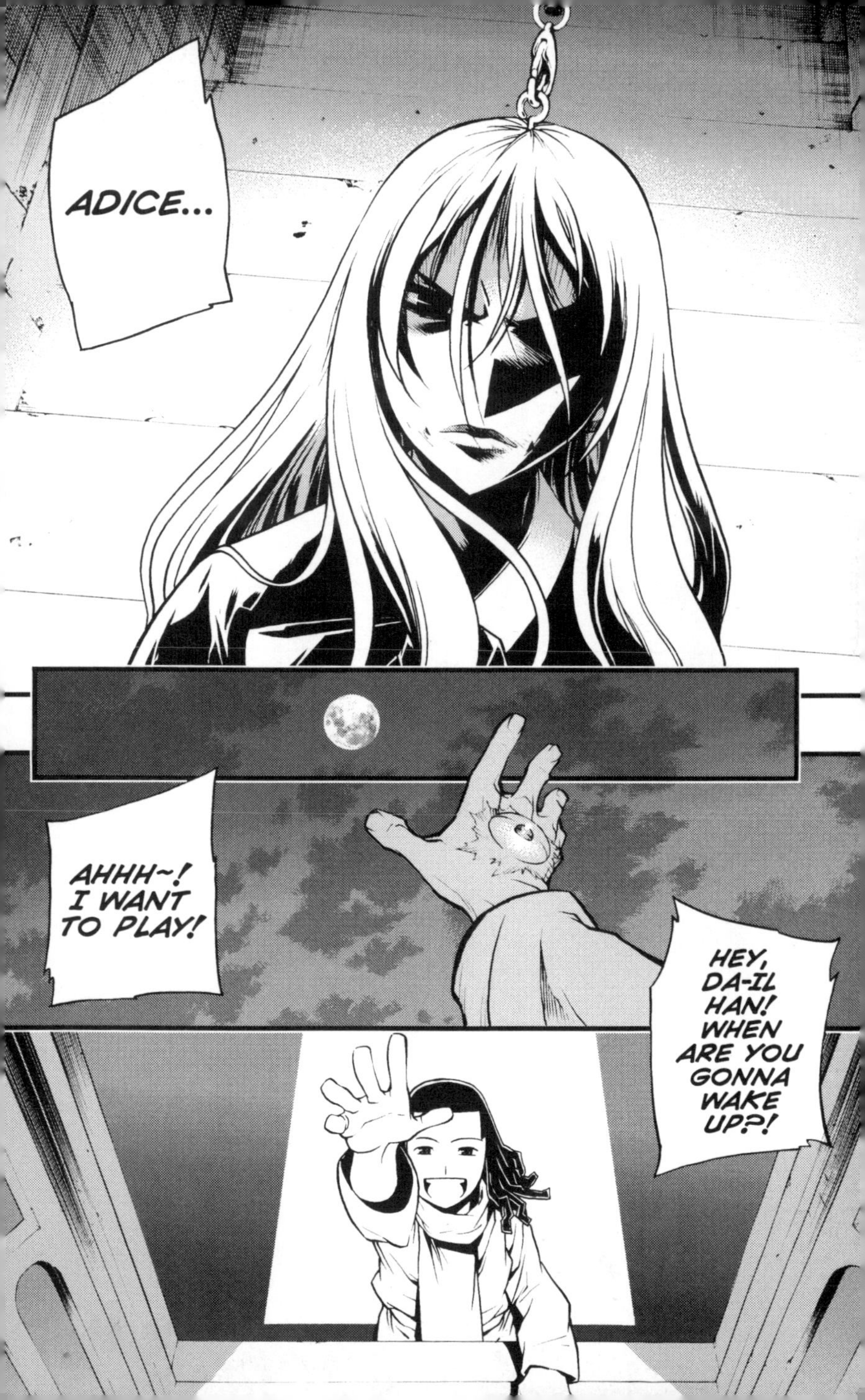
ADICE...
AHHH~! I WANT TO PLAY!
HEY, DA-IL HAN! WHEN ARE YOU GONNA WAKE UP?!

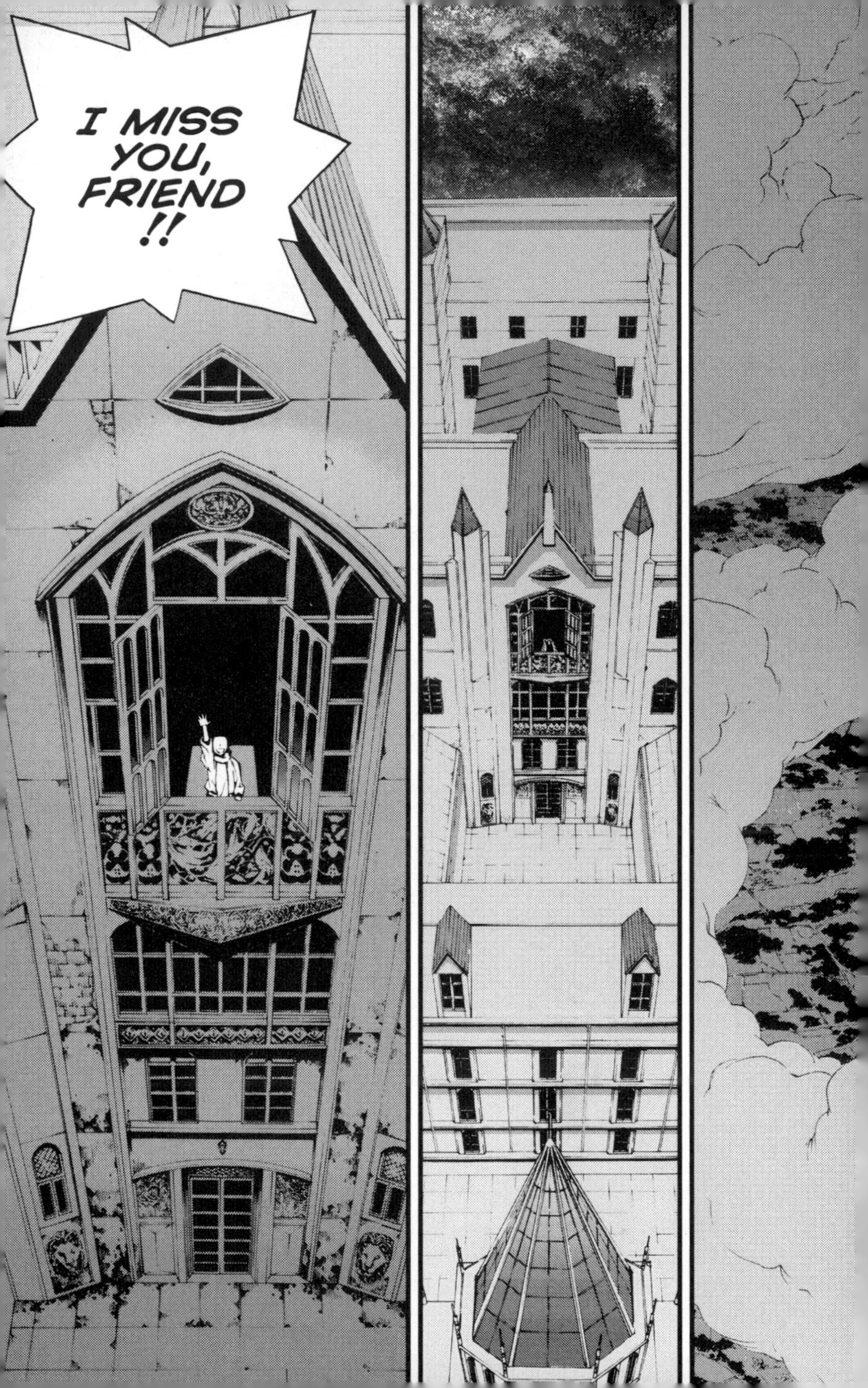
I MISS YOU, FRIEND !!

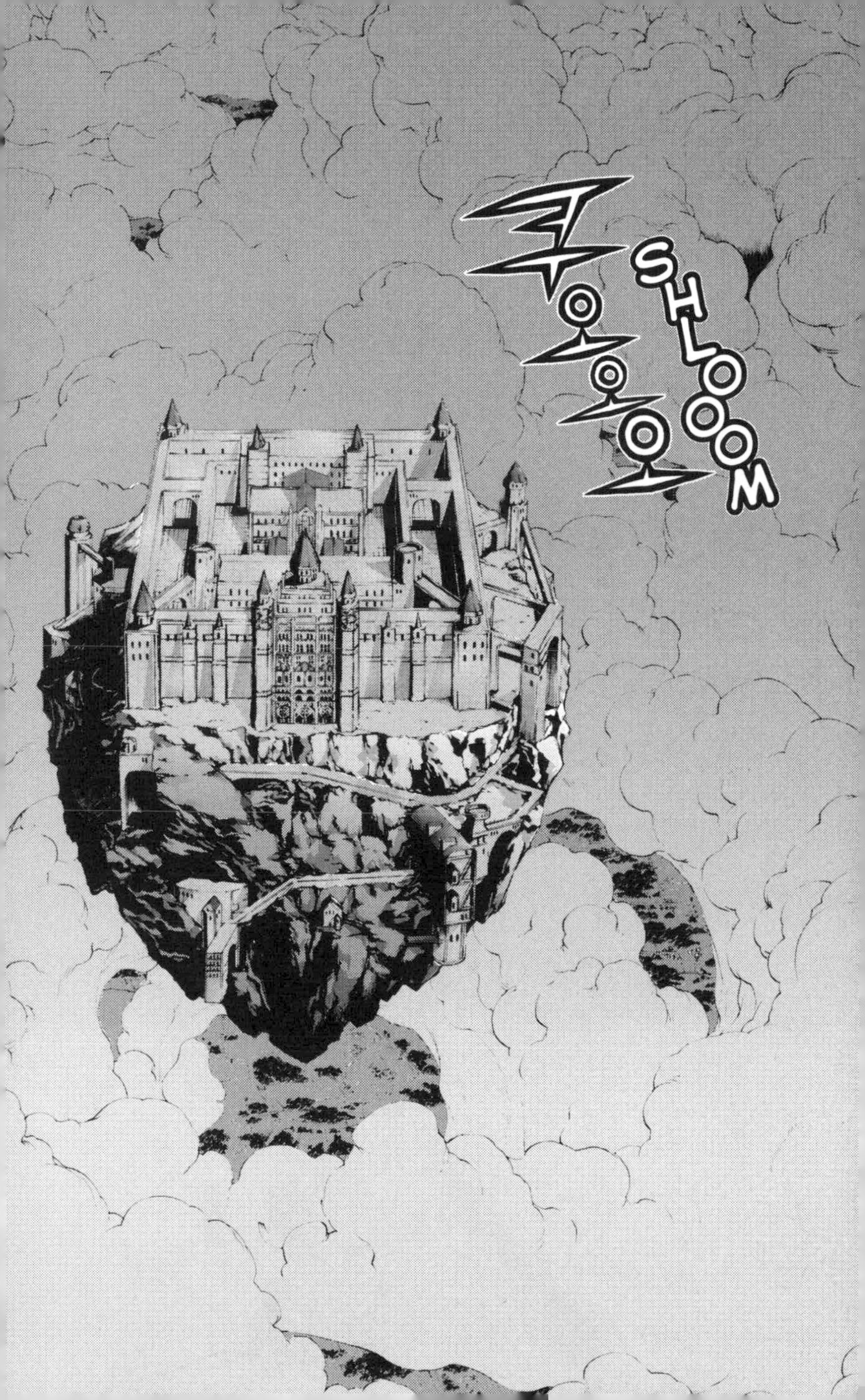
SHLOOOM

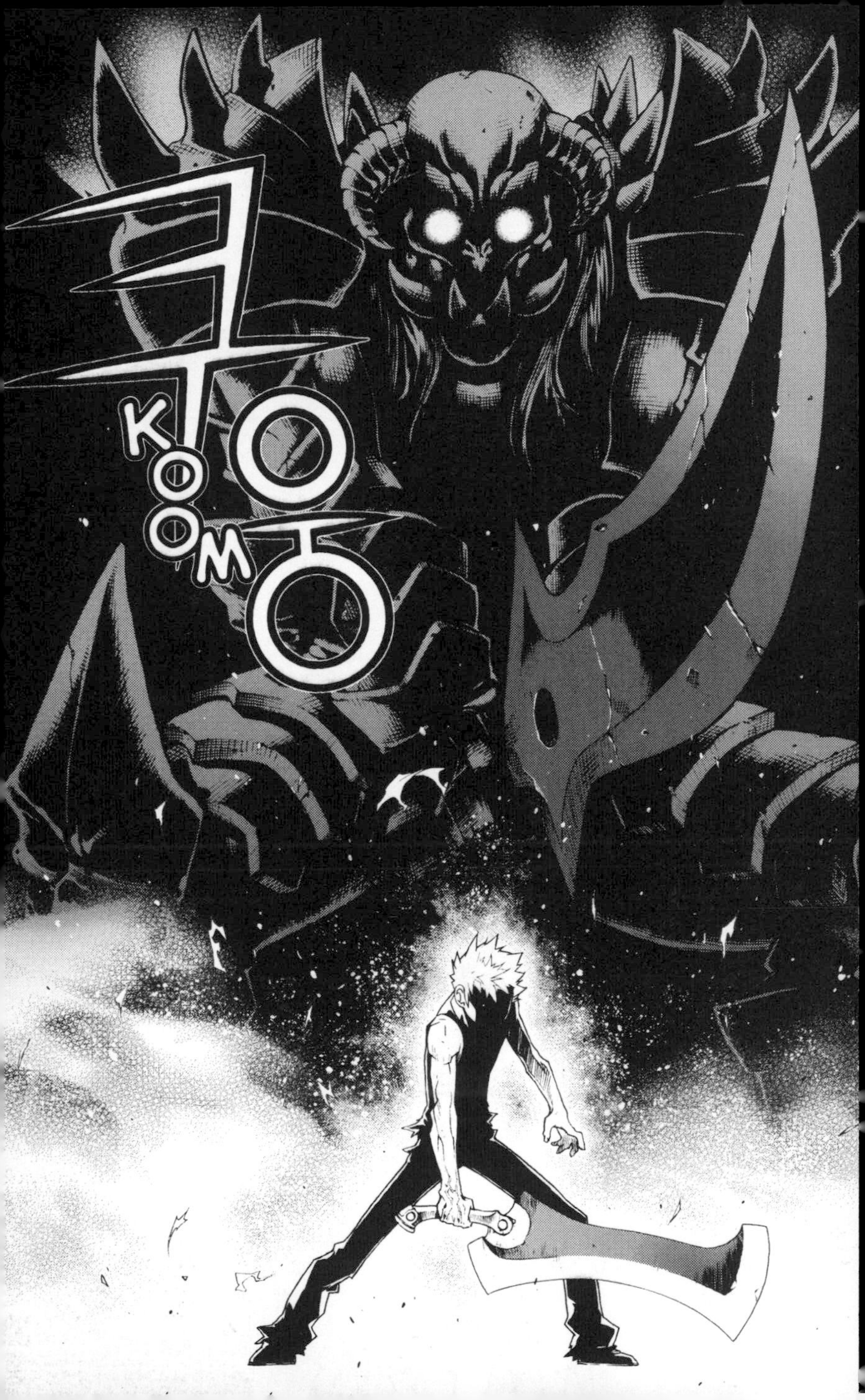
KOOM

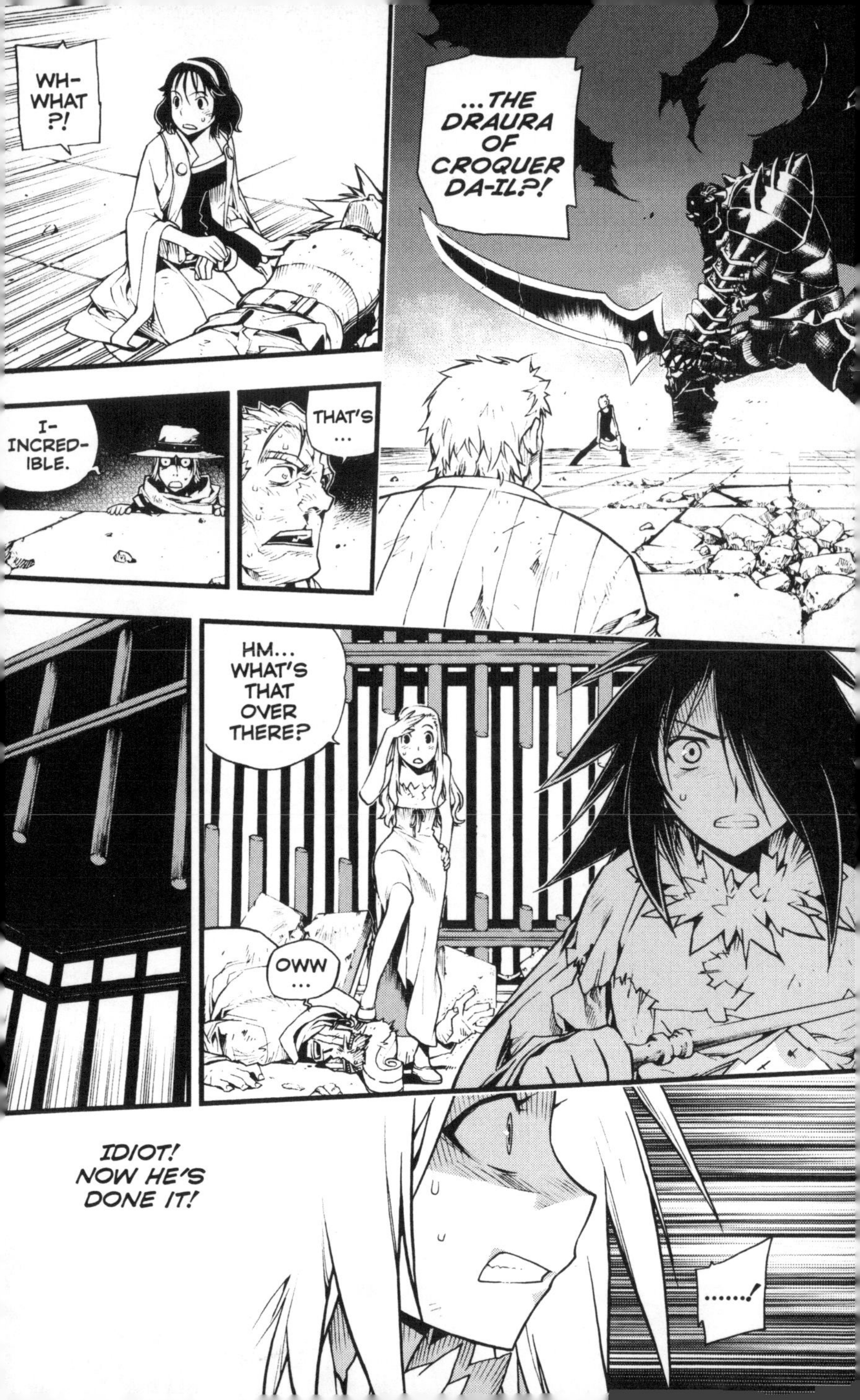
WH-WHAT ?!
...THE DRAURA OF CROQUER DA-IL?!
I-INCRED-IBLE.
THAT'S ...
HM... WHAT'S THAT OVER THERE?
OWW ...
IDIOT! NOW HE'S DONE IT!
.......!

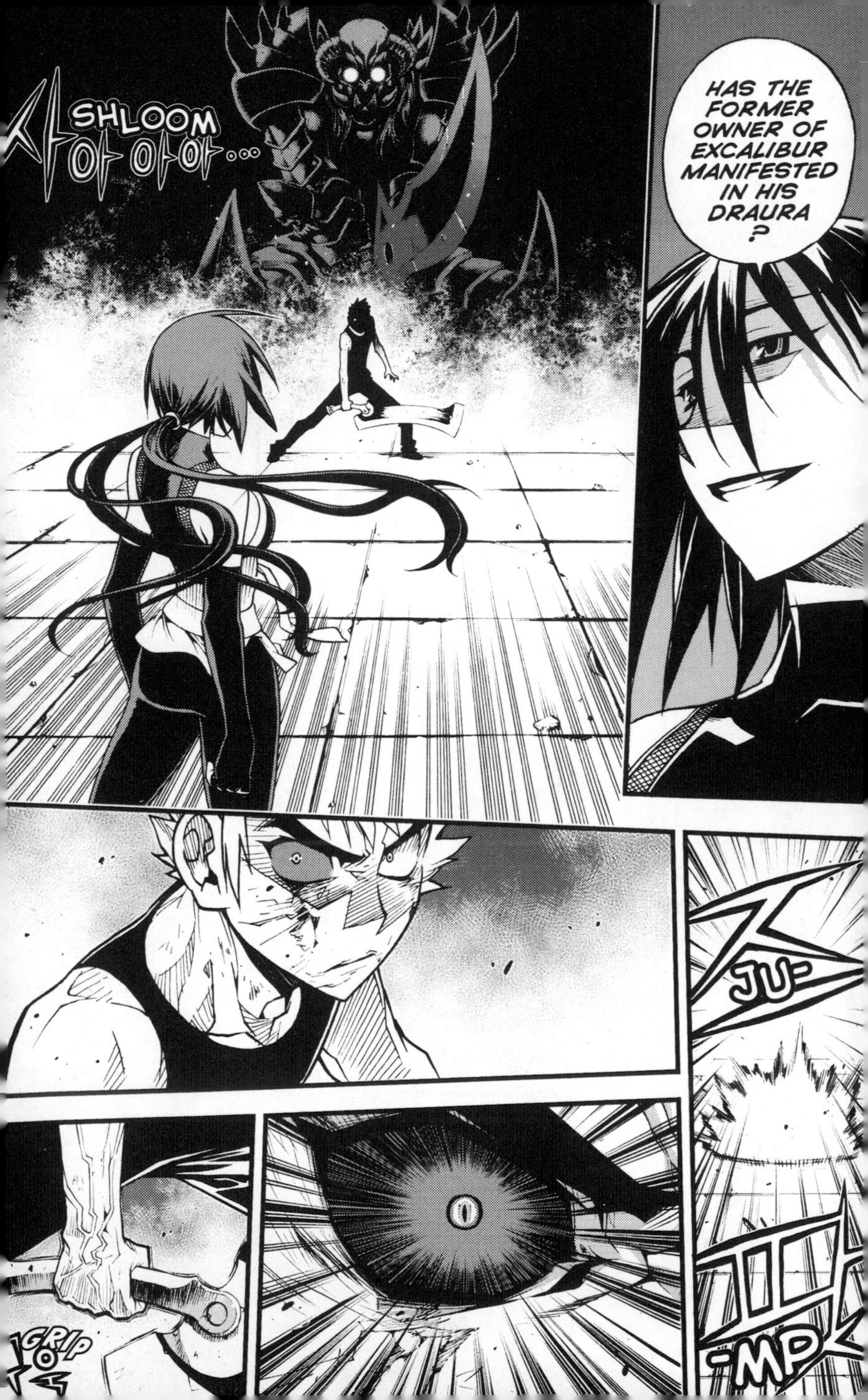
SHLOOM
HAS THE FORMER OWNER OF EXCALIBUR MANIFESTED IN HIS DRAURA ?
GRIP
JU-
-MP

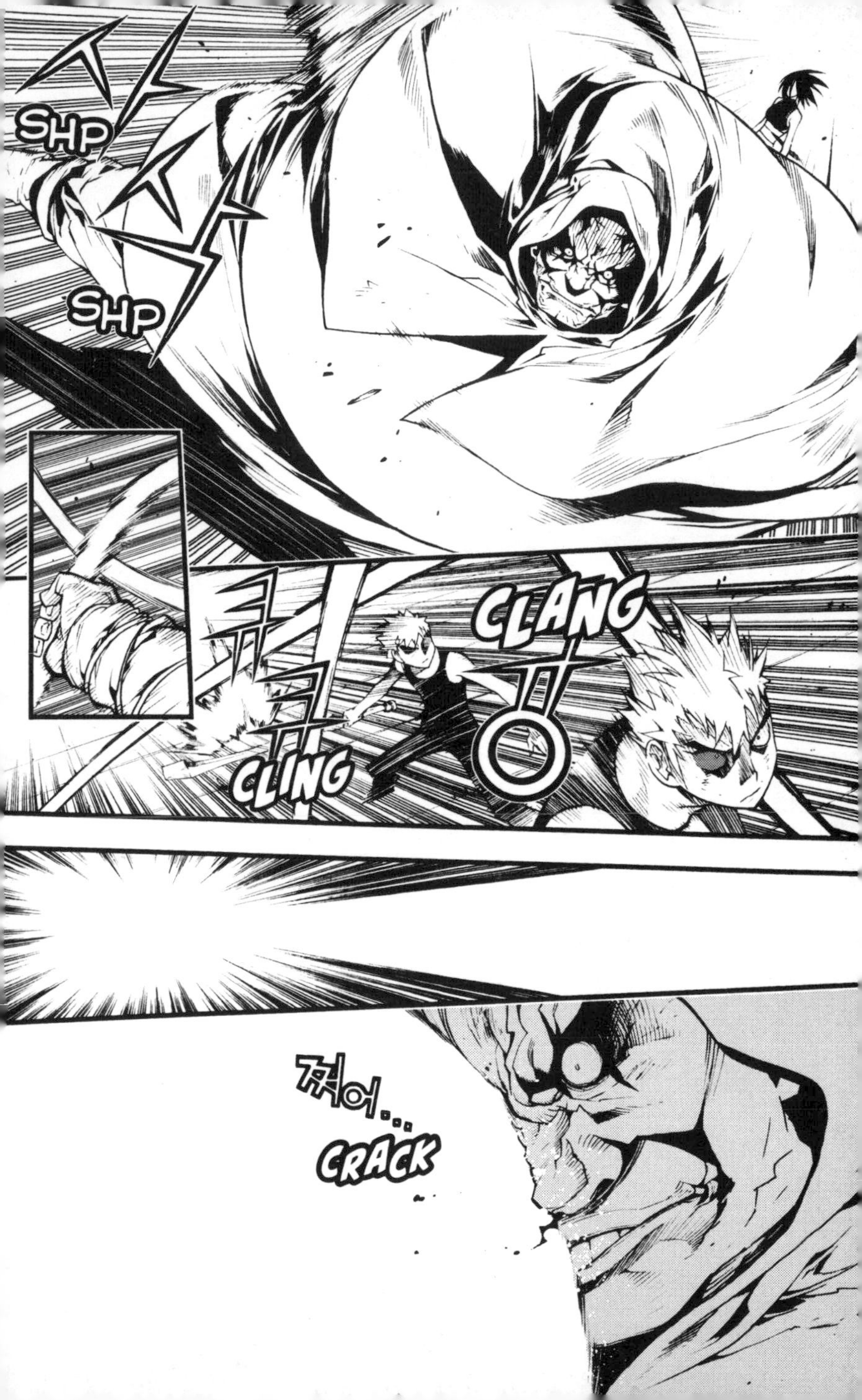
SHP
SHP
CLING
CLANG
CRACK

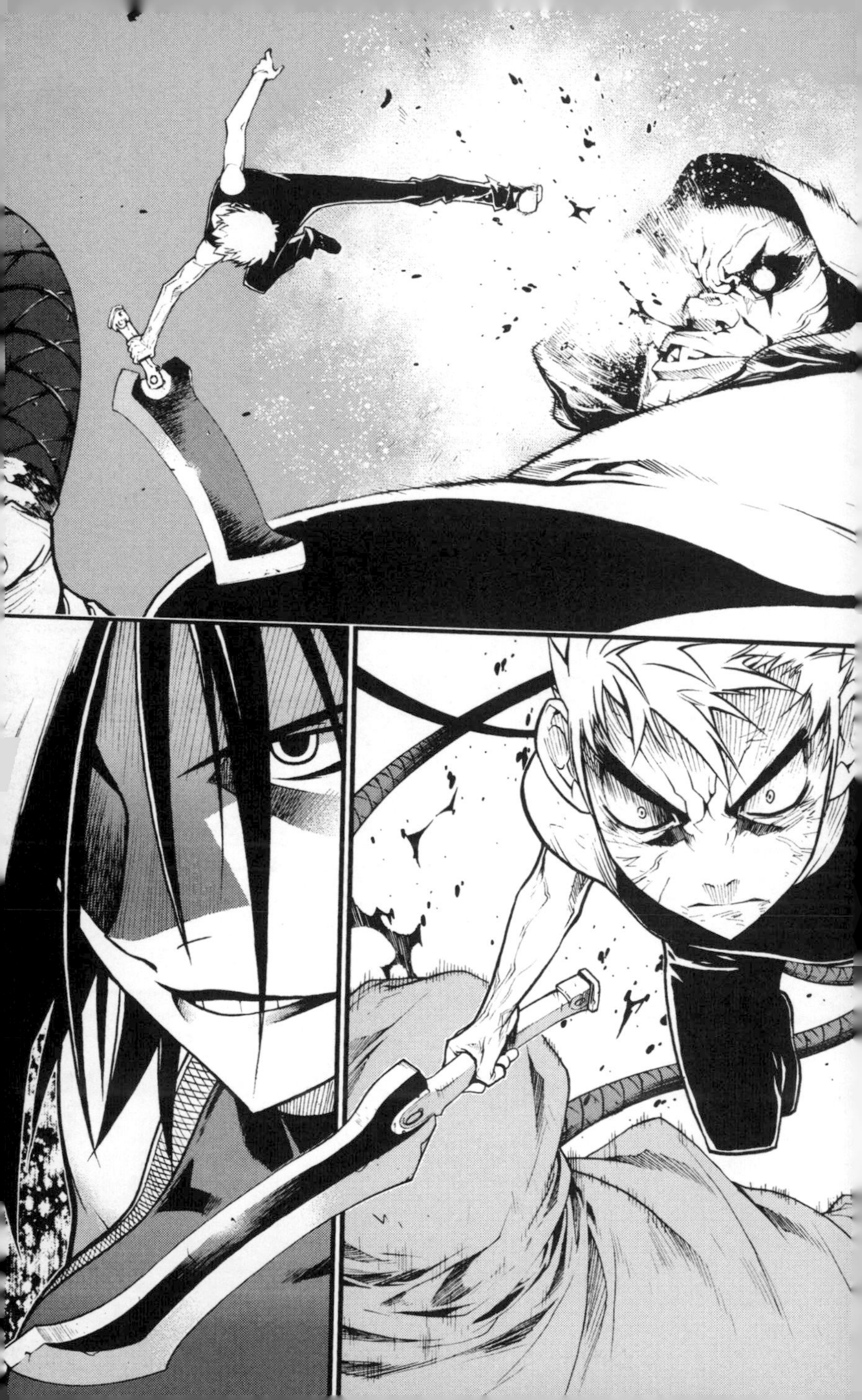

POP 37. EXPLOSION

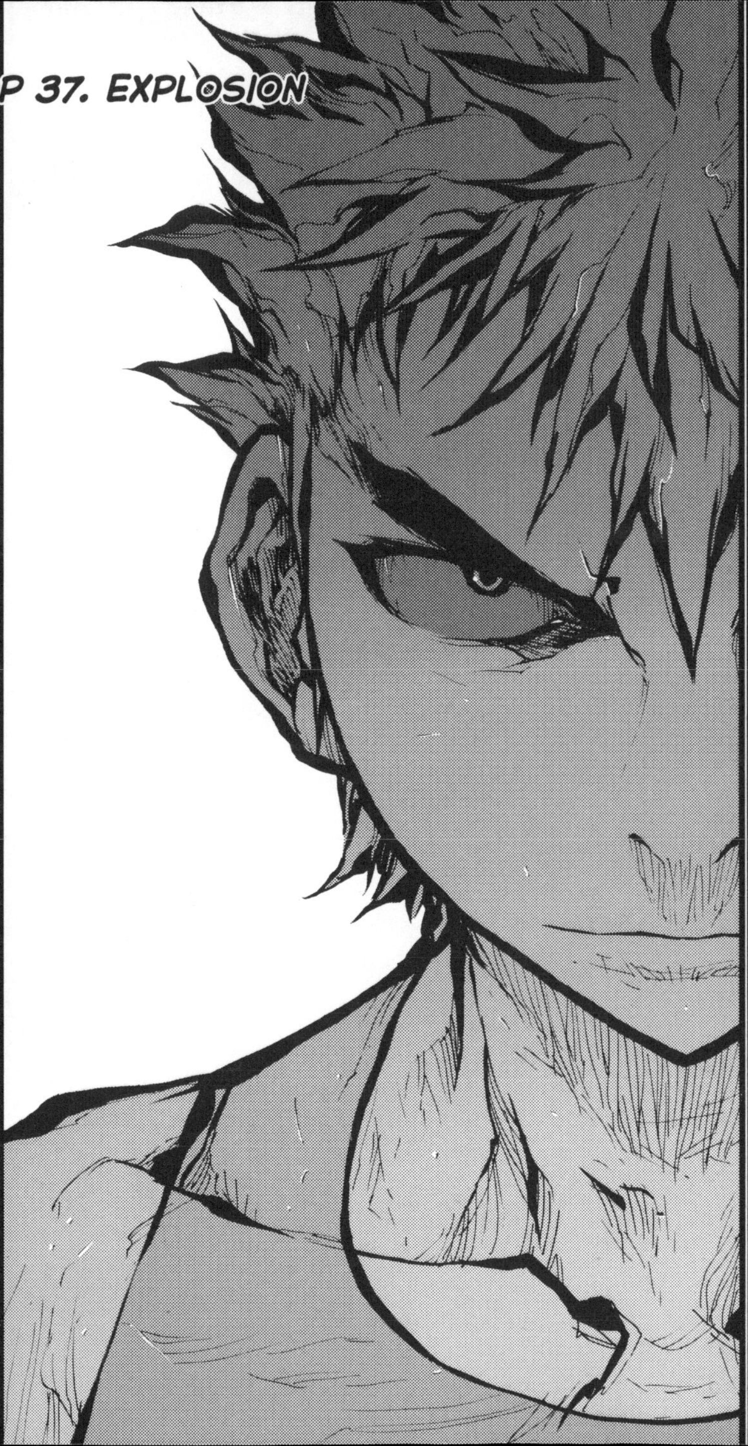

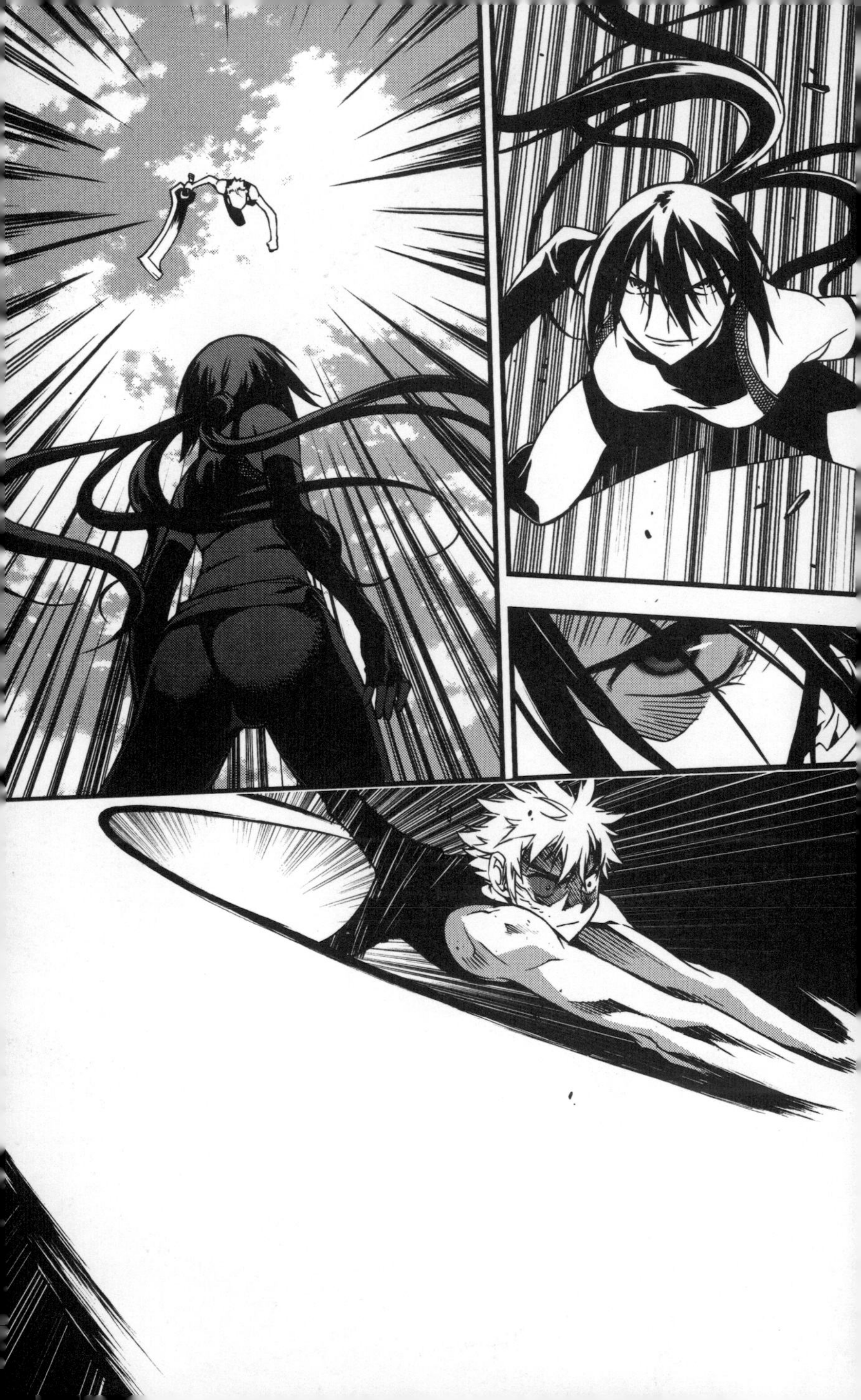

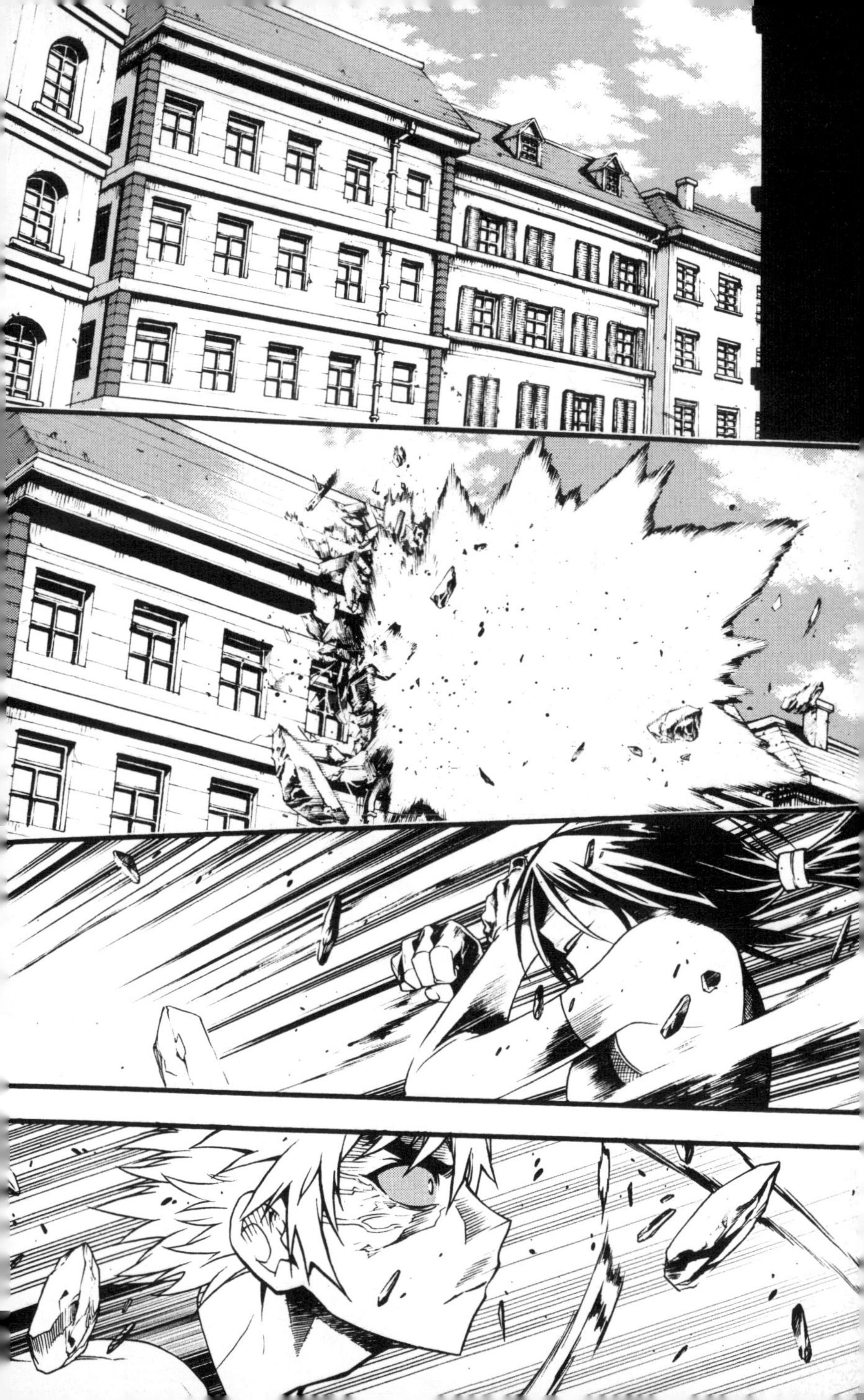

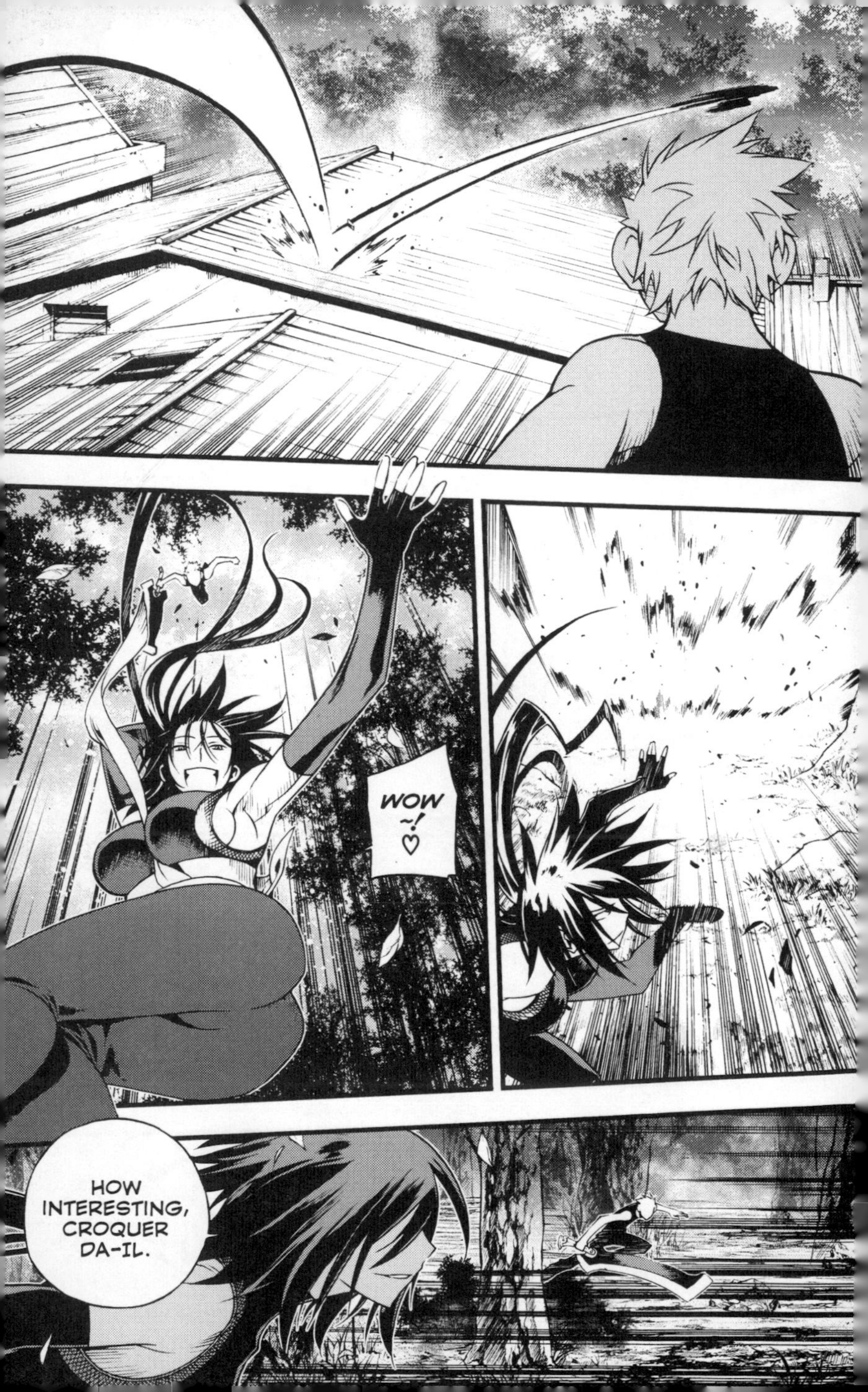
WOW ~! ♡
HOW INTERESTING, CROQUER DA-IL.

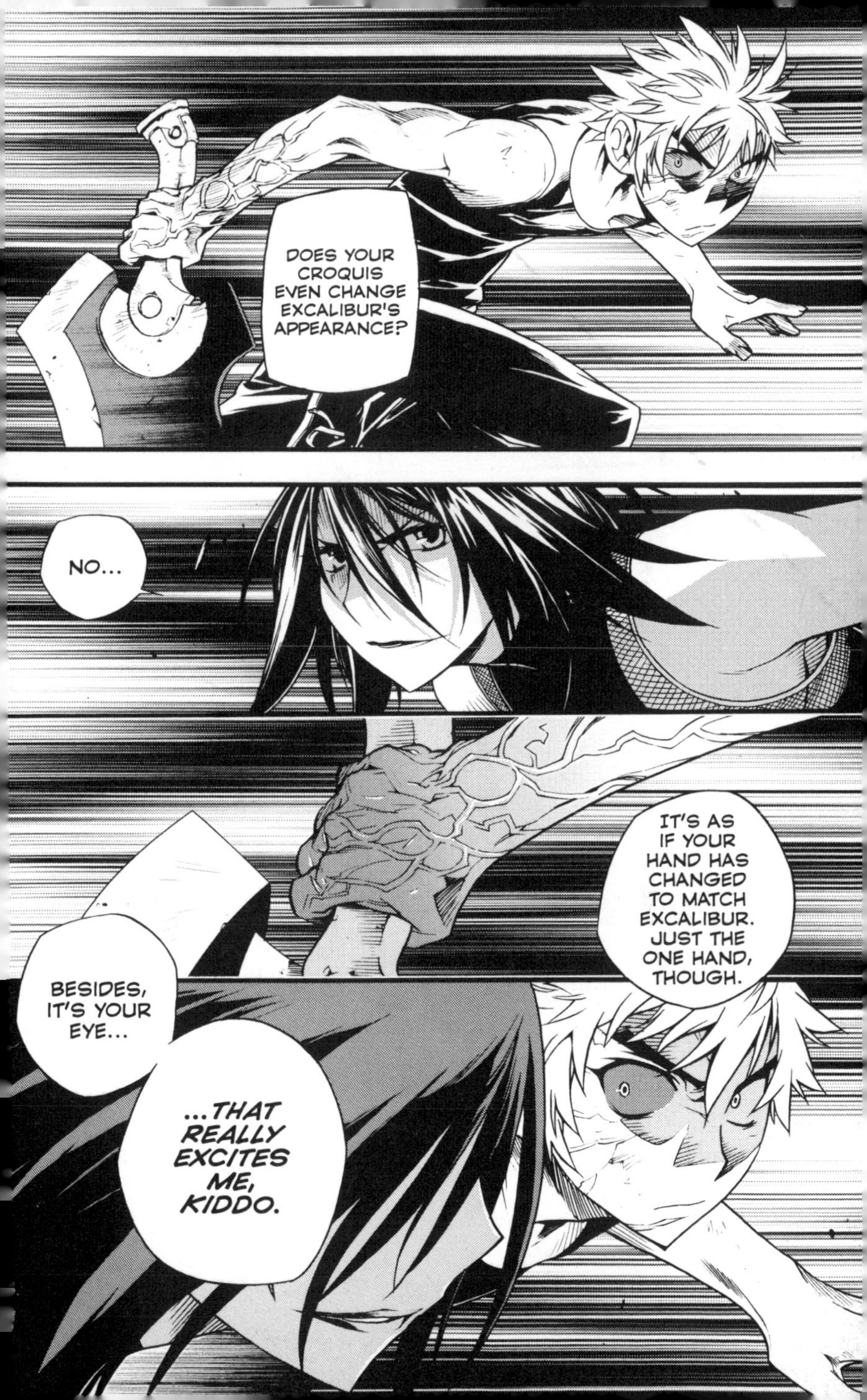
DOES YOUR CROQUIS EVEN CHANGE EXCALIBUR'S APPEARANCE?
NO...
IT'S AS IF YOUR HAND HAS CHANGED TO MATCH EXCALIBUR. JUST THE ONE HAND, THOUGH.
BESIDES, IT'S YOUR EYE...
...THAT REALLY EXCITES ME, KIDDO.

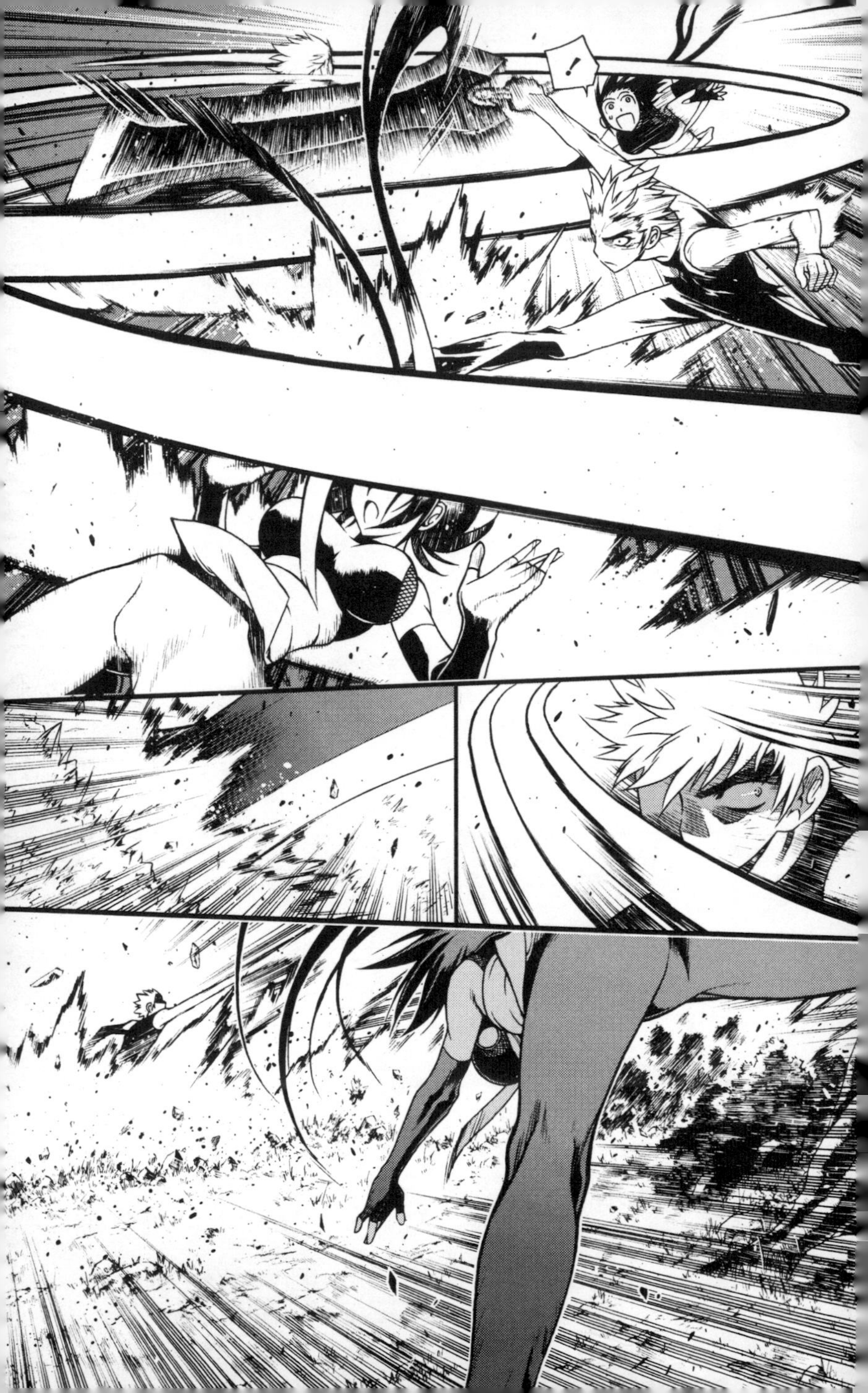
!

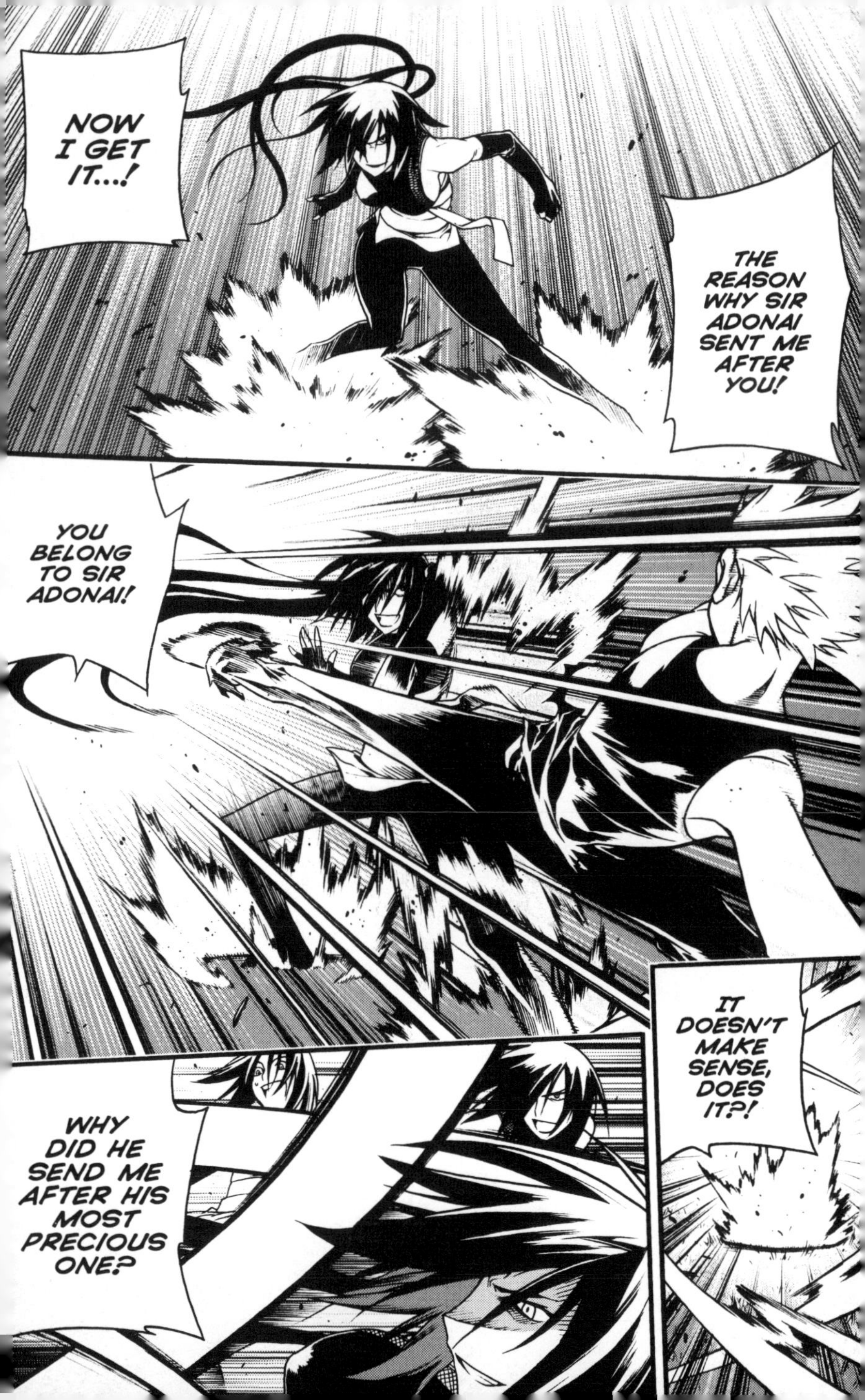
NOW I GET IT...!
THE REASON WHY SIR ADONAI SENT ME AFTER YOU!
YOU BELONG TO SIR ADONAI!
WHY DID HE SEND ME AFTER HIS MOST PRECIOUS ONE?
IT DOESN'T MAKE SENSE, DOES IT?!

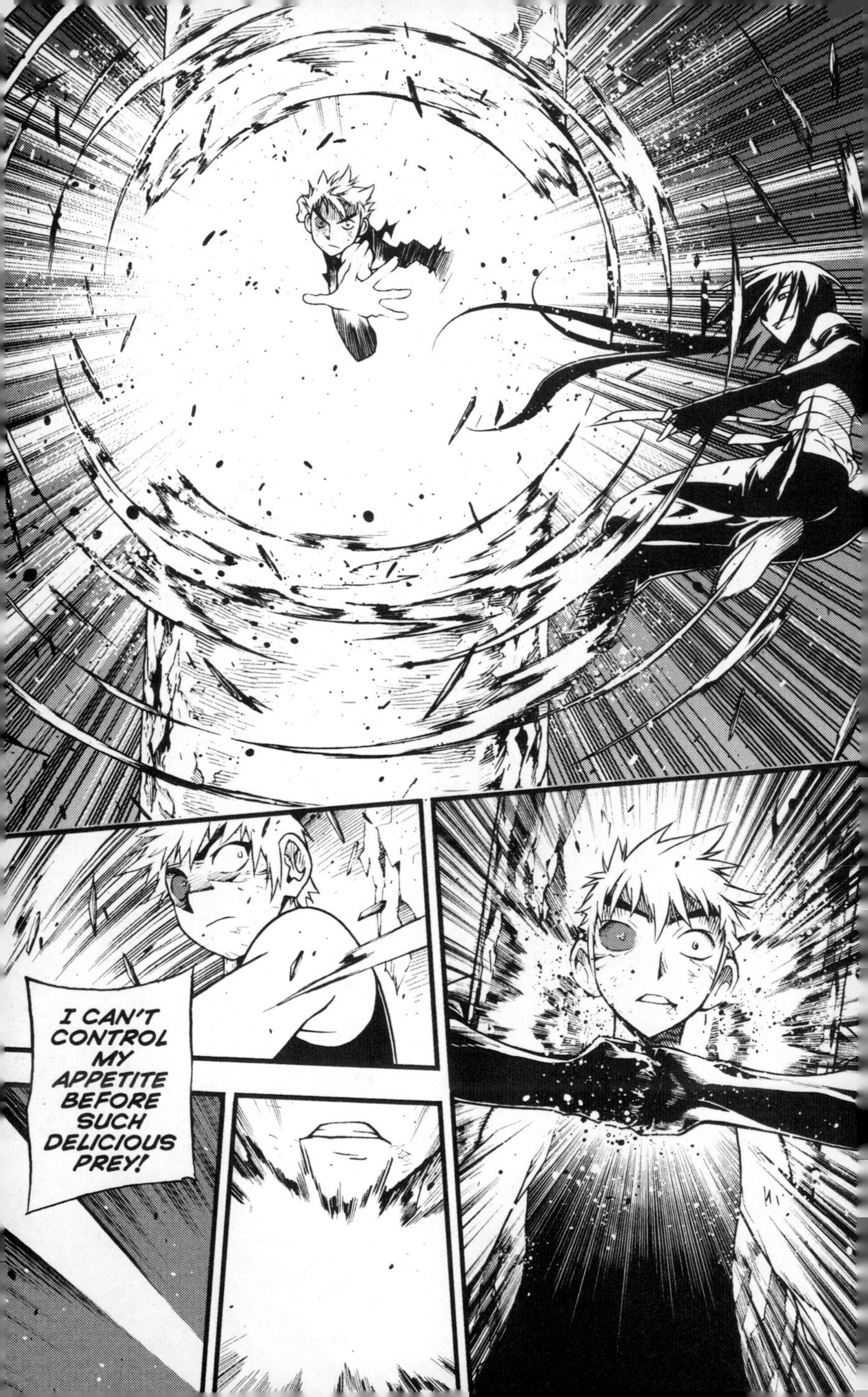
I CAN'T CONTROL MY APPETITE BEFORE SUCH DELICIOUS PREY!

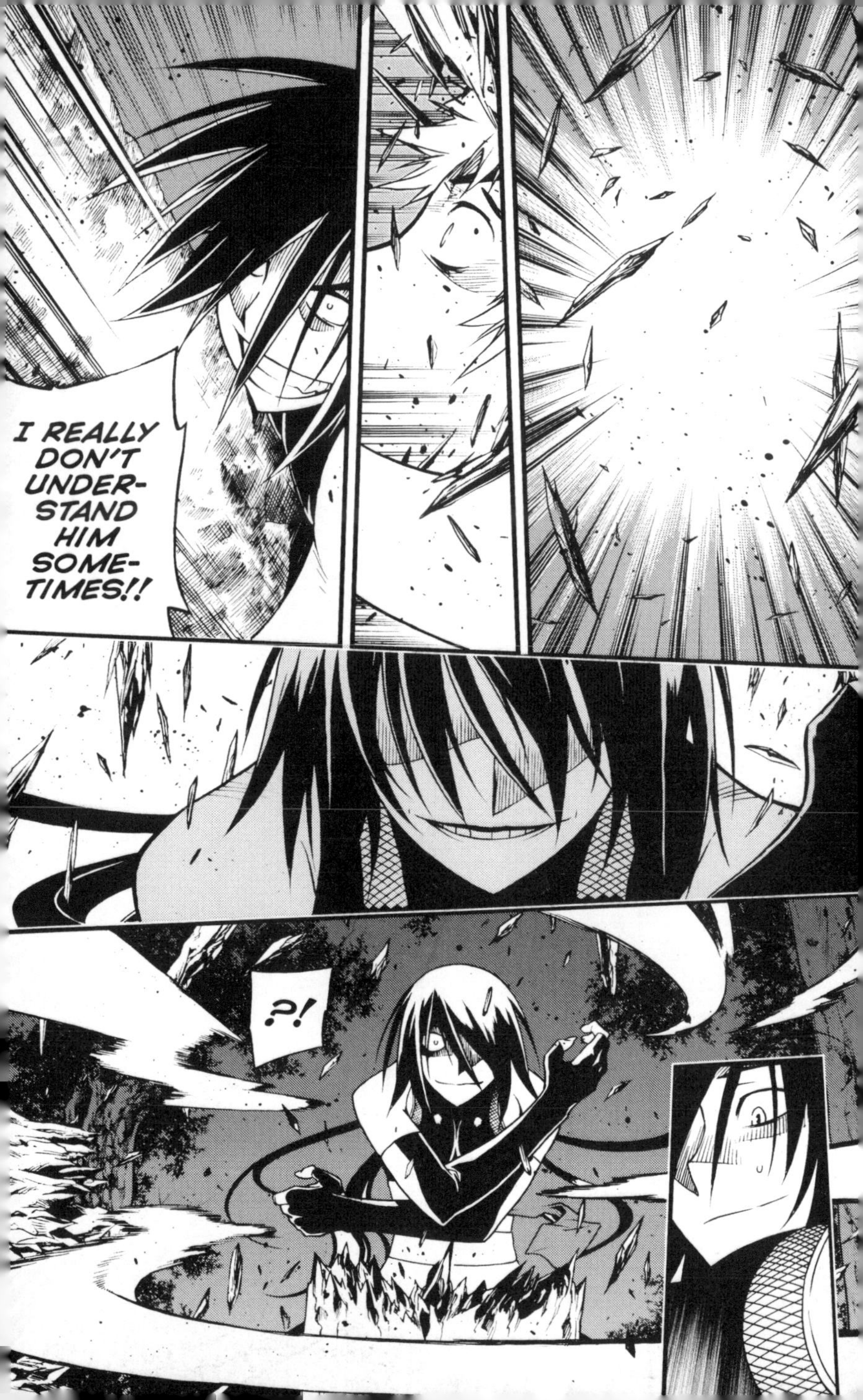
I REALLY DON'T UNDER-STAND HIM SOME-TIMES!!
?!

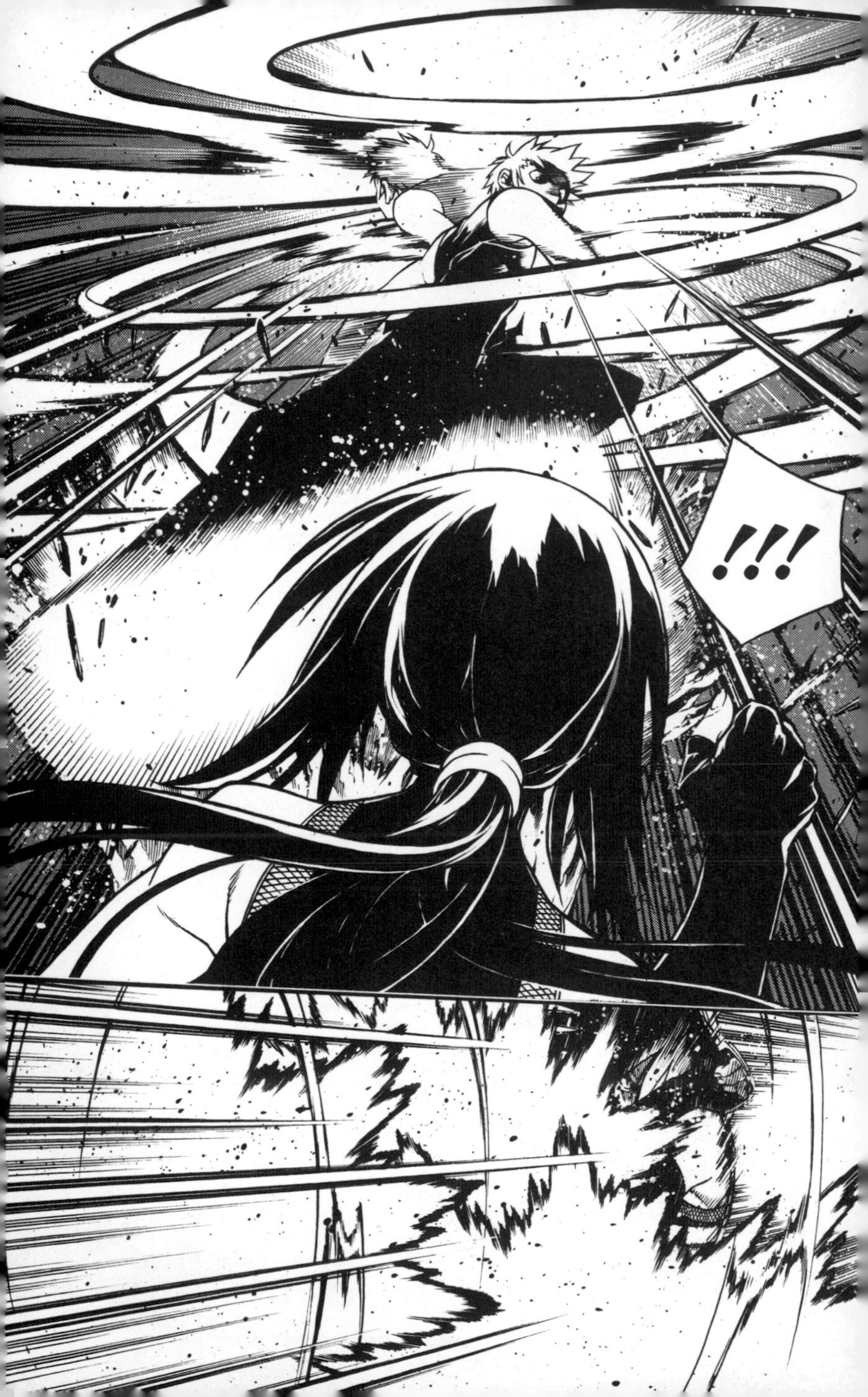
!!!

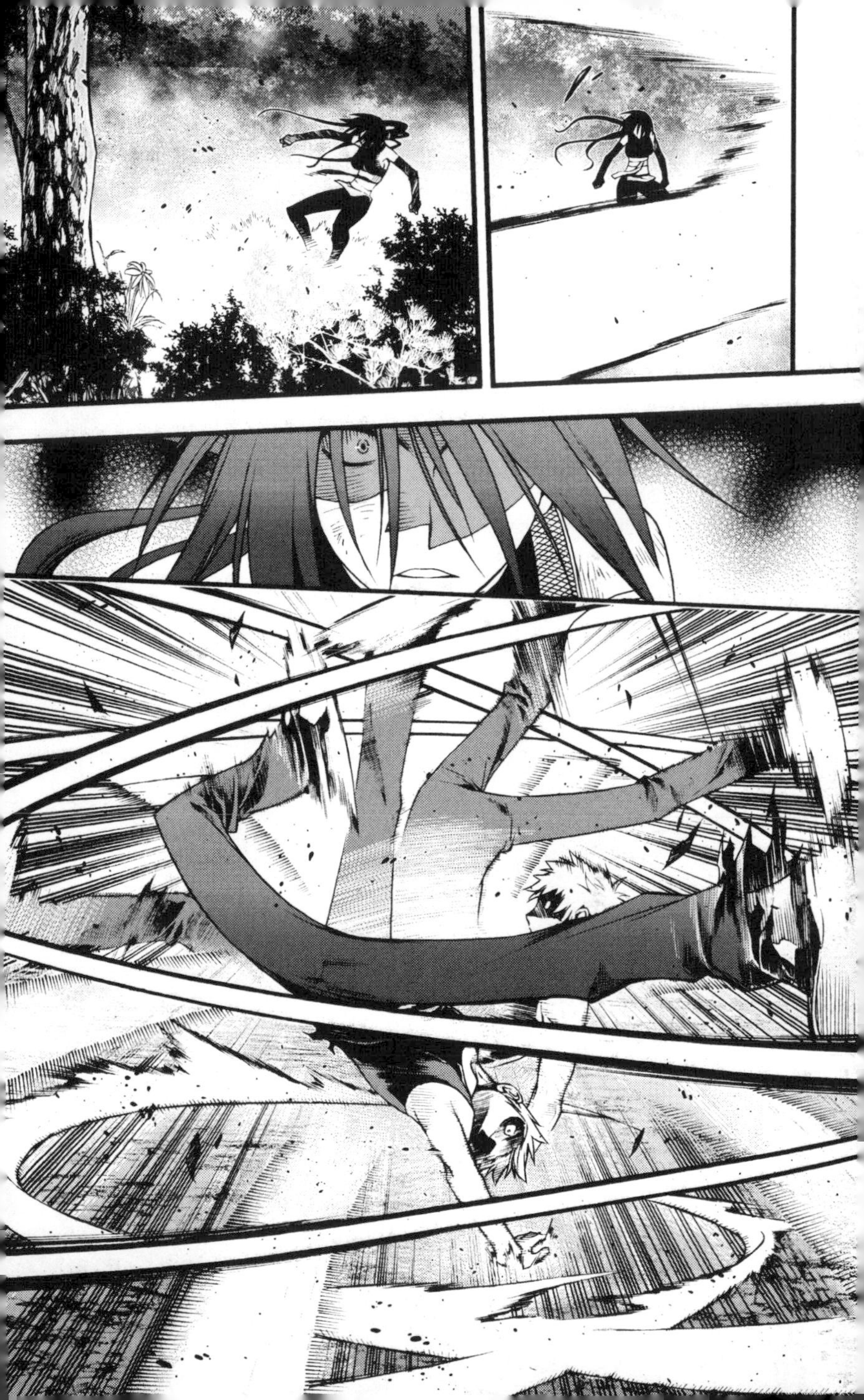

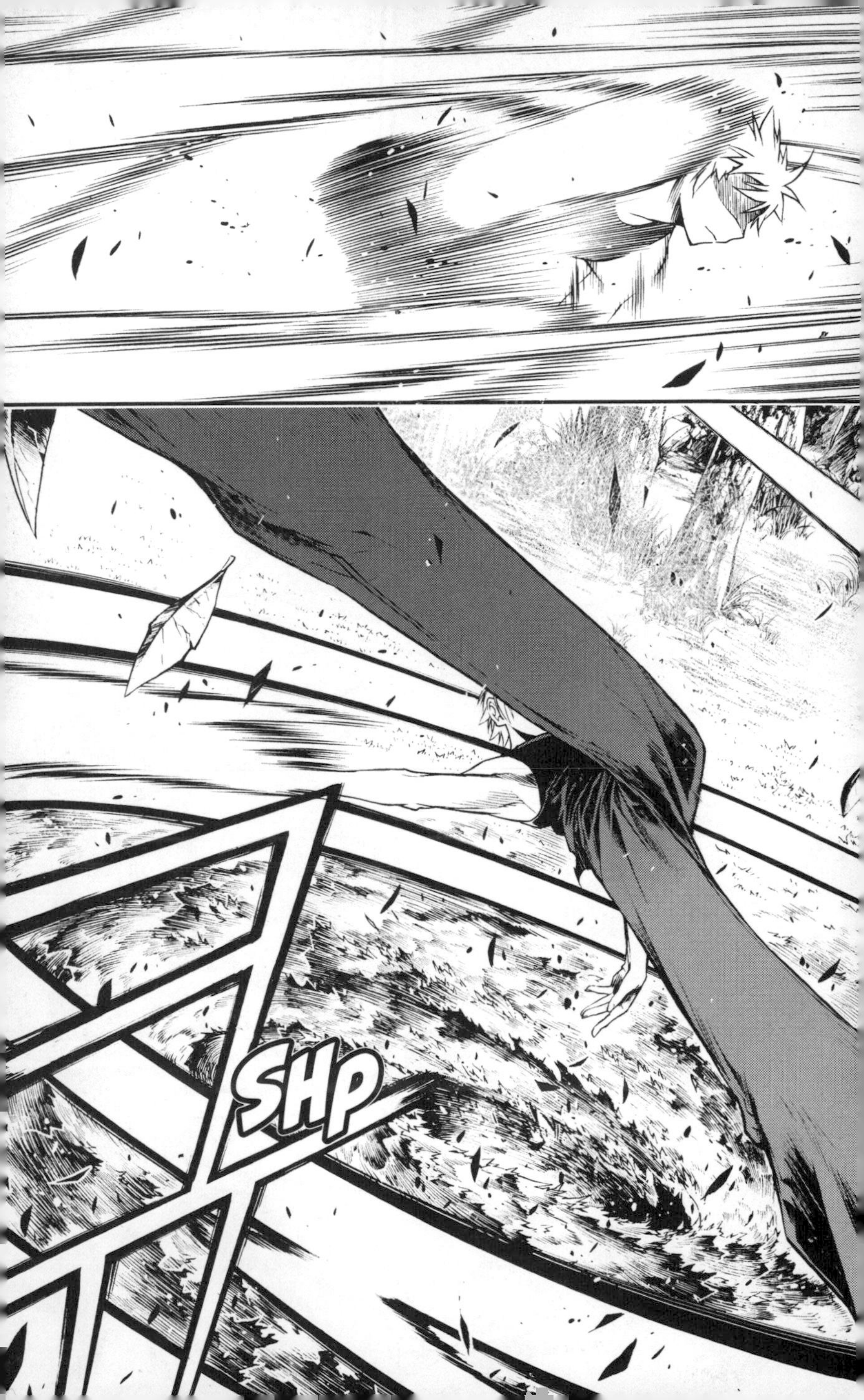
SHP

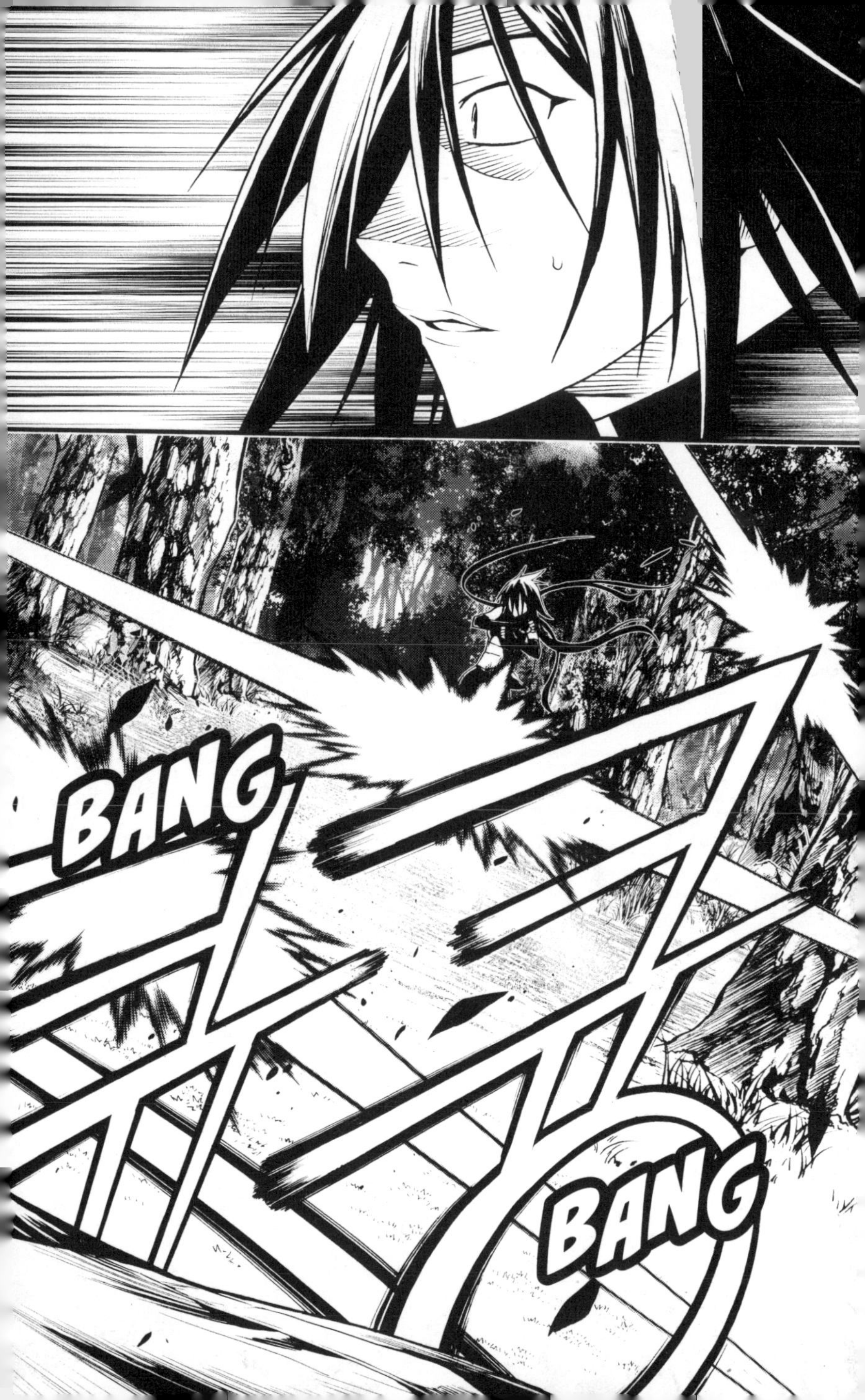
BANG
BANG

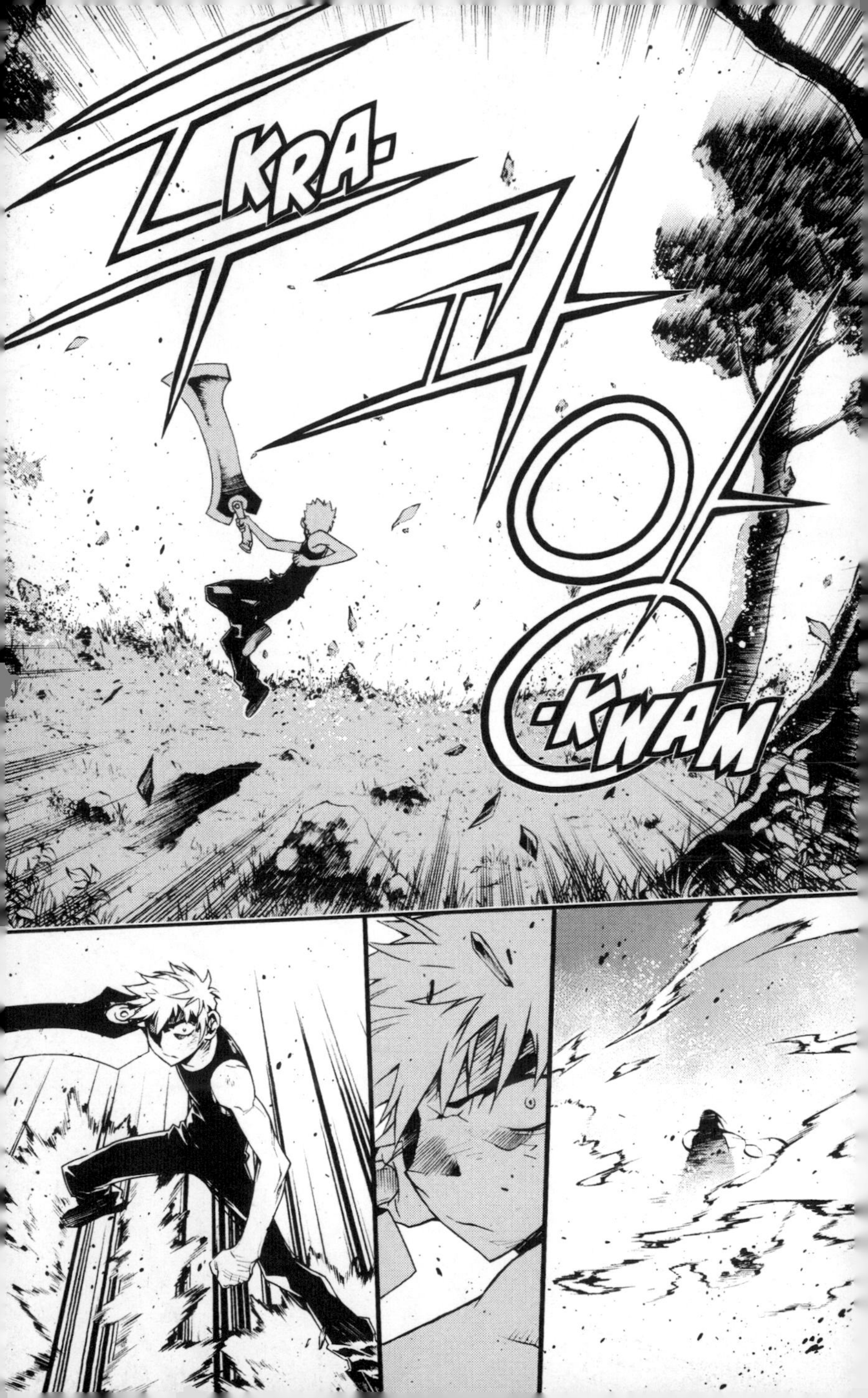
KRA-TTHOOO-KWAM

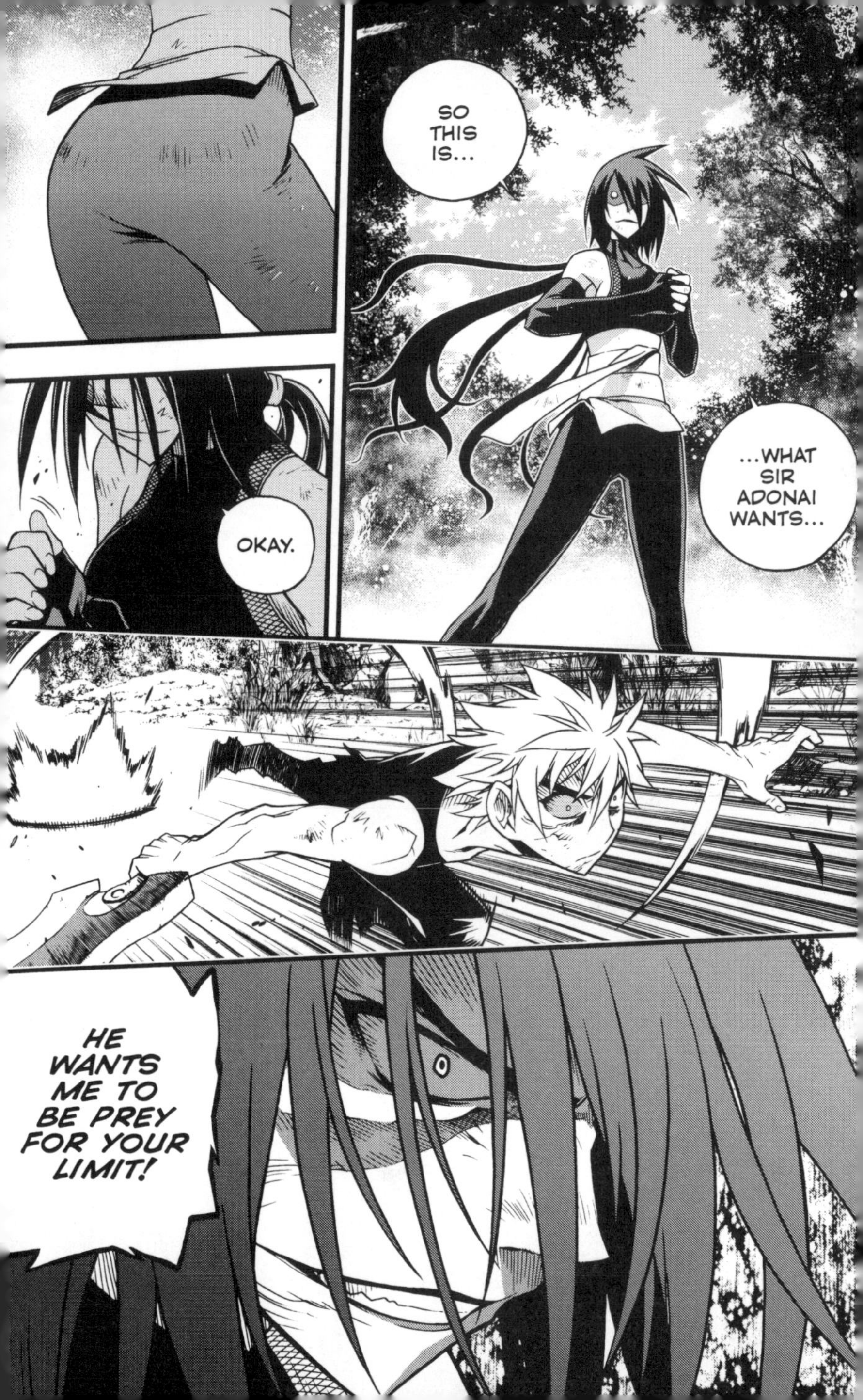
OKAY.
SO THIS IS...
...WHAT SIR ADONAI WANTS...
HE WANTS ME TO BE PREY FOR YOUR LIMIT!

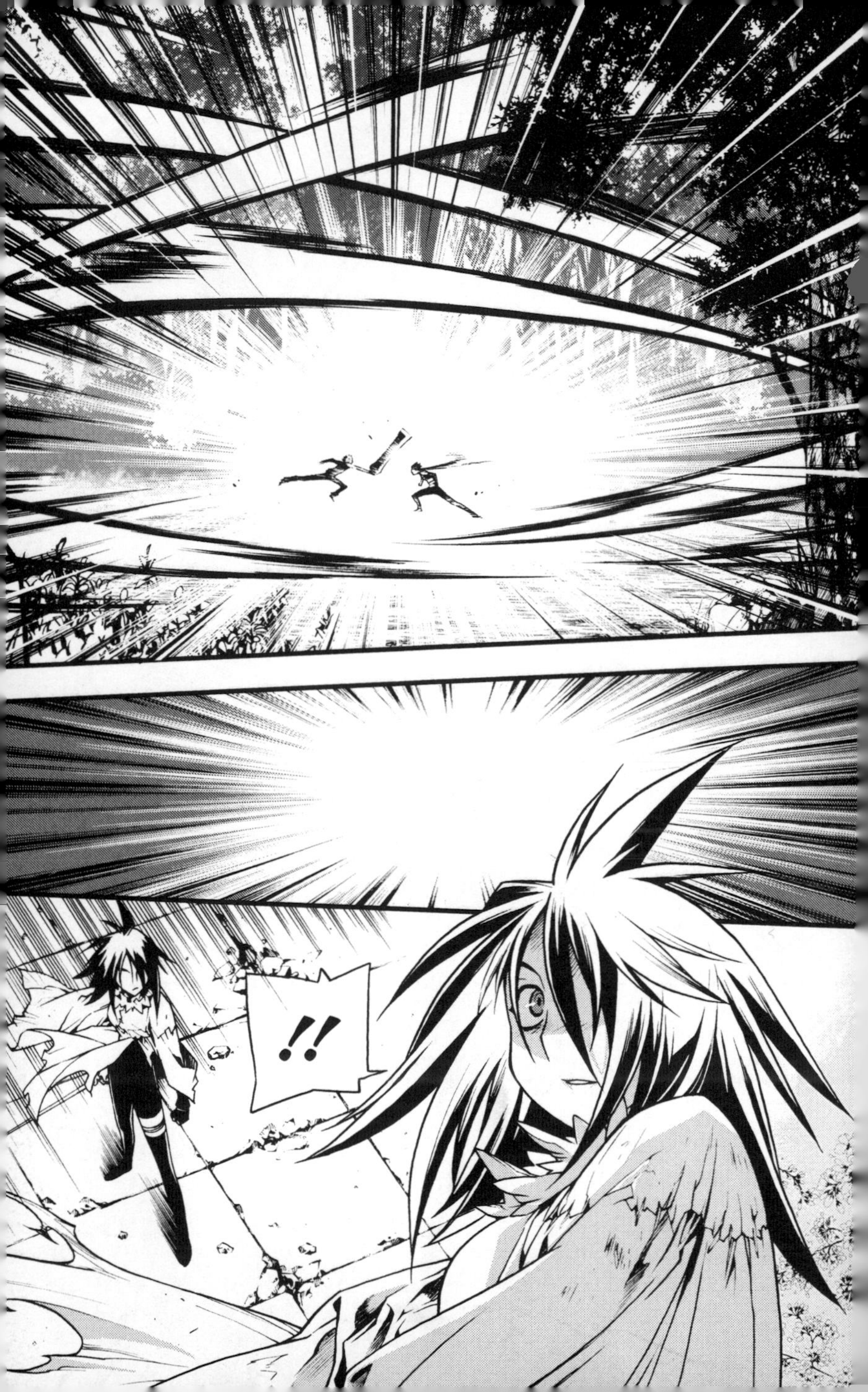
!!

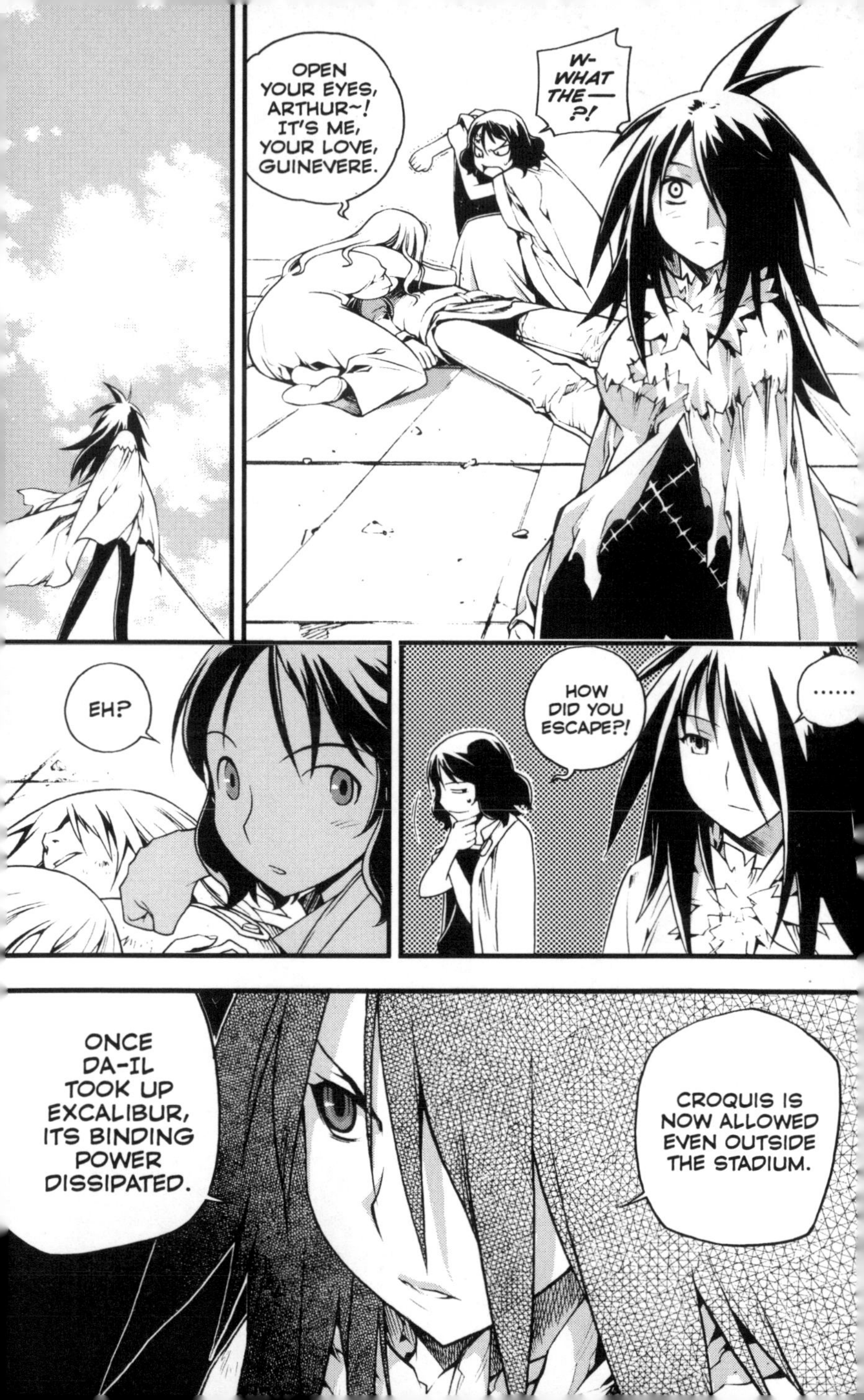
OPEN YOUR EYES, ARTHUR~! IT'S ME, YOUR LOVE, GUINEVERE.
W-WHAT THE—?!
EH?
HOW DID YOU ESCAPE?!
......
ONCE DA-IL TOOK UP EXCALIBUR, ITS BINDING POWER DISSIPATED.
CROQUIS IS NOW ALLOWED EVEN OUTSIDE THE STADIUM.

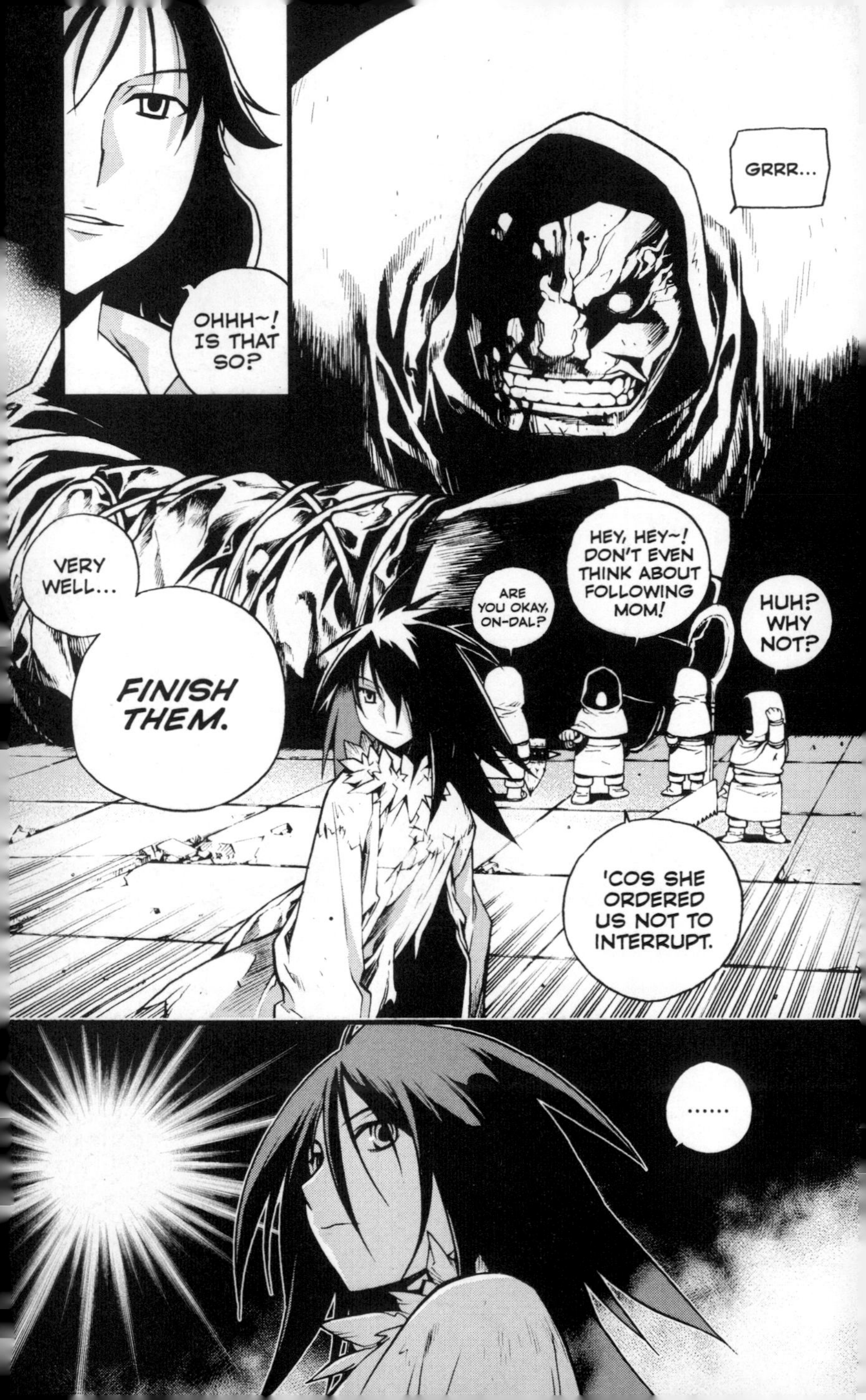
OHHH~! IS THAT SO?
GRRR...
VERY WELL...
FINISH THEM.
ARE YOU OKAY, ON-DAL?
HEY, HEY~! DON'T EVEN THINK ABOUT FOLLOWING MOM!
HUH? WHY NOT?
'COS SHE ORDERED US NOT TO INTERRUPT.
......

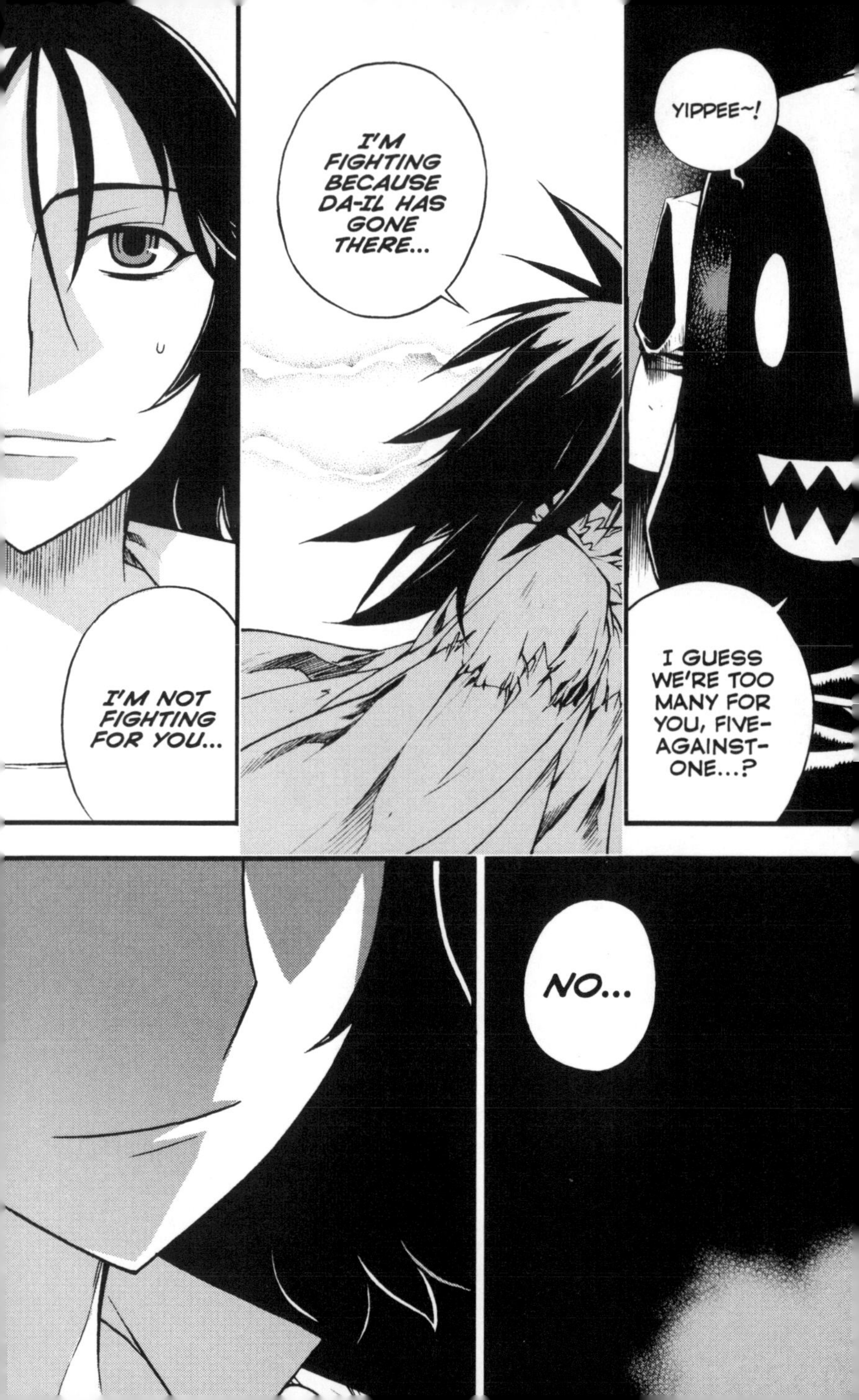
I'M NOT FIGHTING FOR YOU...
I'M FIGHTING BECAUSE DA-IL HAS GONE THERE...
YIPPEE~!
I GUESS WE'RE TOO MANY FOR YOU, FIVE-AGAINST-ONE...?
NO...

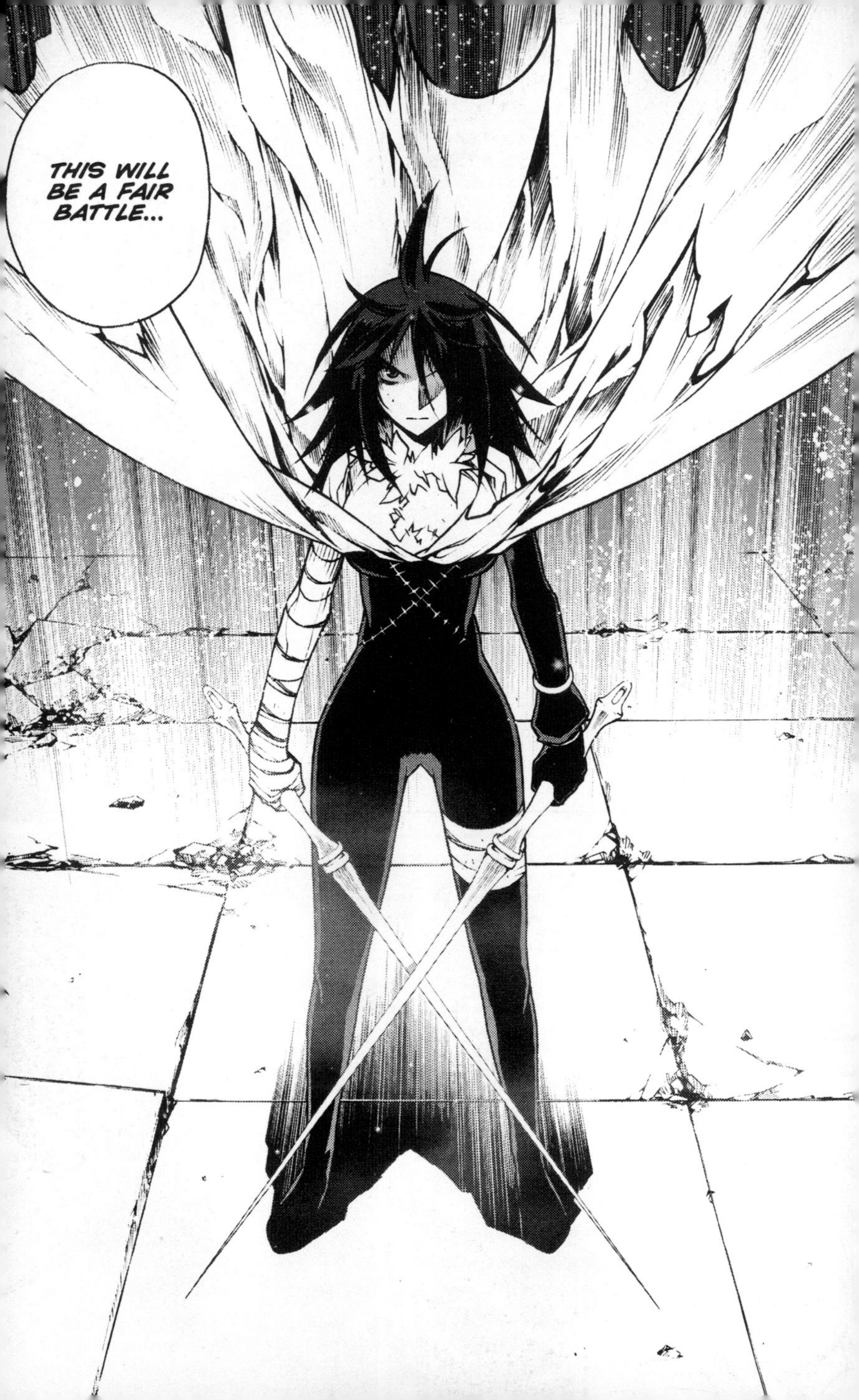
THIS WILL BE A FAIR BATTLE...

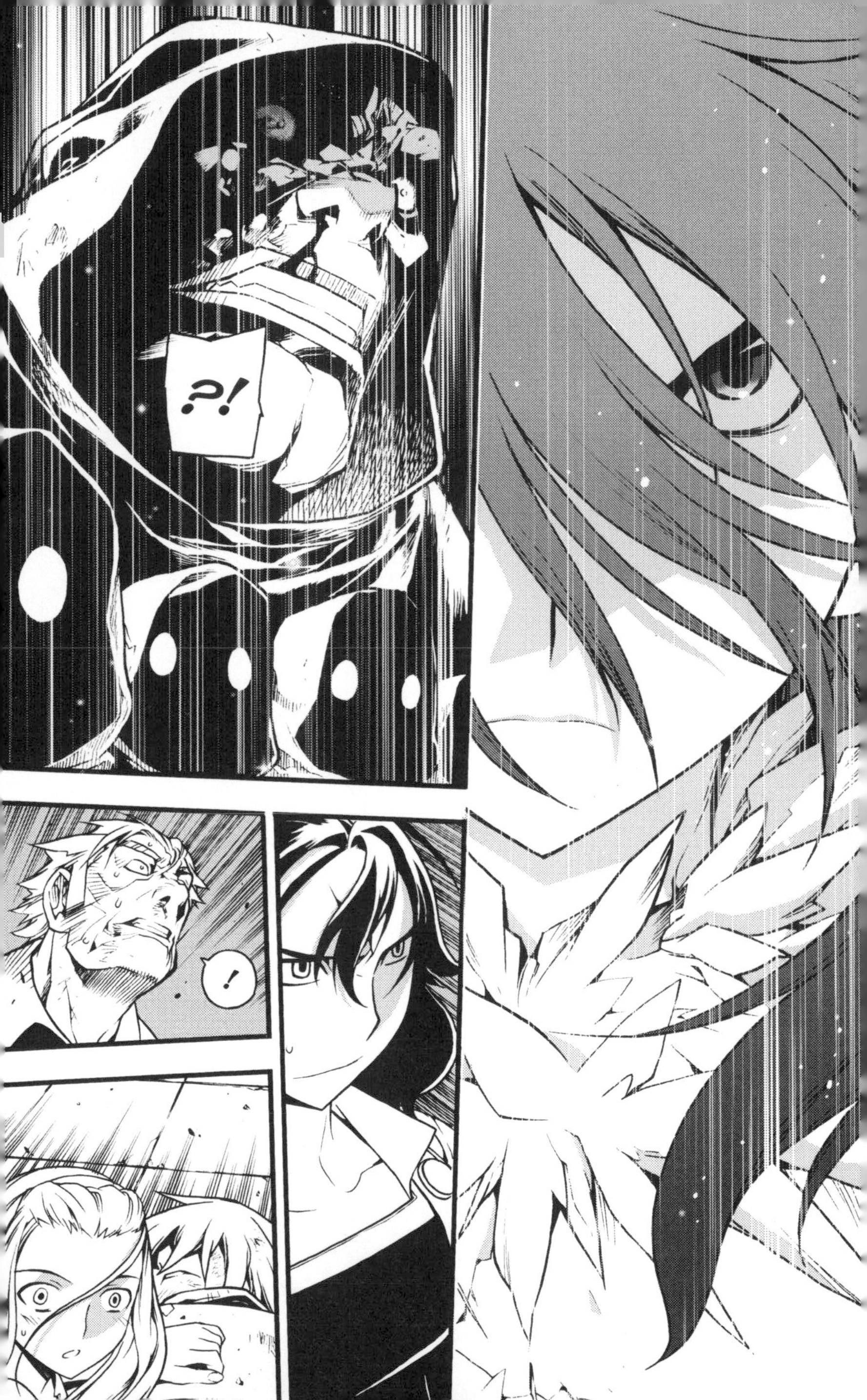
?!
!

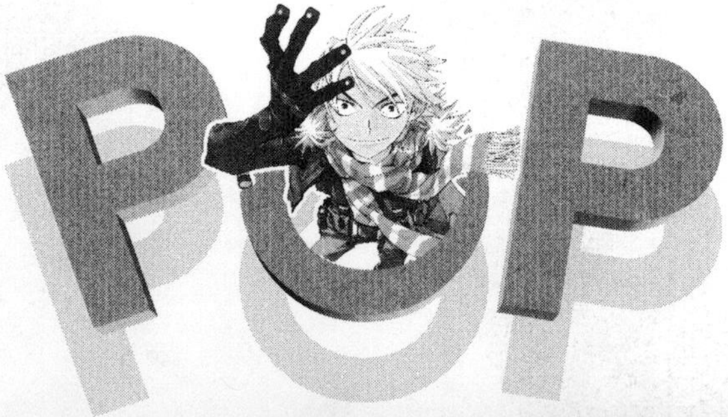
POP

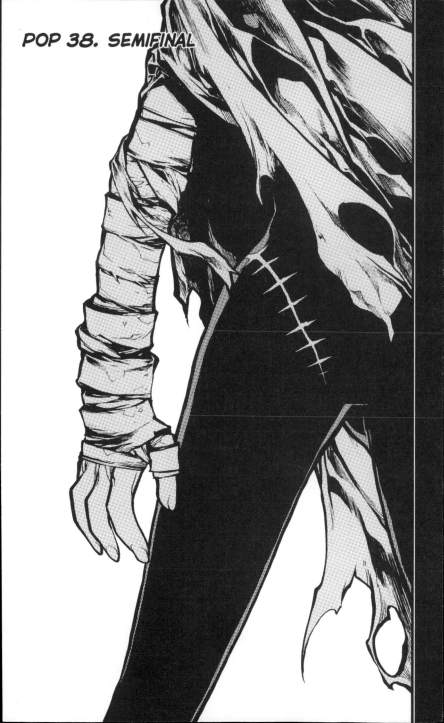

POP 38. SEMIFINAL

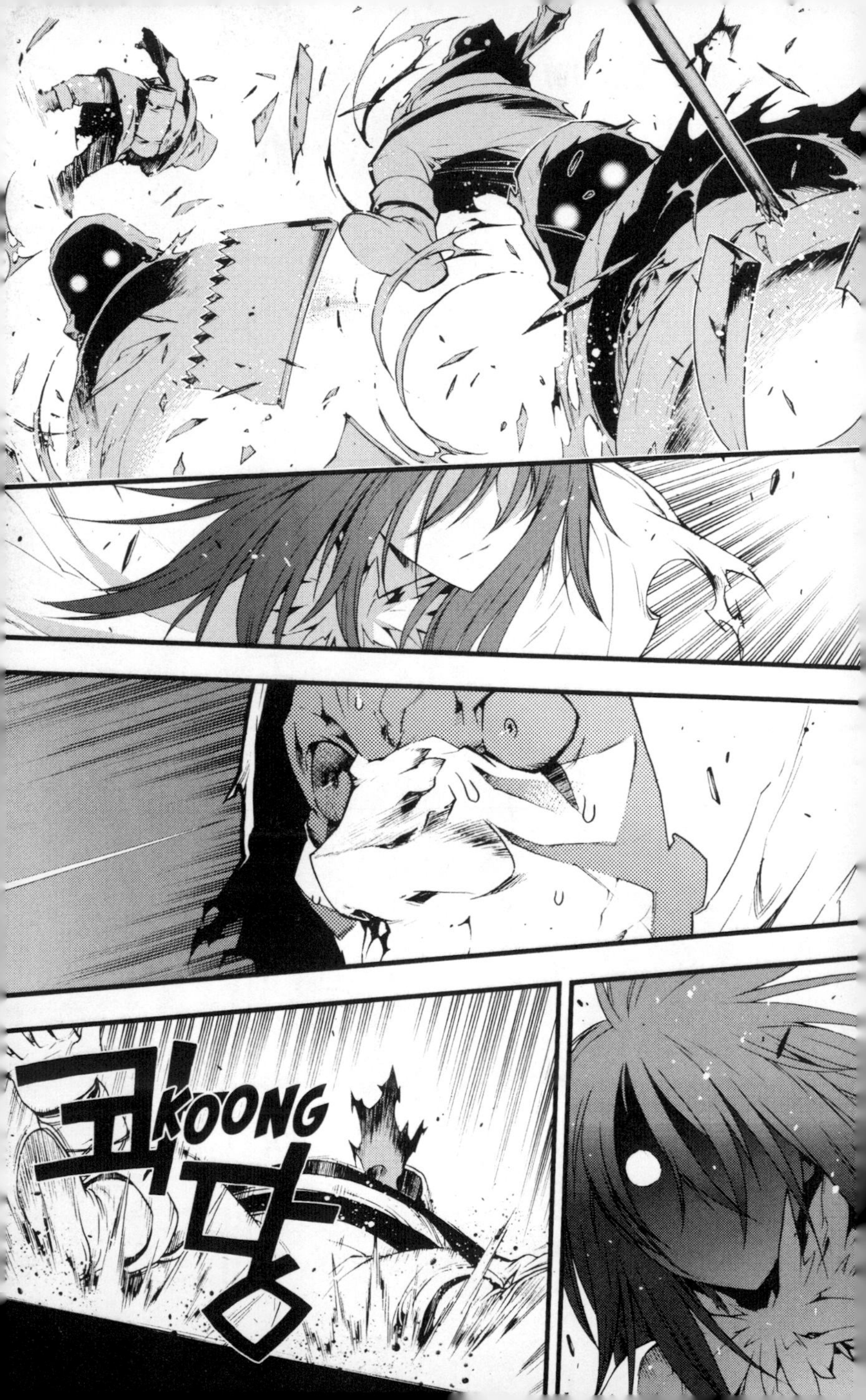
쾅
KOONG

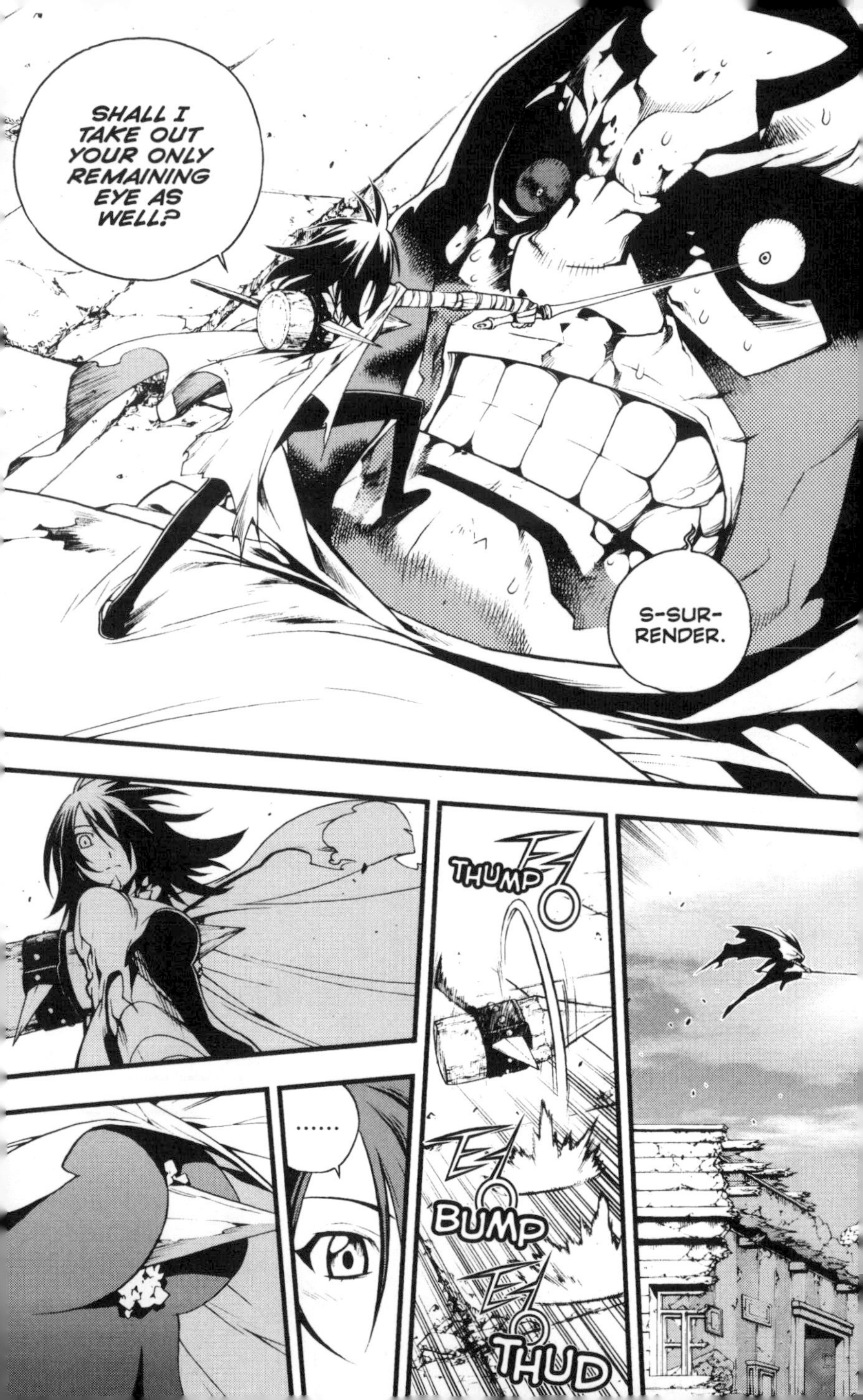
SHALL I TAKE OUT YOUR ONLY REMAINING EYE AS WELL?
S-SUR-RENDER.
THUMP
BUMP
THUD
......

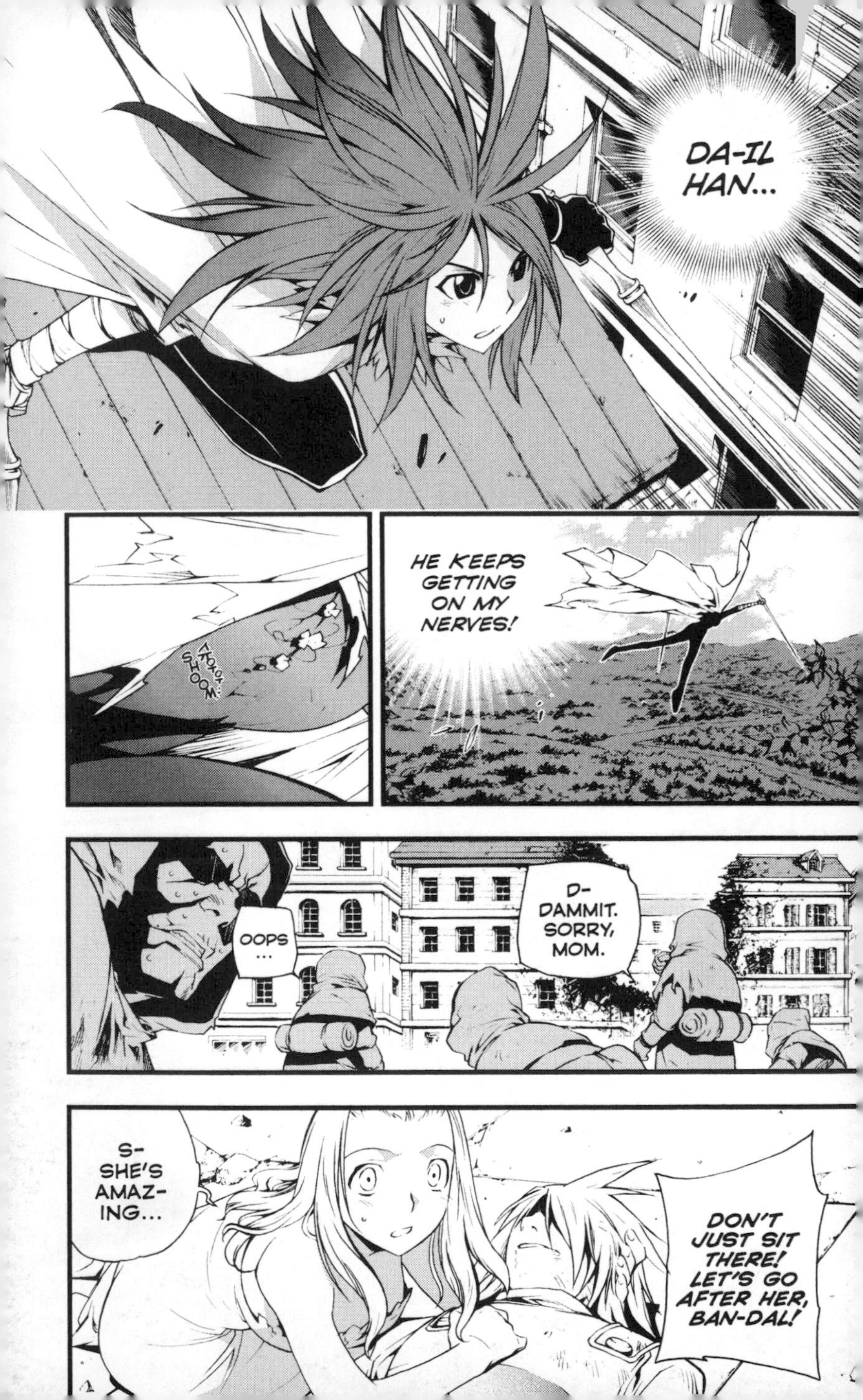
DA-IL HAN...
SHOOM
HE KEEPS GETTING ON MY NERVES!
OOPS ...
D-DAMMIT. SORRY, MOM.
S-SHE'S AMAZ-ING...
DON'T JUST SIT THERE! LET'S GO AFTER HER, BAN-DAL!

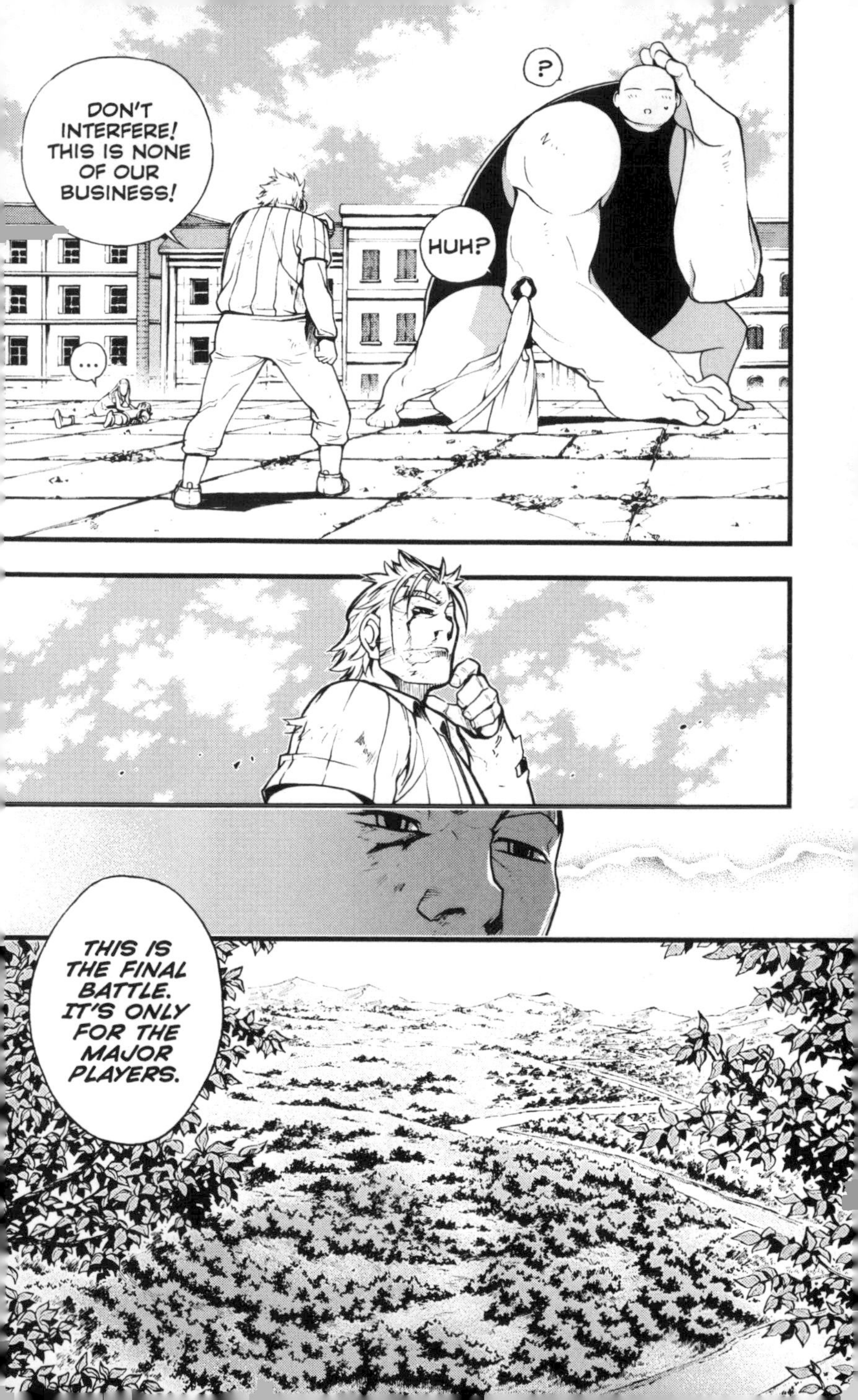
DON'T INTERFERE! THIS IS NONE OF OUR BUSINESS!
?
HUH?
...
THIS IS THE FINAL BATTLE. IT'S ONLY FOR THE MAJOR PLAYERS.

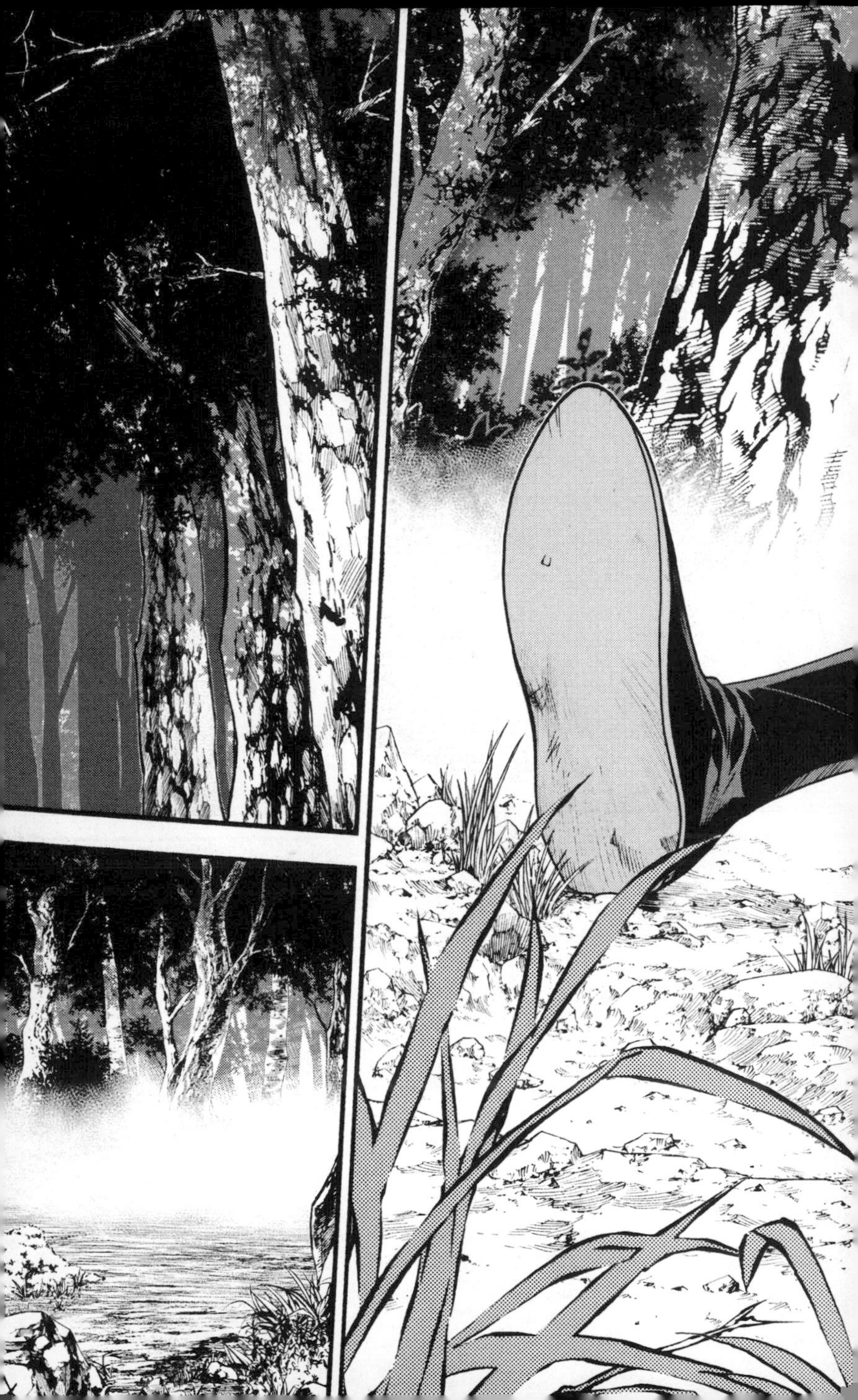

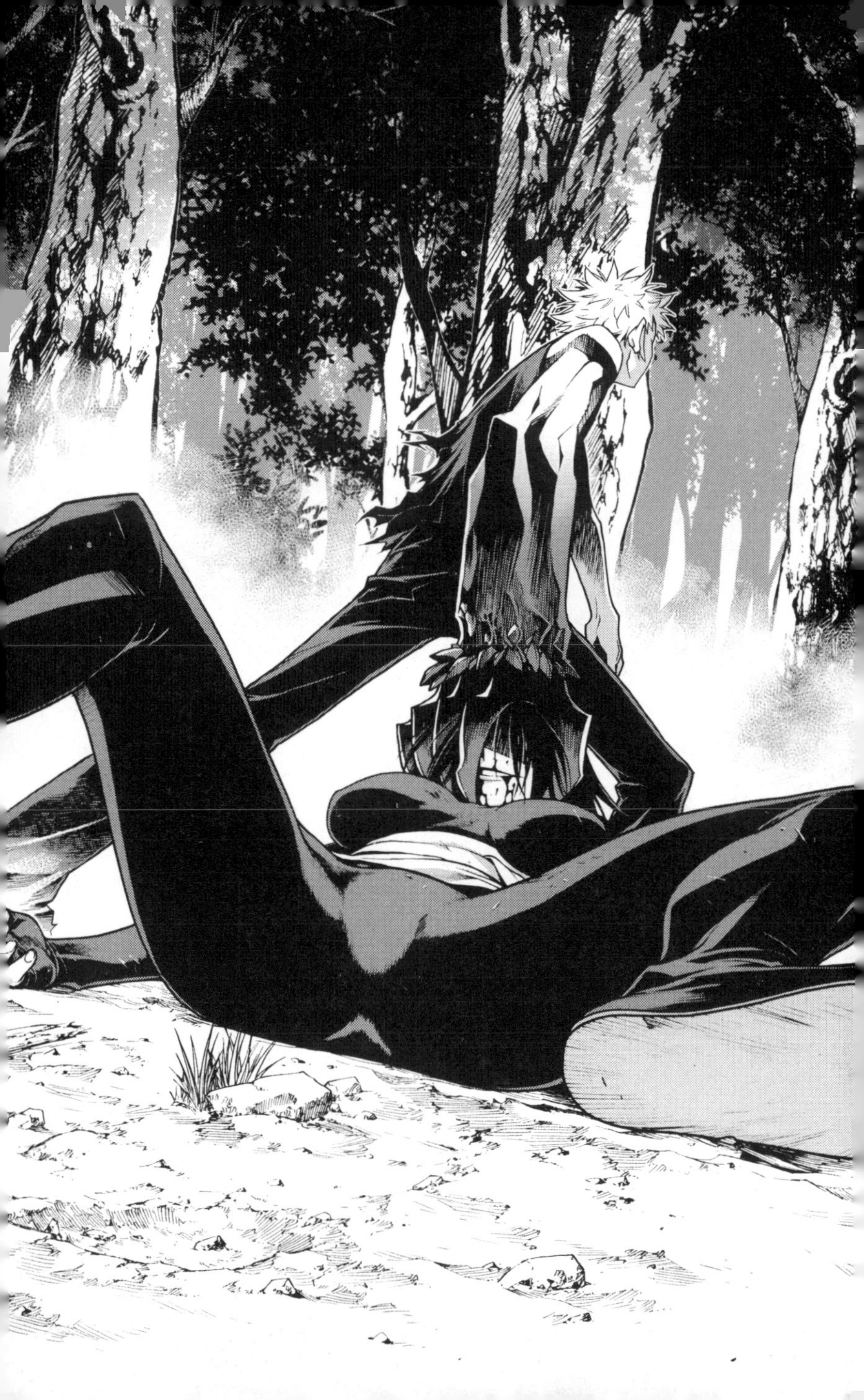

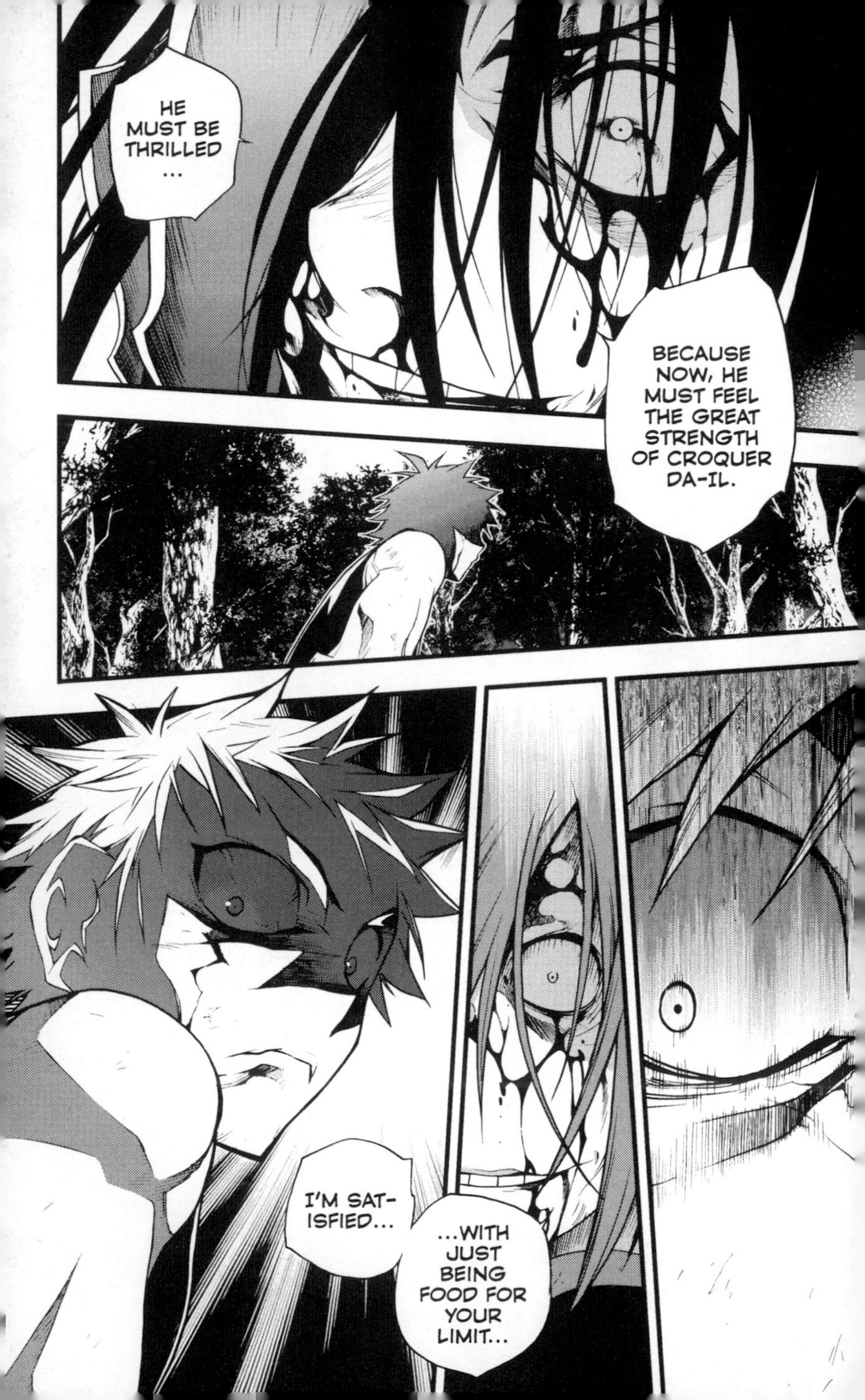
HE MUST BE THRILLED ...
BECAUSE NOW, HE MUST FEEL THE GREAT STRENGTH OF CROQUER DA-IL.
I'M SAT-ISFIED...
...WITH JUST BEING FOOD FOR YOUR LIMIT...

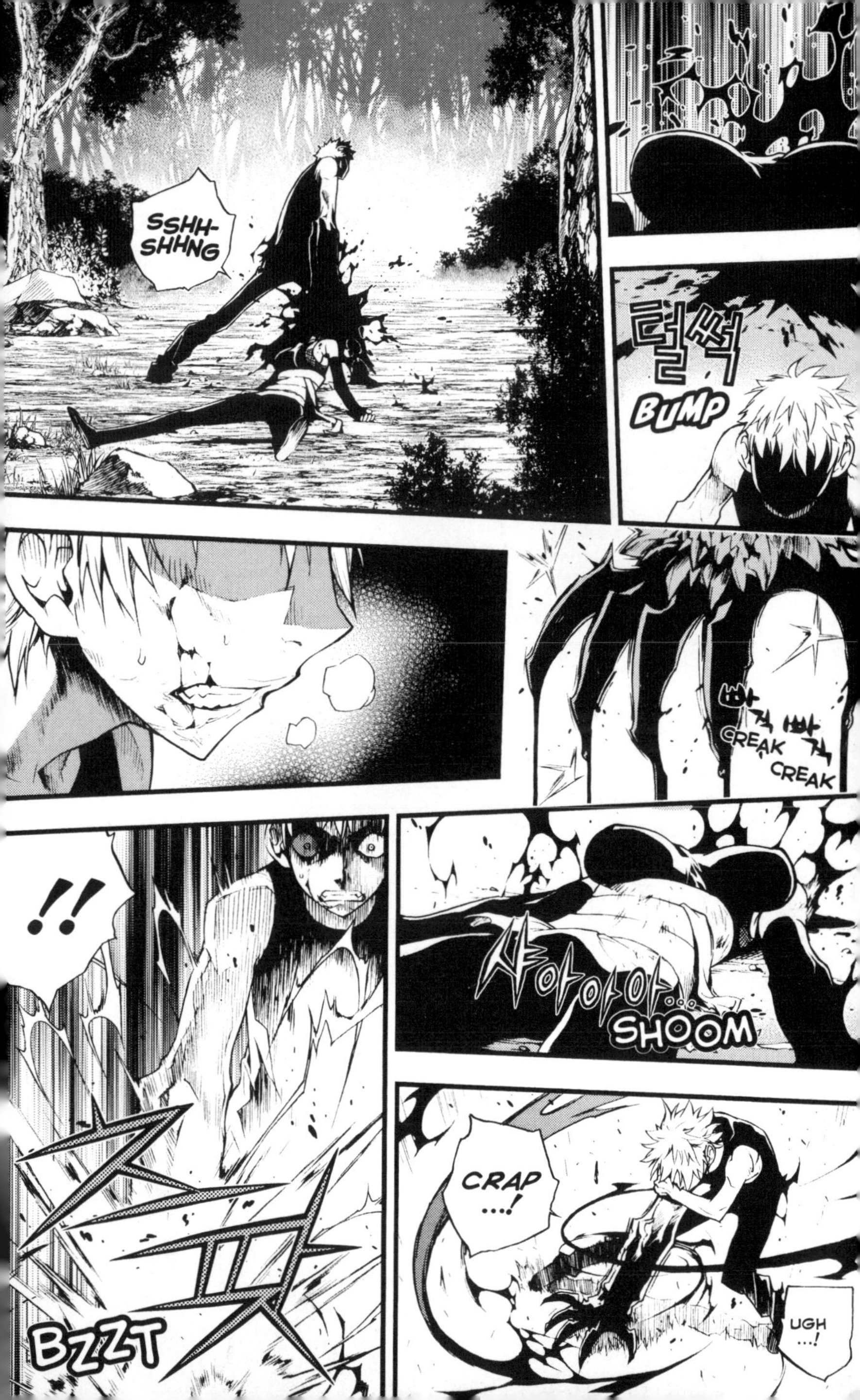
SSHH-SHHNG
털썩
BUMP
빠직 빠직
CREAK
CREAK
!!
BZZT
샤아아아...
SHOOM
CRAP ...!
UGH ...!

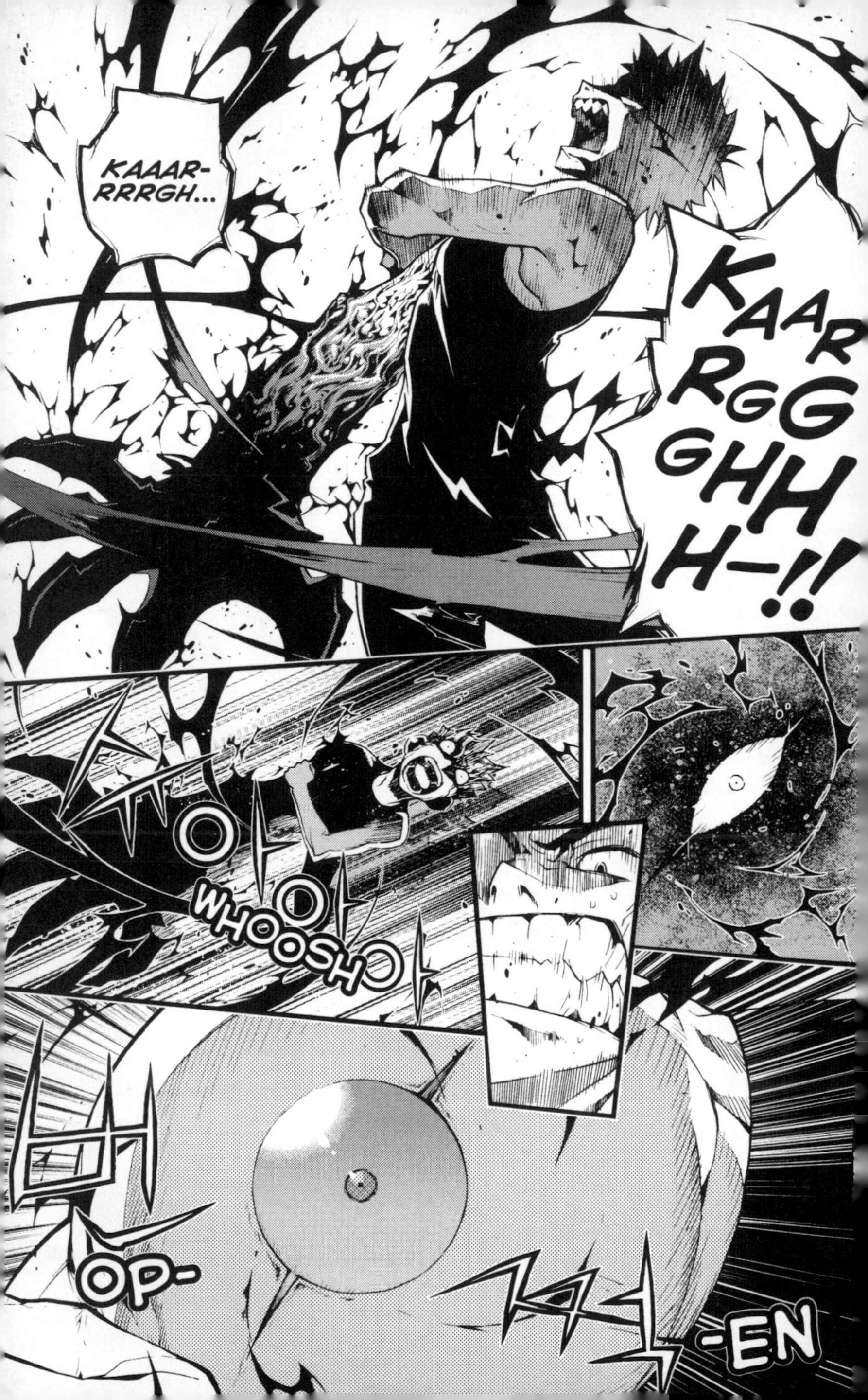
KAAAR-RRRGH...
KAARRGGGHHH–!!
WHOOSH
OP-
-EN

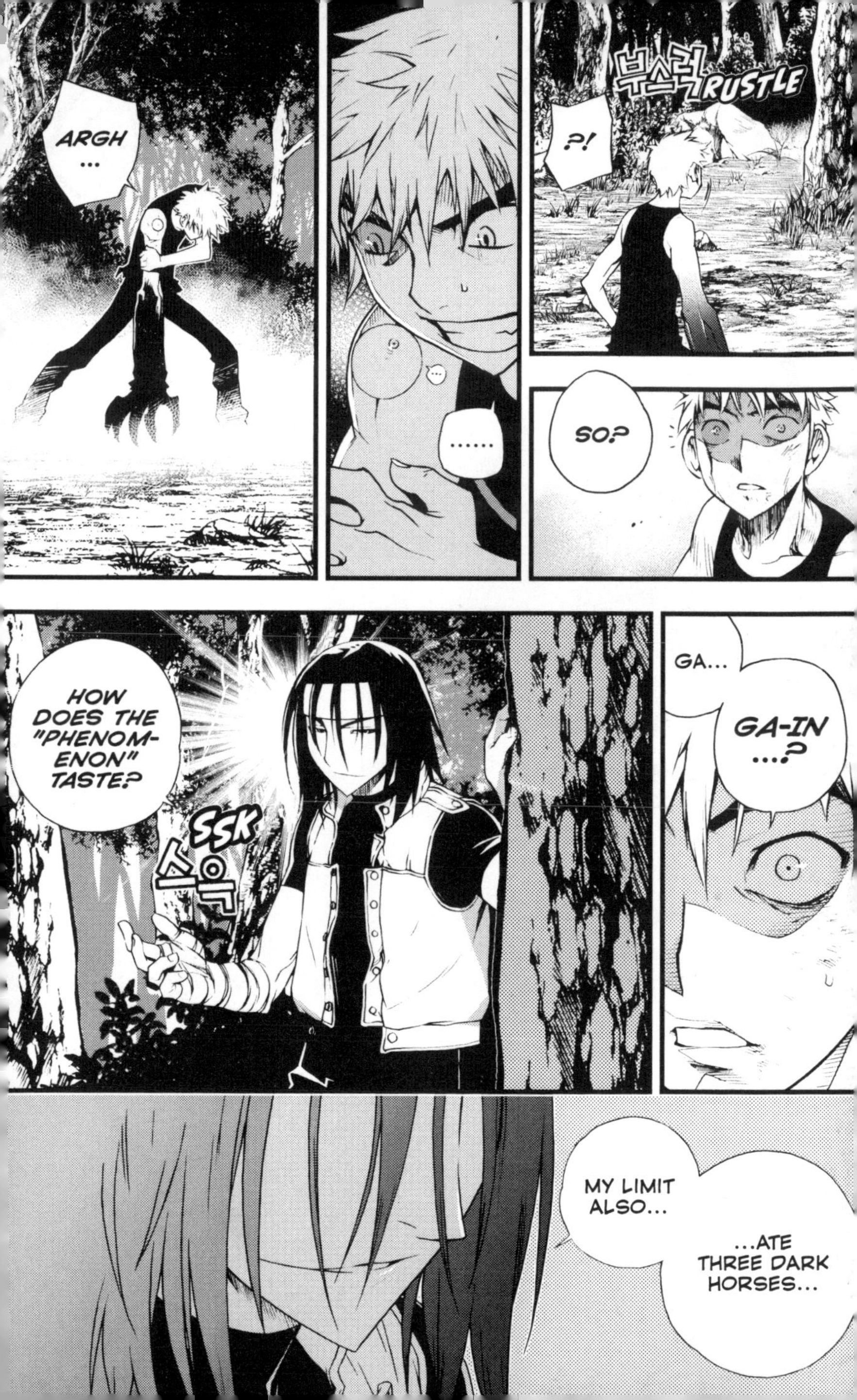
ARGH ...
......
....
부스럭 RUSTLE
?!
SO?
HOW DOES THE "PHENOM-ENON" TASTE?
SSK 스윽
GA...
GA-IN ...?
MY LIMIT ALSO...
...ATE THREE DARK HORSES...

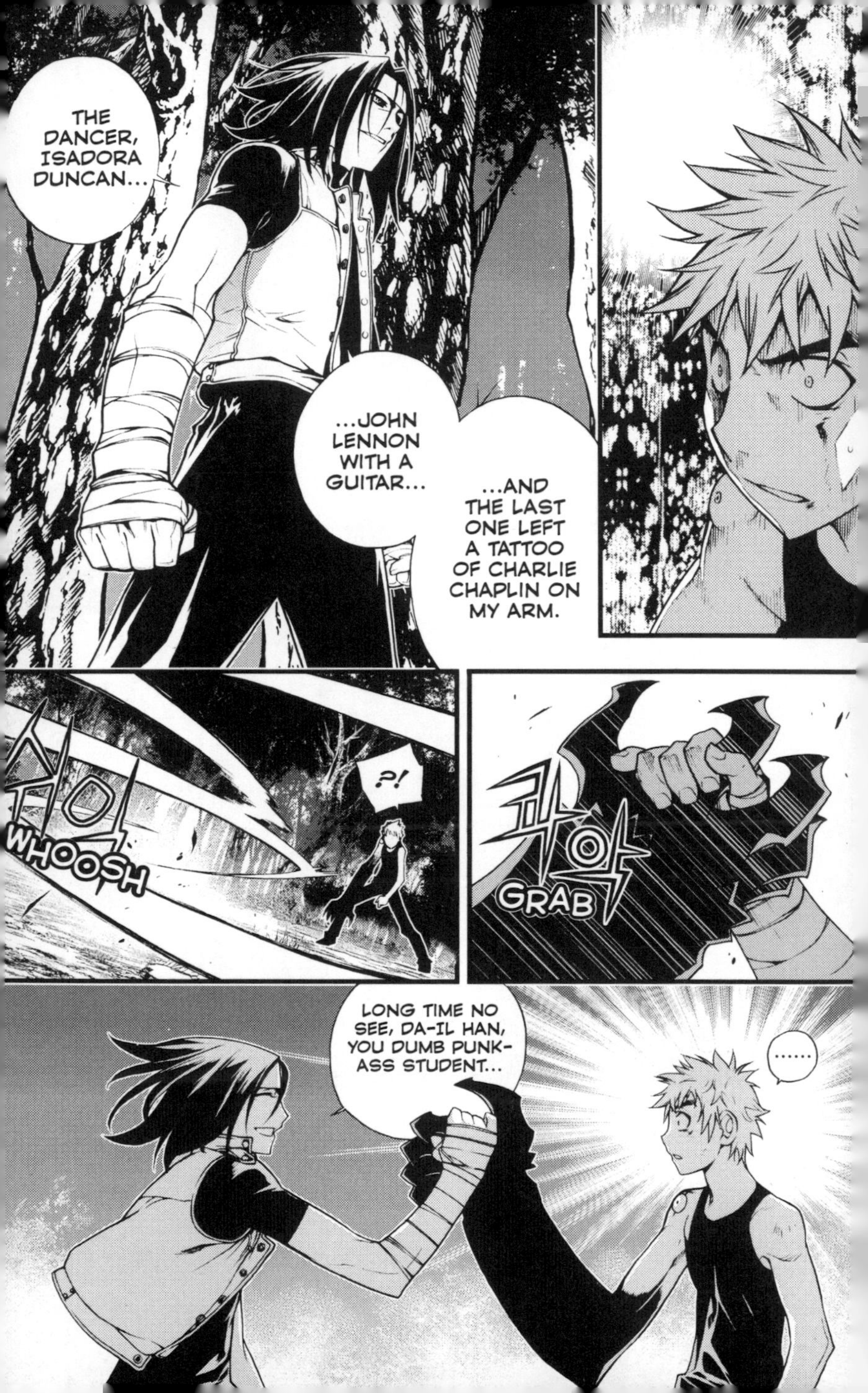
THE DANCER, ISADORA DUNCAN...
...JOHN LENNON WITH A GUITAR...
...AND THE LAST ONE LEFT A TATTOO OF CHARLIE CHAPLIN ON MY ARM.
WHOOSH
?!
GRAB
LONG TIME NO SEE, DA-IL HAN, YOU DUMB PUNK-ASS STUDENT...
......

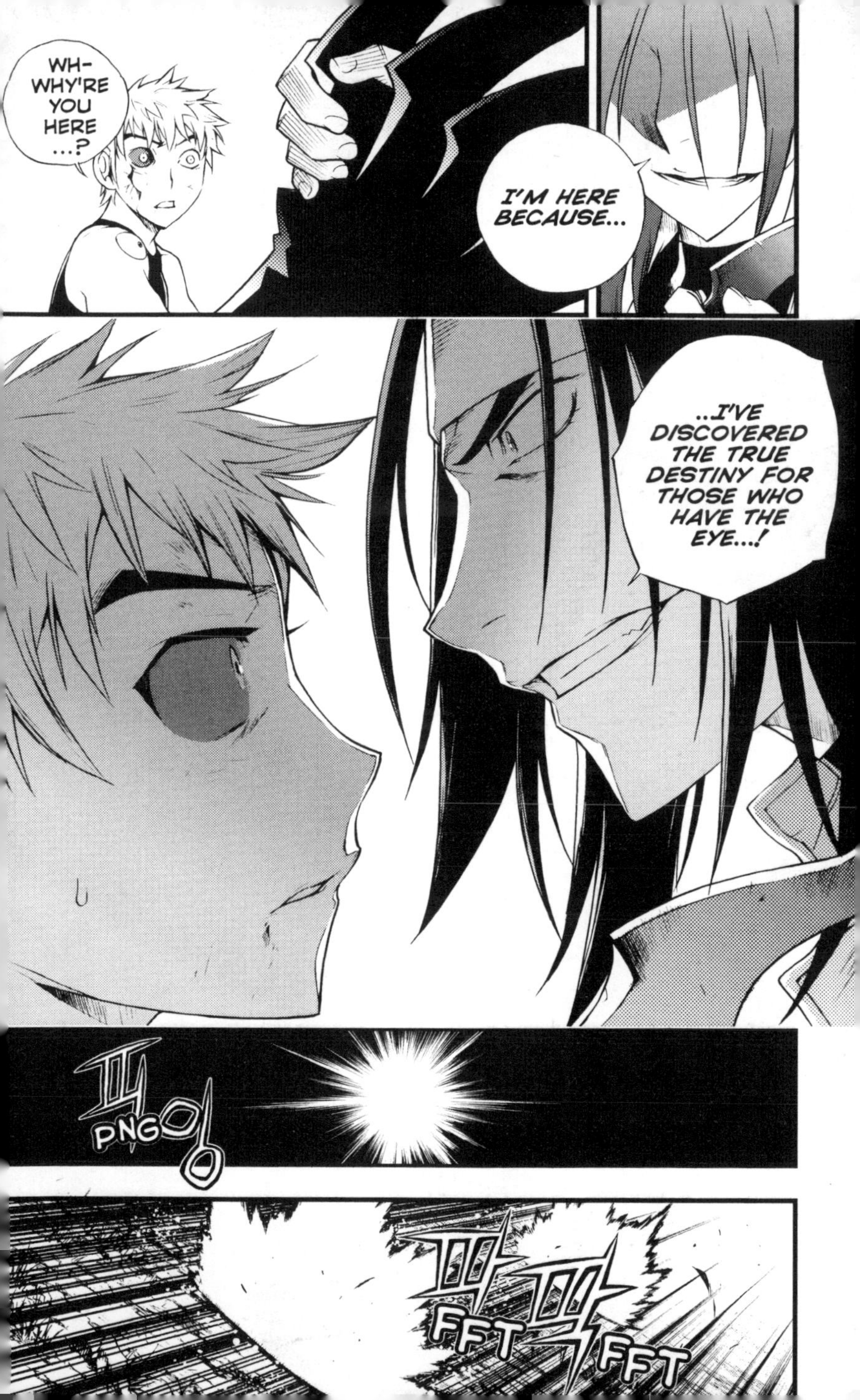
WH- WHY'RE YOU HERE ...?
I'M HERE BECAUSE...
...I'VE DISCOVERED THE TRUE DESTINY FOR THOSE WHO HAVE THE EYE...!
PNG
FFT
FFT

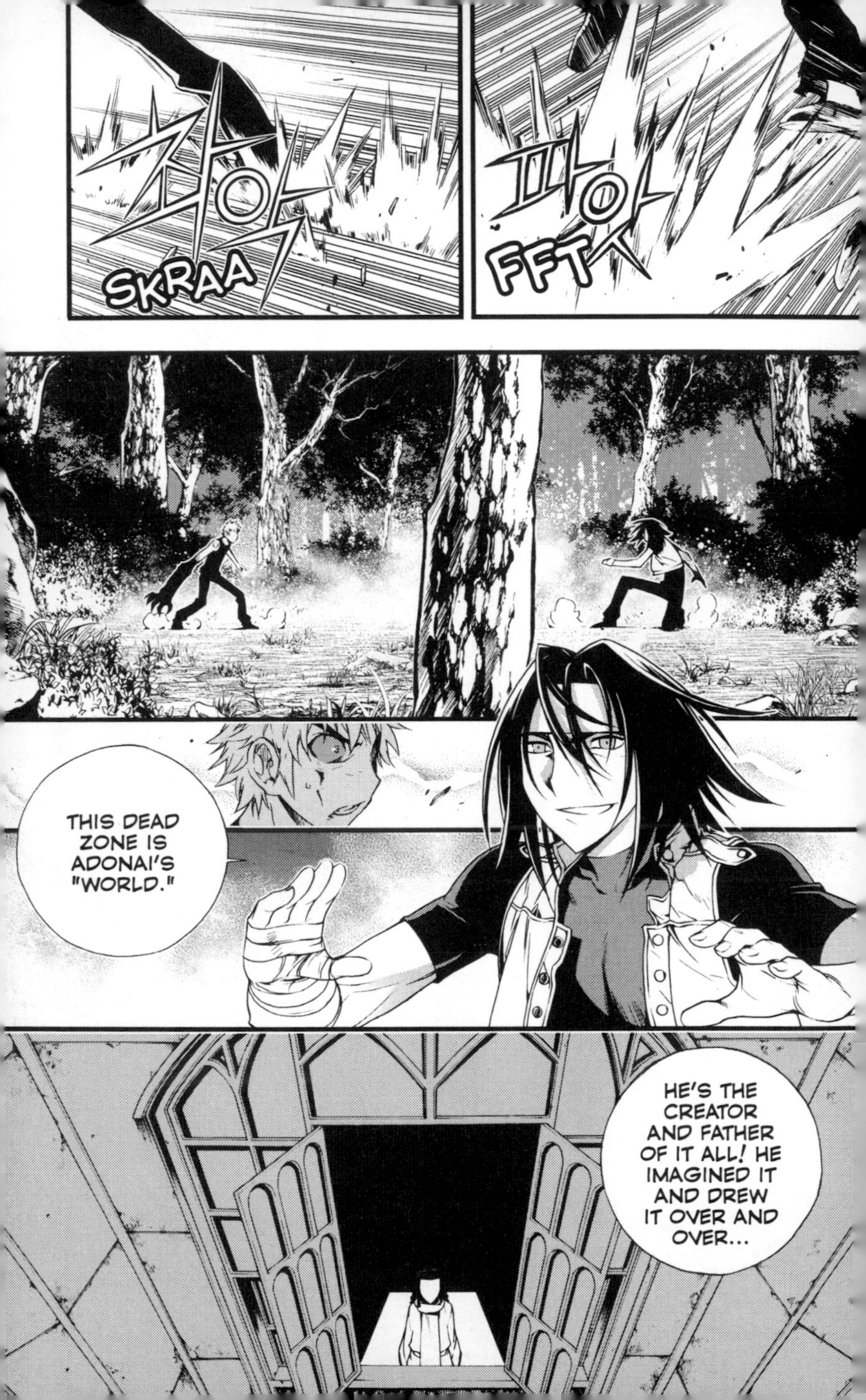
SKRAA
FFT
THIS DEAD ZONE IS ADONAI'S "WORLD."
HE'S THE CREATOR AND FATHER OF IT ALL! HE IMAGINED IT AND DREW IT OVER AND OVER...

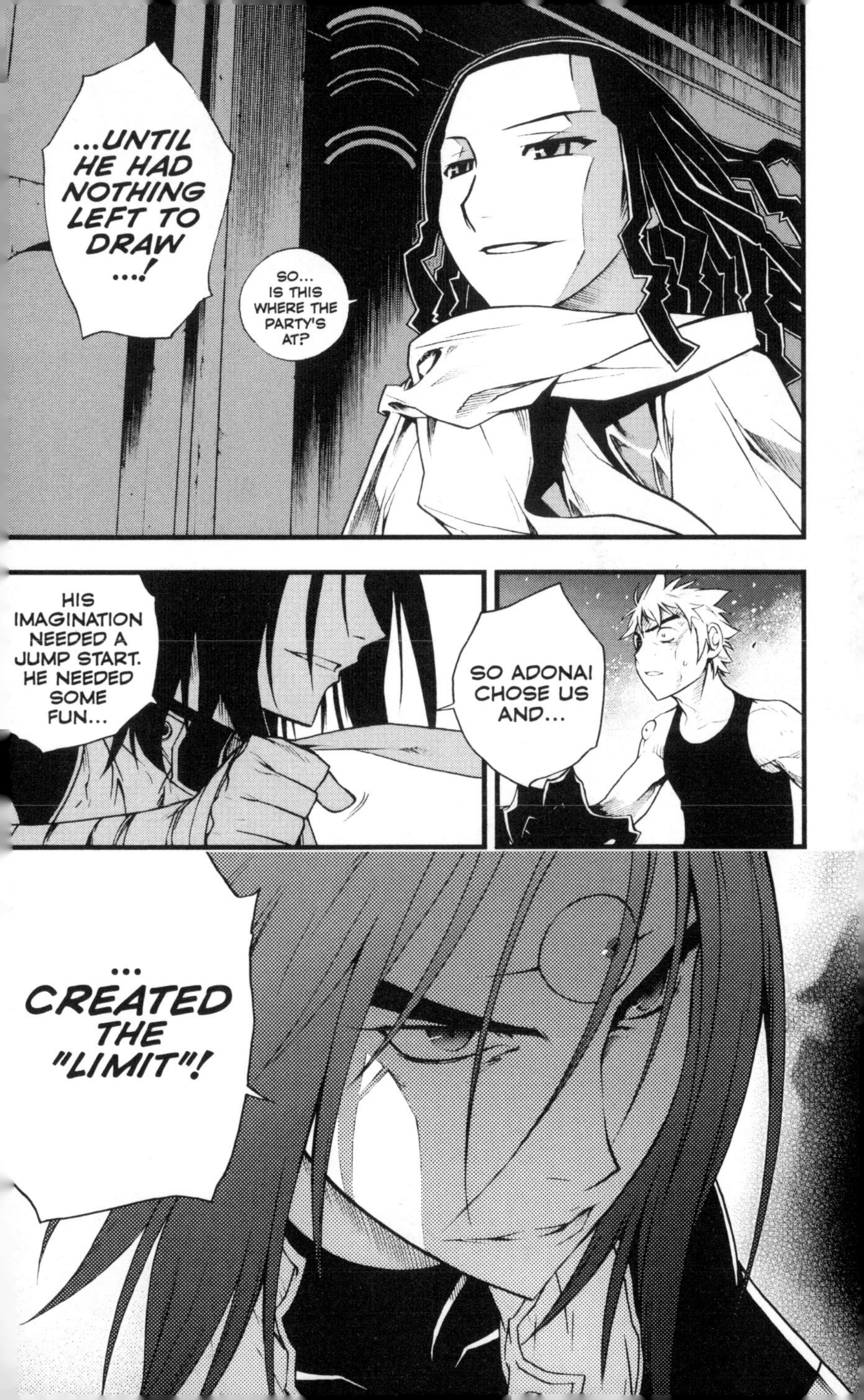
...UNTIL HE HAD NOTHING LEFT TO DRAW ...!
SO... IS THIS WHERE THE PARTY'S AT?
HIS IMAGINATION NEEDED A JUMP START. HE NEEDED SOME FUN...
SO ADONAI CHOSE US AND...
... CREATED THE "LIMIT"!

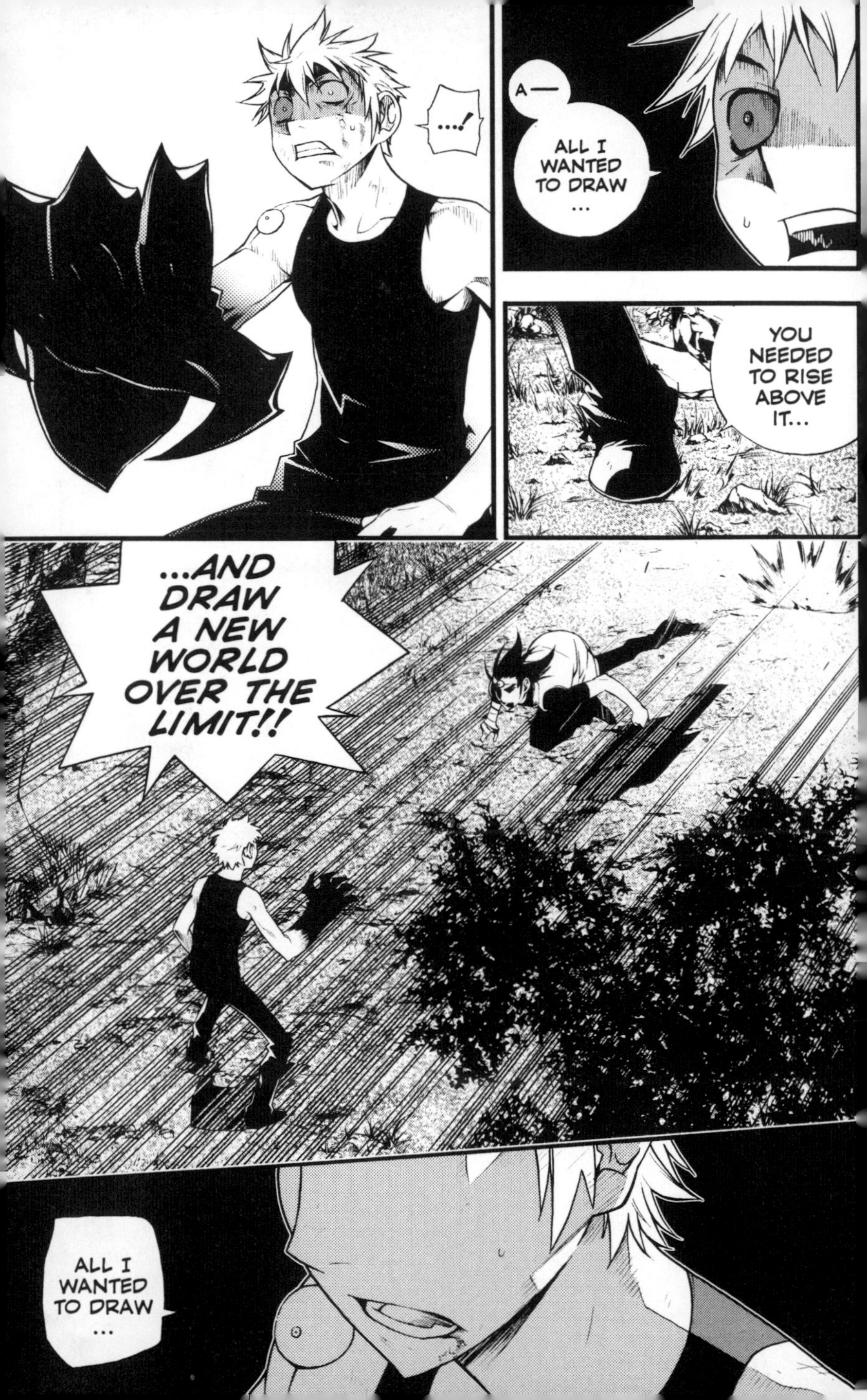
...!
A—
ALL I WANTED TO DRAW ...
YOU NEEDED TO RISE ABOVE IT...
...AND DRAW A NEW WORLD OVER THE LIMIT!!
ALL I WANTED TO DRAW ...

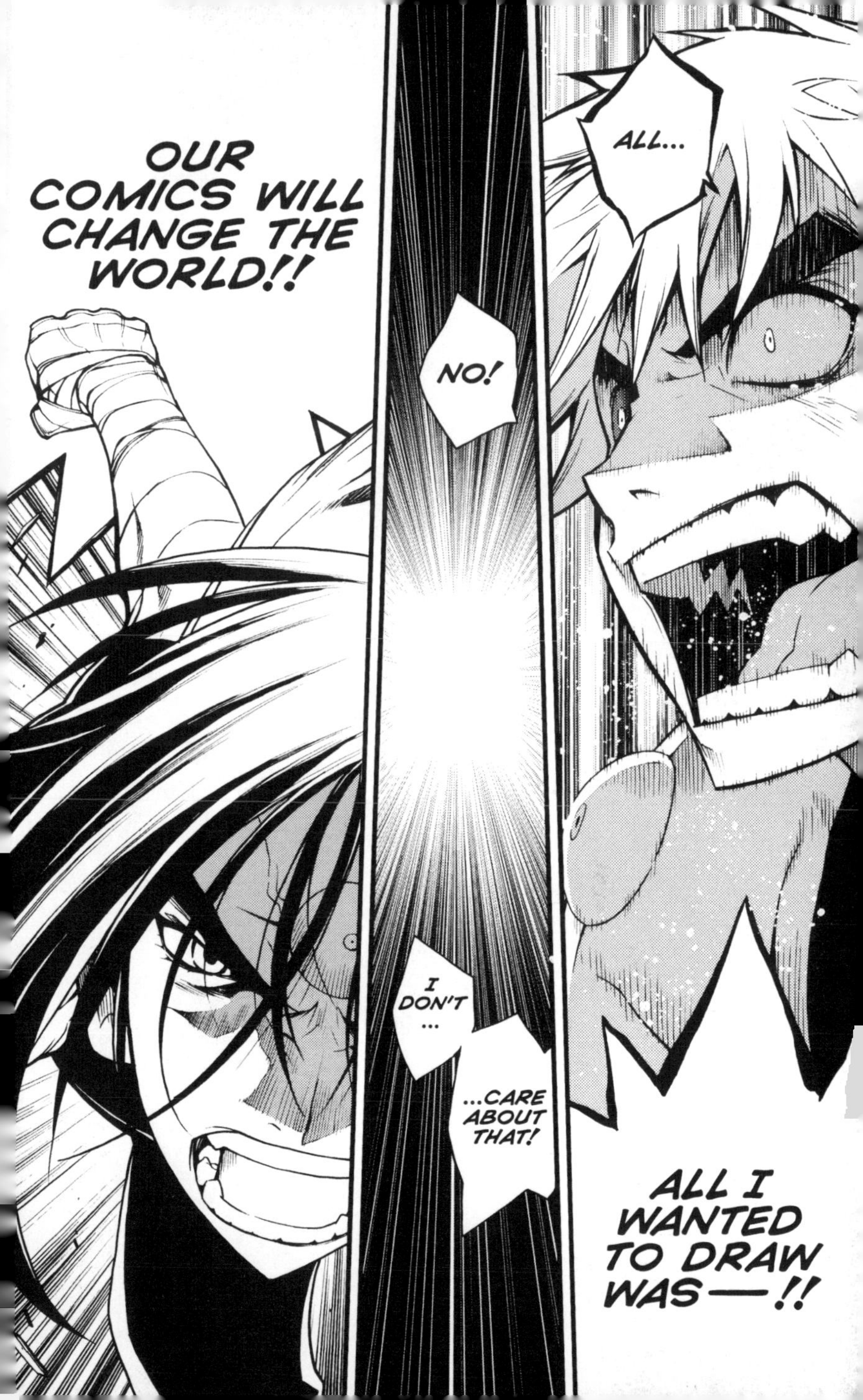
OUR COMICS WILL CHANGE THE WORLD!!
NO!
I DON'T ...
...CARE ABOUT THAT!
ALL...
ALL I WANTED TO DRAW WAS—!!

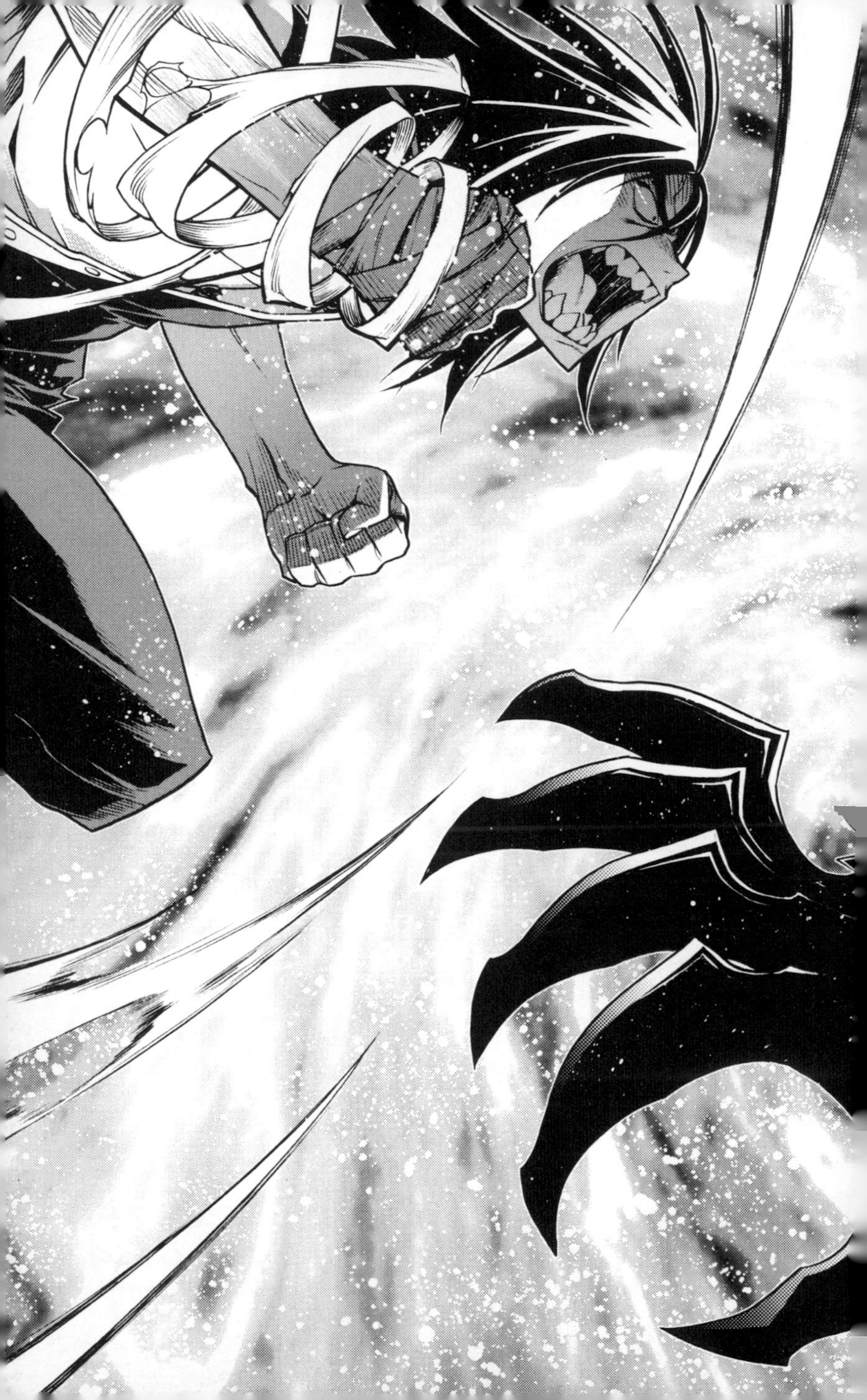

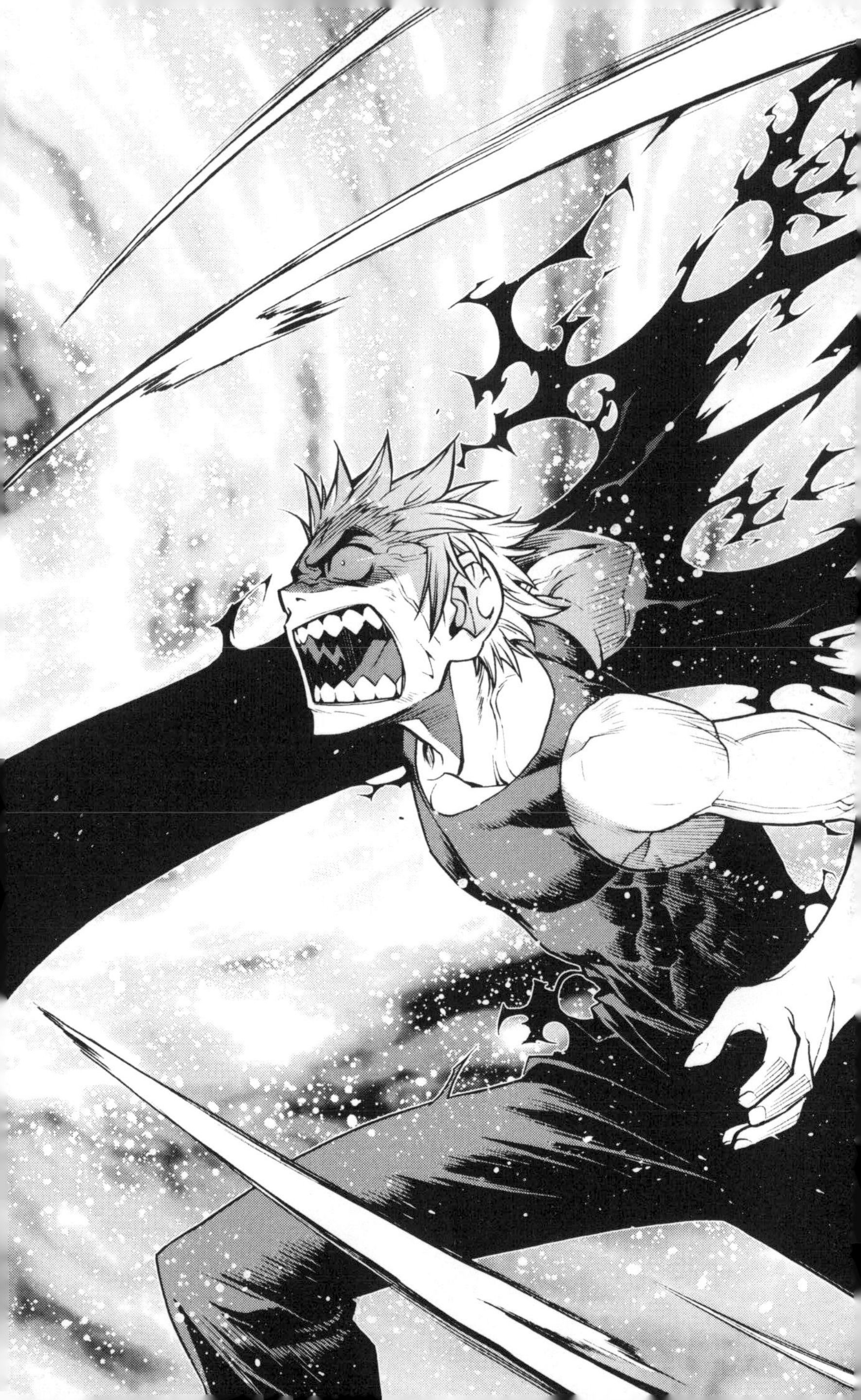

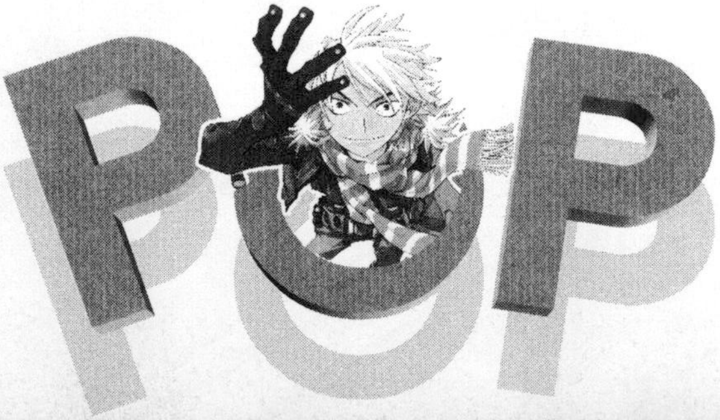
POP

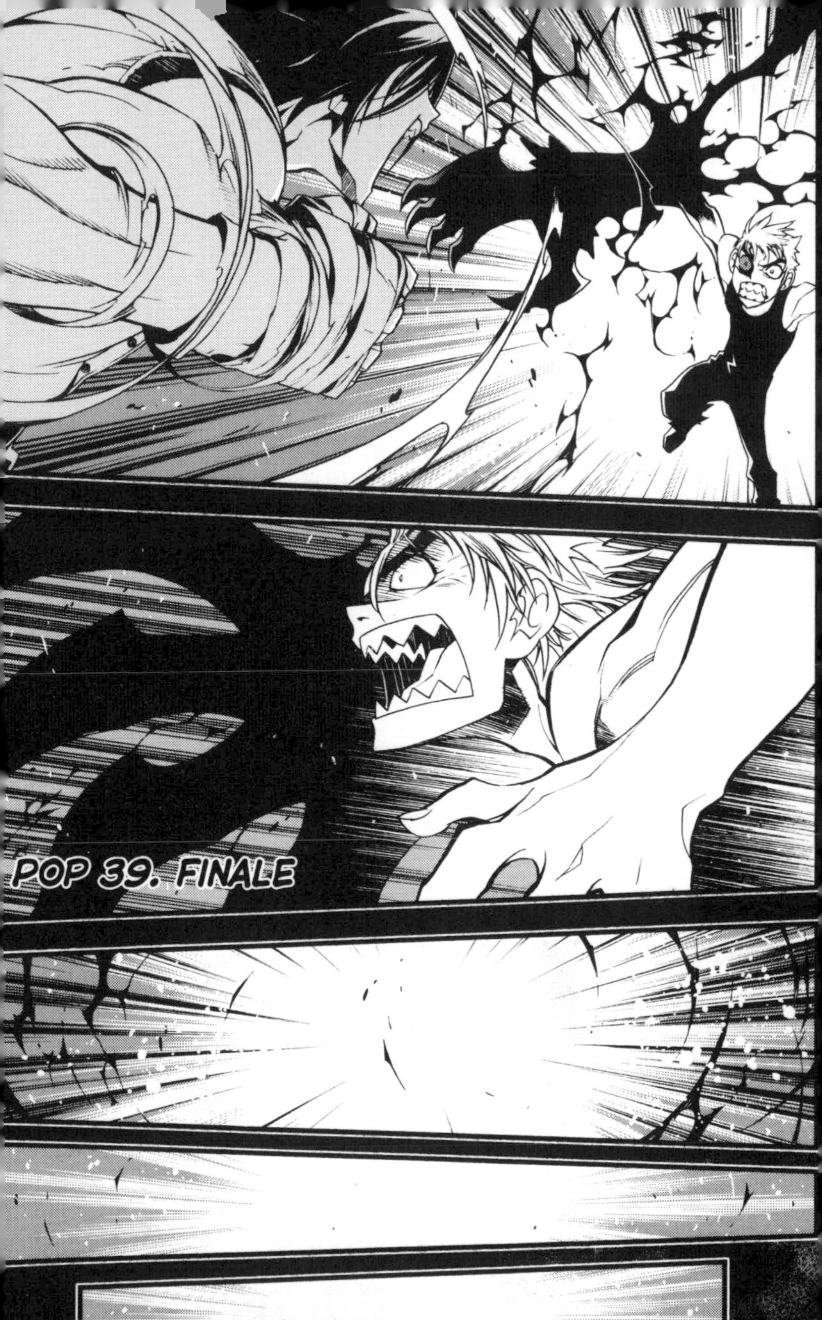
POP 39. FINALE

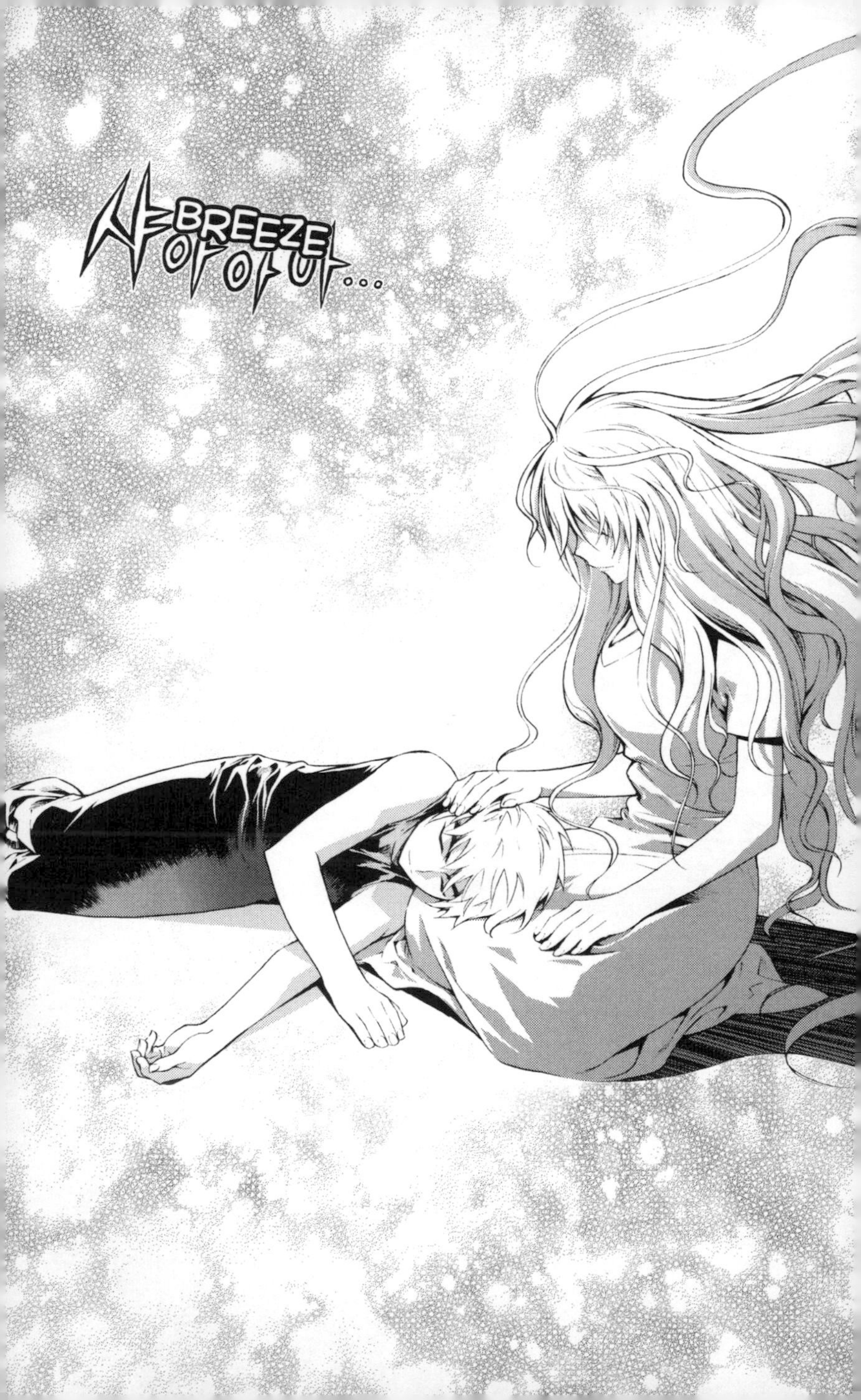
샤아아아...
BREEZE

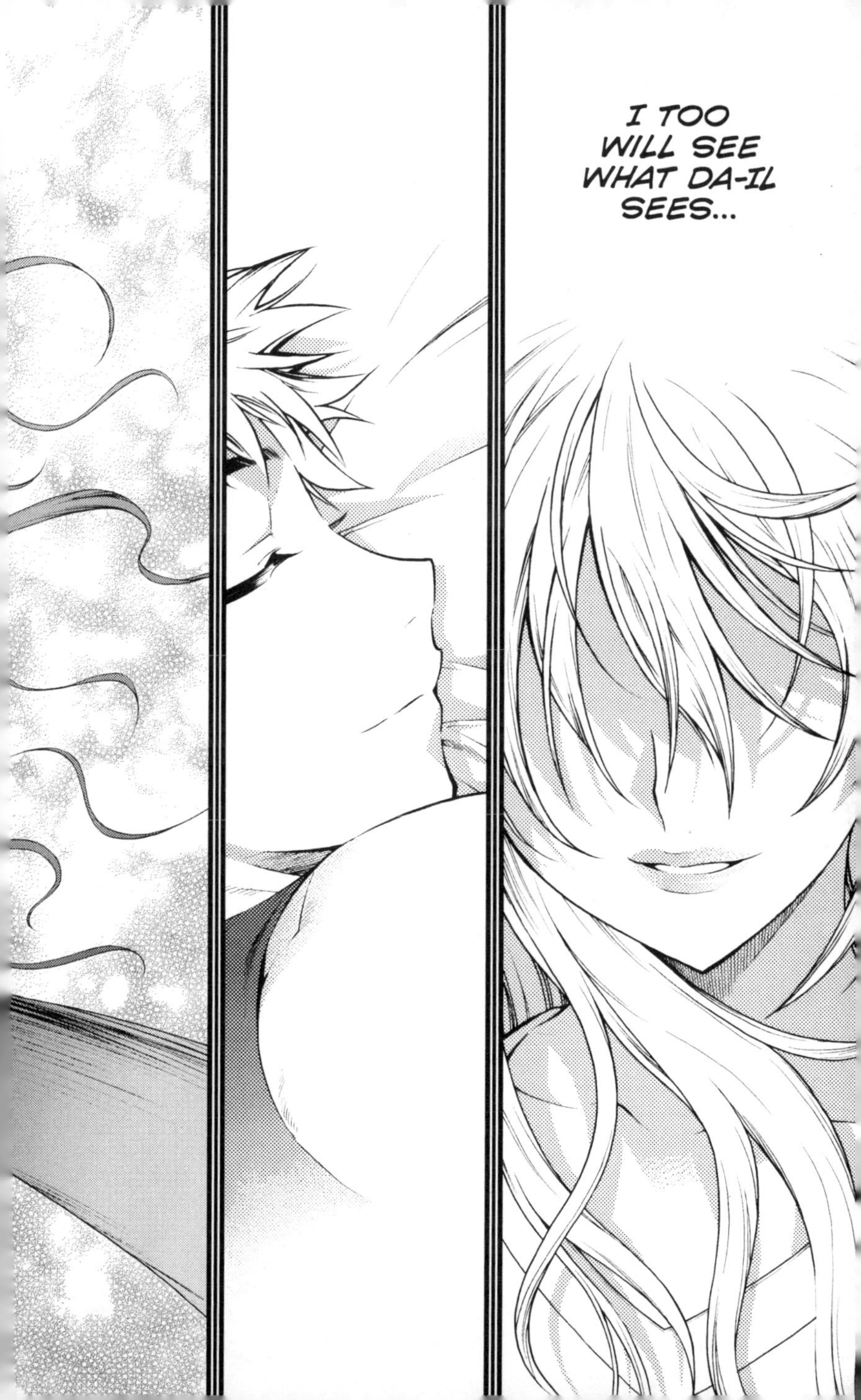
I TOO WILL SEE WHAT DA-IL SEES...

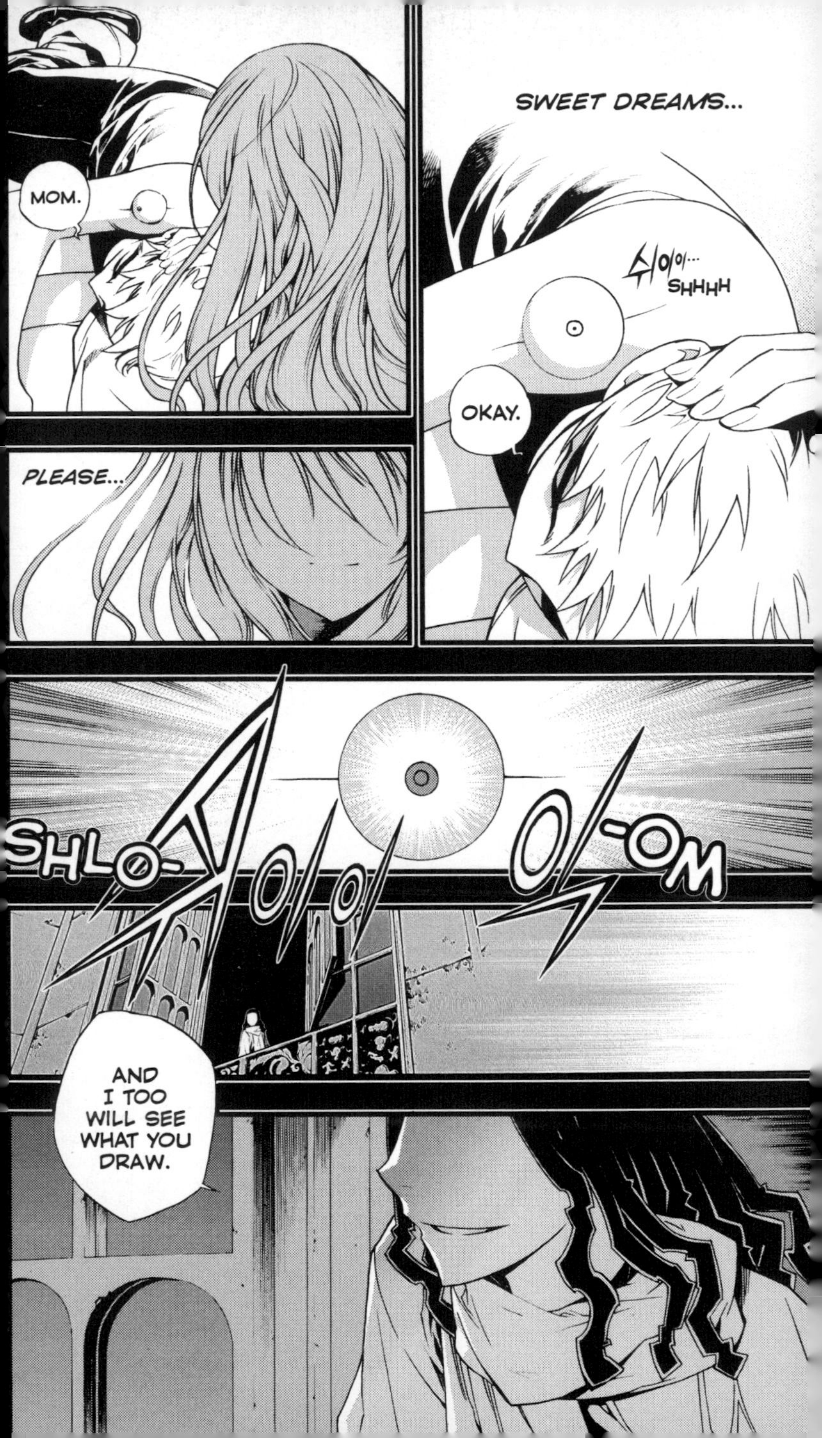
MOM.
PLEASE...
SWEET DREAMS...
쉬이이...
SHHHH
OKAY.
SHLO-
-OM
AND I TOO WILL SEE WHAT YOU DRAW.

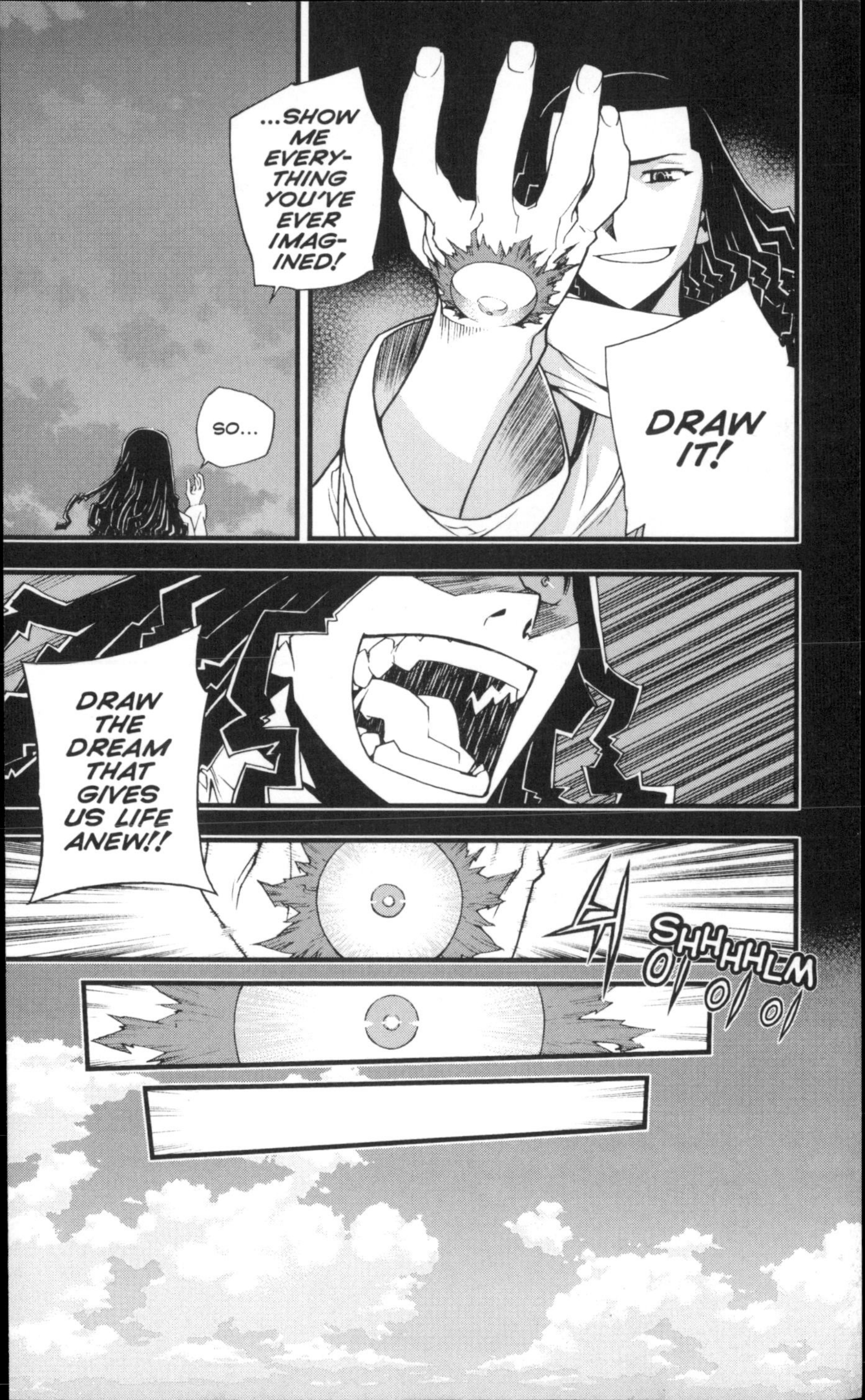
SO...
...SHOW ME EVERYTHING YOU'VE EVER IMAGINED!
DRAW IT!
DRAW THE DREAM THAT GIVES US LIFE ANEW!!
SHHHHLM

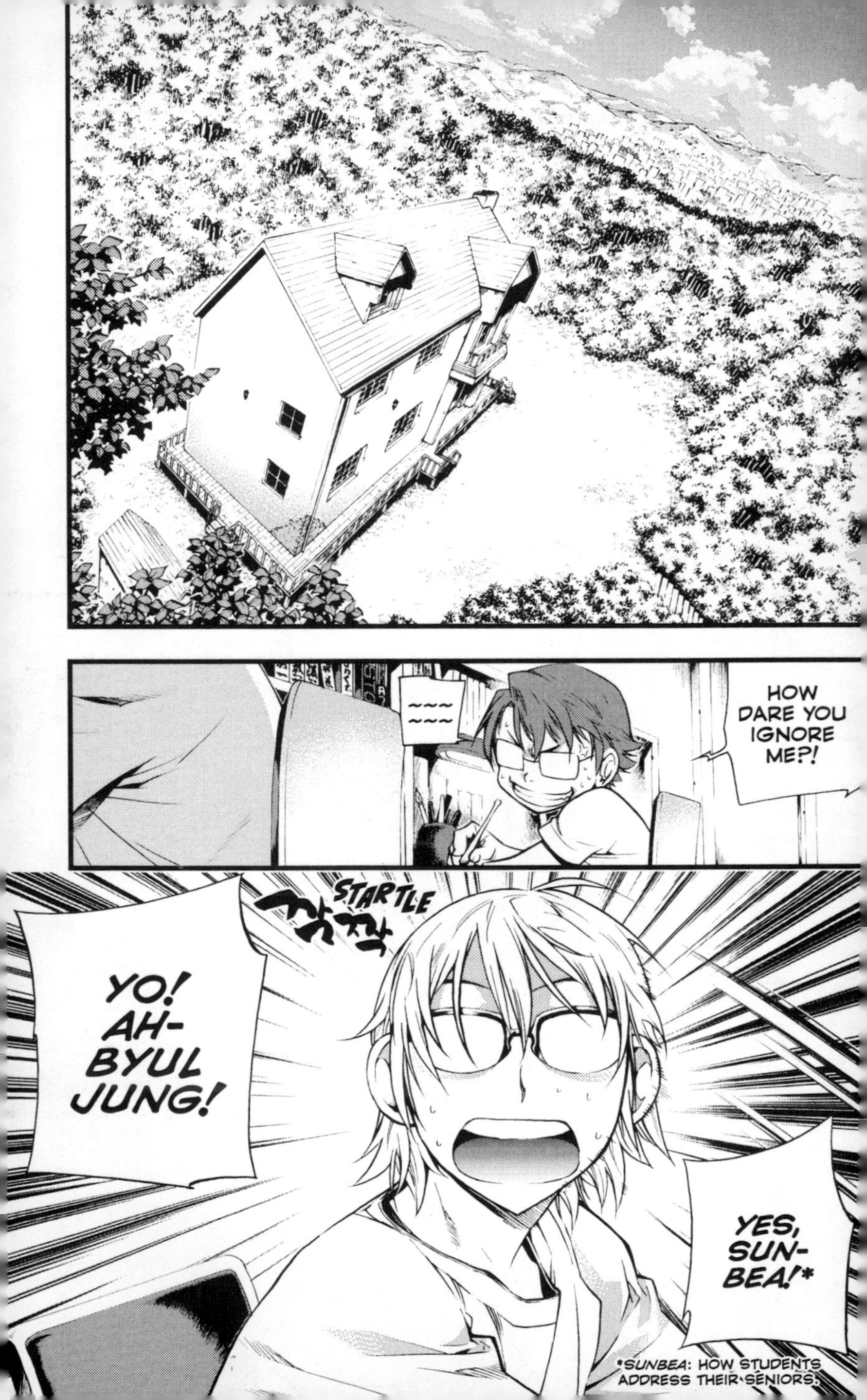
~~~
~~~
HOW DARE YOU IGNORE ME?!
YO! AH-BYUL JUNG!
STARTLE
YES, SUN-BEA!*

*SUNBEA: HOW STUDENTS ADDRESS THEIR SENIORS.

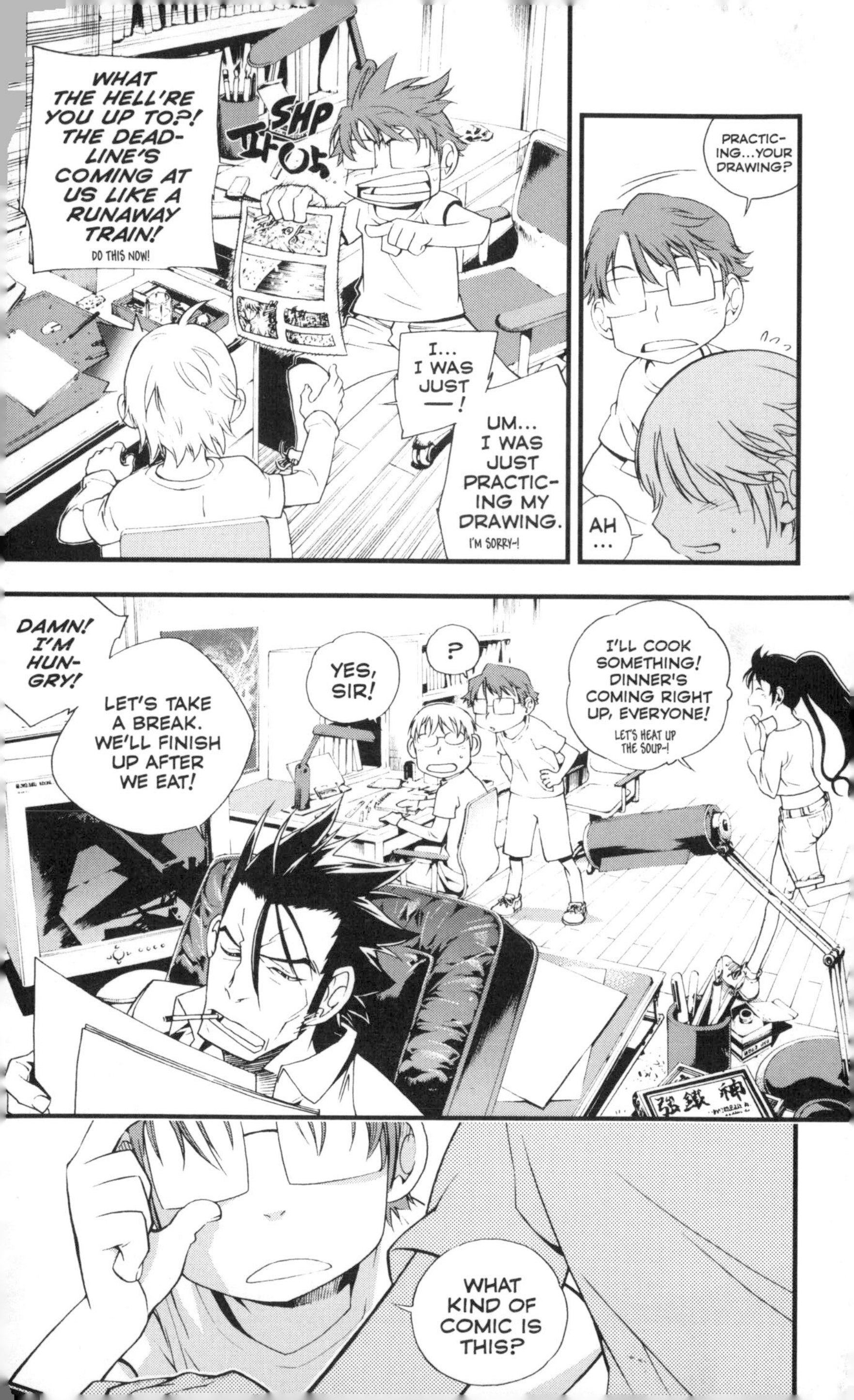
WHAT THE HELL'RE YOU UP TO?! THE DEAD-LINE'S COMING AT US LIKE A RUNAWAY TRAIN!
DO THIS NOW!
SHP
I... I WAS JUST —!
UM... I WAS JUST PRACTIC-ING MY DRAWING.
I'M SORRY~!
PRACTIC-ING...YOUR DRAWING?
AH...
DAMN! I'M HUN-GRY!
LET'S TAKE A BREAK. WE'LL FINISH UP AFTER WE EAT!
YES, SIR!
?
I'LL COOK SOMETHING! DINNER'S COMING RIGHT UP, EVERYONE!
LET'S HEAT UP THE SOUP~!
WHAT KIND OF COMIC IS THIS?

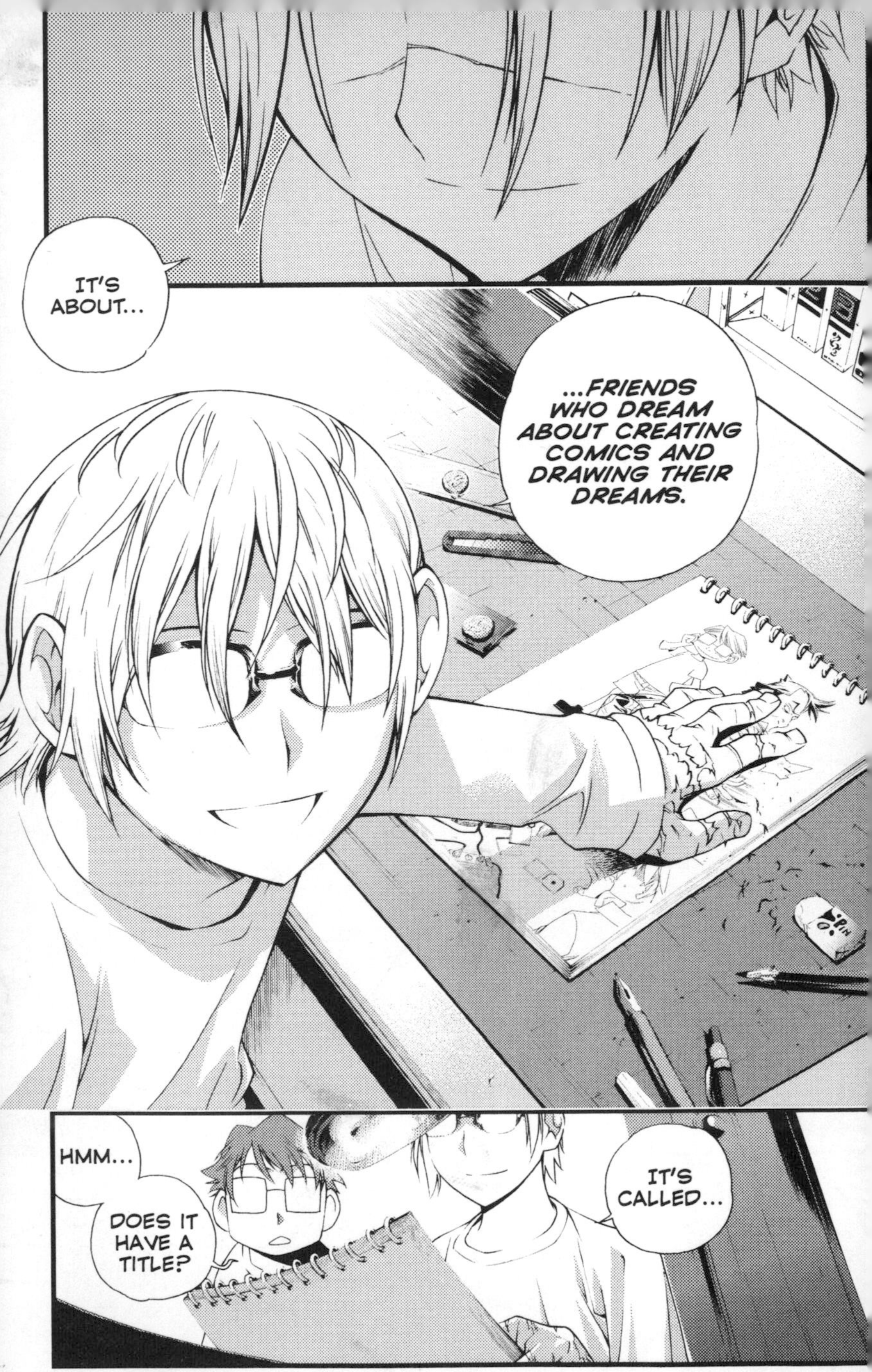
IT'S ABOUT...
...FRIENDS WHO DREAM ABOUT CREATING COMICS AND DRAWING THEIR DREAMS.
HMM...
DOES IT HAVE A TITLE?
IT'S CALLED...

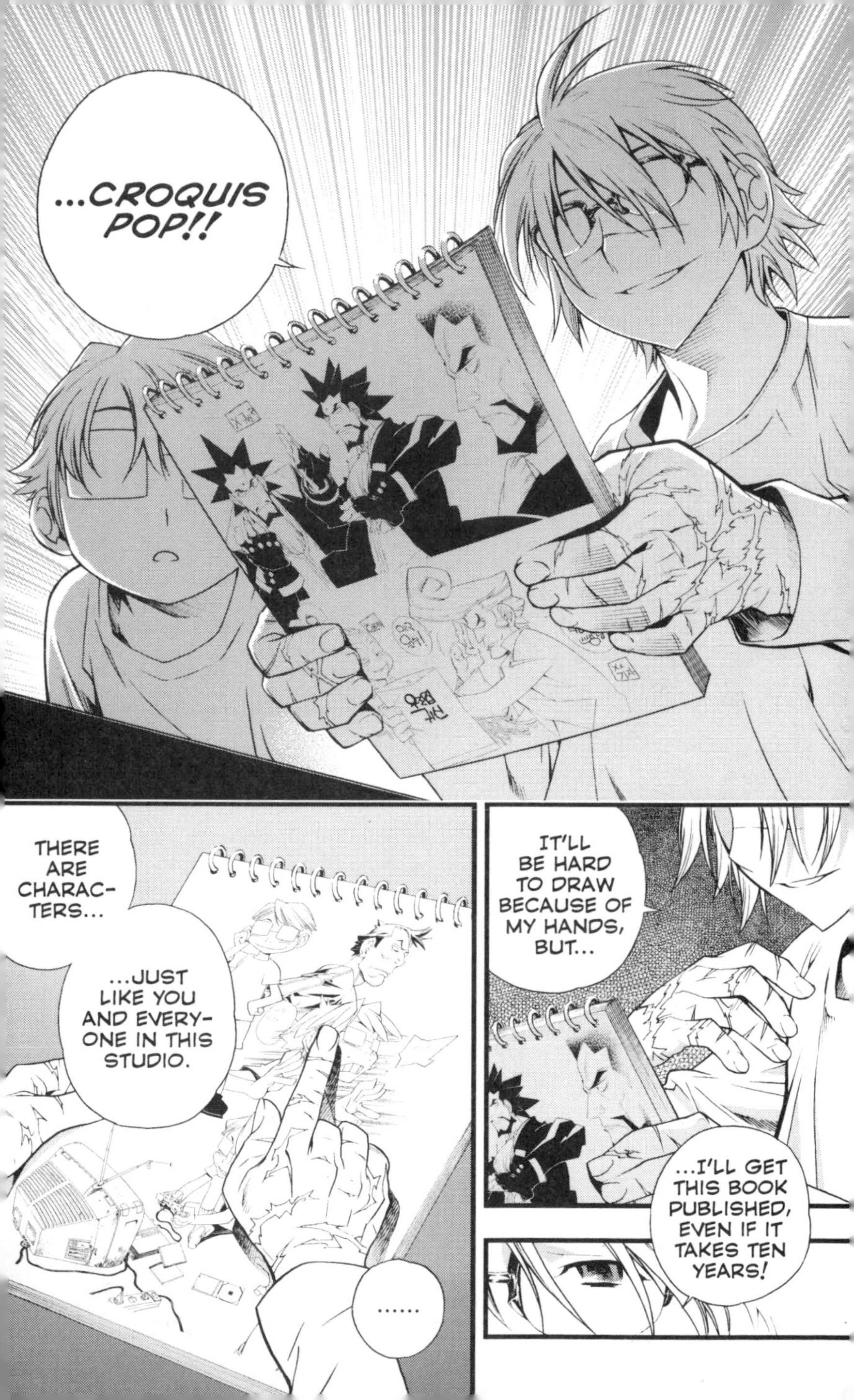
...CROQUIS POP!!
THERE ARE CHARACTERS...
...JUST LIKE YOU AND EVERYONE IN THIS STUDIO.
......
IT'LL BE HARD TO DRAW BECAUSE OF MY HANDS, BUT...
...I'LL GET THIS BOOK PUBLISHED, EVEN IF IT TAKES TEN YEARS!

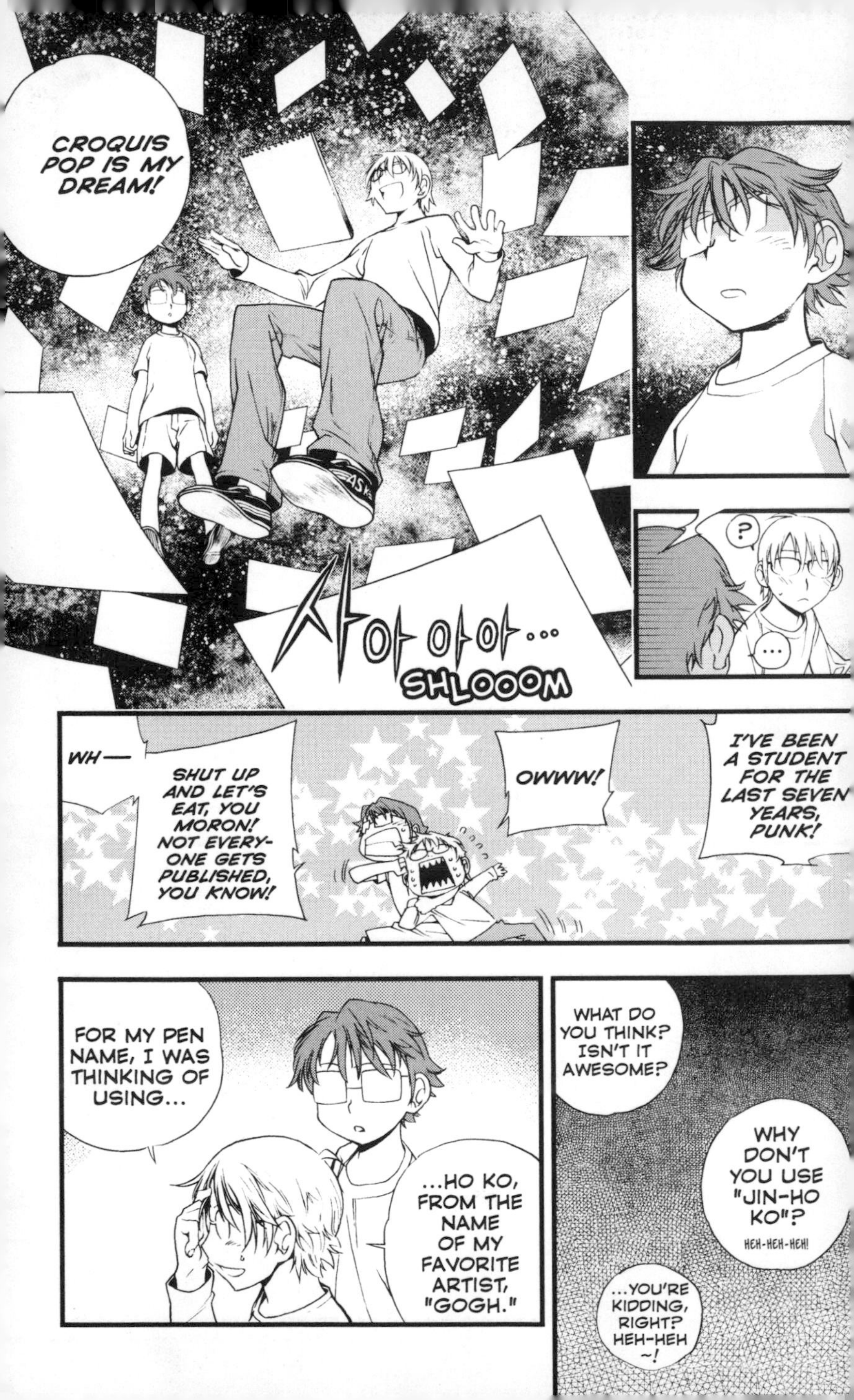
CROQUIS POP IS MY DREAM!
샤아아아...
SHLOOOM
?
...
WH—
SHUT UP AND LET'S EAT, YOU MORON! NOT EVERYONE GETS PUBLISHED, YOU KNOW!
OWWW!
I'VE BEEN A STUDENT FOR THE LAST SEVEN YEARS, PUNK!
FOR MY PEN NAME, I WAS THINKING OF USING...
...HO KO, FROM THE NAME OF MY FAVORITE ARTIST, "GOGH."
WHAT DO YOU THINK? ISN'T IT AWESOME?
WHY DON'T YOU USE "JIN-HO KO"?
HEH-HEH-HEH!
...YOU'RE KIDDING, RIGHT? HEH-HEH ~!

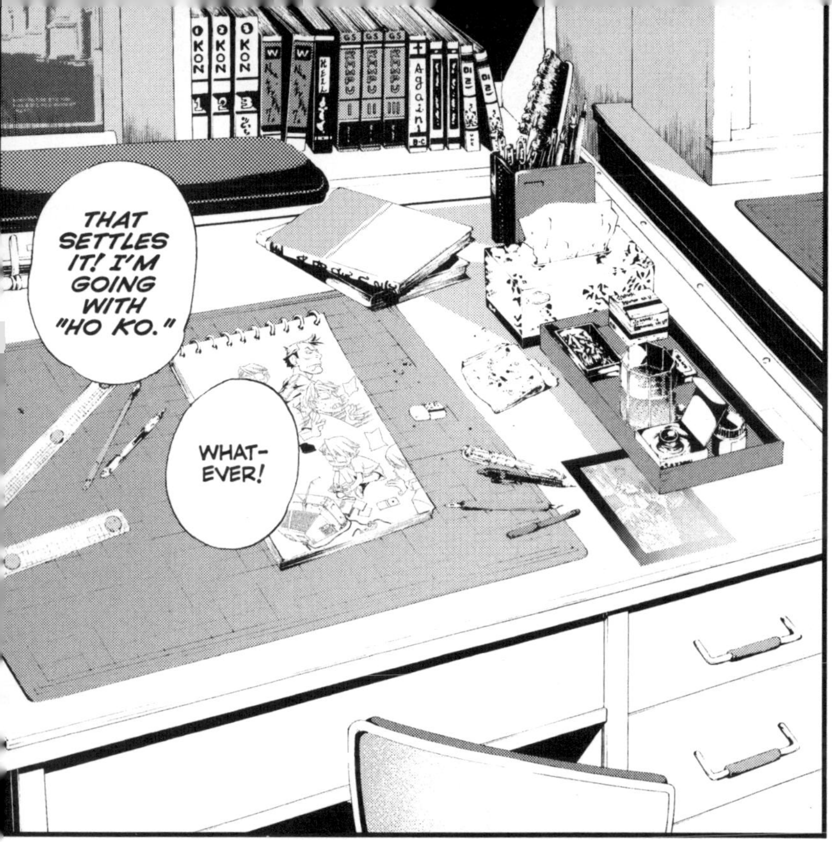
THAT SETTLES IT! I'M GOING WITH "HO KO."
WHAT-EVER!

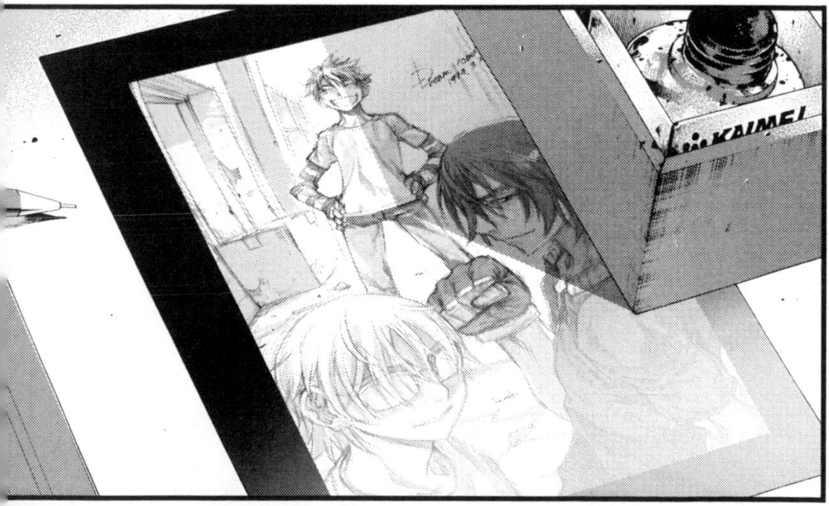

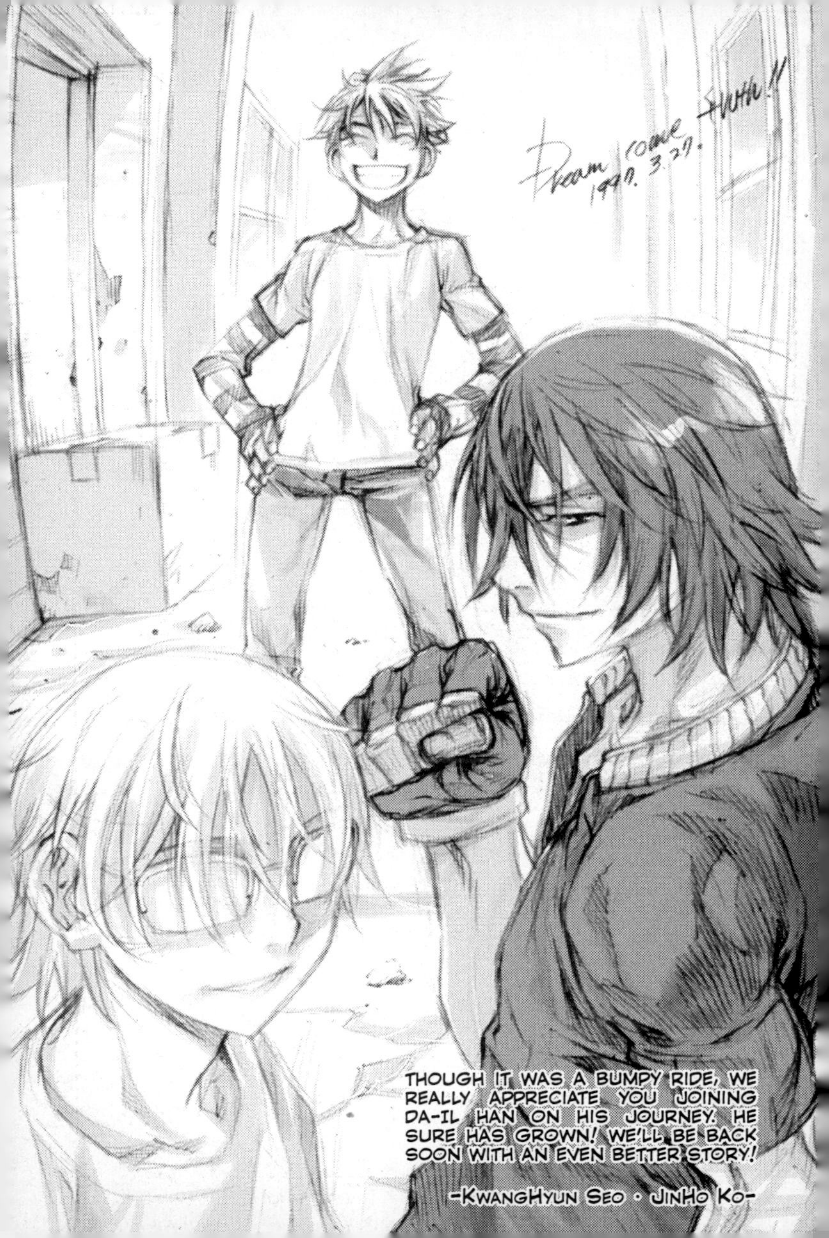
THOUGH IT WAS A BUMPY RIDE, WE REALLY APPRECIATE YOU JOINING DA-IL HAN ON HIS JOURNEY. HE SURE HAS GROWN! WE'LL BE BACK SOON WITH AN EVEN BETTER STORY!
-KwangHyun Seo · JinHo Ko-

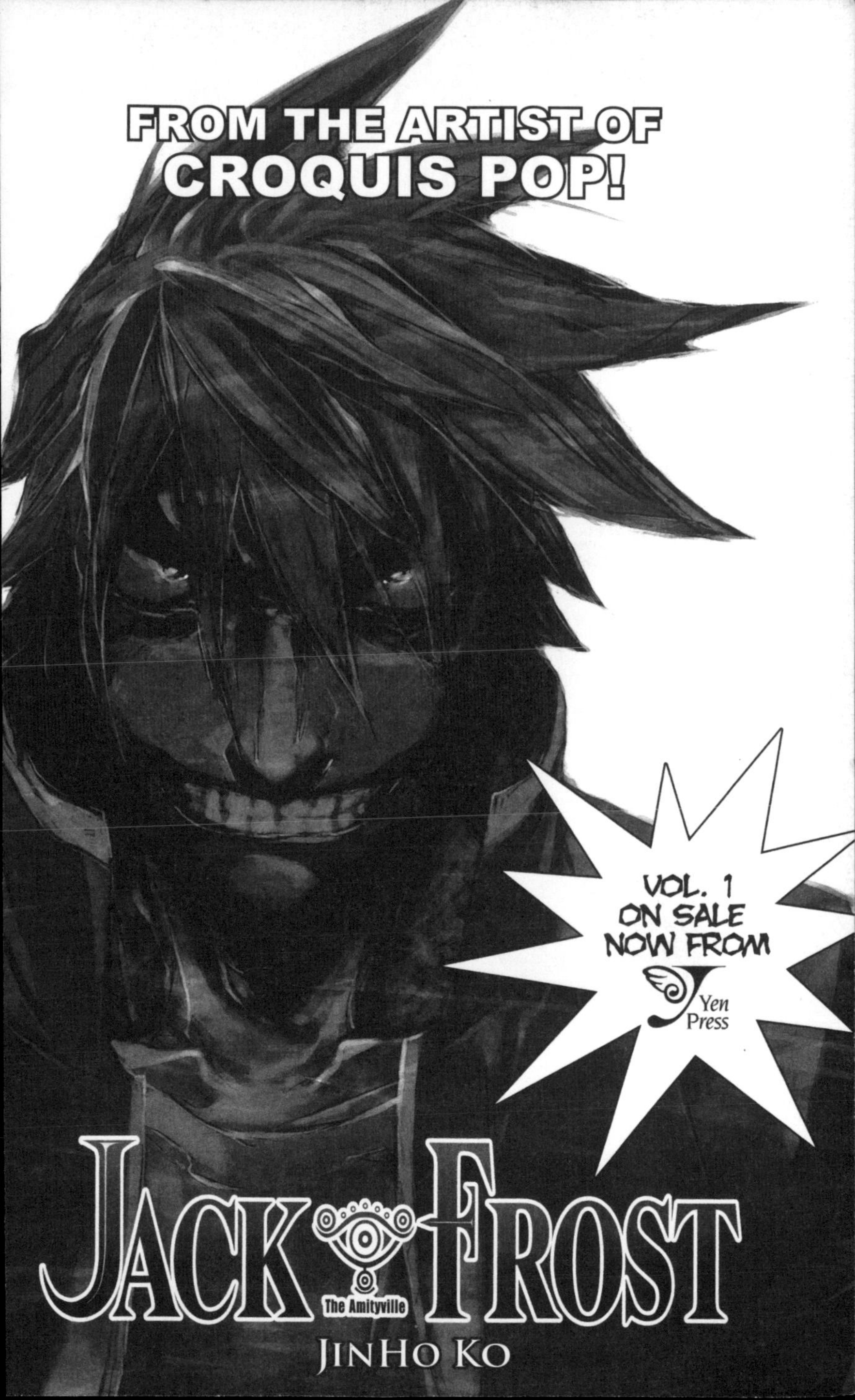

FROM THE ARTIST OF
CROQUIS POP!
VOL. 1
ON SALE
NOW FROM
Yen Press
JACK FROST
The Amityville
JINHO KO

IT'S AN ALL-OUT CAT FIGHT ON CAMPUS...

Cat-lovers flock to Matabi Academy, where each student is allowed to bring their pet cat to the dorms.

Unfortunately, the grounds aren't just crawling with cats...

...an ancient evil lurks on campus, and only the combined efforts of student and feline can hold them at bay...

IN STORES NOW!

CAT
PARADISE

1

YUJI IWAHARA

Yen Press

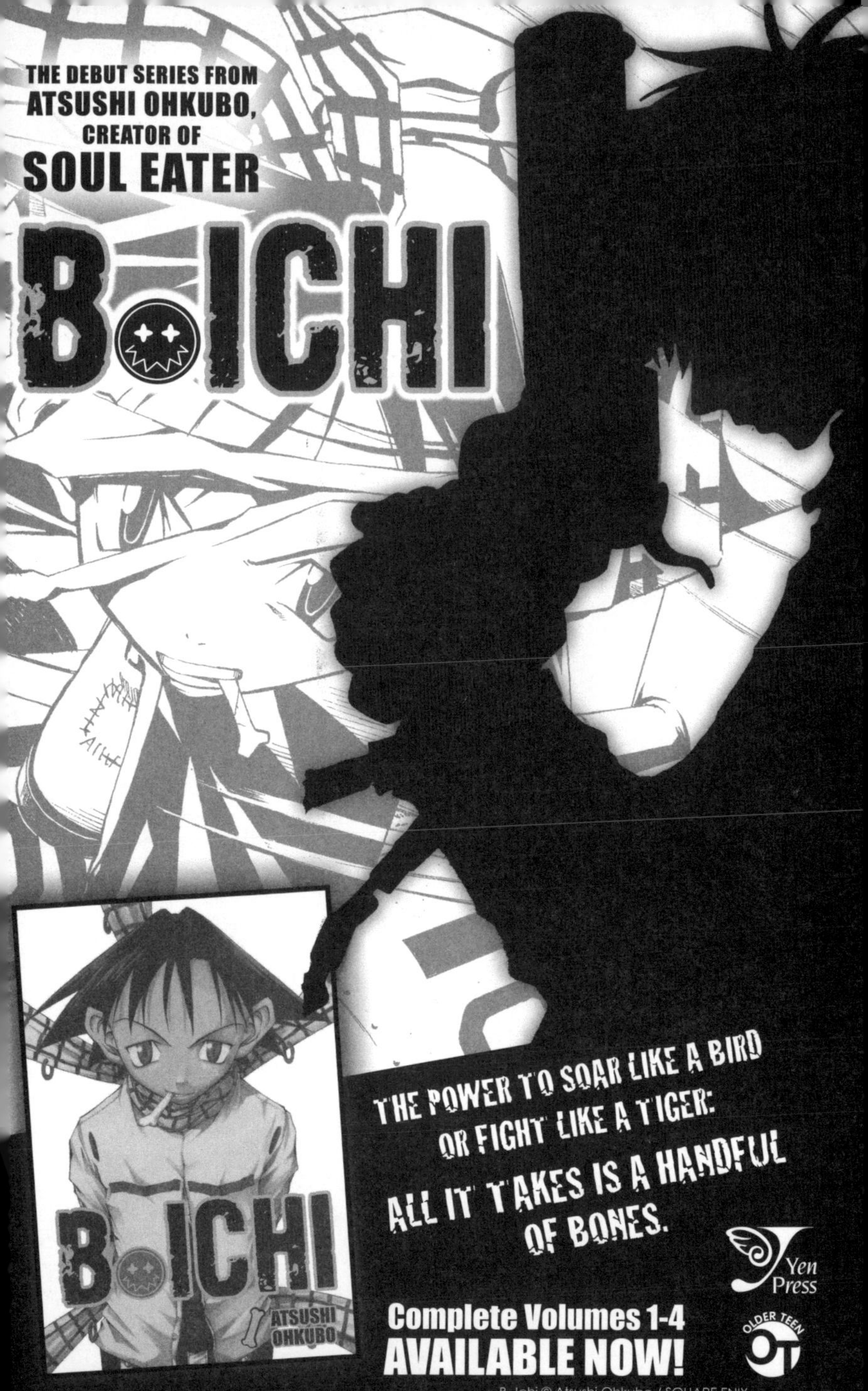
THE DEBUT SERIES FROM
ATSUSHI OHKUBO,
CREATOR OF
SOUL EATER
B. ICHI
B. ICHI
ATSUSHI OHKUBO
THE POWER TO SOAR LIKE A BIRD
OR FIGHT LIKE A TIGER:
ALL IT TAKES IS A HANDFUL
OF BONES.
Yen Press
Complete Volumes 1-4
AVAILABLE NOW!
OLDER TEEN
OT

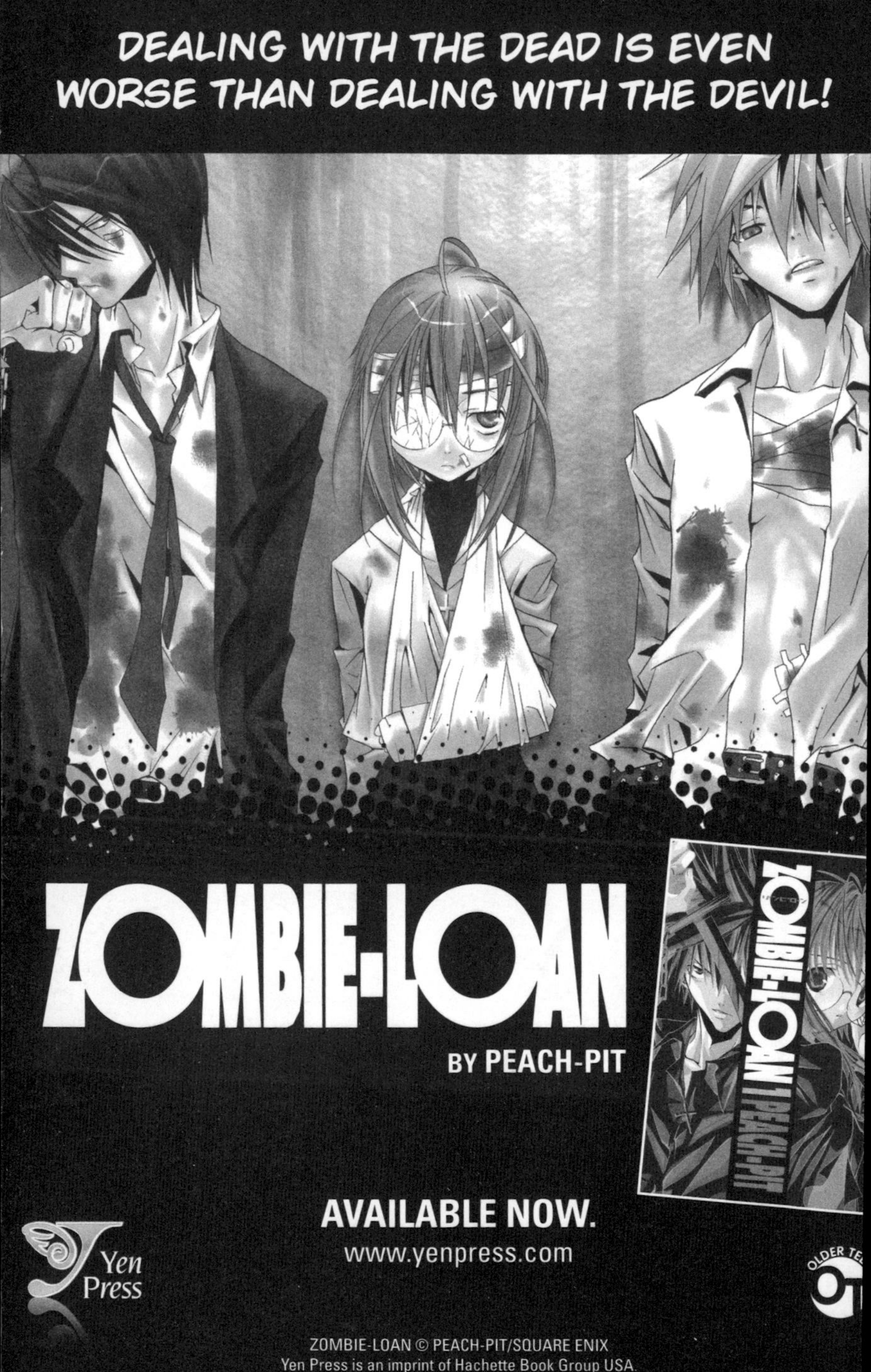
DEALING WITH THE DEAD IS EVEN
WORSE THAN DEALING WITH THE DEVIL!
ZOMBIE-LOAN
BY PEACH-PIT
ZOMBIE-LOAN 1 PEACH-PIT
AVAILABLE NOW.
www.yenpress.com
Yen Press
ZOMBIE-LOAN © PEACH-PIT/SQUARE ENIX
Yen Press is an imprint of Hachette Book Group USA.

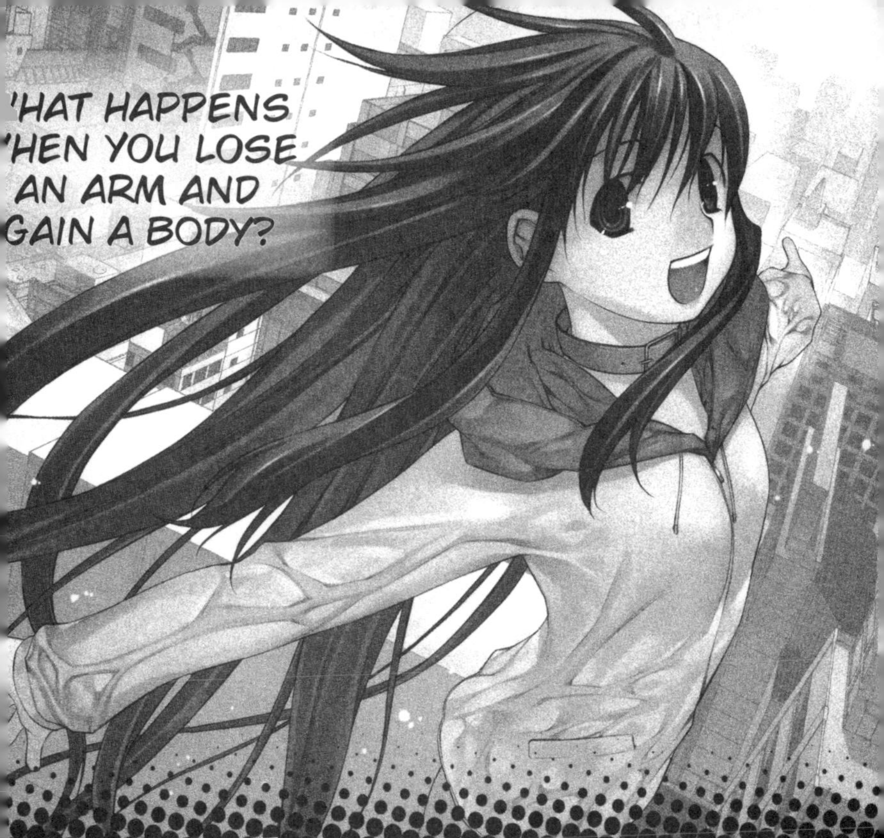
'HAT HAPPENS
'HEN YOU LOSE
AN ARM AND
GAIN A BODY?

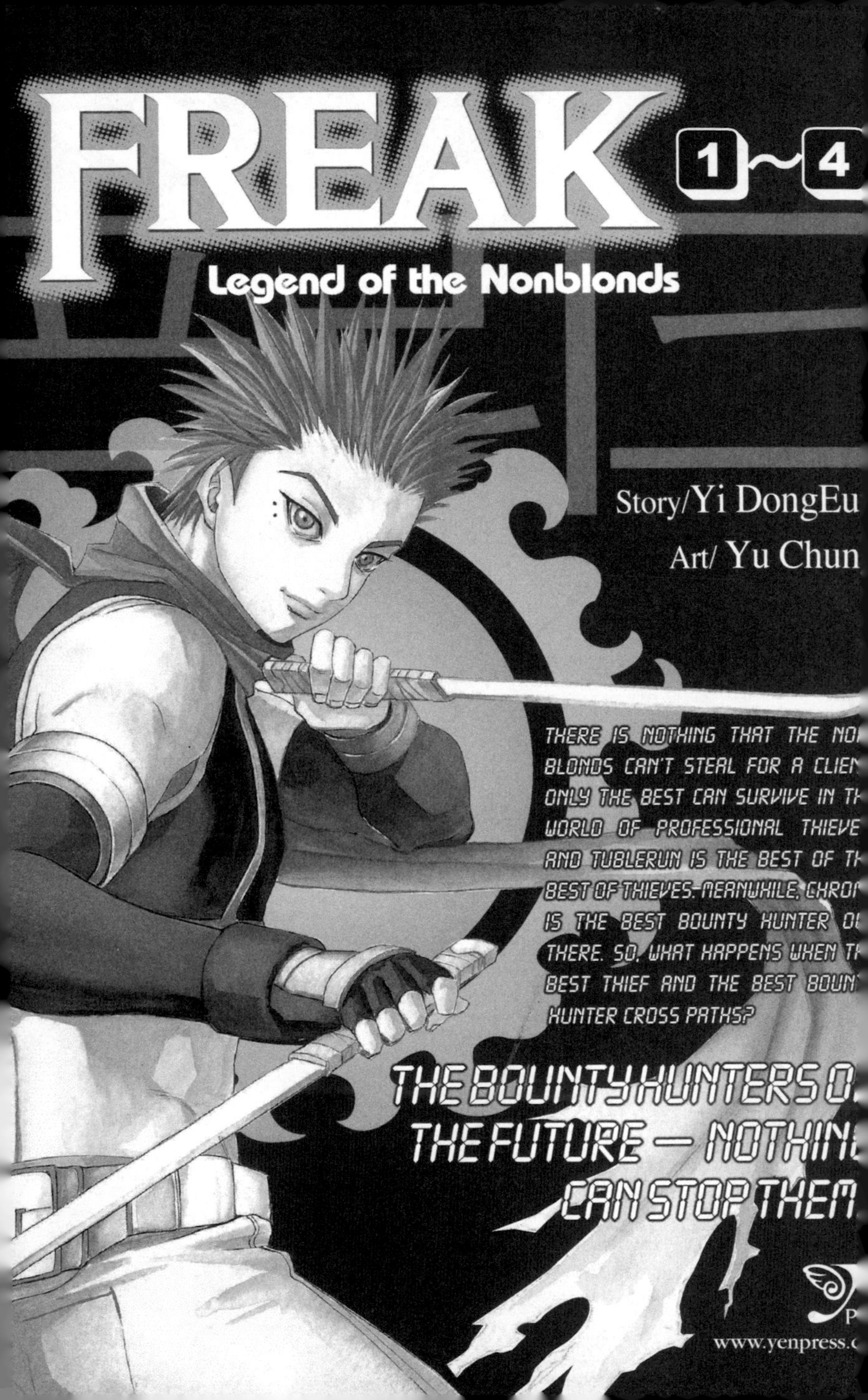
FREAK
1~4
Legend of the Nonblonds
Story/Yi DongEu
Art/ Yu Chun
THERE IS NOTHING THAT THE NO
BLONDS CAN'T STEAL FOR A CLIEN
ONLY THE BEST CAN SURVIVE IN TH
WORLD OF PROFESSIONAL THIEVE
AND TUBLERUN IS THE BEST OF TH
BEST OF THIEVES. MEANWHILE, CHRO
IS THE BEST BOUNTY HUNTER O
THERE. SO, WHAT HAPPENS WHEN TH
BEST THIEF AND THE BEST BOUN
HUNTER CROSS PATHS?
THE BOUNTY HUNTERS O
THE FUTURE — NOTHIN
CAN STOP THEM
www.yenpress.c

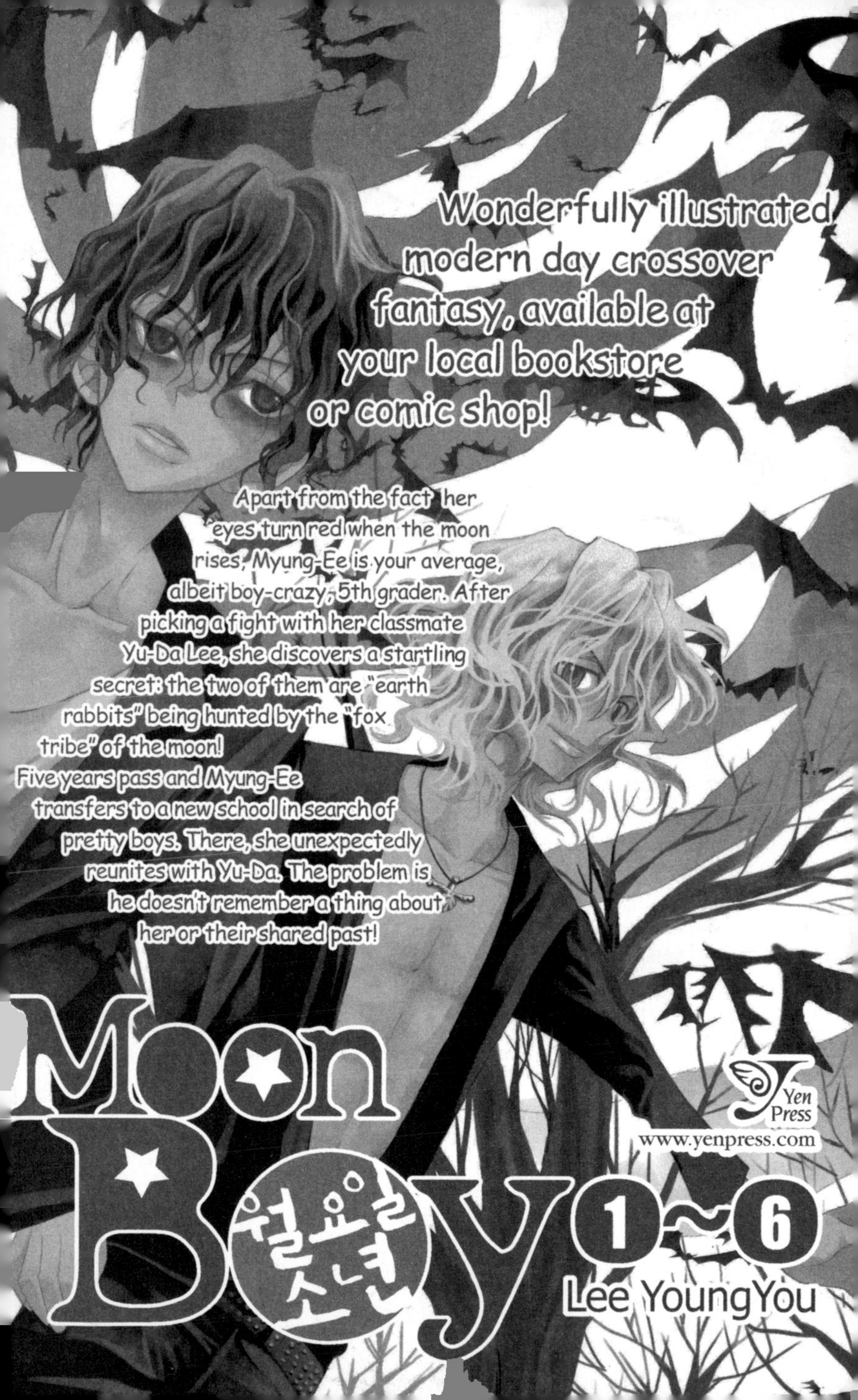
Wonderfully illustrated modern day crossover fantasy, available at your local bookstore or comic shop!
Apart from the fact her eyes turn red when the moon rises, Myung-Ee is your average, albeit boy-crazy, 5th grader. After picking a fight with her classmate Yu-Da Lee, she discovers a startling secret: the two of them are "earth rabbits" being hunted by the "fox tribe" of the moon!
Five years pass and Myung-Ee transfers to a new school in search of pretty boys. There, she unexpectedly reunites with Yu-Da. The problem is he doesn't remember a thing about her or their shared past!
Moon Boy
월요일 소년
1~6
Lee YoungYou
Yen Press
www.yenpress.com

CROQUIS POP ⑥ FINAL

KWANGHYUN SEO
JINHO KO

Translation: JiEun Park
English Adaptation: Arthur Dela Cruz

Lettering: Jose Macasocol, Jr.

Croquis Pop Vol. 6 © 2006 Ko Jin Ho & Seo Kwang Hyun. All rights reserved. First published in Korea in 2006 by Haksan Publishing Co., Ltd. English translation rights in U.S.A. Canada, UK, and Republic of Ireland arranged with Haksan Publishing Co., Ltd.

English translation © 2009 Hachette Book Group, Inc.

Yen Press
Hachette Book Group
237 Park Avenue, New York, NY 10017

Visit our Web sites at www.HachetteBookGroup.com and www.YenPress.com.

Yen Press is an imprint of Hachette Book Group, Inc. The Yen Press name and logo are trademarks of Hachette Book Group, Inc.

First Yen Press Edition: October 2009

ISBN: 978-0-7595-2963-2

10 9 8 7 6 5 4 3 2 1

BVG

Printed in the United States of America